Encyclopedia
of
Assassinations

Also by Carl Sifakis

The Mafia Encyclopedia
American Eccentrics
The Dictionary of Historic Nicknames

Carl Sifakis is a crime reporter and freelance writer.
He lives in New York City.

Encyclopedia of Assassinations

Carl Sifakis

HEADLINE

First published in this edition in 1993
by HEADLINE BOOK PUBLISHING PLC

10 9 8 7 6 5 4 3 2 1

ISBN 0 7472 4236 4

Typeset by
Letterpart Limited, Reigate, Surrey

Printed and bound in Great Britain by
HarperCollins Manufacturing, Glasgow

HEADLINE BOOK PUBLISHING PLC
Headline House
79 Great Titchfield Street
London W1P 7FN

For
Thomas Buchleither

CONTENTS

PHOTO CREDITS

INTRODUCTION

'Assassination is the extreme form of censorship.'
— George Bernard Shaw

In 1975 a modest, heavily illustrated book on assassinations appeared in England. It bore a frontispiece quotation of Benjamin Disraeli, from a speech on the death of Abraham Lincoln in 1865, that said, 'Assassination never changed the history of the world.' Ironically, the title of the book was *Assassinations – the murders that changed history*.

Do assassinations alter the course of history? There are points to be made on both sides. In a limited sense most of the 10 or so assassinations described in that book did provoke some change. The assassination of archduke Francis Ferdinand altered the history of the world by sparking the Great War of 1914. Yet it is equally true that the assassination was merely the spark, and had it not occurred, another immediate cause would have come to the fore, instead. The forces of militarism and the violent expression of economic drives were not to be denied. The same can be said about the 300-odd assassinations presented in this volume.

Julius Caesar? If the plotters' motive was to restore the republic, the assassination was a failure. After only a few years the empire emerged under Octavian, Caesar's heir, who became Augustus Caesar.

Abraham Lincoln? Had he lived perhaps the Reconstruction of the Union would have been slightly less painful, but ultimately it was the passage of time that healed the bitter wounds of the American Civil War.

Czar Alexander II? His assassination in all likelihood

had no effect on the course of Russian history. It took the radicals several decades to learn that one cannot 'kill the czar,' at least not without replacing him with another.

Despite the bulk of evidence to the contrary, public belief in political conspiracy remains rife. In America that has been true since the attempted assassination of President Andrew Jackson by an obviously deranged individual. Jackson himself went to his grave convinced that his assailant, Richard Lawrence, was but a small cog in an intricate Whig plot to kill him. In fact, American political life has been remarkably free of genuine plots. The weight of the evidence in the assassinations of both Kennedys suggests that they were acts by lone, twisted gunmen. The murder that most readily meets the test of conspiracy is clearly that of Martin Luther King, Jr.

Not that American politics is not heavily into personal violence. The period after the assassination of Lincoln is best summed up by a phrase used by James McKinley in *Assassination in America* – 'After Lincoln, the deluge.' While Andrew Johnson held office, 13 political-office holders were shot at and 12 of them were killed. During Ulysses S. Grant's terms from 1869 to 1877, there were 20 attacks and 11 fatalities.

Today, assassination remains hardly a dying institution worldwide. Political assassination exists and has existed ever since humankind formed a body politic.

There are two basic types of assassination – antiestablishment murders and establishment murders.

The antiestablishment assassinations are more readily apparent to the average person; they include the acts of deranged individuals or of dedicated revolutionaries. Although deranged assassins may succeed in their search for power and notoriety, revolutionaries generally fail in their goal of altering society. Throughout the 19th century, for example, the Russian radicals killed czars, aristocrats, generals, and police officials, yet oppressive government persisted.

Every nation on earth, regardless of political persuasion, has utilized assassination to achieve political ends.

For unlike antiestablishment assassination, state-sponsored assassination can work, if not to change history, at least to slow its tide or, quite frequently, to give the establishment continued momentum. In *Terrorism* Robert Liston notes that the first American use of state assassination occurred in 1620 among the Puritans who came to Plymouth, Massachusetts. Seeking to solve the 'Indian problem,' Captain Myles Standish invited the local chief, the chief's 18-year-old brother, and two other braves to his headquarters for a feast.

'Once they were inside,' Liston writes, 'the door was locked. Standish personally hacked one Indian to pieces with his knife, while the chief and the other brave were dispatched by other Pilgrims. The Indian youth was spared long enough to be taken outside and publicly hanged as an example to other Indians.' This was state assassination in its purest form. Indeed, since every country reserves the right to go to war, in which thousands or even millions of people may be killed, why should the state eschew assassination, especially when such a course could forestall the greater bloodshed of war?

Tyrannicide has been debated throughout history. Aristotle's distinction between the altruistic ruler and the self-interested tyrant became standard medieval thought, coupled with the rightfulness of assassination to be rid of a tyrant. Saint Thomas Aquinas differentiated between a usurper, who steals the throne, and a legitimate monarch who misused his or her power. Aquinas could condone the private assassination of a usurper but considered it too perilous to let individuals decide if a properly installed ruler had become a tyrant. In 1415 the Council of Constance condemned a broad defense of tyrannicide but did not exclude its justification under certain circumstances.

By the 16th century the question had assumed life-and-death implications on a broad scale since both Roman Catholics and Calvinists concluded that a ruler who did not hold their religion was automatically a tyrant. In Scotland John Knox held that the defense of his Calvinist faith was all that was necessary to practice assassination.

He was puzzled and frustrated when Queen Elizabeth I of England failed to follow his advice forthwith and execute the Catholic Mary, Queen of Scots.

In France Huguenot writers proclaimed the virtues of tyrannicide; French Catholic writers in turn directed their like arguments against kings Henry III and Henry IV (Henry of Navarre). The Spanish Jesuit Juan de Mariana supported the concept in many circumstances and in fact applauded the assassination of Henry III. Mariana's teachings were often cited as leading to the murder of the popular Henry IV.

Niccolo Machiavelli surveyed the chessboard of Renaissance Italy and described the attributes he felt necessary for a successful prince. He decided that an appetite for assassination and treachery was an important quality, and he chose the notorious assassin Cesare Borgia as his ideal Renaissance prince.

There is little doubt that if we were to name the grandest assassin in history it would be almost impossible not to choose Cesare Borgia. As the Venetian ambassador to the Vatican reported, 'Every night four or five murdered men are discovered, bishops, prelates and others, so that all Rome trembles for fear of being murdered by the Duke.'

This was as fine a tribute as Machiavelli himself could have bestowed upon Borgia. Actually Machiavelli himself remains an enigma to many, and *The Prince* is held by some to have been filled with such cynical opportunism that it may have been intended as satire, as is true of many of Swift's works. But many of Machiavelli's principles have remained with us ever since, used by the great villains of history as well as by every secret police or intelligence service in the world.

Assassinations have been so much a part of human history that it is impossible to quantify them. How would one hazard an estimate? The assassinations offered in this volume necessarily represent only a selection of the most notorious acts of their kind. The killings cited should be regarded as merely starting points for the student of assassinations. As one delves into any one of them, new facts are likely to emerge. Most of them would benefit greatly from a study as intense as that made by the Warren Commission in the case of President John F. Kennedy. And after such a study there would very likely be the same outcries of cover-up. Such was the case in the 1984 murder of Indian Prime Minister Indira Gandhi, with much of India divided by the study and widespread belief in a broader conspiracy and government cover-up.

The case can be made that assassination victims most often not only have a large group of opponents but also dedicated supporters who are given to total adulation. To be hated often has a flip side – the ability to be loved. The murder of Rabbi Meir Kahane, the leader of a militant anti-Arab fringe, on November 5, 1990 – the most recent to be mentioned here given publication deadlines – meets both criteria. Arab gunman El Sayyid a Nosair, himself wounded and captured after the fatal attack, was able to strike not merely at an individual, but to exact great suffering on a broader foe, the dedicated Kahane followers.

Assassination assaults our belief in ourselves. The striking down of a young President revealed our own – and society's – vulnerability. But assassinations are not going to go away. They are in a sense the quintessential crimes of passion, whether nominally executed for God, country, political power, or a misguided drive for social change. Humankind will always find a reason to assassinate others.

A

ABDALLAH ABDEREMANE, Ahmed (1919–1989)
President Ahmed Abdallah Abderemane, the longtime
ruler (with near dictatorial powers) of the Comoro
Islands, off the East African coast, survived coup attempts
in 1983, 1985 and 1987. He was assassinated on November
26, 1989.

At the time of his death, Abdallah had ruled the islands
nation, one of the poorest in the world with an annual per
capita income of $339 (1989), for all but three years since
1972. Abdallah was overthrown in 1975, a month after the
Comoro Islands declared their independence from
France. In 1978 Abdallah returned to power with the aid
of 50 mercenaries headed by Bob Denard, a Frenchman.
In November 1989 he won a referendum that allowed him
to seek another six-year term when he was due to step
down in 1990. The official results showed approval by 92.5
percent of the vote, but observers said the election was
rife with ballot-box stuffing, voter harassment and
destroyed ballots.

The 1989 coup against Abdallah was said to have been
led by Ahmed Mohammed, the former commander of the
armed forces, and Mohammed was said to have been
seized. According to government reports, Abdallah died
in a firefight between the rebels and the members of the
300-man presidential guard, which was far better trained
and better equipped than the regular army forces. The
head of the Supreme Court, Mohammed Djohar, took
over as head of an interim government.

The international consensus soon crystallized that the
real force behind the assassination was the mercenary
Denard, who since Abdallah's return to power in 1978 had

become a very wealthy Comoran with a native wife and substantial real estate and business interests. Faced with growing international criticism, the governments of France and South Africa (which financed the presidential guard) put pressure on Denard to leave the Comoros. France reportedly alternated between offering money to Denard and threatening him with an invasion of Foreign Legionnaires stationed on the nearby island of Mayotte. Denard finally departed in December 1979 with 21 other mercenaries and landed in South Africa. The mercenaries and especially Denard were reported to be continuing into France shortly. (See SOILIH, ALI.)

ABDUL-AZIZ, Ottoman Sultan (1830–1876) There is some question whether the Turkish sultan Abdul-Aziz was murdered or whether he committed suicide a few days after he was deposed in 1876; a case can be made for either possibility. Abdul-Aziz came to the throne in 1861 and for the next decade was busy molding Turkey on the Western European model. However, as the sultan drained the national treasury for his personal excesses, he found it necessary to steer a more Islamic course. He started to rule by willful decree, over the opposition of his more astute ministers, such as Midhat Pasa and army leader Hussein Avni Pasha. The sultan's unpopular alliance in the 1870s with Russia and crop failure in 1873 contributed to his growing unpopularity, as did his lavish expenditures and the soaring public debt.

On May 30, 1876, the two ministers, Midhat and Hussein Avni, headed a coup that drove the sultan from power, and a few days later it was announced that Abdul-Aziz had committed suicide. In the ensuing political ferment, Hussein Avni Pasha was assassinated while attending a cabinet meeting. However, Midhat Pasa continued as grand vizier (chief minister) under Sultan Abdul-Hamid II. Later Midhat was accused of conspiracy against the current sultan and expelled from the country in 1877, only to be recalled in 1878 and restored to governmental position. Finally in 1881 Midhat was stripped of his duties and charged with the assassination of Abdul-Aziz. He was convicted and sentenced to death, but because of protests from Western European countries, he was instead banished to at-Ta'if, Arabia. There in 1883 he was assassinated, almost certainly at the behest of Abdul-Hamid II. (See MIDHAT PASA.)

ABDULLAH IBN HUSSEIN (1882–1951)   Longtime emir of Transjordan, Abdullah Ibn Hussein was throughout his life a close ally (some would say puppet) of Great Britain, and he maintained an army, the Arab Legion, that was trained and commanded by British Brigadier John Glubb Pasha. In 1946 Abdullah became the first king of the new state of Jordan. His longtime ambition was a united Arab kingdom encompassing Syria, Iraq and Trans-Jordan under his rule.

In 1947 Abdullah was the only Arab ruler ready to accept the United Nations' partitioning of Palestine into Jewish and Arab states, which he believed would further his own ambitions. During the 1948 war with Israel, Abdullah occupied the West Bank of the Jordan River and captured the Old City of Jerusalem. Two years later he incorporated the West Bank territory into Jordan, a move that estranged him from his former allies Egypt, Saudi Arabia and Syria, which were seeking the establishment of a Palestinian Arab state on the West Bank. Abdullah also lost considerable popularity within Jordan itself because of his actions.

On July 20, 1951, Abdullah, accompanied by his grandson Hussein, the future king of Jordan, visited the tomb of his father in Old Jerusalem. Abdullah was shot to death there by Mustafa Ashu, a 21-year-old Palestinian tailor and follower of the exiled mufti of Jerusalem. The assassin was killed on the spot by Abdullah's guards.

Abdullah was succeeded for a short time by his son Talal, who abdicated in 1952 because of illness in favor of the 20-year-old Hussein. Almost immediately thereafter Jordan became less pliable to British interests and more so to those of the United States. In 1977 it was revealed that

King Hussein had been a paid agent of the CIA for two decades.

ABU HASSAN   See SALAMEH, ALI HASSAN.

AETIUS, Flavius (?–454)   Roman general and statesman Flavius Aetius was the dominant influence in court during the long reign of Emperor Valentinian III (425–455), who has been described by observers as foppish, lazy and vicious. So great was Aetius's power that envoys from the provinces no longer were sent to the emperor but to him.

In addition to his other less-than-enviable characteristics, Valentinian was also fearful and untrusting, and he fell under the influence of Petronius Maximus, one of Rome's wealthiest men, former prefect of Rome and twice consul. Maximus, whose long-range (and successful) plan was to seize the throne for himself, and the eunuch Heraclius convinced Valentinian that Aetius was plotting against him, a charge that was not true. Aetius was occupied with repelling the advances of Attila the Hun, which he did temporarily at Troyes in 452. However, Maximus's allegations were given credit by the fact that Aetius was trying to espouse his son to the emperor's daughter, Eudocia. Maximus played on Valentinian's fears, suggesting that this would give Aetius a clear motive to assassinate the emperor. Valentinian worked himself into such a frenzy that on September 21, 454, he summoned Aetius and slew him with his own hand.

'Sire,' a member of the court told the emperor, 'you have cut off your right hand with your left.' Within six months Valentinian III would be assassinated as well, part of Maximus's grand designs on the throne. (See VALENTINIAN III, EMPEROR OF ROME.)

AGRIPPINA (the Younger) (A.D. 16–59)   Agrippina the Younger was the mother of Nero, and in her own right a competent ruler (a role she often played during her son's reign) and an accomplished assassin. She is believed to have poisoned her second husband, Caius Crispus, as she did her third, the emperor Claudius. Her driving motivation was to put her son Nero on the throne, and she did so by marrying Claudius and convincing him to adopt Nero as his son and name him as his heir ahead of his own son, Britannicus.

When Nero came to the throne, he let his mother conduct many of the duties of state. Agrippina even had her image face Nero's on Rome's gold coins. Inevitably, friction developed between the two, fueled by Seneca, the great philosopher and dramatist who had tutored Nero. Seneca sought to undermine Agrippina's hold on her son and in this way grasp the effective reins of government in his own hands. Even Burrus, Agrippina's previous ally, whom she had insinuated as prefect of the Praetorian Guard during Claudius's reign, joined against her. Infuriated, Agrippina declared that Britannicus was the true heir to the throne and threatened to unmake Nero by supporting her young stepson. Nero's camp countered by poisoning the youthful Britannicus in A.D. 55.

Agrippina was weakened but not destroyed, and a number of historians have attributed this to an Oedipal fixation on Nero's part. If this were so, it hardly prevented the dissolute emperor from having many other sexual interests. When Nero formed a liaison with an ex-slave named Claudia Acte, Agrippina was outraged. By contrast Seneca and Burrus encouraged the affair as another way to weaken Agrippina. Later Nero became infatuated with Poppaea, the beautiful wife of his friend Salvius Otho. Poppaea refused to be Nero's mistress but offered to marry him if he divorced his wife, the virtuous Octavia. Agrippina fought desperately against the proposed divorce, recognizing that Octavia represented one of her fading points of leverage on her son. Historians such as Tacitus and the gossipy Suetonius say that her defense of Octavia included surrendering her own body to her son. Unfortunately, Poppaea could fight back in kind, and the divorce went through.

It was probably Poppaea's urging – and her taunts that he was afraid of his mother – that finally turned Nero to the assassination of Agrippina. He considered a number of plans, but abandoned the idea of poison since Agrippina was so knowledgeable on the subject and actually took antidotes on a regular basis. The final plot was a bizarre one involving the sabotage of Agrippina's transport ship by constructing it with a collapsible roof. One night in A.D. 59 on a cruise to Baiae in the Bay of Naples, the roof was rigged to collapse in the hope that the entire ship would fall apart. It did not. A friend of Agrippina, Crepereius Gallus, happened to be standing in the cabin at that moment and was killed by the falling timbers. Agrippina and another friend, Acerronia, were reclining on settees and were uninjured. Oarsmen involved in the plot next unsuccessfully tried to capsize the craft by throwing their weight to one side. Realizing it was an assassination attempt and determined to save Agrippina, Acerronia cried out, 'Help, I'm the emperor's mother!' In the darkness the murderous crewmen took her at her word and battered her to death with their oars. In the confusion Agrippina slipped over the side and managed to swim to safety.

Then Agrippina made a fatal mistake. Instead of hurrying to Rome and letting news of the murder attempt circulate, which would have signaled Nero as the obvious perpetrator and constrained him from attempting any further violence against her, she sent a message from Baiae to Nero that she had survived a terrible accident. Nero reacted quickly and with cunning. He threw a sword to the ground and cried out that Agrippina's messenger had been sent to murder him.

Nero dispatched his henchmen to Baiae, where they surprised Agrippina in her bedchamber. According to the historian Tacitus, she presented her belly to an attacker and told him to stab her in the womb that had borne Nero. She was slashed many times, and when the emperor later viewed the uncovered body, he supposedly remarked, 'I did not know I had so beautiful a mother.'

The required cover-up was left to Seneca, who wrote to the Senate in Nero's name, explaining that Agrippina had plotted against the emperor, and upon being detected, had committed suicide. The Senate accepted the story and turned out in a body to greet Nero on his return to Rome, offering thanks to the gods for having saved 'the great Nero.' (See BRITANNICUS; CLAUDIUS, EMPEROR OF ROME.)

Further reading: *A Criminal History of Mankind*, by Colin Wilson; *The Story of Civilization III – Caesar and Christ*, by Will Durant.

AGUIRRE SALINAS, Osmin (1892–1977) The 85-year-old former president of El Salvador was shot to death outside his home in San Salvador on July 12, 1977. In letters sent to radio stations, the Farabundo Marti Popular Liberation Forces claimed responsibility for the murder. The organization was credited with many assassinations in El Salvador, although the total did not begin to approach the numbers killed by government-backed rightists and those employed by powerful landlords seeking to silence advocates of land reform.

The leftist guerrillas assassinated the elderly Aguirre to emphasize how long the land reform movement had sought, unsuccessfully, to achieve economic justice. Farbundo Marti declared it had 'executed' Aguirre for his role in crushing a land reform campaign 45 years earlier, in 1932, when he was chief of police; 30,000 peasants had reportedly died in the police action. A retired army general, Aguirre became president for a few months late in 1944 in a military coup before being ousted early in 1945 in the same manner.

ALCIBIADES (c. 450–404 B.C.) In his day the Athenian statesman and general, Alcibiades, was the most famous man in Athens. Reared in the home of his near relative, Pericles, he was, says Will Durant, 'admired for his eloquence, his good looks, his versatile genius, even his faults and crimes.' Alcibiades suffered no shortage in any of these characteristics: At times he was forced to flee Athens under a death penalty and join the Spartans, the enemies of Athens, only to return to Athens later, hailed as its savior. If it is true, as is often theorized, that an ideal candidate for assassination is one who enjoys great love from a great many people and great hatred from others, Alcibiades met these criteria to the fullest.

In his youth Alcibiades was a frequent companion of Socrates (each was to save the other's life in war), although he never absorbed much of the philosopher's moral and ethical teachings nor did he let them affect his personal behavior. There is little doubt that Alcibiades could have been one of the greatest of Greek leaders, but his unscrupulousness played a key role in provoking the tragic political antagonisms in Athens that were the chief cause of its defeat by Sparta in the long Peloponnesian War.

Although brilliant and fearless in combat, Alcibiades frequently changed sides because of the opposition he constantly invited. Thus he led the Athenian forces, then he joined the Spartan side, then the Persians, then back to the Athenians and then back to the Persians. An aristocrat, he found only one rival for the leadership of Athens after the death of Pericles – the rich and pious Nicias. Since Nicias favored the aristocrats and advocated peace with Sparta, Alcibiades veered in favor of the commercial classes and called for an imperialism that electrified Athenian pride. Durant notes, 'He violated a hundred laws and injured a hundred men, but no one dared bring him before a court.'

Losing some prestige when he was defeated by the Spartans at Mantinea in 418 B.C., Alcibiades promoted the Sicilian campaign in 415 B.C. He was in transit when he was recalled to Athens to stand trial on charges of sacrilege, accused of having led a party in a drunken foray through Athens and knocking off the ears, noses and phalli from the figures of the god Hermes, which stood before many public buildings and private residences as the patron of fertility and the guardian of the home. There were additional charges that Alcibiades and his followers had profaned the Eleusianian Mysteries. Alcibiades started to sail back for Athens, but on learning that his enemies had succeeded in having him sentenced to death in absentia, he, most likely innocent of the charges, turned traitor and journeyed to Sparta, where he advised his former foes on how best to defeat the Athenians.

In Sparta Alcibiades also reinforced his reputation with women by seducing the wife of Spartan King Agis II. The queen bore Alcibiades a son, and she whispered to her friends with considerable pride that he was the father. The Athenian himself told his intimates that he simply could not resist the chance to father a possible future king of Laconia. When the king returned from a military campaign, Alcibiades saw this as the opportune time to head for Asia with a Spartan naval squadron. Hearing that Agis had ordered him killed, Alcibiades took flight, joining the Persian admiral Tissaphernes at Sardis.

In 411 B.C. Alcibiades was able to return to Athens in triumph, the democratic forces having routed the oligarchs. The Athenians, observing how badly the city had fared militarily in recent years, were eager to offer him amnesty for all his intrigues. Alcibiades led the Athenians to a brilliant naval victory at Cyzicus in 410 B.C. In 408 B.C. he recovered Byzantium. However, in 406 B.C. he was unjustly blamed for the defeat of the Athenian fleet at Notium, when his strict orders not to engage the Spartans were disobeyed, and he retired to a castle in Thrace. When the Athenians at Aegospotami facing the Spartans in the Hellespont in 405 B.C. grew increasingly careless, the great military man warned them of the danger. The Athenians chose to ignore his advice, and the entire Athenian fleet was lost to the Spartan admiral Lysander.

Alcibiades's position in Thrace was now untenable, as he faced both Athenian and Spartan wrath. He sought refuge in Phrygia in northwestern Asia Minor, where the Persian general Pharnabazus supplied him with both a castle and a courtesan. Lysander regarded Alcibiades as an eternal future menace and a disturbing influence on Greek politics, and he convinced the Persian king Darius II to order Pharnabazus to kill his guest. Two assassins set fire to Alcibiades's castle, and the Athenian came charging out naked, determined to fight for his life, until his assailants cut him down with javelins and arrows.

It was a brutal end for an Athenian who could have achieved monumental historic fame. When Socrates was later accused of corrupting Athenian youth, Alcibiades was held up as a prime example of his malevolent influence.

Further reading: *The Story of Civilization II – The Life of Greece*, by Will Durant.

ALEXANDER I, King of Yugoslavia (1888–1934) Alexander I of Yugoslavia became king of that patchwork nation in 1921 following the death of his father Peter I. The stresses on a nation made up of Serbia, Croatia-Slovenia, Bosnia, Herzegovina and Montenegro were enormous, and the king faced the near-impossible task of trying to pacify the contending forces that were producing political chaos. Conditions reached a tragic climax in 1928 when Stefan Radich, the Croat leader, was assassinated in Parliament. In 1929 Alexander I abolished the constitution, officially changed the name of the country to Yugoslavia and established himself as dictator.

In 1931 Alexander proclaimed a new constitution, but in fact few of its terms were put into effect. Bitter feelings continued against the king, especially by the Croats, among whom nationalists under Ante Pavelic conspired to assassinate the king with the secret support of Benito Mussolini of Italy.

In 1934 Alexander traveled to France seeking a treaty of alliance, and on October 9 he was motoring by limousine through Marseilles with French Foreign Minister Louis Barthou and French General Alfonse Georges. Suddenly Vlada Chernozamsky, an assassin assigned by Pavelic darted out from the crowds lining the street, jumped to the running board of the automobile and emptied his pistol at the occupants. Alexander was struck twice and died within minutes. Barthou was hit once and would die some hours later. A French general also in the limousine received only superficial bullet wounds. Ironically, the entire assassination and the dying moments of the king were recorded by newsreel cameramen, a film first.

The assassin Chernozamsky did not escape the fury of the crowd. He was smashed to the ground, pummeled with blows and shot in the head, apparently by a policeman. He died a few hours later. Several other conspirators were captured and later sentenced to life imprisonment. Pavelic safely escaped to Italy.

ALEXANDER II, Czar of Russia (1818–1881) On March 1, 1881, as Czar Alexander II of Russia returned to his palace in St. Petersburg after reviewing a military parade, the government was on an 'assassination alert.' Violent radicals had made several attempts on the czar's life, and everyone, Alexander included, fully expected more, despite the fact that by czarist standards he could be classified as a liberal. But although he was known as the 'Emancipator,' it could not really be said he had 'freed' the serfs. What he had actually done was offer them the opportunity to purchase their own lands and therefore pay crushing taxes. Alexander did put through some other feeble reforms, all insufficient to quench the revolutionary fervor spreading in the country.

Radicals in Russia in the 1870s were divided on the use of violence as a way of achieving change. The socialists under the banner of Black Repartition (redivision of the land) advocated nonviolence, while the militant anarchists identified themselves as the 'Will of the People' and urged terror and assassination. The Will of the People were adherents of the late Mikhail Bakunin (1814–1876), an anarchist and himself a follower of Pierre Joseph Proudhon. Bakunin had come into conflict with Karl Marx in the First International and had been expelled. A radical aristocrat, he preached collectivism, atheism and violence to attain social justice.

Police persecution of radicals had been a hallmark of Russian life throughout the century, and the czars became the focal point of protest. Underground newspapers advocated 'direct action' against the government. In 1878, Vera Zasulich, a typesetter for the unauthorized paper *Land and Liberty*, protested the vicious maltreatment of political prisoners and shot General Trepov, the St. Petersburg chief of police. Trepov survived, and the trial of Zasulich was converted by her defense counsel into a trial of police brutality. To the amazement of all, Zasulich was found not guilty. A stunned Czar Alexander ordered her immediate rearrest, but an enthusiastic throng prevented the police action and she was spirited away from the scene and eventually to haven in Germany.

Zasulich became a martyr for the Will of the People, as did the editor of *Land and Liberty*, Sergei Kravchinsky, who later assassinated General Mezentzev, another high police official. He too escaped to exile. These acts of terror evoked harsh police reaction, and in August 1879 the Will of the People determined to assassinate the czar.

Several attempts were made on the czar's life. Late in 1879 Will of the People members attempted to blow up Alexander's train, and two death traps were set at 24-hour intervals on the monarch's itinerary. The first trap was supervised by the brilliant Andrei Zhelyabov, a charismatic Will of the People leader who was born a serf and had won a scholarship to the University of Odessa. The trap failed when the explosives did not detonate.

This meant a further attempt would have to be made by Sophia Perovskaya, a fierce activist and Zhelyabov's lover. Intelligence gathered by the plotters indicated there would be two trains on the track, the first to test the safety of the rails and the second to carry the czar and his entourage. Accordingly, Perovskaya and her comrades let the first train pass and derailed the second. But the plotters had been outwitted. The second train was the decoy and the czar was on the first one.

Other unsuccessful attempts on the czar's life were made, the most spectacular in 1880, the blowing up of the dining room of the Winter Palace. The explosion occurred too soon, only minutes before the ruler and his family were to arrive for dinner. After this, the czar's advisers induced Alexander for a time to reduce public appearances and to limit his travel to waterways. However, within months the czar bridled under such restraints. 'I have already lived longer than any of my race,' he said. 'As to death, I do not personally fear it.'

Will of the People prepared well for the czar's plans to review his troops on March 1, 1881. The route of the royal family was studied, and Zhelyabov and Perovskaya opened a bogus cheese shop in a basement storefront on Malaya Sadovaya Street. The plotters tunneled under the street and planted explosives to blow up the czar's carriage. As backups, four men were to be stationed beyond that spot to carry out bomb attacks if necessary.

Just before the scheduled assassination, Zhelyabov was seized by the police, leaving execution of the plan to Perovskaya. At the last minute, the czar's security guards altered his expected route, bypassing Malaya Sadovaya. The mined-street preparations proving worthless, the action now fell to the backup killers. As the czar's carriage rumbled toward the palace on an unaccustomed route, a 19-year-old student named Rysakov dressed in peasant garb charged out of the crowd and hurled a bomb. The explosion was deafening and the czar's carriage rocked and its door collapsed, but the ruler was unharmed, although a boy in the street, two cossack escorts and several horses were killed.

Several other soldiers were wounded, and the shaken Alexander alighted from the carriage in the snow to survey the situation. The czar tended to some of the wounded and then turned to take a substitute carriage, while the bomb thrower was being dragged away.

Just then a second assassin, Ignaty Grinevitsky, charged forward holding a nitroglycerine bomb enclosed in a glass ball, and hurled it directly under the czar's feet. The ensuing explosion shattered Alexander's legs and blew out an eye. The assassin was mortally wounded and 20 men were killed and many more badly injured. Fragments of bloody flesh covered lampposts and trees, and the snow turned crimson.

Still conscious, the czar managed to gasp to Grand Duke Michael: 'Cold – cold – to the palace, quick – die there.' Alexander died within the hour, surrounded by his family.

If the Will of the People thought the assassination would trigger the revolution, they were sadly disappointed; and after the six principal conspirators were tried and executed, the organization collapsed, as did similar groups.

Under the new czar, Alexander III, police repression intensified and revolutionary progress was stunted for more than a decade. Alexander III thoroughly hated the very word *reform* and was determined to turn the clock back to the autocratic ways of Peter the Great. In the process the czar became even more remote from the citizenry and virtually a prisoner within his own palace. Upon his premature death in 1894, Alexander III was succeeded by his son Nicholas II, the last of the czars, who would also be assassinated, along with the entire royal family, by the Bolsheviks during the Russian Revolution.

ALEXANDER OBRENOVIC, King of Serbia (1876–1903)
Few monarchs in European history proved as unpopular as the authoritarian King Alexander Obrenovic of Serbia, who succeeded his father, King Milan, in 1889 upon the latter's abdication. In 1893 Alexander dismissed the regency council and assumed active leadership of the country. Although popular at first, Alexander soon demonstrated a contempt for public opinion and a dictatorial inclination that frequently ignored the liberal constitution of 1889. In 1893, he abrogated that document and reinstated the constitution of 1869, which limited the powers of the legislature.

His pro-Austrian policies, similar to those of his deposed father, put Alexander in opposition to elements of the army as well as the powerful pro-Russian Radical Party. He dismissed ministers with increasing frequency, and in 1897 he recalled his father from exile and installed him as commander of the armed forces. Alexander met criticism by restricting press freedom as well as freedom of association.

In 1900 Alexander further inflamed public opinion with an unpopular marriage to Madame Draga Masin, a widow and former lady-in-waiting to Alexander's mother, who was 10 years older than the king and had a dubious reputation. Even the king's father opposed the marriage, and the entire cabinet resigned in protest. In reaction to the turmoil caused by the scandal, Alexander instituted a new constitution in 1901, but he soon made a mockery of the document by simply suspending it whenever he wished to engage in some unconstitutional acts.

The final straw was Alexander's apparent determination to name Draga's brother as heir to the throne. Mutinous military officers conspired to end the Obrenovic dynasty once and for all, and on June 11, 1903, they burst into the palace searching for the monarchs, whom they finally discovered cowering in a secret room behind the royal bath. Alexander and Draga were shot repeatedly, then their bodies were slashed with sabers. Finally the corpses were hurled from a window to the courtyard below.

The bloody coup was generally welcomed by the country, and Peter I was brought back from exile and put on the throne.

ALEXANDER SEVERUS, Emperor of Rome (c. 206–235)
Alexander Severus acceded to the throne of Rome in 222 while still in his 16th year, succeeding his depraved cousin Elagabalus, who was assassinated by his own guards. The early portion of Alexander's reign was relatively tranquil for those bloody times. The empire had suffered from a surfeit of degeneracy, and Romans welcomed a prince who, if not particularly adept, was at least mild and virtuous. His mother, Mamaea, was the power behind the throne, and she schooled her son well. Even before Elagabalus was murdered, Alexander's mother had taken pains to make her son popular with the soldiery and especially the Praetorian Guards, who had become

sickened by Elagabalus's unmanliness.

Unfortunately for Alexander, he thus owed his throne to the Praetorians, something neither he nor they could forget. Because of this and the fact that the guards had in recent years made and unmade, fatally, three consecutive emperors, military discipline withered and insubordination grew among the rank and file. Efforts to enforce discipline led to ill feelings by the Praetorians who had put their protege on the throne. For a time the guards focused their wrath on their own prefect, Ulpian. Rising in mutiny, they slew him in the very presence of the emperor, who vainly tried to shield him from their murderous blows. It was an obvious forecast of things to come.

In an effort to regain his hold on the soldiers, Alexander led them in the field against the Persians, who were seeking to drive Rome out of Asia. Alexander's performance was mixed. The Persians under Ardashir suffered some defeats but lost no territory, a result that could not be passed off by Alexander in the Senate as a grand victory. As a result Alexander's standing with the military continued to plummet.

In 235 the emperor had barely ensconced himself once more in Rome when pressure from the German and other barbarian hordes grew critical on the northern frontier. Alexander marched off to meet the new challenge, and the emperor must have felt his fate was almost certainly settled.

The facts are obscure. The soldiers mutinied after the emperor tried to reach an agreement with the enemy near Mainz by offering to pay an annuity for their peacefulness. Alexander, his mother and several of his supporters were slain in the emperor's tent. The troops thereupon proclaimed as emperor a fighting man, the Thracian Maximus. He would rule for three years as Maximinus, a reign marked by awesome bloodletting in Rome that would end in his own assassination and no less than four other proclaimed emperors in a 12-month span, a record even for the empire in decay. (See ELAGABALUS, EMPEROR OF

ROME; MAXIMINUS, EMPEROR OF ROME.)
   Further reading: *The Illustrated World History, vol.* 2,
edited by Sir John Hammerton and Harry Elmer Barnes.

ALFONSO OF ARAGON (1481–1500) Marrying into the
15th-century Borgia family of Rome was always hazard-
ous, and at times deadly, if the family decided that better
prospects turned up elsewhere. The head of the family,
Pope Alexander VI, and his notorious, murderous son
Cesare, regularly used Cesare's young and beautiful sister
Lucretia as bait for improving the lot of the Papal States.
She was first married off in 1493 to Giovanni Sforza of the
powerful Sforza family of Milan, but when Alexander
later allied himself with Naples and Milan allied itself with
the invading French, Giovanni, fearing for his life at the
hands of the Borgias, fled Rome, later charging both
Alexander and Cesare with incestuous relations with
Lucretia. The pope countered in 1497 by annulling the
marriage of Lucretia and Sforza on the dubious grounds of
nonconsummation.
   Then the pope, seeking to cement his ties with Naples,
arranged a marriage in 1498 between Lucretia and the
17-year-old Alfonso of Aragon, possible heir of Naples. It
appears that Lucretia greatly loved her new husband –
some said she had the capacity to love any man – but when
Cesare entered into an alliance with the French king,
Alfonso, fearing for his life, fled. However, within a few
months, finding separation from Lucretia intolerable, he
returned to Rome.
   One day in July 1500 Alfonso was strolling through St.
Peter's Square after supping with the pope when several
supposed pilgrims approached for alms. As he reached for
his money, Alfonso was surrounded, and daggers rose and
fell. Strong and courageous, Alfonso fought back furi-
ously, and with the approach of the papal guards the
would-be assassins took to their heels. The badly
wounded Alfonso was carried to his wife's apartment in
the Vatican, where Lucretia and his sister, Sanchia,
worked tirelessly to save his life. Alfonso and most of

Rome was certain the assassination attempt had been the work of Cesare Borgia.

As Alfonso improved, the pope moved him to quarters closer to his own to make any further attempts on his life less likely. About a month after the original attack, Lucretia and Sanchia left him alone for an hour, and Alfonso peered out the window and saw Cesare approaching with several armed men. Guessing their intent, Alfonso took up a bow and arrow and shot at Cesare, missing. Within seconds Cesare's men burst into the room and strangled and stabbed Alfonso to death.

The citizens of Naples were outraged at the assassination and demanded an inquiry. Pope Alexander VI promised one – and promptly put it out of his mind. Some historians consider the assassination of Alfonso the Borgias' most devious crime, but it was only one among many. As the Venetian ambassador to the Vatican reported, 'Every night four or five murdered men are discovered, bishops, prelates and others, so that all Rome trembles for fear of being murdered by the Duke [Cesare].' In *The Prince* Machiavelli relates how Cesare charmed a group of conspirators against him, inviting them to a banquet to discuss their grievances. The plotters arrived without weapons, and when they sat down to talk, Cesare had them seized from behind and strangled. Others consider the death of the rich Venetian cardinal Giovanni Michele as the most heinous of the Borgias' crimes. The cardinal died after two days of violent intestinal illness, generally ascribed to poison administered by the Borgias so that his wealth would pass to the pope.

Cesare understood that his power stemmed from his father's control of the papacy. Indeed, after Alexander died in 1503, Cesare's fortunes went into an abrupt decline. He lost most of the cities he controlled and died in a minor skirmish fighting in the service of his brother-in-law, the king of Navarre. He was not yet 31.

Alfonso's widow, Lucretia, had married for a third time in 1501, an alliance arranged by Cesare to cement his position at the time in Romagna. Her husband, Alfonso d'Este, son of Ercole I, duke of Ferrara, at first shunned the union because of the Borgias' unsavory reputation. With the death of her father Lucretia ceased to play any role in politics – her involvement in many murders is now discounted by historians, although her vices are undeniable – and she turned to arts and letters. The court of Ferrara became a great center of the Italian Renaissance, and Lucretia in later years turned to religion as neither her father nor brother truly had. She died, much loved, in 1519 at the age of 39.

Further reading: *The Borgias*, by Michael Mallet; *A Criminal History of Mankind*, by Colin Wilson; *The March of Folly*, by Barbara W. Tuchman.

ALFONSO XIII, King of Spain (1886–1941) Perhaps the most famous unsuccessful assassination attempt in Spanish history involved the 1906 effort to murder both the 20-year-old King Alfonso XIII and his queen, Victoria (Ena). During the late 19th century and the early 20th, the heyday of anarchist violence in Europe and most especially in Spain, one of western Europe's most repressive regimes, there were several attempts on Alfonso's life. Few came close except for the 1906 attempt – which proved to be extremely bloody.

On May 31, 1906, Alfonso took Victoria, the daughter of Prince Henry of Battenberg and cousin of King George V of England, as his bride. The announcement of the forthcoming marriage had stirred considerable turmoil in both Britain and Spain, for opposite reasons. On the announcement of the royal engagement Victoria abandoned the Protestant faith, an act that unleashed extremists' cries of 'No Popery' in Britain. Since Victoria bore the title of 'Princess,' her conversion led to government debate. That proved limited, however, since despite her title Victoria was not the recipient of any public monies. In Spain Victoria was attacked by many of the Catholic faithful who viewed her conversion as merely one of convenience and not the act of a convinced Roman Catholic.

Such was the charged atmosphere in Madrid as the royal couple left the cathedral in an open carriage after the ceremony. Security was supposedly stringent, but a man among the spectators easily got close enough to fling a bomb at the couple. The device did not hit the carriage, but in the ensuing explosion and panic, 31 soldiers and spectators were killed. The king and queen were unhurt, and the assassin committed suicide before he could be seized. The immediate fear was that the attempt had had a religious motivation, but the assassin was identified as one Matteo Morales, sometimes known as Matteo Morral, an anarchist.

The next day the queen solidified her position with the Spanish populace by proving her personal courage attending a bull fight where she was wildly cheered by the crowd. In succeeding years Alfonso attempted to rule by making some efforts of reform, but his governments, plagued by continued terrorist acts and assassinations of high officials, constantly lapsed back into repressive phases and finally total dictatorship in 1923. In a short-lived republican reaction, Alfonso was forced in 1931 to declare he was 'suspending the exercise of royal power' and going into exile. He later renounced claims to the throne in favor of his son, Juan.

ALLENDE GOSSENS, Salvador (1908–1973)   On September 12, 1973, Salvador Allende, president of Chile and the first freely elected Marxist head of state in South America, died during a rightist attack on Santiago's presidential palace. Considerable dispute remains about what happened to Allende during the attack, whether he was assassinated or whether, according to the army junta headed by General Augusto Pinochet that succeeded him, he committed suicide to avoid capture and trial by his foes.

Only one person has acknowledged seeing Allende die, his personal surgeon, Dr. Patricio Guijon Klein. Dr. Guijon in many statements over the years has said that Allende killed himself after ordering his staff and bodyguards to leave the palace and surrender; Dr. Guijon had supposedly returned to get his gas mask. The doctor said he saw Allende pull the trigger of an automatic rifle held between his knees, blowing away most of his head. Although Dr. Guijon went to prison on Dawson Island in the Strait of Magellan, like many members of the former government, he was freed after a few months and resumed his practice, leading some to doubt the veracity of his story.

It was known that in 1970, the rightists had assassinated General Rene Schneider, the army's commander in chief, who had pledged support for a freely elected president, even if that president proved to be the Marxist Allende. In 1973 the right insisted it had not killed Allende. The following year, 1974, the Pinochet junta announced that Jose Toha Gonzalez, former interior and defense minister and a close aide of Allende, had hanged himself in a Santiago military hospital. That story was challenged not only by Chilean and foreign leftists but by ecclesiastical authorities and other observers, who doubted that Toha, dying of stomach cancer, had the strength to hang himself.

Allende's three-year Marxist reign was marked by civil disorders and a tottering economy. Later U.S. congressional investigators ascribed some of this to schemes by International Telephone and Telegraph and the U.S. government through the CIA to destabilize the Allende government. Columnist Jack Anderson has said of the corporation: 'ITT operates its own worldwide foreign policy unit, foreign intelligence apparatus, communication network, classification system, and airliner fleet.' Because Allende campaigned on a program of expropriating American businesses, including ITT, the corporation, according to journalist Herb Borock, 'tried to get the CIA to support Allende's right-wing opponent and offered to pay the CIA $1 million to prevent the Chilean Congress from confirming Allende after he was elected.'

After this failed, ITT offered the Nixon administration an 'action plan' to savage the Chilean economy and cause social disorder. President Nixon later set up a special inter-agency group to implement the ITT program, and when the Chile story was publicized by the Church Committee of the Senate, then-CIA Director Richard Helms made misleading statements concerning Chile before the Senate's Committee on Foreign Relations and later pleaded nolo contendere to a misdemeanor charge of failing to testify fully about a covert political operation.

The United States' economic blockade of Chile choked Chile's commerce and produced 300 percent inflation, encouraging the unrest that ultimately resulted in an army coup and Allende's death.

ALP ARSLAN, Seljuq Sultan of Persia (1029–1072) Alp Arslan, the Seljuq (Turkish) Sultan of Persia, reigned from 1063 to 1072. Known as 'the lion-hearted hero,' he conquered Herat, Armenia, Georgia and Syria. His greatest triumph was at Manzikert in Armenia in 1071, when his army of 15,000 Turks defeated a Byzantine force of 100,000 under Romanus IV. When Romanus was taken prisoner and brought before him, the sultan asked of him: 'What would have been your behavior had fortune smiled upon your arms?'

Romanus replied, 'I would have inflicted upon thy body many a stripe.'

Arslan, however, treated his prisoner with all respect, releasing him on the pledge of a royal ransom and even burdening him with lavish parting gifts. Upon his return to Constantinople in disgrace, Romanus was deposed, imprisoned and blinded, then allowed to die from his untended wounds.

A year later the sultan was himself to suffer assassination. Advancing to the Oxus River to conquer Turkestan, Arslan was hindered by enemy fortresses there. Capturing one of the forts on December 15, 1072, the sultan had the governor, Yussuf Kothual, brought before him. A violent argument ensued, and suddenly the prisoner leapt forward and stabbed Alp Arslan to death.

ANANDA MAHIDOL, King of Siam (1925–1946) On the

morning of June 9, 1946, a gunshot sounded in the royal bedchamber of 20-year-old King Ananda (Rama VIII) of Siam. When attendants at the royal palace in Bangkok rushed in they found the dead monarch, a bullet wound in his head. The assassination proved to be one of the most traumatic events in the modern history of Thailand.

Born in Heidelberg, Germany, Ananda was 10 years old and a student in Switzerland when he succeeded his uncle, King Prajadhipok, to the throne in 1935. However, political and military turmoil prevented him from assuming his constitutional role until early 1946. There has never been an acceptable explanation for the assassination, although British authorities attributed it to a Communist plot. However, an analysis of the end result might lead to a different conclusion. The murder of the young king did much to shatter the principle of civilian constitutional government, and led to the return of military rule in Thailand.

AQUINO, Benigno (Ninoy), Jr. (1932–1983) On August 21, 1983 a group of reporters aboard a China Airlines plane bound for Manila listened as Benigno (Ninoy) Aquino, the Philippine opposition leader, outlined his plans on his return from self-imposed political exile in the United States. When the plane landed, Philippine security men escorted Benigno off the plane. The reporters heard gunshots. Aquino lay sprawled on the tarmac, dead.

The alleged gunman, Rolando Galman, was immediately killed by security guards. However, the common opinion in the Philippines and around the world was that members of the Marcos government and the Philippine army had planned Aquino's murder. Much of the speculation centered on General Fabian Ver, the army chief of staff, and Brigadier General Luther Custodio, the airport security chief.

A period of political turmoil followed in the Philippines, with the steady weakening of the Marcos regime as former Marcos supporters defected.

Ninoy Aquino himself was no stranger to strong-arm

politics, having served as mayor of Conception and later governor of Tarlac Province. In 1967 he became the only member of the Liberal Party (of which he was secretary general) to be elected to the Philippine Senate. Marcos clearly regarded Aquino as a potential rival for president, and under the terms of the martial law Marcos had declared in 1972, Aquino was sentenced to death and spent the next eight years in prison. In 1980 he was permitted to go to the United States for open-heart surgery. Marcos never expected Aquino to return, and when he did the stage was set for his assassination. The inept way it was carried out, with the transparent blaming of a lone gunman, doomed Marcos's rule.

The overconfident Marcos called early elections, and a team of observers from the U.S. Congress concluded that Marcos had tried to steal the election. Television news coverage showed the bodies of murdered campaign workers for Corazon Aquino, Benigno's widow. Nevertheless, for a time CIA Director William Casey and President Ronald Reagan tried to shore up Marcos, who had been a longtime ally of the United States. In time, however, the Reagan–Casey view could not withstand the avalanche of incriminating evidence. U.S. support withered, and on February 25, 1986, Marcos was deposed by an uprising of a portion of the Philippine army and the dramatic appearance of 'People Power' – civilians who kneeled in front of Marcos's tanks to protect pro-Aquino military units. Marcos fled into exile in Hawaii (where he died September 28, 1989), and Mrs. Aquino was elevated to the presidency of the Philippines.

Further reading: *Impossible Dream – The Marcoses, the Aquinos, and the Unfinished Revolution*, by Sandra Burton.

ARAMBURO, Pedro Eugenio (1903–1970) On May 29, 1970, two men dressed as army officers came to the home of former Argentine President Pedro Eugenio Aramburo, claiming they were there to arrange personal protection for him. Mrs. Aramburo admitted the men and then left to go shopping. The men actually were kidnappers and were seen leading Aramburu at gunpoint to a waiting car, where two accomplices had been waiting.

Aramburu rose through the military ranks and by 1951 he was made a brigadier general by dictator Juan Peron. Aramburu was one of the leaders in Peron's ouster in 1955 and was named provisional president, pressing the fight against all Peronist organizations until the 1958 elections. He then retired to private life reemerging in 1963 for a failed run at the presidency.

Within a few days of the kidnapping more than a dozen communiques were issued by various political organizations, from all over the political spectrum, claiming to have Aramburo. In time the Juan Jose–Valle–Montoneros Command, a Peronist group named for a Peronist army general executed in 1956, came to be regarded as the actual kidnappers. The Valle Command issued a communique headed 'Peron will return,' and announced that Aramburo was to be tried by a revolutionary tribunal for his part in the execution of 27 Peronist leaders in the unsuccessful 1956 coup. On June 1 the Valle Command announced that Aramburo had been found guilty and that he would face a firing squad. The group said it was 'impossible to negotiate his release.'

In a note the following day it was stated that Aramburo had been executed, but then a June 3 statement said the execution would not be carried out until June 4. These conflicting statements fueled wild speculation, including the theory that Argentine President Juan Carlos Ongania had actually had Aramburo kidnapped because he feared that the former president was plotting against him. In any event, the government was thrown into chaos, and on June 8 a junta made up of the commanders of Argentina's army, navy and air force forced Ongania from office and pledged to 'establish order' in the country and name a new president. In early July Juan Peron, living in exile in Spain, called for a revolt in Argentina and pledged to return 'at any moment I can be useful for something.' Then on July 16 Aramburo's body was found in an old farmhouse near Timote, some 300 miles west of Buenos Aires. He had been shot twice in the chest. By now it had been established that the Valle Command had been the kidnappers.

The police later identified Fernando Abal Medina, 23, as the mastermind of the kidnapping; he remained at large. In the end three individuals were charged in the assassination – Peron sympathizer Carlos Maguid, a 27-year-old television scriptwriter who drew an 18-year sentence, student leader Ignacio Velez, 27, who got 32 months, and Roman Catholic priest Alberto Carbone, 46, who was given a two-year suspended sentence as an accessory in the kidnapping.

The following year Peronist-inspired chaos enveloped the country, and Juan Peron returned to Argentina. In 1973 he once more became president, an office he held until his death in 1974.

ARSES, King of Persia (?–336 B.C.) Arses, King of Persia, succeeded to the throne in 338 B.C. only because of a number of assassinations carried out by the infamous eunuch Bagoas, who was for many years the real master of the empire. Arses was the youngest son of King Artaxerxes III, and as such had not been likely to ascend the throne. However, Bagoas, after many years of controlling Artaxerxes III, became annoyed by the king's occasional lapses to self-rule and decided to have him assassinated. Surveying the king's sons, Bagoas decided the young Arses would make a likely puppet, and upon murdering Artaxerxes, he also eliminated all Artaxerxes' older sons.

Arses did not reign long enough to have much of an impact on Persian history. The main foreign policy event was the invasion of Asia Minor by Philip II of Macedonia after Arses rejected Philip's demand for reparations for Artaxerxes' aid to the city of Perinthus against the Macedonians. On the home front Arses quickly became upset with the tyrannical control Bagoas was exercising and concluded he had to be rid of him. The king conspired to poison the eunuch, but the cunning Bagoas struck first, assassinating Arses and all his children, thus ending the direct family line. Bagoas next put on the throne a relative of the former king, Darius III. (See ARTAXERXES III, KING OF PERSIA; BAGOAS; DARIUS III, KING OF PERSIA.)

ARSINOE III, Queen of Egypt (c. 235–204 B.C.) The sister and wife of the dissolute Ptolemy IV Philopator, Queen Arsinoe III of Egypt enjoyed great popularity with the people. However, she was unable to prevent the steady erosion of the Ptolemaic kingdom under the debauched rule of her husband and his royal ministers. In 217 B.C. Arsinoe accompanied her brother to Raphia on a campaign of conquest in Palestine and gained the affection of the Egyptian soldiery even before their great victory over the troops of the Middle Eastern Seleucid kingdom.

Following the victory Arsinoe married her brother. About 210 B.C. she gave birth to the future Ptolemy V Epiphanes, but thereafter was confined to the palace on orders of the king, who spent his time with his male and female favorites. Arsinoe III's efforts to influence her husband's governmental or even personal behavior proved fruitless. When Ptolemy IV died in 205 B.C., Arsinoe regained power, as the mother of Ptolemy V, and was expected to move against the corrupt ministers who had brought the dynasty to its low ebb. However, the royal ministers were able to delay the enthronement of the new ruler until they arranged the murder of Arsinoe III.

Neither the king's nor queen's death was announced until the child Ptolemy was put on the throne. News of Ptolemy IV's death caused no public remorse, but large elements of the population rioted on learning of the queen's assassination. There was, in time, a rallying to the new ruler, and a measure of order was restored.

ARTAXERXES III, King of Persia (?–338 B.C.) As king of Persia, Artaxerxes III is known as both an energetic and a cruel leader. While cruelty certainly marked his reign, much of his energy emanated from the power behind the throne, the murderous and cunning eunuch Bagoas, without whose advice Artaxerxes III frequently refused to act. To secure his throne, Artaxerxes put to death virtually all of his relatives.

Artaxerxes launched a number of campaigns to reconquer Egypt and to put down revolts by the Phoenician cities and the princes of Cyprus. His mainstays of support were Bagoas and Mentor of Rhodes, who formed a close alliance with Bagoas. Eventually Bagoas ruled the Persian court and the upper satrapies, while Mentor took on the task of restoring the power of the empire in the west.

By 340 B.C. the Persian empire came under intense pressure from Philip of Macedonia, who attacked the cities of Perinthus and Byzantium. As the threat of the Macedonian invasion increased, friction developed between the king and his eunuch adviser. Finally in 338 B.C., Bagoas decided he needed a more pliant monarch on the throne and had the king and his elder sons killed, ensuring the succession of Artaxerxes III's youngest and presumably weakest son, Arses. In due course the eunuch would murder Arses as well. (See ARSES, KING OF PERSIA; BAGOAS.)

ATRAKCHI, Albert (1955–1985) On August 20, 1985, Albert Atrakchi, administrative attaché to the Israeli embassy in Egypt, was submachine-gunned to death in a car in a Cairo suburb. With him at the time were two other embassy employees – his 24-year-old wife, Illana, and Mazal Menashe, who were both wounded. It was the first fatal attack on an Israeli diplomat in Egypt since the two countries resumed diplomatic ties in 1979, and it occurred some four years after the assassination of Anwar Sadat, the Egyptian president who resumed diplomatic ties with Israel. Egypt's Revolution, a previously unknown organization, issued a statement of responsibility for the slaying, saying it had attacked 'members of the Israeli intelligence' and intended to do so 'until the Israeli enemy leaves the country.'

Both Egyptian and Israeli officials condemned the

attack and at the time appeared to be making an effort to keep the incident from derailing the slow improvement of the developing relationship between the two countries.

AURELIAN, Emperor of Rome (c. 212–275)   While the decline of the Roman Empire is generally thought to have begun in 211 with the death of the emperor Severus, that decay was arrested from time to time during the reigns of more or less competent rulers, and especially from 270 to 275, when Aurelian sat on the throne. He succeeded the not-incompetent Claudius II and defended the empire against the onslaught of the barbarians as well as ambitious monarchs in neighboring Zenobia, Palmyra and elsewhere. Autocratic but statesmanlike and certainly a brilliant soldier, Aurelian regained Britain, Gaul, Syria Egypt, Spain and Mesopotamia, and thus revived the glory of Rome; he won the accolade 'Restorer of the World' from grateful and proud Romans.

Aurelian ruled over a revived empire with magnanimity, restoring many fallen monarchs to favor and endowing them liberally. By increasing the distribution of free food in Rome, he did more for the plebeians than any of his predecessors. Has Aurelian solidified his rule and principles for a couple of decades, the decline of the empire might well have been arrested for scores of years, but the venality rampant in a sick Rome proved decisive. In 274 Aurelian launched a major military campaign against Persia. While on the march in 275, Aurelian was assassinated by a group of his officers who had apparently been misled by the emperor's secretary to believe that they had been marked for execution. The killing was a limited affair, not the start of a broad-based rebellion, as demonstrated by the fact that the legions, loyal to the memory of the dead emperor, did not attempt to name a successor, awaiting instead the decision of the Senate. Aurelian's widow, Ulpia Severina, continued to administer the government for six months until the Senate decided on the elderly Tacitus as the new ruler in 276. The soldiery, still mourning Aurelian, concurred.

B

BAGOAS (?–336 B.C.) One of the most amazing and awesome figures in Persian history, the eunuch Bagoas was for a number of years the most powerful figure in the empire, towering over kings, crowning them, and removing them by assassination when it suited his purposes. Bagoas was the commander in chief of the Achaemenid forces that conquered Egypt in 343 B.C., and he accumulated great wealth by seizing sacred writings from Egyptian temples and reselling them to the Egyptian priests for exorbitant sums.

In Persia Bagoas became more than merely the power behind the throne. His control was so complete that for a number of years King Artaxerxes III did virtually nothing without first consulting him. By 338 B.C. some friction developed between the king and the eunuch, and Bagoas murdered Artaxerxes. He also killed all the king's sons except the young Arses, whom he placed upon the throne. Two years later, when Arses opposed some of Bagoas's acts, the king set in motion a plan to poison the eunuch. Bagoas, however, struck first, having the king killed along with all his children.

Bagoas then decided that a collateral heir to the family, the satrap of Armenia, should be enthroned. He was, as Darius III. Bagoas was sure he had picked a pliable puppet, but Darius proved to be of sterner mettle and sought to exercise power on his own. Bagoas attempted to correct his misjudgment by poisoning the king, but Darius III had schooled himself well in Bagoas's methods. The king had become aware of the plot through spies, and when the eunuch tried to give Darius the poison, Darius forced Bagoas to drink the poison himself, thus ending the great assassin's reign of terror. (See ARSES, KING OF PERSIA; ARTAXERXES III, KING OF PERSIA; DARIUS III, KING OF PERSIA.)

BAHRAM VI CHUBIN, King of Persia (?–591) A general without royal blood, Bahram VI Chubin seized the Sasanian throne of Persia in 590 through the assassination of King Hormizd IV. Bahram had been Hormizd's top general and had gained much renown in repelling a Turkish invasion. However, in 589 he was defeated by the Romans and was treated with sneering disrespect by the king. When shortly thereafter two of Hormizd's brothers-in-law, Bostam and Bindoe, staged a palace coup, Bahram withdrew the support of the army from the king. In the ensuing disorder Hormizd was assassinated.

The throne should have passed to Hormizd's son Khosrow (or Chosroe) II, but Bahram forced the heir to flee to Mesopotamia. Khosrow was saved from capture by the military exploits of Bindoe, who lost out in the power struggle with Bahram. In 591, with Byzantine support, Khosrow returned to drive Bahram from the throne. The restored king set about avenging the assassination of his father, executing many of the conspirators, including Bindoe, whose support he had had to rely upon to achieve victory. Bahram was pursued to Turkistan by agents of the king and assassinated. A popular Middle Persian romance sketches the colorful career of the rebel general who for a short time became a king. (See HORMIZD IV, KING OF PERSIA; KHOSROW II, KING OF PERSIA.)

BANDARANAIKE, Solomon West Ridgway Dias (1899–1959) It is not freedom of speech so much as 'freedom of language' that is the driving force of the revolutionary and even terrorist ardor that dominates politics in many countries of the world, perhaps none more so than Ceylon in recent decades. It was such a burning issue that proved fatal to Solomon West Ridgway Dias Bandaranaike, the Prime Minister of Ceylon from 1956 to 1959. Oxford educated, Bandaranaike was a Christian converted to

Buddhism. This might have satisfied the religious situation, but the official language remained a searing problem. Political opponents castigated the prime minister on the ground that the interests of the Sinhalese and their tongue was being disadvantaged compared to those of the Tamil, the language among the peoples of Ceylon and South India.

The opposition to Bandaranaike became so strong that many of his own colleagues abandoned him, and he was forced to form a new government with a razor-thin majority. In parliament, the prime minister was the recipient of many threats of physical violence, which he tended to ignore. Outside observers felt the prime minister's position was secure since he was recognized as one of the greatest patriots of 20th-century Ceylon. However, on September 25, 1959, Bandaranaike was sitting on the veranda of his official residence when two Buddhist monks requested an audience. One of them, Talduwa Somarans Thero, pulled a gun from under his robes and shot the prime minister at close range. Bandaranaike died the next day.

BARDAS   See MICHAEL III, BYZANTINE EMPEROR.

BARNHILL, John (1906–1971)   In 1969 the violence that had plagued Northern Ireland in the 1920s returned with a vengeance, with 195 persons killed there by early December 1971. Strictly speaking, the first political assassination of the period did not occur until December 12, 1971, when John Barnhill, a right-wing member of the ruling Unionist Party, was murdered by members of the left-wing 'Official' branch of the Irish Republican Army.

According to Barnhill's wife, he was shot by gunmen when he opened the front door of their mansion in Strabanne, about 200 yards from the Republic of Ireland border. They then dragged his body to the living room, where they placed a bomb under him and blew up the mansion.

The Officials released a statement in Dublin in which they took responsibility for the assassination but contended they had merely intended to destroy the house. They insisted that Barnhill had been shot after he attacked two raiders who asked him and his wife to evacuate before the explosion. The statement said the bombing was in 'reprisal for the destruction of working-class homes throughout the province' by the British army.

British officials charged that the Irish government had failed to stop terrorists from moving freely across the border. In turn, John Lynch, prime minister of the Irish Republic condemned the Barnhill killing but denied protecting the terrorists and called for a United Nations observer team to ensure stability in the border area. Shortly before the Barnhill assassination Lynch had also said that the constitution of a united Ireland was negotiable, and indicated a willingness to write in accommodations for the Protestants of Northern Ireland. This was in response to a proposal by Labour Party leader Harold Wilson looking toward eventual Irish unification. Nothing came of these proposals, and assassinations and other terrorist acts continued unabated.

BARRIENTOS, Rene　See QUINTANILLA, ROBERTO.

BEATON, David (c.1494–1546) David Beaton, (also spelled Bethune), the Scottish statesman and cardinal who became archbishop of St. Andrews in 1539, learned his suppression of church reformers from his uncle James Beaton, primate of Scotland, chancellor and David's direct predecessor as archbishop of St. Andrews. It was James who burned the first Scottish martyr, Patrick Hamilton, in 1528 and after that several other reformers.

Dubbed princely, able and dissolute by historians, David Beaton began his political career in 1529 and became a trusted counselor of King James V. At Beaton's urging the king rejected the reformist policy of Henry VIII of England. Beaton sought to maintain a close alliance between Scotland and France as a counter to England and arranged James's two successive marriages to French noblewomen.

When James died in 1542 Beaton was imprisoned by James Hamilton, the earl of Arran, who became regent for James's daughter, Mary Stuart. However, in 1543 Arran changed sides and Beaton was freed and became chancellor and the virtual ruler of Scotland. He launched a massive prosecution of Protestants, and his policies so frustrated Henry VIII that Henry launched an abortive invasion of Scotland in 1544, instructing his army to destroy everything in its path, 'putting man, woman and child to fire and sword without exception where any resistance shall be made,' and particularly 'sparing no creature alive' in Beaton's St. Andrews.

Beaton nevertheless retained his power, becoming papal legate that same year. On March 1, 1546, Beaton had the popular reformer George Wishart burned at the stake. More than anything else, this act triggered Protestant opposition to Beaton, and Sir James Kirkcaldy, Norman Leslie and other Scottish gentlemen offered to help the English 'burn places belonging to the extreme party in the Church, to arrest and imprison the principal opponents of the English alliance, and to apprehend and slay the Cardinal himself.' Henry VIII embraced the plot enthusiastically and promised £1,000 on account for expenses. For a time the plotters were unable to get to Beaton, but on May 20, 1546, a large band of nobles and cutthroats gained entry to St. Andrews Castle and caught the Cardinal almost *in flagrante delicto*, or as John Knox, the Scottish reformer and founder of Presbyterianism, put it, 'busy at his accounts with Mistress Ogilvy that night.' They slew Beaton and hanged him for good measure.

Knox, at the time an almost unknown and undistinguished Scottish priest, was a member of the assassination party and reveled in the deed. 'Now, because the weather was hot,' he related, 'it was thought best, to keep him from stinking, to give him salt enough, a cope of lead . . . to await what exequies his brethren the bishops could prepare for him. These things we write merrily.'

BECKET, Thomas (c.1118–1170) It may be said that

Thomas Becket was assassinated twice, once physically and later by one of the most inventive methods of character assassination through a posthumous alteration of his name. A confidant and most worldly companion of King Henry II of England, Becket served as chancellor beginning in 1155 and for several years always sided with the king in his struggles with the clergy.

In 1161 Archbishop Theobald of Canterbury died. Henry hit upon what he was sure was the solution to his political problems: He would install Becket as archbishop of Canterbury, and with his man as both chancellor and archbishop, Henry's power troubles with the clergy would vanish. In the eyes of respectable churchmen Becket hardly qualified for the position, being, mildly put, a most secular type and too much the king's friend.

Becket too agreed with that view, expounding the position that the head of the church should be a spiritual man. Finally, though, he bowed to the king's wishes, and in June 1162 was consecrated as archbishop.

Henry's plans quickly went awry. Thomas Becket changed overnight. He resigned as chancellor – immediately ruining Henry's grand design – and took his episcopal obligations with a seriousness that the king and almost no one else had anticipated. His career was marked by a long series of quarrels with Henry, as he opposed the king's interference in ecclesiastical affairs. As archbishop, Becket insisted that church lands taken away in the Conquest be returned. He defied the king's authority to try to punish anyone connected with the Church, insisting they were subject only to church law and courts. He further enraged the king by excommunicating dissolute nobles.

Finally Becket was forced into exile in France for more than six years. When he returned, he was as aggressive as ever, although he realized the king would probably seek his head. As Becket opposed the king on one matter after another, Henry exploded in rage. 'What cowards have I about me,' he cried, 'that no one will rid me of this lowborn priest?'

Four of his knights – William Tracy, Hugh de Morville, Reginald Fitzurse and Richard Briton – hastened to Canterbury with a retinue of heavily armed soldiers and confronted Becket in the cathedral before the altar of Saint Benedict. When Becket refused an ultimatum to withdraw a number of excommunications, Fitzurse slashed him with his sword. The other knights joined in. It was a slaying that shocked Christendom and ensured Becket's rapid canonization to sainthood.

For a time Henry denied any responsibility for the assassination, insisting he had not called for Becket's murder but simply had asked a rhetorical question.

In this period we also find the origins of Becket's name as Thomas a Becket, which appears to have been an attempt to brand Becket as somehow not quite English. Becket was born in England, and although his parents were of French origin, there seemed to have been no contemporary use of the *a*. The name doctoring has lasted for centuries, however, since Becket's name to this day probably appears with the *a* more often than without.

In the end Henry II paid a grim price for Becket's assassination, doing penance under orders from the pope. The king walked barefoot in a pilgrim's gown and hair shirt through the streets of Canterbury to Becket's tomb in the cathedral, there confessing and asking pardon. The king bared his back and all the monks at Canterbury lashed him seven times each, giving him hundreds of welts.

Thomas Becket had finally won his struggle with Henry II.

BEN BARKA, Mehdi (1920–1965)   The Ben Barka Affair of 1965 produced a major rift between France and Morocco, and involved not only an act of state terrorism but the active cooperation of another country's counter-intelligence agency, or at least a portion of it. Mehdi Ben Barka had been a leader in the fight for Moroccan independence and had served three years under house arrest until 1954. Later he became an opposition leader against the Moroccan government and King Hassan II, whom he had served as tutor when Hassan was a prince.

Ben Barka had lived in exile in France since 1963, but his activities remained a thorn in the side of the Moroccan government. He was abducted from his Paris home on October 29, 1965, and was never seen again. In the criminal investigation that followed it was learned he had been brought to the villa of a notorious ex-convict by a member of France's counterintelligence agency, the SDECE (Service de Documentation Exterieure et de Contre-Espionage), and two French police inspectors. The following day an SDECE agent met Moroccan interior minister General Mohammad Oufkir and some members of the Moroccan security at Orly Airport and drove them to the villa. There was later court testimony that General Oufkir had tortured Ben Barka with a dagger, and subsequently Ben Barka was seen no more.

The scandal led to the recall of ambassadors from France and Morocco, and French president Charles de Gaulle called the abduction and apparent assassination one 'organized abroad with the complicity of French special services or police.' The Moroccan government dismissed the matter, calling it 'a purely French affair.' A shake-up of the SDECE followed, and Premier Georges Pompidou was relieved of the responsibility of getting reports from the agency.

After a trial, General Oufkir was found guilty in absentia and sentenced to life imprisonment, but Morocco did not release the interior minister to the French and King Hassan II continued to voice support for him. In 1972 Oufkir committed suicide after being identified as the mastermind of an unsuccessful attempt to assassinate the king. (See HASSAN II, KING OF MOROCCO.)

BERNADOTTE, Count Folke (1895–1948) Military officer, humanitarian and diplomat Count Folke Bernadotte had a long career with the Swedish government in several important fields. A nephew of King Gustav V, Bernadotte headed the Swedish Red Cross during World

War II, arranging the exchange of many prisoners of war and saving an estimated 20,000 inmates of Nazi concentration camps. Because Bernadotte was respected by all combatant nations in Europe, Heinrich Himmler used him as a conduit for an unsuccessful offer that would have had Germany surrender unconditionally to the United States and Great Britain but not to the Soviet Union.

In May 1948 the United Nations Security Council sent Bernadotte to Palestine to arrange a truce between Israeli and Arab troops, and Bernadotte won the grudging acceptance from both Israel and the Arab states to a U.N. ceasefire. However, his proposal that Arab refugees be allowed to return to their homes in what had become Israel earned him a number of threats against his life. On September 17, 1948, Bernadotte and his French aide-de-camp were assassinated in their car on a Jerusalem street.

For decades the assassination was credited to Jewish extremists, the Stern Gang. Once led by Yitzhak Shamir, the Stern Gang was the most militant of the underground bands seeking to establish the Israeli state. It was not until September 1988, however, that two former guerrillas of the group appeared on Israeli radio and television to admit their roles in the Bernadotte murder. A former leading member, Yehoshua Zeitler, told the Israeli public he had decided to reveal what had happened because, he said, he feared that the U.N. would again seek to force concessions from Israel that would threaten its survival. Meshulam Markover declared he led the four-man assassination squad in a jeep that cut off Bernadotte. Three guerrillas jumped out, according to Markover, and one of them, Yehoshua Cohen, now deceased, fired the fatal shots that killed both men.

The Stern Gang, formally known as Lohamei Herut Israel (Fighters for the Freedom of Israel), had previously split from another underground organization, the Irgun, led by Menachem Begin. The Stern Gang gained its new name from its first leader, Avraham Stern, who was shot to death while in the custody of British police charged with a U.N. mandate over the territory. On Stern's death,

Yitzhak Shamir became one of the three commanders of the group.

Following the 1988 media revelations, Shamir, then prime minister of Israel, declared through a spokesman that he had not played a role in the killings since the group had officially disbanded six months previous to them.

BETANCOURT, Romulo (1908–1981) – Attempted Assassination One of the most important failed assassination attempts in Latin American history occurred on Venezuelan Armed Forces Day, June 24, 1960, as President Romulo Betancourt was being driven to preside over the military parade in Caracas. There was a fierce explosion and the presidential limousine was hurled across the street and engulfed in flames as sixty pounds of explosives packed in two suitcases were detonated in a nearby parked car. Remarkably, Betancourt, Defense Minister Josue Lopez Henriques and the minister's wife, all riding in the backseat, were only slightly injured. However, Colonel Ramon Armas Perez, chief aide-de-camp to the president, the chauffeur and a bystander were killed.

It was determined that the ammonium-nitrate bomb had been put together 500 miles away in Ciudad Trujillo, and the 'godfather' of the operation was Rafael Leonidas Trujillo, the longtime dictator of the Dominican Republic. In fact Trujillo was present at a discussion on June 17 in which a small group of conspirators met in the home of Trujillo's brother, Pipi, for instructions on the operation of the bomb by a radio and electronics man named Johnny Abbes. Also present among the conspirators were some Venezuelans who were to carry out a coup d'etat once Betancourt was dead. When the assassination failed, there was no coup.

This had not been the first attempt Trujillo had made on the liberal Betancourt. While the latter was earlier in exile in Cuba, Trujillo had tried to have his agents inject him with poison in broad daylight on a Havana street.

It was not simple political philosophical differences that provoked the second attempt on Betancourt's life, but rather more pressing problems for Trujillo. In Cuba Fidel Castro had come to power, and in America the Eisenhower administration was obsessed with the idea that Trujillo's oppressive regime was laying the seeds for another Communist menace in the hemisphere. The United States was also having trouble mobilizing political forces in Latin America against Cuba; previously such democratic leaders as Betancourt, Jose Figueres of Costa Rica and Governor Luis Munoz Marin of Puerto Rico had warned Washington that its efforts to isolate Castro were doomed unless the United States first demonstrated that it also opposed right-wing dictators in general and Trujillo in particular. Even the 1956 kidnapping of Columbia University lecturer Dr. Jesus de Galindez and his apparent murder by Trujillo agents had not goaded Washington to strong action against the Dominican dictator, despite the enormous uproar throughout Latin America.

It was apparently to relieve this pressure that Trujillo ordered the abortive Betancourt assassination. After Trujillo's failure, Venezuela, Costa Rica and Puerto Rico renewed strong pressure on the United States, and Betancourt warned U.S. Secretary of State Christian Herter, 'If you don't eliminate him, we will invade.'

Ten months later Trujillo himself was eliminated. (See DE GALINDEZ, JESUS; TRUJILLO MOLINA, RAFAEL LEONIDAS.)

Further reading: *Trujillo*: *The Death of the Goat*, by Bernard Diederich.

BETHUNE, David   See BEATON, DAVID.

BIAYENDA, Emile Cardinal   See NGOUABI, MARIEN.

BIKO, Steven B. (1947–1977)   Few deaths caused stronger condemnation of the white South African government and its harsh efforts to maintain apartheid than that of Steven Biko, who was one of the most influential black student leaders, the central figure in the country's black consciousness movement, founder of the South African

Students Organization and cofounder of the Black Peoples' Convention. On August 18, 1977, Biko was in police custody in Port Elizabeth, under arrest for writing pamphlets that allegedly incited violence and stirred unrest among blacks in the city.

On September 12 Biko died while in police detention. Authorities claimed he died of a hunger strike he had begun on September 5. Opposition leaders demanded an inquiry, and the U.S. State Department protested Biko's death, calling for an investigation and describing the dead man as 'another victim of the *apartheid* system and the . . . security legislation which supports that system.' The *Rand Daily Mail*, South Africa's leading liberal newspaper, pointed out in an editorial that people don't die from a hunger strike of only seven days.

Sticking to the official explanation, Justice Minister James T. Kruger told a meeting of the ruling National Party, 'Biko's death leaves me cold.' He insisted Biko had been given adequate medical supervision during his fast and added that it was 'his democratic right' to starve himself to death. By September 17, under a drumbeat of criticism, Kruger admitted that there might have been some irregularities in Biko's death. He now agreed Biko had not died of starvation and said he had learned that Biko had been driven to Pretoria from Port Elizabeth on September 11, 24 hours before his death.

A later autopsy revealed the cause of Biko's death as extensive head wounds. Under questioning at an inquest by a lawyer for the Biko family, witnesses testified that Biko had been kept naked and chained in his cell while held in Port Elizabeth. They also said he had been covered with only a blanket when transported by car to Pretoria, a 750-mile drive taking 14 hours. However, Pretoria's chief magistrate, Marthinus J. Prins, found after the three-week inquest that the South African police were blameless in the affair. The magistrate ruled 'the available evidence does not prove that the death was brought about by any act or omission involving or amounting to an offense on the part of any person.' This decision provoked a new round of protest worldwide.

In 1979 Biko's family received 65,000 rand, about U.S. $76,000, in an out-of-court settlement of a suit against the South African police, who made the payment 'without admission of liability.'

BORGIA, Juan (1477–1497) Of the many murders committed during the heyday of the Borgias, the assassination of one of that family's members remains subject to speculation and dispute. Had Juan Borgia, the younger son of the dissolute Pope Alexander VI, been murdered by his brother, Cesare Borgia? It was a logical question to ask about the notorious Cesare, who earned the admiration of Niccolo Machiavelli and served as the model for the latter's classic on politics, *The Prince*.

Juan was Alexander VI's favorite, and the pope saw in him a great political future. Originally that role was to be played by the two brothers' elder half-brother, Pedro Luis, who became duke of Gandia. As was common with second sons, Cesare was guided to a religious career, one for which he was eminently unsuited even in the days of high-living churchmen. He was better known for his hunting parties, his innumerable amorous affairs and his lavish wardrobe, rather than for any dedication to ecclesiastical duties.

When Pedro Luis died in 1488, Cesare hoped to be saved from the church, but his father bypassed him in favor of Juan as the heir to his dukedom. Alexander also installed Juan as commander of the papal army in 1496. Cesare was delighted when the papal troops under Juan suffered a major defeat near Bassano in January 1497, thwarting Alexander's plans for extending papal territories.

On June 14, 1497, Juan and Cesare took supper with their mother, accompanied by two footmen and a mysterious masked man who had joined them during the meal. Juan had been seen frequently in public with this mystery man and seemed very attached to him. After the meal they rode off with the masked man sharing Juan's horse.

At a certain point Juan and the masked man decided to go off on their own, despite Cesare's warning that Rome was dangerous after dark. Juan was never seen alive after that. A Tiber boatman saw a man leading a horse with what appeared to be a body across the saddle. He thought he heard someone speak the words, 'my lord.' This was followed by a splash.

When Juan failed to turn up, the river was dragged and his body was fished out. He had been stabbed nine times, and his purse was intact. At first the general belief was that enemies of the pope, such as the Sforza family or the Orsini family, were behind the assassination, but suspicion shifted to Cesare. As historian Barbara W. Tuchman writes, 'In the bubbling stew of Rome's rumors, no depravity appeared beyond the scope of the Borgias.'

The pope himself was gravely affected by his son's murder, and he locked himself away in the Vatican for three days. When he emerged, he committed himself to a program of reform to make up for his own sins, which he felt had caused God's wrath to descend on Juan. Alexander's newfound devotion did not last long, however, and thereafter he shortly pulled Cesare out of his cardinalate in his need for a trusted secular lieutenant. There remains considerable dispute whether Cesare had had his brother assassinated. Some present-day historians tend to doubt it, but there is no doubt that from that period on the Borgias committed many more deceits and assassinations.

Further reading: *The Borgias*, by Michael Mallett; *A Criminal History of Mankind*, by Colin Wilson; *The March of Folly*, by Barbara W. Tuchman.

BORIS III, King of Bulgaria (1894–1943)   The death of King Boris III of Bulgaria was announced on German radio on August 28, 1943. The cause of death, however, has remained a form of historical multiple choice. It has variously been reported as due to a heart attack, self-inflicted gunshot or poisoning, or more likely an assassination. What is known is that just before his death Boris III had a stormy interview with Adolf Hitler.

Boris III became king of Bulgaria when his father, Ferdinand I, abdicated in 1918. However, the real power in the country passed to political strongman Aleksandur Stamboliski, the head of the Bulgarian Agrarian party. There followed over four years of struggle between the king and Stamboliski, who held the post of prime minister. In 1923 Stamboliski was murdered and the king was generally considered to have been involved in the plot. The king did not, however, gain a strong hold on the nation for more than another decade, being himself the subject of numerous terrorist attacks, including two attempts on his life within a few days in April 1925.

In 1934 a military dictatorship replaced the constitutional government Boris had established to win back the support of the peasants. Boris III found he could maneuver well in the atmosphere of military control and slowly reasserted his power. In 1935 he succeeded in installing Georgi Kyoseivanov, a personal favorite, as prime minister, and within a few years Boris III was dictator in all but name.

Boris maneuvered his foreign policy close to Great Britain, but finally, under pressure from the Nazis in 1941, he joined the Axis powers and declared war on Great Britain. Hitler, however, found the king only a reluctant ally. While the monarch participated in the invasion of Yugoslavia and Greece, he resisted declaring war on the Soviet Union. In August 1943 the king had his fateful meeting with Hitler and died immediately thereafter. Because Hitler would not countenance anything less than total support from his allies, he would have taken a hard line against any show of resistance or independence. Just the previous month Benito Mussolini had been forced to resign in Italy when the majority of the Fascist Grand Council voted him out. One theory is that Mussolini's downfall may well have determined Boris III's fate. (See STAMBOLISKI, ALEKSANDUR.)

BOUDIAF, Mohammed (1919–1992) In an assassination muddied by imprecise factual reports, Mohammed Boudiaf, the president of Algeria's ruling military council, was killed on June 29, 1992 in a hail of machine-gun fire as he was speaking in Annaba, on the country's east coast. The killer, dressed in a military uniform, shot at the podium and hit Boudiaf in the neck and back. According to varying accounts of witnesses, gunfire erupted between the presidential guards and other soldiers. It was reported that 41 persons were wounded in the attack, which apparently also included grenade explosions.

The president was flown to a military hospital on the outskirts of Algiers but died shortly afterwards. Meanwhile, initial reports indicated that the unidentified assassin had been shot by presidential bodyguards, but the government later said he had been captured. Interior Minister Larbi Belkhair later identified the killer as a member of an élite security force and that he 'leans in an Islamic direction.' Subsequently, the suspect was identified as Lt. Lembarak Boumaraf, a 26-year-old secret service agent in a unit charged with the president's safety.

Other stories circulated that there had been two assassins, one of whom was killed and the other arrested. There were additional reports that as many as a dozen of Boudiaf's guards, including some commanders, had been arrested in connection with the assassination. Among the groups mentioned as possible plotters in the killing was the fundamentalist Islamic Salvation Front (FIS), which had been on the verge of sweeping parliamentary elections five months earlier before the military seized the government to prevent that victory. Boudiaf, a hero of Algeria's liberation war, living in voluntary exile for 29 years, was recalled and placed in power by the army. Also under suspicion were the military itself and the former ruling party, the National Liberation Front (FLN), both groups having had differences with Boudiaf.

In his speech – which was in dedication of a new cultural center – Boudiaf said, 'We must know that the life of a human being is very short. We are all going to die. Why should we cling so much to power? Other peoples have overtaken us by technology and science. Islam . . .' His words were then cut off by the deadly gunfire.

BREDOW, Kurt von   See SCHLEICHER, KURT VON.

BRITANNICUS (A.D. 42–55)   The son of Emperor Claudius and the notorious Messalina, the young Britannicus
could be described as a youth ripe for assassination within
the intricate intrigues swirling around the Roman throne.
When Agrippina the Younger, the sister of Caligula,
married Claudius, she was determined to make her son,
Nero, emperor. She induced Claudius to name Nero as
his heir to the throne, ahead of his natural son, Britannicus.

After Agrippina poisoned Claudius and Nero became
emperor, she acted for a time as the de facto ruler of
Rome, her son being distracted by other interests and
pleasures. However, Nero was egged on to trim his
mother's authority by a number of courtiers, especially
his tutor, the philosopher-dramatist Seneca. Aware of
these machinations, the infuriated Agrippina announced
that Britannicus was the true heir to the throne and
threatened to topple Nero. The 18-year-old emperor
solved that vexing problem with typical imperial
resourcefulness – assassination. Nero procured the
services of an accomplished poisoner named Locusta,
who is presumed to have been the supplier of the
poison that had previously dispatched Claudius.
Britannicus, despite his tender years, was always
cautious when dealing with Nero and always had his
food sampled by a taster. At a banquet in 55 Britannicus tried a drink after his taster, found it too hot and
asked that some water be added to cool it. It was the
water that was poisoned, and Britannicus went into
violent and painful convulsions until he died. Nero gazed
on coolly, noting that such attacks were common to
epileptics. Thus Nero adroitly checkmated his mother,
who eventually fell herself to Nero's hired assassin. (See
AGRIPPINA THE YOUNGER; CLAUDIUS, EMPEROR OF
ROME.)

BUBACK, Siegfried (1920–1977)   On April 7, 1977, Siegfried Buback, West Germany's chief federal prosecutor, was riding with his driver and bodyguard in a Mercedes in Karlsruhe, Germany, the home of the country's highest court. Two men on a motorcycle pulled up next to the car at a traffic light, and the pillion rider opened up on the car with a submachine gun. Buback and his driver died instantly, and the badly wounded bodyguard would die five days later. The assassins switched from the motorcycle to an automobile and were driven away by a third member of the hit team.

Buback had been coordinating the federal and state investigations into terrorism in West Germany and had been acclaimed for the successful arrest of the Baader-Meinhof gang leaders in 1972. He had been the chief prosecutor at their trial, which had been in progress since May 21, 1975.

The Baader-Meinhof leaders' trial was completed, and on April 28, 1977, Andreas Baader, 33, Jan-Karl Raspe, 32, and Gudrun Ensslin, 36, were sentenced to life imprisonment for several murders, as well as 15 additional years for other terrorist activities. All three were later said to have committed suicide in prison, although their supporters claimed they had been murdered. In May one of the three men sought for Buback's murder, Guenther Sonnenberg, was wounded in a gun battle near the Swiss border. (A woman charged with other terrorist acts was captured at the same time.) (See SCHLEYER, HANNS-MARTIN.)

BUCKINGHAM, George Villiers, First Duke of (1592–1628) Immensely charming, George Villiers, the first duke of Buckingham, was introduced to King James I of England in 1614 just as that monarch, notorious for his attraction to handsome young men, was tiring of his Scottish favorite, Robert Carr, earl of Somerset. Within five years, after a number of prestigious advancements, Buckingham had become lord high admiral and was dispensing the king's patronage. Among those who enjoyed the duke's bounty were many of his relatives, and

Buckingham soon alienated the upper classes from the crown.

Buckingham's intrusion into international politics proved to be disastrous, finally leading to various moves in Parliament to have him dismissed. James I disregarded such calls, as did King Charles I, who succeeded to the throne in 1625. Buckingham and Prince Charles had been very close, and as monarch the latter stood by Buckingham against all attacks even though Buckingham became known as the virtual king of England. In late 1625 Buckingham launched a huge land and sea campaign against the Spanish port of Cadiz, but, poorly organized and equipped, it proved a colossal failure. Buckingham was impeached by Parliament, but the king countered by dissolving that body to prevent any trial.

Buckingham went on to failure after failure, such as an attempt to relieve the French Protestant (Huguenot) port of La Rochelle being besieged by French government troops. There were also charges of Buckingham's sale of honors and accepting bribes from the East India Company. Still Charles I successfully repelled all attempts to dismiss Buckingham, even though virtually all elements of society opposed his friend, including the upper and lower classes, the Puritan zealots and especially the military veterans left impoverished because they were unable to collect their arrears in pay.

Among this latter group was one John Felton, a naval lieutenant, who had served at Cadiz and La Rochelle, where he was seriously wounded. Now Felton lay hungry in a London garret, brooding about his inability to collect the pay owed him, to say nothing of the promotion he had expected. Felton read many of the anti-Buckingham pamphlets, bought a butcher's knife and walked 60 miles from London to Portsmouth, where Buckingham was in the process of readying yet another expedition to La Rochelle. On August 23, 1628, Felton gained access to a dimly lit hallway of Buckingham's headquarters. As the duke prepared to make his toilet, Felton plunged his knife into the duke's chest. Buckingham made an effort to draw his sword, crying out, 'God's wounds, the villain hath killed me!' He died shortly later, with his wife in attendance. Felton was cornered in the kitchen, where he surrendered.

The electrifying news of Buckingham's assassination spread rapidly, prompting much rejoicing in London. Felton himself was cheered by crowds on his journey to the capital for trial. By then he was contrite and sent his apologies to the widow, begging her forgiveness. She gave it, and Felton was executed without torture, a concession the king felt obliged to make.

Buckingham's death did not cure England's ills, and his exercise of power had done much to fuel the tensions that eventually exploded in the civil war in 1640 between the royalists and the forces of Parliament.

Further reading: *George Villiers, First Duke of Buckingham,* by H. Ross Williamson.

BUCKLEY, William (1928–1985) The kidnapping of CIA Beirut station chief William Buckley by Islamic terrorists in Lebanon on March 16, 1984, was to have a profound impact on the intelligence activities of the United States and was to give considerable impetus to the arms-for-hostages scandal that bedeviled the final days of the Reagan administration. In the attempt to free Buckley, CIA Director William Casey authorized or ignored efforts clearly violating administration policy for dealing with hostage takers.

In his White House office, Lieutenant Colonel Oliver North concocted a plan to utilize a Middle East informant of the Drug Enforcement Administration to buy Buckley's freedom. North informed Robert C. (Bud) McFarlane, the National Security Adviser, that $200,000 could win the release of two American hostages, including Buckley. McFarlane approached President Ronald Reagan with the proposal and won approval for the money to be raised by private sources. North had a source in mind, Texas billionaire H. Ross Perot, who did provide the money.

On June 7, 1985, North sent a top secret memo to McFarlane in which he said the $200,000 would be merely a down payment. North declared he had met with the DEA 'asset' and wrote, 'The hostages can be bribed free for $1 million apiece.' North added, 'It is assumed that the price cannot be negotiated down, given the number of people requiring bribes.' McFarlane approved the plan and the $200,000 was sent.

On October 4, Islamic Jihad, the terrorist group claiming to have taken Buckley, announced his execution, and eight days later a blurred photograph purporting to show Buckley's corpse appeared in a Beirut newspaper. Islamic Jihad said his execution had been ordered in retaliation for an Israeli bombing of the Palestine Liberation Organization base in Tunisia. However, there was no real proof of when the photograph was taken.

Later it would be concluded that Buckley had died in June 1985 of either extreme torture or lack of medical care – or both.

Further reading: *Veil: The Secret Wars of the CIA 1981–1987*, by Bob Woodward.

BURGOS CATHEDRAL MURDER   See GUITERREZ DE CASTRO, S. GUITTEREZ.

C

CACERES, Ramon   See HEUREAUX, ULISES.

CAESAR, Julius (102?–44 B.C.)   Although the soothsayer's warning to Julius Caesar to 'beware the Ides of March' is included in Suetonius, Plutarch and Appian, it may well be legend. What is true is that on March 14, 44 B.C., Caesar engaged a number of friends in a dinner discussion on the question: What is the best death? His own answer: 'A sudden one.'

At the time Caesar stood at the pinnacle of his power. He had survived being proscribed (officially ordered to be killed) by Sulla when he was forced to flee Rome in 81 B.C. Able to return in 78 B.C. on Sulla's death, he began a political career as a member of the Democratic, or Popular, Party. In 60 B.C., after winning considerable honors in war in Spain, Caesar formed the First Triumvirate, comprising Pompey, Crassus and himself. Later, after Crassus was killed in war in the east, Pompey joined forces with the Senate in opposition to Caesar's ever-increasing power.

In 49 B.C. Caesar refused to return to Rome from Gaul at the Senate's command; instead he crossed the Rubicon with his armies and commenced civil war. The result was total victory for Caesar with Pompey's assassination in 48 B.C. in Egypt.

Caesar returned to Rome and stood as dictator and emperor in all but name. As was often his custom, Caesar sought the support of his former enemies by pardoning them, but their opposition continued. In 44 B.C. Caesar planned to leave Rome on March 18 to begin a great military campaign in the East: He would capture Parthia to avenge Crassus, march around the Black Sea and pacify Scythia. He would travel the Danube and conquer Germany. Then with the empire secure he would return to Rome with untold honors and spoils and enough wealth to end the city's economic woes. He would then be powerful enough to ignore all opposition and to name his successor.

Few in Rome who learned of Caesar's great campaign doubted he would succeed. The aristocracy, foreseeing their extinction by the return of a triumphant Caesar, joined the republicans in the Senate who still hoped to restore the republic. But all depended on Caesar's being assassinated before he left.

What was so amazing about the assassination plot was how extensive it was without Caesar's learning of it. There were 60 members of the conspiracy, and all held their peace. Critical to the plot was Marcus Brutus, who was recruited by Gaius Cassius after he had involved several other senators, as well as some investors who had lost income with Caesar's restriction of their collection of provincial taxes. Also among the plotters were some of Caesar's own generals who were dissatisfied with their spoils of war. Brutus was an important ingredient in the plot because he had wide repute as a virtuous Roman. He was believed to be a descendant of the Brutus who had put the kings to flight almost five centuries before. His mother was Servilia, and, says Appian, 'It was thought that Brutus was Caesar's son, as Caesar was the lover of Servilia about the time of Brutus' birth.'

Plutarch reports that Caesar also believed Brutus to be his son. Will Durant would later add, 'Possibly Brutus himself shared this opinion, and hated the dictator for having seduced his mother and made him, in the gossip of Rome, a bastard instead of a Brutus.'

After much hesitation, Brutus concluded assassination was the only honorable course, but he insisted, with tragic consequences, that Caesar's loyal friend Marc Antony be spared.

Caesar left for the Senate on March 15, shortly before a friend arrived to tell him he had just learned of a plot.

Caesar arrived at Pompey's theater, where the Senate was to meet, and a tablet bearing the full information of the plot was thrust into his hand. Caesar did not read it but entered the theater and sat down. Marc Antony came moments later but was delayed in conversation outside the hall by one of the conspirators.

Tillius Cimber, a senator, approached Caesar with a petition to allow the return of his brother, whom Caesar had banished from Rome. This allowed the other senators and conspirators to crowd around. With swiftness Tillius seized Caesar's robe at the neck and tore it open, the attack signal. From behind Caesar, Casca, a tribune of the people, who was to strike the first blow, thrust his dagger at Caesar's throat, but the blade only grazed the target's chest. Caesar grasped Casca's arm and threw him off balance, but in the process he left his side open. He received a second wound, this more serious, probably from Casca's brother. Cassius then stabbed Caesar in the face.

Now the other conspirators took courage and attacked. Caesar staggered under a series of wounds, yet defended himself though half-blinded by his own blood. He still saw well enough when Brutus came forward to strike him.

'Some have writen,' Suetonius says, 'that when Marcus Brutus rushed at him he said, in Greek, "*kai su teknon*" [You, too, my child].'

It was said that when Brutus stabbed him in the groin, Caesar ended all resistance. He drew his robe over his face and head and submitted to the final blows, falling at the foot of Pompey's statue. Caesar was granted what he regarded the 'best death.'

Learning what had happened, Antony, disguised as a slave, fled and made it safely to his home. In the end Antony and Caesar's adopted son, Gaius Octavius, the future Augustus Caesar, were to gain the upper hand, and the assassins, already hated by the Roman populace, would be killed. Marcus Brutus threw himself on a friend's sword after being defeated in battle.

Did Caesar's assassination change the history of Rome?

Historians debate the point, but certainly the republican plotters accomplished little with the ending of Caesar's dictatorship, as it was replaced by Augustus and the imperial Caesars who followed him. The empire and not the republic was the legacy of the assassination. (See POMPEY THE GREAT.)

Further reading: *The Story of Civilization III – Caesar and Christ*, by Will Durant.

CALIGULA, Emperor of Rome (A.D. 12–41)   A number of historians have marveled at the fact that the Roman emperor Caligula managed to rule Rome for four years. Caligula killed capriciously; his sexual vices were abominable even by Roman imperial standards; and, perhaps worst of all in the view of many high-stationed contemporaries, he squandered the entire treasury of the greatest empire the world had ever known.

When Caligula came to the throne, he had 2.7 billion sesterces in the treasury, thanks to Tiberius's skillful management of funds. Within a scant few years Caligula had spent it all – and much more besides. He bathed himself not in water but in perfume. He gave banquets that cost as much as 10 million sesterces. He spent an incredible sum to have ships anchored in a double line three miles long and covered with planks and earth so he could ride back and forth, because a soothsayer had once told the young Caligula that he had as much a chance of becoming emperor as he did of riding dry-shod over the Bay of Baiae.

To keep the funds coming in Caligula levied a sales tax on all food, instituted wage taxes and even levied a tax on the earnings of prostitutes ('as much as each received for one embrace'). He victimized rich men by accusing them of treason and having them condemned to death so that their fortunes went to the treasury.

Declaring himself a god, Caligula committed incest with all three of his sisters, and even forced his sister Drusilla to divorce her husband and marry him, making her heir to the throne. For any woman of rank for whom he devel-

oped a desire, Caligula sent letters of divorce in her
husband's name and then ordered them to his embrace. In
between four marriages – the first three ending in rather
quick divorce, with one ex-wife specifically forbidden to
have relations with any man thereafter – Caligula enjoyed
a number of homosexual interludes.

Many died at Caligula's hands. He enjoyed fencing with
gladiators with a wooden sword, and once, when a
gladiator went down deliberately, Caligula pulled a dagger and stabbed him to death, then showed off the bloody
weapon in triumph. Told once that the price of raw meat
for the wild animals in the circus had risen, he decided
criminals would do as well. He described Rome as 'the
city of necks waiting for me to chop them.' In the middle
of a banquet he delighted in reminding his guests that he
could have them all killed where they reclined. And when
embracing a wife or mistress he would announce brightly,
'Off comes this beautiful head whenever I give the word.'

Caligula had come to the throne thanks to assassination, when Macro the prefect of the Praetorian Guard,
smothered the feeble and ailing Tiberius. For a time after
coming to the throne in A.D. 37 Caligula accepted Macro
as a valued and trusted adviser. The following year,
however, he had Macro killed.

In all his excesses, Caligula sought to ensure the loyalty
of the Praetorians by rewarding them with money and
gifts. But even they were not exempt from his lapses into
capricious murders. One day a number of the guards,
headed by the tribune Cassius Chaerea, murdered the
emperor in a secret passage of the palace leading to the
palatine games. As word of the assassination filtered
through the city, many Romans feared Caligula was up to
one of his deadly tricks, seeking to discover who would
rejoice at his reported death.

As though to confirm the assassination, other guards
hurried to the palace and proceeded to kill Caligula's wife
and dash out his young daughter's brains against a wall.
The guards then found Caligula's 50-year-old uncle Claudius cowering in terror. Lame and a stammerer, Claudius

was regarded as an idiot. The guards proclaimed him emperor, and fearing the army's might, the Senate confirmed the choice. In fact, most members of that body thought it a shrewd choice. After four years of dealing with a raving lunatic they would now face merely a harmless dolt. (See CLAUDIUS, EMPEROR OF ROME; TIBERIUS, EMPEROR OF ROME.)

CALINESCU, Armand (1893–1939)   Armand Calinescu, prime minister of Romania, made the most persistent effort of any political figure to try to crush that country's notorious fascist and anti-Semitic Iron Guard. In 1938 Calinescu, then minister of the interior, ordered the arrest of Iron Guard members, and in November of that year the group's longtime charismatic leader, Corneliu Z. Codreanu, was taken into custody. While he and 17 of his followers and aides were being moved from one prison to another, all were shot and killed, according to Calinescu's department, by a lone gunman who was 'unknown and unapprehended.'

The government's stability was at least for a time assured. However, the Iron Guard had not been destroyed by the drastic action. On September 21, 1939, Calinescu, now prime minister, was assassinated by members of the Iron Guard as he was driving to his home. The Iron Guard was instrumental in bringing Marshall Ion Antonescu to power in 1940. Antonescu, a friend of Hitler, joined the war on the Nazis' side, but he also crushed the Iron Guard after it had served its purpose. After the war Antonescu was shot as a war criminal.

CALVO SOTELO, Jose (?–1936)   Jose Calvo Sotelo, a Spanish monarchist and a finance minister in Miguel Primo de Rivera's government, was assassinated on July 13, 1936, after being kidnapped from his Madrid home by left-wing gunmen. His bullet-ridden body was found near a cemetery outside the capital.

The murder, which is regarded as the start of the Spanish civil war, followed one of the most dramatic sessions in Spanish parliamentary history just 48 hours earlier. Calvo Sotelo had bitterly attacked the republican government. Rising to answer him was Dolores Ibarruri, who would gain worldwide recognition in the civil war as 'La Pasionaria' – The Passion Flower – who responded, 'This is your last speech!' It was. During and after the war, the Franco government maintained that La Pasionaria had instigated the killing. She denied it. The actual murder was carried out by a Captain Condes of the Civil Guard, who eluded capture and died in the early fighting in the war.

CANALEJAS Y MENDEZ, Jose (1854–1912)   Spain during the reign of Alfonso XIII, from 1886 through 1930, has been described by many historians as a near stranger to moderation. Anarchists and other radicals and revolutionaries engaged in numerous terrorist acts, including assaults on royalty and chief ministers of the country. The government's response was massive, brutal, reflexive retaliation, which frequently led to international outcry, as mass arrests and tortures were used against both likely and unlikely suspects.

Some have argued that from time to time Alfonso sought to alleviate the terror and occasionally reined in his prime ministers from their more brutal excesses, but the nation continued under the yoke of censorship, limited suffrage and stern restrictions on the right to hold political meetings. As the repression continued, Alfonso XIII was subjected to several assassination attempts, as were his chief ministers. Both the successful and unsuccessful acts resulted in mass killings and injuring of innocent bystanders in bomb plots. In September 1893 Prime Minister Martincz de Campos survived a bomb attack in which his horse was destroyed under him and six persons were killed. In 1897 Prime Minister Canovas del Castillo was assassinated.

In 1912 it was probably inevitable that Prime Minister Jose Canalejas y Mendez would fall to an assassin. Canalejas was perhaps the most repressive premier of

Alfonso XIII's reign and had resigned several times when the king sought to apply a standard of mercy to the government's more odious excesses. However, just as inevitably, the king found it necessary to recall him to office. On November 12, 1912, Canalejas y Mendez started for the ministry of the interior to engage in discussions aimed at new and sterner measures against revolutionary opposition. At that time the anarchist forces, even those divided among one another on several points, had agreed that Canalejas y Mendez was the leading obstacle to their aims and thus a more important target than the king himself. As Canalejas y Mendez reached the government building, an anarchist gunman named Manuel Pardinas stepped from the shadows and killed Canalejas with a single shot. The assassin then fired a bullet into his own brain.

The violence did not bring down the king, who continued to rule until forced into exile 19 years later, in 1931, when the short-lived Spanish republic was proclaimed.

CANBY, Brigadier General Edward R. S. (1817–1873)
Brigadier General Edward R. S. Canby, the only U.S. general officer to be killed by Indians, was slain by Kintpuash, the chief of a band of Modocs, in an assassination mired deep in intrigue, both red and white, with little credit on either side.

Ironically Kintpuash, called Captain Jack by white settlers, had always advocated peaceful relations with whites and had managed to control the firebrands within the band, even after his father, the previous chief, was massacred by white settlers. Under Jack in the late 1850s and early 1860s the Modocs carried on friendly and mutually rewarding trade with the mining town of Yreka, California. However, under an 1864 treaty the Modocs were moved onto a reservation with the Klamath Indians in southern Oregon.

The Modocs were not happy there, due to tension with the Klamaths and a shortage of promised food and other supplies. In 1870 Jack led his band of 150 men, women and children back to their old homeland. When the army tried to force them back to the reservation, the band fled into the lava beds south of Tule Lake, a forbidding area of fissures, caves, pits and ridges, from which it was impossible for the army to root them out.

Shortly after arriving at the lava beds, Jack and his band were joined by a smaller group of Modocs led by Hooker Jim that had killed 14 settlers on the way. Then came the Hot Creek Modocs, who had recently split from Jack's band. Barely surviving a lynching by whites, they felt only war could save the tribe. Hooker Jim and the Hot Creek Modocs quickly joined forces to question Jack's leadership and to force him into full-scale war with the army. Instead, Jack continued to ride out of the lava beds to meet with white men whom he felt he could trust and who indeed trusted him and sought to make peace. In subsequent negotiations with General Canby, Hooker Jim was guaranteed amnesty, but meanwhile the Modoc War continued unabated.

In April 1873 new negotiations were offered to Jack. Hooker Jim and his supporters opposed any negotiation, fearing that Jack would agree to surrender them. Instead they threatened to remove Jack or even kill him, unless he agreed to go to the conference and kill the peace commissioners, including Canby.

'Why do you want to force me to do a coward's act?' Jack demanded.

'It is not a coward's act,' Hooker Jim replied. 'It will be brave to kill Canby in the presence of all those soldiers.'

The argument continued for several days. On the morning of April 10, Jack called his men together and asked to be relieved of the order to kill Canby and the others. 'My heart tells me I had just as well talk to the clouds and wind,' he said, 'but I want to say that life is sweet, love is strong; man fights to save his life; man also kills to win his heart's desire; that is love. Death is mighty bad. Death will come soon enough.' He warned his listeners that should they renew the killing, all of them would die, including their women and children. He noted he had promised the peace commissioners to commit no acts of violence as long as the peace talks continued. 'Let me show the world that Captain Jack is a man of his word.'

Hooker Jim spoke next. 'You have to kill Canby. Your talk is good, but now it is too late to put up such talk.'

Jack asked for a vote. Of the 50 present only about a dozen backed his position. Still, Jack sought to maneuver, saying he would kill Canby but only after telling him what the Modocs wanted. 'I will ask him many times. If he comes to my terms, I shall not kill him. Do you hear?'

To this all present agreed.

The peace conference was held the following day, Good Friday, with army troops at a distance. Captain Jack made a number of demands, including a new reservation near Tule Lake and the lava beds, and the withdrawal of the troops invading the lava beds. Amnesty for Hooker Jim and the others was not even touched on. Getting no satisfactory promises, Jack drew a pistol from his coat and fired at Canby. The weapon misfired. Canby was frozen in astonishment. Then the pistol fired successfully and Canby fell dead. One of Jack's companions, Boston Charley, shot Reverend Eleazar Thomas to death. The other three commissioners escaped, and Jack led his men back to the lava beds to await the inevitable army onslaught.

Battles waged for four months, and although the Modocs generally won the fights, they continued to lose men. In the war of attrition the Modocs were reduced to butchering their horses for food; they also suffered from a lack of water. Hooker Jim argued constantly with Captain Jack, and finally Hooker Jim and his men abandoned the chief who had given them sanctuary and then had refused to surrender them to Canby. Jack was reduced to 37 warriors to battle more than 1,000 soldiers.

Hooker Jim and his band surrendered to the army and offered to lead the military to Captain Jack in exchange for amnesty. General Jefferson C. Davis accepted those terms. After a fruitless effort to convince Jack to surrender, his pursuers finally cornered him in a thicket. With him were three warriors who had stayed loyal to him to the end.

Captain Jack and several of his followers were brought before a military tribunal for the assassination of Canby and Thomas. Among those who testified against Captain Jack were Hooker Jim and his followers, who won their freedom in the process. The defendants were afforded no lawyer but were permitted to cross-examine the witnesses. However, most understood little English and spoke it even less well. During the proceedings soldiers were busy constructing a gallows leaving little doubt about the outcome.

Contemptuous of the proceedings, Captain Jack refused to cross-examine Hooker Jim, but in his final address said: 'Hooker Jim is the one that always wanted to fight, and commenced killing and murdering. . . . Life is mine only for a short time. You white people conquered me not; my own men did.'

Captain Jack was hanged on October 3, 1873, along with three others. The next night, Jack's body was secretly disinterred and embalmed, and was shipped east as a carnival attraction. Later the body was obtained by the surgeon general and placed in his museum.

In 1974 the members of the Modoc and Klamath tribes were paid $49 million by the federal government for the earlier seizure of their tribal lands.

Further reading: *Bury My Heart at Wounded Knee*, by Dee Brown; *The Modocs and Their War*, by Keith A. Murray.

CANOVAS DEL CASTILLO, Antonio (1828–1897)
Antonio Canovas del Castillo had been prime minister of Spain several times from 1875 to 1897, serving under both Alfonso XII and Alfonso XIII and standing for a stern reaction to terrorism, which in turn was at least in part a revolutionary reaction to government oppression. In June 1896 a bomb was hurled at a religious procession in Barcelona. Eleven persons died and another 40 were

injured. In response, Canovas launched a campaign of mass arrests, and torture was used to extract confessions. Four alleged terrorists were garrotted, and 76 more persons were sent to prison in the aftermath of the case. A French newspaper's account of the tortures used by the government security forces led to an outcry worldwide.

Canovas brushed aside such criticisms as well as vows of vengeance by radical groups, who insisted their members had been falsely accused. On August 9, 1897, the prime minister and his wife were taking the waters at Santa Agueda in the Basque Mountains when they were approached by a pleasant-looking blond man, an Italian anarchist named Angilliolo. The man drew a revolver and shot Canovas to death. Madame Canovas threw herself on the man, crying, 'Assassin!'

'I am not an assassin,' Angilliolo gravely replied. 'I am an avenger.' The avenger was in due course garrotted.

CAPTAIN JACK See CANBY, BRIGADIER GENERAL EDWARD R. S.

CARACALLA, Emperor of Rome (A.D. 188–217) Emperor Caracalla was noted in Roman history both for the great baths he built for Rome and for his bloodbaths, which were almost unmatched in the violent history of the empire. The son of the brutal but not inefficient Emperor Severus, Caracalla shared the throne in 211, upon his father's death, with his younger brother, Geta. Severus advised his sons: 'Make your soldiers rich and do not bother with anything else.' Both brothers ignored the advice and instead went about plotting to murder each other.

Caracalla proved much more treacherous than his brother and in 212 finally succeeded in killing Geta, in the arms of their mother, the dying youth's blood soaking into her garments. Thereafter Caracalla unleashed a brutal bloodbath that claimed the lives of an estimated 20,000 real or imagined Geta partisans.

Caracalla went on slaughtering throughout the five

years of his solitary reign. He was particularly brutal in his expeditions against the German tribes in 213 when he senselessly massacred an allied German force. Caracalla preferred military activities to civil rule, and so he turned over most governmental duties to his mother, Julia Domna, which arrangement produced Caracalla's crowning malignancy. He flew to Alexandria in outrage because the city wits had referred to his mother and himself as Jocasta and Oedipus. However, after arriving Caracalla appeared in a benevolent mood and invited much of the city's youth to a mammoth celebration on the parade grounds. Then his soldiers surrounded the unwitting youths and mowed them down.

Despite the emperor's penchant for massacre, historians have credited Caracalla with some major achievements, particularly the colossal baths of Rome and his edict of 212, which accorded Roman citizenship to all free inhabitants of the empire (although this has been viewed by many as simply a way to increase the taxpayer rolls).

Caracalla likened himself to Alexander the Great, assuming the surname *Magnus*, 'the great.' He organized his legions in Alexander's style and adopted imitations in dress, weapons, behavior; he even traveled the routes of Alexander. In 216 he launched a military campaign against Parthia. However, his officers were not as keen on the campaign as was the emperor. Caracalla's behavior had grown more unpredictable, and he was attracted to magical religious practices that made his officers all the more nervous. When the prefect Macrinus discovered that Caracalla was preparing his downfall, an assassination plot was perfected and the emperor was stabbed to death at Carrhae in 217. Macrinus, whose role in the murder was concealed, proclaimed himself emperor. The soldiery concurred, especially since Macrinus bullied a reluctant Senate to proclaim the late Caracalla a god.

Further reading: *The Reign of Caracalla*, by D. C. Mackenzie.

CARAUSIUS, Usurper Emperor of Britain (?–293) An

officer in the Roman army, Marcus Aurelius Mausaeus Carausius was little more than an embezzler who established a short-lived independent Britain. Born in what is today Belgium, Carausius proved valorous in battle, and the emperor Maximian put him in charge of a fleet to subdue the barbarian pirates of the North Sea.

Carausius found it rewarding to allow the pirates to carry out raids before striking at them, seizing their booty as his own, and sending only token sums to Rome. Outraged, the emperor sentenced him to death, but this did not lead any of Carausius's followers to betray him, as he prudently shared his profits liberally. Carausius came to control Britain and northern Gaul, and he established an independent monarchy, taking for himself the title of Augustus. He then recruited the barbarian pirates to his cause and became the ruler of the western sea. Efforts by Maximian and coruler Diocletian failed to dislodge the usurper, and in 290 they were temporarily forced to acknowledge his rule in Britain.

Finally, the newly appointed Caesar Constantius I made inroads into Carausius's domain, and the latter's own top general, Allectus, assassinated him in 293. Allectus took the throne himself but proved less successful in repelling the Roman forces. In 296 Constantius I killed him in battle in southeast England.

Further reading: *Who Was Who in the Roman World*, edited by Diana Bowder.

CARNOT, Sadi (1837–1894) Sadi Carnot, an engineer turned statesman, served as president of France from 1887 to 1894, when he was assassinated. The early 1890s saw the greatest explosion of terrorist activities in France. By and large Carnot was popular with the people, although a total of 10 governments rose and fell during his presidency. He was not popular with French anarchists, especially after the execution of an anarchist bomber named August Vaillant. Vaillant was from the ranks of the unemployed, having been put out on the streets at the age of 12. In December 1893 Vaillant threw a bomb into the

Chamber of Deputies. By all accounts it was a small bomb, probably intended to alarm rather than kill, but the French courts thought otherwise; and Vaillant was sentenced to death.

Carnot declined to grant a reprieve or reduce the sentence, causing Vaillant's comrades to launch a number of terrorist attacks after the execution was carried out. A young Italian anarchist, Santo (or Sante) Caserio, decided to take personal vengeance on President Carnot.

On June 24, 1894, Carnot delivered a speech at a Lyon exposition. Upon leaving, the president informed the police that they should allow persons along the route to approach his open carriage if they wished. Holding a rolled-up newspaper, Caserio strode forward. He pulled a six-inch dagger from the newspaper and plunged it into Carnot's stomach, shouting *'Vive la revolution! Vive l'anarchie!'* Carnot died a short time later.

Caserio was almost lynched on the spot by the crowd, but he survived to be tried and executed. He went to the guillotine on August 16, 1894, shouting *'Vive l'anarchie!'*

Carnot was buried in the Pantheon next to his illustrious grandfather, Lazare Carnot, the famous 'Organizer of Victory' of the French Revolution.

Further reading: *A Criminal History of Mankind*, by Colin Wilson.

CARRANZA, Venustiano (1859–1920)   One of the more conservative leaders of the Mexican Revolution, Venustiano Carranza was the son of a powerful landowner who became active in politics in 1877. Although linked to the reactionary government of Porfirio Diaz, he joined Francisco Madero against Diaz in 1910. After Madero was assassinated by Victoriano Huerta, Carranza joined with more radical revolutionaries such as Zapata, Villa and Obregon to force Huerta to flee the country in 1914. Carranza established a provisional government, and with the aid of General Alvaro Obregon, he defeated Pancho Villa's army in 1915, establishing his primacy in most of the country.

Carranza became constitutional president in 1917, but he failed to carry out the provisions of the new constitution calling for reforms in land ownership, natural resources, labor organizations and other social programs. As a result, throughout his term Carranza faced growing social unrest as well as continued opposition by Villa and Emiliano Zapata, who demanded immediate social reforms. The Zapata problem was eliminated in April 1919 when the great peasant leader was assassinated, clearly at Carranza's behest.

Little more than a year later the same fate would befall Carranza as well. With his term of office ending in December and being barred by the constitution from running for reelection, Carranza sought to deny the office to Obregon and instead to install as president his ambassador to Washington, Ignacio Bonillas. Violence erupted throughout the country, and many Obregon followers were imprisoned, shot or executed. An attempt to kill Obregon in Mexico City failed, and he issued a call for civil war. A number of more radical generals supported Obregon, and in the rebellion Carranza was forced to flee when on May 5, 1920, he was informed that several rebel armies were within 30 miles of the capital. With typical efficiency Carranza proceeded to empty the entire national treasury, and seized the dies from the mint and the national archives, in preparation for a move to Veracruz. More than 10,000 Carranza supporters and their relatives jammed the railway station for a mass evacuation as the rebels pushed closer. The train convoy got just beyond Rinconada, in the state of Pueblo, where the rail lines had been destroyed. In any event, Veracruz had fallen to the rebels.

Carranza and a few of his followers fled into the mountains on horseback. They stopped in the small village of Tlaxcalantongo because of a fierce rainstorm, and Carranza took refuge in a mud hut. Informers led forces under Rodolfo Herrera to Carranza's hideaway, and before dawn broke, Carranza awoke to gunfire and shouts of '*Muera Carranza!*' and '*Viva Obregon!*' Resistance was useless, and Carranza was shot to death. (See OBREGON, ALVARO; VILLA, PANCHO; ZAPATA, EMILIANO.)

Further reading: *A History of Mexico*, by Samuel II. Mayo.

CARRERO BLANCO, Admiral Luis (1903–1973) In the early 1970s Spanish dictator Francisco Franco had two potential successors in mind upon his death. A confirmed monarchist, he was determined that when he died Prince Juan Carlos would become chief of state. But to make sure the prince did not fall prey to liberal ideas, Franco had tapped Admiral Luis Carrero Blanco, his prime minister and the number two man in his regime, to keep matters on a rightward course. But Carrero Blanco was not destined to play that role. On December 20, 1973, he was murdered in the heart of Madrid by members of Euzkadi Ta Askatasuna (Basque Homeland and Liberation), or ETA. Formed in 1959, the ETA pursued the struggle for freedom for the Basques, a hardy, industrious and independence-oriented people who inhabited the Pyrenees Mountains in both Spain and France and who spoke a language unrelated to any other European tongue. The Franco regime vigorously opposed any national independence movement by the Basques.

The Carrero Blanco assassination took months of elaborate planning. Posing as sculptors, two men rented a basement room near the San Francisco de Borja Church, where the 70-year-old prime minister entered for mass each morning. The plotters tunneled to the middle of the street, where Carrero Blanco's car passed after mass. This took weeks of digging, and in the meantime 100 pounds of plastic explosives was smuggled to the site, carried in several Christmas-wrapped packages to divert suspicion, and constructed into a massive bomb.

The fatal explosion was so powerful it not only killed Carrero Blanco, his chauffeur and his police bodyguard outright, but it blasted a 25-foot hole in the street and blew parts of the car over the top of the five-story church and onto a balcony on the other side. The ETA justified the assassination as revenge for the killing of nine Basque militants by the government.

A period of stern crackdowns followed, and eventually 14 suspects were arrested. In 1978, three years after the death of Franco, King Juan Carlos's government announced a full amnesty for the 14. This bow to Basque nationalism, as well as an easing of antiterrorist legislation and reform of the security forces, did not bring an end to revolutionary activities. Between 1977 and 1982 a total of 20 army officers, eight of them generals, were killed by the group, whose membership has been estimated at about 600. (See LAGO, GENERAL VICTOR.)

Further reading: *The Terrorists*, by Christopher Dobson and Ronald Payne.

CASTILLO ARMAS, Carlos (1914–1957) On July 26, 1957, a member of the Guatemalan palace guard, 20-year-old Romero Vasquez Sanchez, turned his rifle on President Carlos Castillo Armas in the presidential palace, and shot him to death. Before others could intervene, Vasquez killed himself as well.

Castillo Armas had become president in 1954 after leading a successful, United States-supported revolt against the Communist regime of Colonel Jacobo Arbenz Guzman, the so-called Red Colonel, who had previously offended the United States for many of his left-wing policies and especially for the government's expropriation of the United Fruit Company's interests in Guatemala. John Peurifoy, the U.S. ambassador to Guatemala, was believed by most Latin American watchers to have been one of the principal architects of the revolt.

An ardent anti-Communist, Castillo Armas reversed many of the programs instituted under Arbenz Guzman, especially the agrarian reforms, and he returned much of the land to its original owners. Under Castillo Armas there was also a purge of leftists and their sympathizers in the government and unions. Castillo Armas would have done well to extend his purge to his own presidential guard, since his killer was later revealed to have been discharged from the regular army in 1955 for Communist leanings and was later fired from a government television network job as 'suspicious.' Nine other palace guards were arrested as possible accomplices but were later freed.

Former President Arbenz Guzman fled the country and lived out his years in exile. In 1971, he drowned in scalding water in his bathtub, leading to speculation that he too had been murdered.

CASTRO, Fidel (1926–) – Attempted Assassination The attempt by the United States Central Intelligence Agency to assassinate Cuba's Fidel Castro stands as one of the most bizarre examples of government sponsored assassination attempts. Few plots to kill a government leader have received more publicity than the supposedly super-secret Operation Mongoose.

The CIA clearly advocated the elimination of Fidel Castro at least as early as December 1959, and the matter was discussed at special meetings in January and March 1960. According to Dr. Ray S. Cline, a former deputy director for intelligence of the CIA, 'At an NSC [National Security Council] meeting on March 10, 1960, terminology was used suggesting that the assassination of Castro, his brother Raul and Che Guevara was at least theoretically considered.' According to Cline, in his book *The CIA under Reagan, Bush & Casey*, high officials clearly 'thought they had been authorized to plan Castro's assassination.' However, he adds, 'whether President Eisenhower or Dulles or President Kennedy had actually intended to authorize Castro's murder is simply not clear from the records.' Cline insists he himself knew nothing of the plots at the time.

Perhaps the most salient point in the entire Castro story was that the CIA, for all its intelligence capabilities, clearly lacked any method of penetrating Castro's Cuba. It is this fact that forced the agency to engage in a bizarre recruitment program, which Cline puts in the best light:

'Once the assumption was made that it was essential to get rid of Castro by assassination, it was not illogical to try to do it through the Mafia, since its former Havana gambling empire gave them some contacts to work with and since a gangland killing would be unlikely to be attributed to the U.S. Government.'

Thus the curtain went up on the comic-opera plots to kill Castro. Names that float about in this incredible operation include Chicago Mafia boss Sam Giancana, underworld mastermind Meyer Lansky, flamboyant mobster Johnny Roselli, Tampa crime boss Santo Trafficante Jr., the eccentric Howard Hughes and Hughes's executive officer Robert Maheu, among many others.

Because of his Las Vegas connections and his long-suspected relationship with the CIA, Hughes was the perfect conduit for bringing the parties together. Hughes ordered Maheu to find suitable Mafia killers to carry out the operation. Maheu recruited Johnny Roselli, the Chicago mob's overseer in Las Vegas, and his boss, Giancana, and apparently through them Tampa's Trafficante. In retrospect, probably only the CIA and Hughes thought there was a real plot to get Castro.

The operation was in actuality a bald-faced Mafia scam. The CIA concocted all sorts of ludicrous plans, such as trying to blow the Cuban leader off the ocean floor while he was satisfying his passion for skin-diving, injecting deadly poison into him with a specially prepared 'pen,' letting him puff on some poisoned cigars, and contaminating his clothes with fungus spores and tubercle bacilli. There was even a zany plot for infecting Castro so that his beard would fall out, thus ruining his macho image.

When the CIA suggested to Roselli a simple Capone-style ambush with machine guns blazing, Roselli patiently pointed out that such Chicago rubout tactics were not practical since there was little chance that the killers could get away and the survival instincts of hit men were always a shade higher than those of political assassins.

The underworld took the CIA down the primrose path with one phony story after another. Trafficante simply sat on any operations assigned to him, coming back instead with thrilling tales of derring-do for the intelligence men – hit men constantly seemed to have their boats shot out from under them just as they neared the Cuban shore. CIA scientists came up with a liquid poison that would kill in two or three days and turned it over to Trafficante to transmit to his phantom Cuban contacts. Trafficante flushed the poison down the toilet. There is absolutely no record of any CIA money or equipment – assorted guns, detonators, explosives, poison, boat radar and radios – ever getting to Cuba.

In time some government agents even theorized that Trafficante had sold out to Castro and was feeding him all sorts of intelligence, not only on the plots to kill him but on the anti-Castro movement in Florida among Cuban refugees. Trafficante had always had only a small piece of the mob casino business in Cuba before the Castro takeover, and it was felt that if he sold out to Castro he would be in a perfect position for a major slice of the action if the Cuban leader ever allowed gambling to return.

Undoubtedly the mobsters enjoyed swindling the CIA, but their main interest, as well as that of the shadowy Maheu, was to utilize the agency to keep other government investigators, such as the FBI, off their backs and out of underworld activities.

Eventually the CIA determined it was being duped and pulled the plug on Operation Mongoose. However, to this day there are elements within organized crime, and some without, who remain uncertain whether the 1975 murder of Giancana – just prior to his scheduled appearance before the Senate committee headed by Frank Church inquiring into government assassination plots – and the 1976 killing of Roselli were the work of the mob or of the CIA. The CIA's alleged motive was to keep secret the embarrassing details of Operation Mongoose.

Further reading: *The CIA Under Reagan, Bush & Casey*, by Dr. Ray S. Cline; *The Last Mafioso*, by Ovid Demaris; *The Mafia Encyclopedia*, by Carl Sifakis.

CAVENDISH, Lord Frederick Charles (1836–1882) A protege of William Gladstone and viewed as the future leader of the Liberal Party in England, Lord Frederick Cavendish took on the thankless task of chief secretary to the lord lieutenant of Ireland and goodwill emissary to Ireland at the peak of the Irish crisis of 1882.

On May 6, 1882, the evening after he had made the crossing to Dublin, Cavendish was walking across Phoenix Park with Thomas H. Burke, the permanent under secretary for Ireland, when they were attacked by several Irish assassins armed with knives. Despite spirited resistance by Frederick, both targets were killed.

The following year four of the assassins, members of a secret organization called the Invincibles, were betrayed and were hanged for the murders.

Oddly, Cavendish's assassination was to have a profound influence on the anarchist movement in the United States. A German anarchist, Johann Most, who had been expelled from his homeland and was living in England, praised the Irish assassins. He was expelled from England, and he traveled to the United States. Most became one of the more important anarchist leaders in America, but he suddenly retracted his support for the Cavendish assassination and announced he no longer approved of 'the propaganda of the deed.' He also condemned a young anarchist named Alexander Berkman who had tried to kill millionaire Henry Frick during the Homestead Steel Strike. Most's conversion seems to have been caused at least in part by the fact that Berkman had previously replaced Most as the love interest of the vibrant radical Emma Goldman. Still, Most's denunciation of the Cavendish assassination convinced many American anarchists to curb their violent inclinations. Despite the hysteria in the United States about anarchists, their acts of terror and murder never approached the levels of European countries.

Further reading: *A Criminal History of Mankind*, by Colin Wilson.

CERMAK, Anton J.   See ROOSEVELT, FRANKLIN DELANO.

CHAKA, King of the Zulus (c.1787–1828) A military if not a political genius, Chaka, or Shaka, was the great founder of southern Africa's Zulu Empire. Even though much that is said of Chaka is 'white man's history,' there can be no doubt that he was an extraordinary tyrant by any standard.

At the time of Chaka's birth, about 1787, various small chiefdoms among the Nguni were being combined into confederacies. Chaka's early years were spent in the service of Dingiswayo, who controlled the Mthethwa Confederacy. In 1816 Chaka became head of the Zulu Confederacy, wresting control from his half-brother. (By birth Chaka was the son of a Zulu chief, but because the marriage of his parents was considered incestuous, he had been forced to spend his youth with other clans.)

As leader, Chaka organized the young men into regiments, separating them from all forms of civil life and instilling in them rigid discipline. He also altered the traditional method of warfare by substituting short stabbing spears for the previously favored assegais, or javelins. Within two years Chaka had built an awesome army that swept away all opposition between the Tugela and Pongola rivers. Chaka next defeated his two major foes, the Ndwandwe and the Qwabe, and conquered the rest of Natal; then in a series of tribal wars he depopulated much of southern Africa. But he never developed the political skills needed to complement his military prowess, seeking merely to extend his personal dominion over as wide an area as possible. The key to Chaka's power was his ability to instill fear in those he ruled. He frequently carried out scores of executions daily, guaranteeing minimal opposition to his will.

Two women played major roles in Chaka's life, his mother and his wife Nandi. He left no offspring, despite his harem of 1,200 women, since he killed any concubines who became pregnant.

When Nandi died in 1827 this, together with the death of his mother about the same time, caused Chaka to turn openly psychotic. In his grief he initially caused 7,000 Zulus to be killed or sacrificed. For a year no crops could be planted and no milk could be used. Any woman becoming pregnant was killed, along with her husband, as were thousands of milk cows. Thus, Chaka ordained, even the calves might know what it was to lose a mother. Chaka also increased his external warfare, ordering his forces to cut a swath all the way to the boundaries of the Cape Colony. When his warriors returned home in triumph expecting a seasonal respite, Chaka instead ordered them north on another extermination sweep. Now at last anger overcame fear, and Chaka's fate was sealed. An assassination party headed by two of Chaka's half-brothers, Dingane and Mhlangana, stabbed him to death on September 22, 1828. Dingane became chief.

Even though mismanaged by Dingane and his successor, Chaka's armed nation continued as an awesome power until it was finally defeated by the British in the Zulu War of 1879. In a sense Chaka's depredations had guaranteed the success of the whites. Chaka had triggered great tribal massacres that left two million dead, so that when the Boer Great Trek of the 1830s passed through vast ravaged areas, there was virtually no one left to oppose them.

Further reading: *The Washing of the Spears: A History of the Rise of the Zulu Nation under Shaka and its Fall in the Zulu War of 1879,* by D. R. Morris.

CHAMORRO, Pedro Joaquin (1920–1978) There was never any doubt that the assassination of Pedro Joaquin Chamorro, a Nicaraguan newspaper editor, was the handiwork of the dictatorial regime of Anastasio Somoza Debayle. Chamorro, editor of his family-owned *La Prensa* and an outspoken opponent of the Somozas since the 1940s, was shot to death in Managua on January 10, 1978. Three men in a car forced Chamorro's vehicle to a curb and, using two rifles and a machine gun, pumped 18 bullets into their victim.

The Somoza government immediately condemned the

murder and said it would spare no effort to find the assassins. Hardly anyone took the pledge seriously. About 50,000 persons escorted Chamorro's coffin from the hospital to his home on the night of January 10, and the next morning some 30,000 mourners came to pay their respects. That night tens of thousands of protesters rioted in the capital, setting fire to buildings and automobiles, looting stores and stoning policemen, soldiers and firemen. Business and labor leaders in succeeding days called a general strike to demand a real investigation of the Chamorro assassination, and several parties demanded Somoza's resignation.

The Chamorro killing united diverse elements in Nicaragua, and although Somoza fought back with both repressive actions and promises of reform, he was finally forced to flee the country in mid-1979. The opposition then splintered with the leftist Sandinistas taking effective control. Ironically, the Sandinistas for a time suppressed *La Prensa*.

By the late 1980s, pressure from without and economic problems from within forced the Sandinistas first to loosen up politically and finally to agree to free, internationally monitored elections in February 1990. The anti-Sandinistas coalition, the National Opposition Union, somewhat disorganized and beset with internal disputes (being composed of disparate elements ranging the political spectrum from liberal to moderate to extreme right wing) nominated as their candidate Chamorro's widow, Violeta Barrios de Chamorro, who shocked the world by defeating the heavily favored incumbent, Daniel Ortega Saaneda. (See SOMOZA DEBAYLE, ANASTASIO.)

CHOSROE II See KHOSROW II, KING OF PERSIA.

CICERO, Marcus Tullius (106–43 B.C.) The most illustrious victim of vengeance after the assassination of Julius Caesar was none of the assassins but rather the noted Roman orator, statesman and philosopher Marcus Tullius

Cicero. He knew nothing of the conspiracy but approved it as an accomplished fact, and he turned his often venomous oratory against Marc Antony.

Cicero had been a magnificent survivor for years. In 63 B.C. he exposed Cataline's conspiracy in a famous series of speeches in the Senate. In 60 B.C. he refused Caesar's invitation to join his alliance with Crassus and Pompey, considering their acts unconstitutional. Banished by Clodius in 59 B.C., he was recalled by Pompey in 45 B.C. Thereafter Cicero unsuccessfully sought to estrange Pompey from Caesar. When Pompey later did split with Caesar, Cicero joined Pompey to some extent and continued, not without considerable bravery, to oppose Caesar.

After Caesar's murder, Cicero spoke in the Senate in favor of a general amnesty, although he continued to oppose and denigrate Antony. Cicero felt Antony would be protected by Octavian, Caesar's adopted son, whose skills Cicero seriously underestimated. Unfortunately for Cicero, Caesar's heir learned of the senator's true feelings toward him. Cicero had told others in confidence: 'The young man should be given distinctions – and then be disposed of.'

That as good as marked Cicero for death. Octavian left the killing to Marc Antony. Cicero fled by boat, but buffeted and sickened by the sea, he ordered the craft to land so that he could spend the night at his home at Formiae. The next morning, December 7, 43 B.C., Cicero resolved to remain there to await his assassins rather than face the choppy waters. However, his devoted slaves forced him into a litter and started for the ship. Just then Antony's henchmen approached. The servants wanted to do battle, but Cicero ordered them to yield. As Plutarch reports it, Cicero, 'his person covered with dust, his beard and hair untrimmed, and his face worn with troubles,' eased the chores of the soldiers by stretching forth his head so that it might be more readily chopped off.

Cicero's head and hands were presented to Antony and Antony's wife Fulvia, in Rome. After duly admiring them for a time, Antony had them put on display on the speaker's platform at the Forum. One of the most controversial figures in history, Cicero has been criticized for his vacillation, indecision and egotistical manner, but, most historians agree, his shifting alliances reflected the changes in the political scene more than his own failing. Cicero certainly held to a belief in constitutional government and the rule of law, but the majority view is that his misfortune lay in not protecting himself sufficiently while holding to his ideals.

Further reading: 'Cicero,' *Plutarch's Lives; The Story of Civilization III – Caesar and Christ*, by Will Durant.

CLAUDIUS, Emperor of Rome (10 B.C.–A.D. 54) The case can be made that Claudius was one of the better Caesars of Rome, although few authorities are as laudatory as Robert Graves in *I, Claudius*. Claudius was crowned emperor by the Praetorian Guard upon their assassination of the tyrant Caligula.

Although no Caligula, Claudius did reveal some of the same unseemly traits of his much-despised predecessor. It has been said that when Claudius became annoyed with the failure of mechanical devices used in the arena, he ordered the carpenter responsible to fight the lions. Claudius displayed what the historian Suetonius called a 'cruel and sanguinary' disposition by making a point of watching the more sadistic executions by torture. A roster of some of his executions, said Suetonius, included Appius Silanus, father of his son-in-law; Cneius Pompey, his eldest daughter's husband; two nieces, 35 senators and 300 knights.

Before becoming emperor, Claudius, whose physical disabilities included partial paralysis, stammering and limping, showed a knack for survival. Augustus and Tiberius tried to keep Claudius from public view as much as possible, but Caligula enjoyed him as a harmless figure of fun and allowed him to become consul in A.D. 37. As a result, Claudius had the time to devote himself to studying and learning and became expert in a number of subjects, such as history, biography, linguistics and even gambling;

he authored many works in these fields.

Indeed, when he became emperor he proved rather competent, and insisted to the Senate that he always feigned idiocy as a method of survival of the various palace intrigues. He corrected many of the legal excesses of Caligula, restored many confiscations and cut taxes. He thanked the army for supporting his rise to power, but at the same time executed the assassins of Caligula on the ground that it was not prudent to condone the murder of an emperor.

Some historians insist the excesses in Claudius's reign were really the excesses of his wives, Messalina and Agrippina the Younger, and of his scheming advisers. Certainly Messalina carried even the royal palace to new depths of sexual excess, including her 'duel' with a prostitute to determine who could satisfy the most lovers in a single night. When the empress found resistance or fear on the part of a new lover, she would reportedly appeal to Claudius for his aid in making the object of her affection more compliant. Messalina, say some historians, reciprocated by giving him some attractive housemaids for bed partners. Although the gossipy Suetonius found Claudius 'immoderate in his passion for women,' he did bestow upon him a unique accolade for the time as being 'wholly free from unnatural vice.'

Finally Messalina went too far by 'marrying' a handsome youth named Caius Silius 'with pomp and all accustomed rites.' Claudius learned that Messalina was planning to have the emperor assassinated so that Silius could be put on the throne. Instead he ordered Messalina and Silius and other ardent admirers of his wife slain, including hundreds who had taken part in the empress's orgies.

After that Claudius decided to marry Agrippina the Younger, his niece and Caligula's sister. This violated the laws against incest, so Claudius appeared before the Senate and persuaded them to change the law to ensure the stability of the throne and the good of the state. However, Agrippina was not the ideal instrument for such stability, as her life's motivation was to see her son Nero become emperor. To achieve this, she convinced Claudius to adopt Nero as his son and place him next in the order of succession ahead of the young Britannicus, Claudius's natural son.

As empress, Agrippina carried on a reign of terror, executing any female rivals to her hold on Claudius and on any men whom it seemed possible Claudius might accept as his heir in place of Nero. Claudius, described as 'weakened by ill health, many labors, and sexual enterprise,' took years to finally attempt to halt Agrippina's intrigues. He decided to alter the succession by naming Britannicus his heir.

Agrippina then realized she must risk all to win the throne for Nero. With the aid of a notorious poisoner named Locusta she fed Claudius poisoned mushrooms. The emperor languished for 12 hours in agony, unable to speak, before dying. Later the Senate deified Claudius, but this was a mere formality to please the citizenry and did not reflect the true attitude of the senatorial aristocracy, which was utter contempt. That being the case, the Senate also saw little reason to oppose Nero's accession. With dark wit, Nero could not help noting that mushrooms must be the food of the gods, since Claudius ate them and achieved divinity. (See AGRIPPINA THE YOUNGER; BRITANNICUS; CALIGULA, EMPEROR OF ROME.)

Further reading: *Claudius: The Emperor and His Achievements*, by Arnaldo D. Momigliano; *A Criminal History of Mankind*, by Colin Wilson; *I, Claudius*, by Robert Graves.

CODREANU, Corneliu Z. (1899–1938) The founder and leader of the Romanian Fascist group known as the Iron Guard, Corneliu Z. Codreanu was a fervent anti-Semite and an extreme rightist. Becoming active in anti-Semitic groups during his college days, Codreanu founded the National Christian League in 1923. He was committed to violence to achieve his purposes and was tried in 1925 for the murder of a police officer, but he was acquitted. He left the country immediately thereafter but returned in 1927 to take up the leadership of the league, which by then was called the Legion of the Archangel Michael. The following year he merged his group with another equally rightwing group, the Brothers of the Cross, headed by another extremist, Michael Stelescu. The new group was called the Iron Guard, with Codreanu at its head.

The Iron Guard aped the street violence, political brawling and anti-Semitic activities of the German Nazis, and the group was clearly responsible for the assassination of Prime Minister Ion Duca in 1933. Codreanu also learned from Hitler the virtue of assassinating rivals within the movement. In 1936 Codreanu had Stelescu murdered while he was a patient in a hospital.

In 1938 the fragile Romanian government outlawed the Iron Guard and sought to act decisively to eliminate Codreanu and his followers. On November 30, 1938, Codreanu and 17 of his followers who had been arrested were being transferred from one prison to another when they were all shot to death. The communique of the justice ministry simply said they had been shot by a gunman who remained 'unknown and unapprehended.' (See CALINESCU, ARMAND; STELESCU, MICHAEL.)

COLIGNY, Admiral Gaspard de (1519–1572)   The assassination of the gifted Admiral of France Gaspard de Coligny was the act that triggered the Massacre of St. Bartholomew in 1572. Coligny had embraced the Huguenot cause, and on the death of Henry II in 1559 he developed a much closer relationship with the young Charles IX, despite the strong opposition of Charles's mother, Catherine de' Medici.

In time Catherine de' Medici seemed to be amenable to courting the Huguenots, and her opposition to the admiral appeared to ebb. Catherine even decided to marry off her daughter Marguerite to Henry of Navarre, the leader of the French Huguenots. However, together with the country's chief Catholic family, the House of Guise, and her youngest son, the future Henry III, Catherine plotted Coligny's assassination. Four days after the wedding of Henry of Navarre and Marguerite, a gun was fired at Coligny as he left the king's palace, and he fell, wounded, to the ground.

Coligny survived. The Huguenots, many of the major leaders having poured into Paris for the wedding, were furious and talked threateningly of revenge.

Catherine decided to strike the first blow once more. On August 24, just six days after the wedding, armed men battered their way through Coligny's door. The admiral was stabbed to death, and his body was dragged into the street and hacked to pieces, the action being supervised by the Catholic leader Henry, Duke of Guise. Meanwhile, in the Louvre, where the Huguenot nobles were staying as the king's guests, the bloodletting continued. The Huguenot nobles were dragged from their beds and slaughtered. With the dawn of Saint Bartholomew's Day the general massacre ensued, and mobs attacked Huguenot houses, killing the inmates, men, women, children and babes. In all, Coligny's assassination was followed by the slaughter of from 3,000 to 4,000 victims over the next three days in Paris alone. Henry of Navarre survived only by temporarily reconverting to Catholicism.

A measure of the ferocity of the religious feelings of the period is found in historian Warren O. Ault's comment in *Europe in Modern Times*: 'The head of Coligny was sent to the pope, who, happy in the extermination of so many heretics, ordered a medal to be struck.' (See GUISE, HENRY, DUKE OF; HENRY III, KING OF FRANCE.)

Further reading: *Catherine de' Medici and the Lost Revolution*, by Ralph Roeder; *The Later Years of Catherine de' Medici*, by Edith Sichel; *The Story of Civilization VIII – The Age of Reason Begins*, by Will and Ariel Durant.

COLLINS, Michael (1890–1922) Michael Collins was one of the great Irish nationalist heroes of the Anglo-Irish War of 1919–1921, but he fell an assassination victim in the civil war that followed.

Collins had joined the Irish Republican Brotherhood in his teens and fought in the Easter Rising in 1916. He was imprisoned until December of that year, and in December 1918 he was elected as a Sinn Fein (an Irish nationalist movement) member of the Dail, or Irish Assembly, where he was a leader in declaring the Dail for the republic. With Sinn Fein President Eamon De Valera and Vice President Arthur Griffith both in prison, Collins as minister of home affairs carried much of the burden of power.

In February 1919 Collins planned and carried out De Valera's dramatic escape from Lincoln jail, after which Collins served as minister of finance and more importantly as director of intelligence of the Irish Republican Army. Because of his masterful role as chief planner of IRA activities against the English, a price of £10,000 was put on his head by Britain.

With the truce of July 1921 De Valera sent Collins and Griffith to London as peace negotiators. It was not a role that could possibly enhance Collins's standing with many Irish republicans, since there was no way the complete Irish program would be accepted by London. When Collins signed the treaty of December 6, 1921, he did so recognizing it was the best compromise to be obtained at that point in time: The treaty allowed Ireland to emerge as an independent republic with dominion status, but it also required partition of the North and an oath of allegiance to the crown. De Valera rejected the treaty, but Collins managed to win narrow approval of the measure in the Dail.

Griffith became president and Collins chairman of the Irish Free State, but the Free State's operations were obstructed by antitreaty republicans and internecine fighting broke out. Collins at first refrained from hitting back at his former comrades, but when IRA insurgents seized the Four Courts in Dublin, civil war became unavoidable. When Griffith suddenly died on August 12, 1922, Collins, already in command of the Free State army, assumed the leadership of the government.

Ten days after Griffith's death, Collins made an inspection tour in his home county of Cork. IRA ambushers learned of his presence in the area on the morning of April 22 and prepared an ambush at Bealnamblath on the Macroom-Bandon road. That evening the ambushers were starting to give up their vigil when a convoy consisting of a motorcycle outrider, Collins's open touring car, a Crossley tender and an armored car came into view. In the resulting gunfire, Collins was hit in the back of the head by a ricocheted bullet.

After the assassination of Collins the bloodletting intensified; ultimately, the loss of Irish lives in the civil war proved much greater than that in the previous fighting with the British.

Further reading: *The Green Flag,* by Robert Kee.

COMMODUS, Emperor of Rome (A.D. 161–192)   History has recorded one period of the Roman empire when it was dominated by five successful rulers in a row as representing the empire in all its grandeur. They were Nerva, Trajan, Hadrian, Antonius and Marcus Aurelius. The record was broken when Lucius Commodus, the son of Marcus Aurelius, acceded to the purple in the year A.D. 180. At the age of 19, Commodus was known as brilliant but abysmally degenerate.

Immediately on becoming emperor, Commodus abandoned his late father's efforts to safeguard the northern borders from pillaging tribesmen and raced back from the battles to Rome for bizarre personal pleasures and tyrannical rule, or, as H. G. Wells observes in *The Outline of History,* 'an age of disorder.' He changed the name of Rome to Commodiana and gave himself the name of Hercules, claiming to be the reincarnation of that god. Dressed as Hercules in lion's skin and bearing a club, Commodus took part in degrading spectacles in the arena. He 'fought' against carefully chosen opponents, whom he dispatched with his sword. He boasted of killing literally thousands of foes with only his left hand. Will Durant notes that 'tales of unbelievable cruelty [have been] transmitted to us: Commodus ordered a votary of Bellona to amputate an arm in proof of piety; forced some women devotees of Isis to beat their breasts with pine cones till they died; killed men indiscriminately with his club of Hercules; gathered cripples together and slew them with arrows. One of his mistresses, Marcia, was apparently a Christian; for her sake, we are told, he pardoned some Christians who had been condemned to the Sardinian mines. Her devotion to him suggests that in this man, described as more bestial than any beast, there was some lovable element unrecorded by history.'

Few of Commodus's subjects would have accepted even this last pale accolade, and a few years into his reign plots were formed against this depraved emperor. His aunt Lucilla led a conspiracy to kill him, but Commodus discovered it and had her executed. Commodus became so panicked that he regularly suppressed all dissent. Senators were executed by the score. Out of fear, Commodus raised incompetent favorites to posts of power and then surrendered them to the foes they provoked. Finally, it became clear that no one was safe from his caprices, and even members of his own disreputable household joined the plots. A plot carefully nurtured by Laetus, the prefect of the Praetorian Guard, was developed in A.D. 192, and Marcia gave Commodus a cup of poison. When the poison worked too slowly an athlete the emperor kept to wrestle with strangled him in his bath.

Further reading: *The Story of Civilization III – Caesar and Christ*, by Will Durant.

CONSTANTINE VI, Byzantine Emperor (770–797) Constantine VI became the Byzantine emperor in 780 on the death of his father, Leo IV, but real power lay in the hands of his mother, Irene, as regent. During the regency one of the most divisive issues of the empire, the question of the veneration of icons, came to the fore once again. The use of icons had been prohibited in 730, but the religious Irene sought to restore their use.

After years of laying the groundwork for such a change, she called for a general church council in 786 to review the subject. When the council met in Constantinople their assembly was broken up by the Iconoclast soldiers, who were opposed to icon worship. Undeterred, Irene sponsored another council the following year, this one recognized by both the Roman Catholic and Eastern Orthodox churches. This Seventh Ecumenical Council met at Nicaea and restored the cult of images.

As Constantine VI grew older, his mother sought to retain supreme power, but in 790 the army (still largely Iconoclast) placed her under confinement and declared Constantine VI the sole ruler. Unfortunately for the empire and for Constantine himself, he proved to be less than the cleverest of rulers. In 792 he foolishly pardoned his mother and allowed her to return to the court. Carefully, Irene reassumed much of her power as a coruler. She also conspired to weaken her son's popularity. Because she knew it would encourage the church and the public to denounce her son, she encouraged him in his plans to divorce his wife and marry his mistress, Theodote.

By 796 Irene, through the use of public opinion and lavish bribes, developed a civil and military party against her son. In August 797 the opposition forces struck. Constantine was seized and locked up in the lower depths of the palace. Then by the order of his mother, Constantine's eyes were put out. He died shortly thereafter.

It has been argued by some that Irene had not sought the death of her son, but merely wanted to ensure that he could never again retake the throne. However, there is much to be said for the thesis of the contemporary Byzantine historian Theophanes that the blinding was intentionally done in such a way that it was sure to kill him.

Irene continued to rule for another five years, but the reign was a disaster within and without. All of Europe shuddered at her treatment of her son, her armies in the East were demoralized and the Saracens seized many rich provinces. Only her religious supporters remained, and they were unable to prevent a coup by a number of officials and generals. Irene was exiled to Lesbos and died in 803.

Her treatment of Constantine VI notwithstanding, Irene's zeal in restoring the use of icons and her patronage of monasteries raised her to an exalted place among the saints of the Greek Orthodox Church. Her feast day is August 9.

COSTELLO, Seamus (1939–1977)   The competing forces in the struggle for Irish independence became more crowded and confused with the appearance of the Irish National Liberation Army in 1975. It was the fighting arm of the Irish Republican Socialist Party founded by Seamus Costello, a former adjutant general of the Irish Republican Army. The republican movement until that time was split between the Official and Provisional IRAs. The Provos emphasized violent action against the British presence, while the Officials sought to develop a political alternative line, one aimed at forging a nonsectarian working-class alliance of Catholics and Protestants to achieve immediate socioeconomic objectives in Northern Ireland. Regarding the Provos as no more than sectarian gunmen, the Officials called for a 1972 ceasefire against the British. There was, however, no unanimity within the Official movement, and Costello felt that the ceasefire commitment was a needless concession. He declared it was possible to straddle the Official and Provo views. In December 1974 Costello led a splinter group called the Irish Republican Socialist Party, which drew to its banner the likes of Bernadette Devlin-McAliskey.

If the Officials eschewed violence against the British, they did not grant the IRSP the same bye. Warfare broke out between the two groups, starting with the murder of two IRSP members. The following year saw a bloody, incestuous feud culminating in the shooting death of Billy McMillan, the Officials' leader in Belfast.

For a time a truce was arranged, but on October 5,

1977, Seamus Costello was shot down on a crowded Dublin street, in what was taken as belated revenge for the McMillan assassination.

It is doubtful whether Costello's Irish National Liberation Army (INLA) ever had more than a hard-core strength of 100, and quite possibly considerably less than that, but the murder of Costello energized his followers to greater efforts at assassination to maintain their identity. In 1979 they achieved their most notable strike in this regard with the murder of Conservative politician and war hero Airey Neave with a bomb planted on his car in the House of Commons carpark.

But without Costello's guidance the INLA fell into a mode of dissent and feuding and mutual suspicion – due partly to the massive penetration of the ranks by informers – and they became known as 'mad gunmen.' While this internal dispute continued, the INLA kept up its battle with the Officials and to a lesser extent with the Provos. The opposition by this latter group was somewhat softened when three members of the INLA starved themselves to death along with seven Provos in the 1981 Hunger Strike.

But the main preoccupation within the INLA remained an internal orgy of bloodletting, culminating in early 1987. Among those killed at this time were Gerard Steenson, or 'Dr. Death' (one of the most feared killers of the period), as well as the notorious terrorist Dominic McGlinchey's wife, who was murdered in front of her children.

A truce was arranged through two Catholic priests, but by the late 1980s it appeared that Catholic opinion of the INLA was so negative it was assumed that the Seamus Costello organization was probably beyond repair and that the remnants of the INLA were likely to be absorbed into the Provisional IRA. (See NEAVE, AIREY.)

Further reading: *Combating the Terrorists*, edited by H. H. Tucker; *The Terrorists*, by Christopher Dobson and Ronald Payne.

CROSS, James R.   See LAPORTE, PIERRE.

D

DALLA CHIESA, General Alberto   See LA TORRE, PIO.

DARIUS III, King of Persia (c.380–330 B.C.)   Darius III became the last king of the Achaemenid dynasty in Persia in 336 B.C., thanks to wholesale assassination. The notorious regicide and eunuch Bagoas poisoned Darius III's two predecessors, Artaxerxes III and Arses. Since this represented the end of the direct family – Bagoas eliminated all Arses' children as well – the eunuch was able to enthrone Darius, the satrap of Armenia and a relative of the assassinated king. Bagoas was startled to find that Darius III did not prove to be a puppet king, and he determined to poison him as well. However, Darius III was forewarned and in a dramatic confrontation forced Bagoas to drink the poison himself.

As ruler, Darius III reconquered Egypt, which had proclaimed its independence following the death of Artaxerxes. But the real threat to Persia came from the Greeks under Philip II of Macedonia, who had formed the League of Corinth with a number of Greek states to retake the Greek cities under Achaemenid rule. Darius III gained a brief respite from this attack when Philip II was assassinated. Some historians have speculated that Darius III instigated the murder. In any event, this solved nothing for Darius III, as Philip's son, Alexander the Great, crossed the Hellespont at the head of a powerful army.

At first Darius III avoided direct conflict with Alexander but finally met him at Issus in 333 B.C. The Persians suffered a massive defeat and Darius fled the field, leaving his mother, wife and children to the mercy of the Greeks. Darius tried to make peace with Alexander, offering friendship and huge ransoms for his family. Alexander ignored the offers, keeping up the pressure by moving into Mesopotamia, or modern Iraq. The two forces met on a wide plain some 20 miles north of the village of Arbela.

One estimate of the contending forces allows Alexander 47,000 seasoned soldiers and Darius 250,000, although many of these were motley elements drafted from the eastern part of the Persian Empire. The battle proved to be Alexander's greatest military victory, as he split the Persian army and inflicted great damage. The Persians lost between 40,000 and 90,000 men, while Alexander lost between 100 and 500 men. As gaping holes were ripped in the Persians lines and Darius III's chariot driver was killed by a javelin, the King panicked, mounted a horse and once again fled the scene of battle. Leaderless, the Persians broke into a complete rout.

Darius III abandoned Babylonia, Susa and Persepolis to Alexander but still hoped to rally his forces in eastern Iran. With Alexander in hot pursuit, Darius III sought refuge in Bactria (modern Afghanistan), but he was taken captive by his own governor, Bessus. As Alexander closed in, Bessus had Darius III stabbed to death, and as a peace gesture left the corpse for Alexander to find. Darius III had led the Persian Empire to its destruction. (See BAGOAS.)

DARLAN, Jean (1881–1942) French naval officer and government official Jean Darlan was commander in chief of the French navy at the outbreak of World War II. With the fall of France he vacillated between loyalty to Vichy France, and indeed to Hitler, and allegiance to the Allies. Despite this, both Winston Churchill and Franklin D. Roosevelt envisioned a role for Darlan as a counter to the troublesome Charles de Gaulle. Of the latter Churchill looking at the Free French emblem was to say: 'The most difficult Cross I have ever had to bear is that of Lorraine.'

When the invasion plan for North Africa was drawn up, Roosevelt and Churchill refused to allow French forces to take part, producing predictable outrage from de Gaulle.

To try to lure the French forces in North Africa to the Allied cause, it was decided to bring in General Henri Giraud, de Gaulle's main rival for leadership of the Free French. However, the Algerian French leaders, after accepting an armistice, refused to obey Giraud. The Allies then turned to Darlan instead, further outraging the de Gaulle supporters, who regarded the admiral as a collaborator.

During the invasion of Algeria, Darlan happened to be in Algiers, and he agreed to cooperate with the Allies, putting all French forces in North Africa at their disposal.

On December 24, 1942, an obscure young Frenchman named Bournier de la Chapelle was admitted to the admiral's presence by a pass issued by Darlan's own staff. He shot Darlan to death. The assassin was quickly tried, convicted and executed. It was never determined beyond all doubt whether he was a de Gaulle supporter and whether he had been prompted in his act. In any event Darlan was eliminated as a competitor of de Gaulle, who also proved far more popular than Giraud with the French people. Churchill and Roosevelt were stuck with their 'Cross' to bear.

DARNLEY, Henry Lord   See RIZZIO, DAVID.

DASS, Arjun (1939–1985) Following the murder of Prime Minister Indira Gandhi in 1984 by several Sikh assassins, anti-Sikh rioting broke out in India. It was said that Sikh extremists thereupon drew up a 'hit list' of 16 Indian political figures held responsible for instigating the riots. Arjun Dass, a leading supporter of new Prime Minister Rajiv Gandhi and a powerful voice in the ruling Congress Party, was designated as one bearing such responsibility. Another was Lalit Maken, a labor union leader and member of the Indian Parliament. On July 31, 1985, Maken and his wife were shot to death in their home in New Delhi.

Then on September 4, 1985, two Sikh gunmen raided Dass's council office and shot Dass and his bodyguard to death and severely wounded six others. Three Sikhs were arrested for the murder, and police reported a fourth man committed suicide by drinking poison.

The Dass assassination was also considered to be a follow-up to the murder two weeks earlier of the political leader of moderate Sikh forces, Harchand Singh Longowal, by militants determined to disrupt new elections in the Sikh-dominated Punjab state. (See LONGOWAL, HARCHAND SINGH.)

DAUD KHAN, Mohammad See TARAKI, NUR MOHAMMAD.

DE GALINDEZ, Jesus (1914–1956) In March 1956, Dr. Jesus de Galindez, a Spanish Republican exile and a professor of international law at Columbia University, disappeared from his apartment on New York's lower Fifth Avenue. He had last been seen on March 12 after delivering a lecture in Hamilton Hall to his graduate seminar in Latin American government. A number of civil rights groups and Latin American, Spanish, and Catholic labor organizations asked Attorney General Herbert Brownell Jr. to investigate the possibility that de Galindez was 'the victim of a political crime' by agents of Dominican Republic dictator Rafael L. Trujillo. De Galindez had fled Spain to the Dominican Republic in 1939 and shortly went to work as a legal adviser for the Trujillo regime in the Department of Labor and National Economy. Seven years later he fled to the United States, bearing ample documentation of the brutal excesses of Trujillo, and he became a lecturer at Columbia and an articulate critic of Trujillo.

This guaranteed bloody vengeance on de Galindez by Trujillo. As described by journalist Bernard Diederich, author of the most definitive study of the Trujillo assassination: 'For Trujillo, human life was a cheap commodity. Like the Roman emperor Caligula, he cared more for his horse than humans. Of the many dictators Latin America endured, none used power with such extravagance or tyranny as this amoral man. He would murder an enemy with icy indifference, then arrange an impressive funeral and dictate the obituary.'

Trujillo shrugged off the de Galindez disappearance insisting he knew nothing of the disappearance and branding de Galindez a 'Communist.' Many theories surfaced about the disappearance, one being that he had been burned alive in the furnace of a Trujillo ship that sailed out of New York. The actual story of barbarism and betrayal came out only after the assassination of Trujillo five years later. De Galindez had been drugged and flown to Monte Crisi, the Dominican Republic, by a young American pilot and would-be soldier of fortune, Gerald Lester Murphy. He was then transferred to a plane piloted by Captain Octavio de la Maza and brought to Ciudad Trujillo.

The dazed and weakened de Galindez was brought to one of Trujillo's gaudy residences and presented to the dictator. Trujillo, dressed in riding clothes and carrying a riding crop, tried to force the scholar to eat an anti-Trujillo treatise he had recently completed. When de Galindez proved unresponsive, Trujillo beat him with the riding crop and then turned him over to his torturers. De Galindez was stripped naked, handcuffed and tied to a pulley, and lowered into a vat of boiling water. Later the corpse was fed to the sharks in the Caribbean near San Cristobal.

That hardly ended the horror of the de Galindez affair. Pilot Murphy, a 23-year-old New Jerseyan, was spending money with abandon since hauling his mystery passenger to the Dominican Republic. He was working as a well-paid pilot in that country and was flying between there and Miami. He was also bragging. Then the Trujillo security chief who had recruited Murphy died, and Murphy disappeared. That eliminated two men who had direct knowledge of the de Galindez kidnapping. The third was the other pilot, Tavio de la Maza, a member of an important family in the country that had long supported Trujillo.

Tavio was arrested and jailed for the murder of Murphy, with whom he'd become friendly since their joint flight. Some days later Tavio's body was returned to his wife with the explanation that he had committed suicide by hanging himself with mosquito netting tied to a pipe. Tavio supposedly left a suicide note, which was shown to the U.S. charge d'affaires, Richard H. Stephens. In it Tavio said Murphy had made homosexual advances to him, and he had rejected them. There was a struggle and Murphy had fallen into the sea. 'For this reason remorse is killing me and that is why I am putting an end to my life,' said the note.

The FBI later examined the suicide note and branded it a forgery, which hardly worried Trujillo. However, a chain of events was set in motion, and conspirators laid plans for the assassination of Trujillo, which was accomplished four years later. Dominant among the conspirators were revenge-minded members of the de la Maza family. (See TRUJILLO MOLINA, RAFAEL LEONIDAS.)

Further reading: *Trujillo: The Death of the Goat*, by Bernard Diederich.

DE GAULLE, Charles (1890–1970) – Attempted Assassinations General Charles de Gaulle, the great figure in French history during and after World War II, had the distinction of being listed in popular texts as one of the 'great survivors' of all time, having been subjected to no less than 31 documented attempted assassinations. Throughout his career de Gaulle attracted the enmity of the left, right and center. During the war he was subjected to attacks by pro-German, or at least anti-British, Frenchmen.

However, the most serious attempts on de Gaulle's life occurred during his presidential reign because of the loss of colonial Algeria by France. Rightists in France, including many refugee French Algerians, held de Gaulle responsible for the loss of the longtime colony. De Gaulle, bowing to the tide of history, had called for Algerian self-determination, which was tantamount to giving it independence and causing the expulsion of thousands of French colonists.

On September 8, 1961, de Gaulle and his wife Yvonne were traveling by car to their country home when a bomb made of 100 pounds of plastic explosive was set off alongside 15 liters of napalm. The explosion caused a sheet of flame to envelop the roadway, but the general ordered his police driver to continue right through the flames at well over 70 miles an hour. No convictions were obtained for the crime, although suspicion centered on the Organisation de l'Armee Secrete (OAS), a secret military group that opposed de Gaulle's Algerian policies.

There was no doubt of that group's guilt the next year. On August 22, 1962, de Gaulle was once more riding home in his Citroen with his wife and the same driver, this time followed by an identical dark Citroen with secret service agents and preceded and followed by a number of motorcyclists. Lying in ambush was a handpicked 15-man OAS assassination team armed with submachine guns, hand grenades and Molotov cocktails. However, the convoy was proceeding at such a rapid speed that the assassins did not see de Gaulle's car until it was passing. A desperate barrage of gunfire succeeded in blowing out a front tire and the rear window of de Gaulle's car, which for a moment skidded out of control until the driver could manage to straighten the vehicle and speed to safety. De Gaulle's only injury resulted from a cut finger when he brushed glass splinters off his coat.

A massive investigation followed, and several of the OAS conspirators were arrested among the hundred caught up in the search. A military court, sitting at the fort at Vincennes, judged 15 defendants, nine present and six in absentia, guilty. The court swept aside the defense claim that it had merely wanted to take de Gaulle prisoner to put him on trial for illegal acts. Six of the defendants (three of whom were absent) were sentenced to death and the other nine were given prison terms varying from three years to life. Two of the three in custody had their sentences commuted to life by de Gaulle, but he refused to do the same in the case of Air Force Lieutenant Colonel Jean-Marie Bastien-Thiry whom de Gaulle himself had decorated with the Knights' Cross of the Legion of Honor just two years earlier.

On March 11, 1963, only a week after the death sentence was passed on him, the colonel was awakened in his cell at 4 A.M. and informed by his lawyers that he was to be executed.

'Am I the only one to be executed?' he asked. Informed that he was, he asked, 'Are the others pardoned?' and was told they were. After he was served coffee, Bastien-Thiry died before a firing squad.

The last known attempt to kill de Gaulle occurred on July 1, 1966. As the president was being driven to Orly Airport for a flight to the Soviet Union, his car passed a parked car on the Boulevard Montparnasse that was loaded with about a ton of dynamite, but the bomb never went off. It had been planted by a group of students who had formerly belonged to the National Resistance Council, another group for the preservation of French Algeria. They had gone off the night before the planned assassination to commit a robbery for funds with which to flee abroad and had been apprehended during that crime.

DEWEY, Thomas E. See SCHULTZ, DUTCH.

DIDIUS JULIANUS, Marcus, Emperor of Rome (c. A.D. 132–193) Didius Julianus, a wealthy Roman senator, may be said to have achieved the throne in a more bizarre way than any other ruler, perhaps the most striking example of the empire in decline and decay. Didius Julianus bought the throne at auction.

On March 28, A.D. 193, the previous emperor, Pertinax, was assassinated by his own Praetorian Guard for his foolhardy attempt to enforce discipline on his palace soldiery. The rampaging guardsmen then found themselves in a quandary: They had no successor handy. They offered the scepter to several senators, all of whom refused. Pertinax had been popular among Romans, and it was understood that any successor might have to face considerable wrath from the populace.

An unknown soldier then suggested a solution: The throne could go to the Roman citizen who paid the highest price for it. Other Praetorians pounced on the idea, suggesting it be done by public auction. The historian Herodianus tells of a soldier who then scrambled up the embankments surrounding the city and raced along, bellowing in a loud voice: 'The Empire is for auction! The Empire is for auction!'

One who reacted most favorably to the offer was 61-year-old Didius Julianus, the wealthiest senator in Rome and one later characterized by Edward Gibbon as 'a vain old man.' Didius Julianus made for the auction, as did Sulpicianus, the father-in-law of the murdered Pertinax. The bidding boiled down to a contest between these two, with Sulpicianus bidding 240 million sesterces, which has been translated in mid-20th century U.S. currency to $800 for each of the 12,000 Praetorian Guards. Didius Julianus topped that with an offer of the equivalent of $1,000 per soldier. The Roman Empire was going, going, gone.

As his first act, Didius Julianus went to the Senate to announce his reign. The Senate, cowed by the armed Praetorians, confirmed him. From the Senate Didius Julianus proceeded to the royal palace, getting much-needed protection by the guards from stone-throwing citizens.

'A magnificent feast was prepared by his order,' Gibbon writes, 'and he amused himself till a very late hour with dice and the performances of Pylades, a celebrated dancer. Yet it was observed that, after the crowd of flatterers dispersed and left him to darkness, solitude and a terrible reflection, he passed a sleepless night; revolving most probably in his mind his own rash folly, the fate of his virtuous predecessor, and the doubtful and dangerous tenure of an empire, which had not been acquired by merit, but purchased by money.'

Perhaps Didius Julianus entertained some thoughts that

in time his rule would win acceptance, but he was doomed on his first night in the royal bedchamber. Meetings were held by rebellious citizens, and messengers were dispatched to the combat legions in the far corners of the empire, calling on their commanders to act against this affront to Rome. On the Danube, near the present site of Vienna, a shrewd and cruel ex-lawyer and general, Septimius Severus, acted. He offered his soldiers a bounty of $2,000 each if they would leave their posts and march on Rome. It was an offer the soldiers could not refuse.

In Rome Didius Julianus became aware of Severus's march and sent runners to keep him informed of the progress of the Danube legions. He lost interest in administration of the government, naming his son-in-law governor of Rome. He drilled his unhappy Praetorians to resist the battle troops, and for a time sought to use elephants in a battle attack, a plan soon discarded as few soldiers could ride the beasts. Didius Julianus ordered the vacillating Senate massacred, but then withdrew the order. Severus reached Ravenna, which Didius expected to offer resistance. It did not.

The emperor sent out private assassins, but they found it impossible to get near Severus, who maintained a personal guard of 600 men. Didius Julianus sent a messenger to Severus offering him half the empire and ordered the messenger to kill the general if he refused the offer. Severus listened and then simply had the messenger put to death. Didius Julianus then sent out a party of priests and vestal virgins to block Severus. They failed, and the emperor concentrated on sacrifices and other magical rites to stop his foe.

Severus kept coming. He and his men, fully armored, traveled the 800 miles to Rome in 40 days – an incredible 20 miles a day. They reached Rome on June 3, 193, and violated all custom by coming into the capital in full battle dress. Only Severus himself bowed to tradition by wearing civilian dress.

Didius Julianus, deserted by his guards, was found trembling in his palace. A group of about a dozen ordinary soldiers led him to the baths of his apartment.

'What harm have I done?' Didius Julianus cried out. 'Have I put anybody to death?' The soldiers laughingly threw the emperor down and beheaded him. After a bought-and-paid-for reign of just 66 days Didius Julianus was succeeded on the throne by Septimius Severus.

Further reading: *Decline and Fall of the Roman Empire*, by Edward Gibbon.

DIEM, Ngo Dinh See NGO DINH DIEM.

DMITRY, The False (?–1606) In what became known as the Time of Troubles (1598–1613) in Russia, no less than three pretenders to the czarist throne appeared, all claiming to be Dmitry Ivanovich, the son of Czar Ivan the Terrible. Dmitry had died mysteriously at the age of nine in 1591, during the reign of his older brother Fyodor I.

An official inquiry was conducted by a leading *boyar* (elite noble), Prince Vasily Shuysky, who concluded that the young Dmitry had stabbed himself to death during an epileptic fit. His mother insisted the child had been murdered, but she was forced to take the veil, and her relatives were banished from Moscow. Czar Fyodor I died in 1598 and was succeeded by his brother-in-law Boris Godunov. Around 1600 a pretender appeared, claiming to be the real Dmitry. According to some historians, he was a former member of the gentry who became a monk, one Grigory Bogdanovich Otrepyev. In any event there is little doubt that this youth truly believed he was the heir to the throne, and he took up residence in Moscow in 1601–1602, calling himself Prince Dmitry.

Threatened with official reprisal, this Dmitry fled to Lithuania, where he rallied support for his claim among Lithuanian and Polish nobles and the Jesuits. In 1604 the False Dmitry invaded Russia at the head of an army of adventurers and cossacks. Although he was defeated several times on the field, the False Dmitry continued to gain adherents throughout southern Russia. The real opening for the pretender came early in 1605 when

Shuysky suddenly declared that Dmitry had not died in 1591 and that the pretender was the true Dmitry. Czar Boris died suddenly in April, and major elements of the governmental armies shifted their allegiance to Dmitry. Meanwhile Shuysky and a number of other *boyars* settled any possible disputes about contenders for the throne by murdering Boris's infant son and heir, Fyodor II.

The *boyars* pledged loyalty to the False Dmitry, who entered Moscow in triumph and was crowned czar. Unfortunately for Dmitry, he soon antagonized Russian society by increasing Polish influence at court and marrying Marina Mniszek, the daughter of a noble Polish family. Influenced by his wife and her Jesuit supporters, Dmitry planned to join an elaborate Christian alliance aimed at driving the Turks from Europe. Sensing the growing disaffection for Dmitry and his policies, Shuysky switched positions again, declaring Dmitry to be an impostor after all.

Shuysky was banished for a time but rallied other *boyars* to his banner, and on May 17,1606, they and their armed retainers invaded the Kremlin. Dmitry defended himself with considerable valor and slew many of his assailants with his own hand until he was overcome and killed.

The False Dmitry's body was hauled to the place of executions and left exposed there with a ribald mask over his face and a flute placed in his mouth. Later the corpse was burned and his ashes shot from a cannon in the direction of Poland as a warning against further resurrections. Shuysky was proclaimed Czar Vasily IV.

However, the grim warning did not prevent yet more bizarre pretensions to the throne. Rumors spread through the superstitious countryside that Dmitry had not died in the coup, and in August 1607 a second False Dmitry appeared, claiming to be the first. He gathered considerable support among cossacks, Lithuanians, Poles and other rebels who had supported the first Dmitry and still fought Czar Vasily. The second pretender set up a rival court to Moscow in the Tushino in the North, and with

Marina Mniszek's formal recognition of the pretender as her husband, the second Dmitry became as powerful as the czar in Moscow.

Vasily was forced to seek the aid of Sweden to regain control of northern Russia, and this show of force caused the second False Dmitry to flee his headquarters. However, the alliance with Sweden provoked Poland to war with Vasily. The Poles advanced toward Moscow, as did an army under a reinvigorated second False Dmitry. In July 1610 Vasily was dethroned and forced to take monastic vows. The second Dmitry failed to reach Moscow, however, and in December he was fatally wounded by one of his own followers, variously recorded as an accident or a willful attack.

Within months a third False Dmitry appeared, and by March 1912 he succeeded in ravaging the environs of Moscow and other cities. However, in May he was betrayed, turned over to Moscow and executed. The Time of Troubles, with the three False Dmitrys seeking the throne, ended.

Further reading: *A History of Russia*, by Nicholas V. Riasanovsky.

DOE, Samuel Kanyon (1951–1990) Samuel Doe, a 28-year-old master sergeant in the Liberian National Guard who dropped out of the 11th grade, became president-dictator of Liberia in April 1980 after engineering the assassination of President William R. Tolbert, Jr. Ten days after the killing of Tolbert, Doe invited foreign reporters to watch 13 senior Tolbert government officials, including most of the former cabinet, marched nearly naked through the streets of Monrovia, tied to seaside posts and shot to death at point-blank range.

Doe's international reputation never fully recovered from this brutal display, and human rights groups later had grounds to continue attacking Doe's violent rule. The U.S. State Department's 1989 human rights report declared 'Brutality by police and other security officials during the arrest and questioning of individuals is fairly common, and there has been no evidence of Government efforts to halt this practice.' During Doe's reign more than 20 army officers and senior government officials were executed on charges of being involved in various coups. Doe's power was based on the Krahn tribe of which he was a member, and most opposition emanated from members of the Mano and Gio tribes.

By 1989 the main opposition was led by Charles Taylor, who had been involved in a failed 1985 coup but had escaped to the Ivory Coast. From there Taylor organized an insurgent army that invaded Liberia. The Taylor forces faced bitter internal feuds and a Gio tribesman, Prince Johnson (the given name is a common one in Liberia and connotes no royal status), split from the Taylor rebels with his own armed force. In the ensuing three-sided civil war, Taylor took control of the Liberian countryside while Johnson wrested control of the downtown of the capital city of Monrovia. Doe maintained only control of the executive mansion area, but resisted all offers to aid him to evacuate the country.

In the warfare an estimated 5,000 persons were killed and finally five West African nations organized a 'peacekeeping' force seeking to prevent further bloodletting. The peacekeepers, opposed by Taylor but welcomed by Johnson, proved ineffective, and the fighting continued. At one point the Taylor forces inaccurately reported having killed Johnson, who persisted in charges that Taylor, a former cabinet member serving in the Doe government, had embezzled $1 million in government funds, and that Taylor had gotten arms and money from Libya, an accusation Taylor denied.

In August 1990 Taylor announced he had signed a cease-fire agreement with President Doe, a move that could isolate Johnson. Then in a surprise development on September 9, Doe left his heavily fortified executive mansion stronghold and appeared at the peacekeeping force headquarters in Monrovia's port area. He was apparently about to meet with Johnson. There was some indication Doe was preparing to leave the country under the peacekeeping force's protection.

Prince Johnson arrived 15 minutes later and it was reported an argument followed. A gun battle broke out and dozens of Doe's heavily armed bodyguards were killed. Doe himself was shot in both legs. Then Johnson's men continued the rampage from room to room, rooting out Doe's soldiers and slaughtering them on the spot. The Johnson attack was so well executed and the inactivity of the peacekeeping force so evident that some African and Western diplomats voiced concern that the peacekeeping troops had acted in collusion with Johnson's rebels.

The wounded President Doe was transported to Johnson's base camp on the outskirts of Monrovia, and Johnson announced that Doe would not be killed but would be brought to trial on charges of corruption. The following day Johnson was reported to have been seen interrogating Doe at length about the whereabouts of large amounts of money he was supposed to have embezzled.

The next day Doe's mutilated body was put on display at a local hospital.

Meanwhile Prince Johnson declared himself president until elections could be held. Western diplomats said that it was not at all certain that Johnson would relinquish control and that the Taylor-Johnson conflict still had to be resolved. Furthermore, the Doe forces were still considered a potent force in the continuing struggle. (See TOLBERT, WILLIAM R., JR.)

DOLLFUSS, Engelbert (1892–1934) The murder of Austrian chancellor Engelbert Dollfuss on July 25, 1934, was German dictator Adolf Hitler's first attempt to use assassination as a method of conquest. By 1934 Dollfuss had gained the endearing nickname throughout Europe of Millimeternich due to his diminutive stature and his popularity for his resistance to the Nazis. Because he defied Hitler, it was generally overlooked elsewhere that Dollfuss was himself guiding his country toward full dictatorship along fascist lines, as established by his admired (and admiring) friend Benito Mussolini in Italy. Dollfuss resorted to civil war to smash the Social Democrats who controlled Vienna, bombarding the workers' flats in the city, killing 1,000 men, women and children and wounding upward of 4,000 more. Victorious, Dollfuss suppressed all parties other than his own, including the rather feeble Austrian Nazi Party.

Nevertheless, urged on by Hitler, the Austrian Nazis attempted a violent takeover in July 1934. On the morning of July 25 they succeeded in seizing a few buildings, and at noon 154 members of the SS Standarte 89, dressed in Austrian army uniforms, managed to penetrate the federal chancellery. Confronted by a number of the SS raiders in his private office, Dollfuss tried to argue them out of the coup. One of the leaders, Otto Planetta, ignored Dollfuss's plaints and shot him through the throat at a range of two feet. The assassins held the building for several hours while Dollfuss, still breathing, begged fruitlessly for medical aid. He died about 6 P.M., but the coup was smashed shortly thereafter by Austrian forces.

Hitler had been getting telephone updates on the action while attending a performance of *Das Rheingold* at the annual Wagner Festival at Bayreuth, but later, upon collapse of the coup, the Fuhrer denied any connection with the attackers and denounced them for assassinating Dollfuss. Thirteen of the assassins were hanged, several shouting 'Heil Hitler!' from the scaffold. When, four years later, Hitler took over Austria in the bloodless Anschluss, one of his first acts was the release of those still in prison for the attempted coup in 1934.

Further reading: *The Rise and Fall of the Third Reich*, by William L. Shirer.

DOMITIAN, Emperor of Rome (A.D. 51–96) Widely described in antiquity as one of the worst of the Roman emperors, Domitian is today regarded by some historians as too maligned a ruler who actually possessed many good qualities including a stern competence, in addition to his morbidity, egocentricity and cruelty. In fact, Domitian's reign of terror against the senatorial aristocracy was perhaps unparalleled in the bloody history of Rome.

Domitian ascended the throne in A.D. 81 upon the death of his brother Titus. While some held that Domitian was involved in his brother's death, there is no credible evidence to support that theory. Domitian's early reign was marked by his stern rule and his determination to achieve autocratic power. In 88 Domitian was faced with the revolt of one of his provincial governors, the senator Lucius Antonius Saturninus. Domitian successfully put down the revolt and thereafter systematically purged the Senate of those he suspected of harboring disloyalty toward him.

He demanded to be treated as a god himself and bestowed divinity upon his father, brother, wife and sisters. On the throne he encouraged visitors to embrace his knees. In 89 he banished all philosophers from Rome because they supported the Senate, and a few years later he banished them from all of Italy. Among these were Dio Chryostom and Epictetus. Domitian executed a number of Christians, including his nephew Falvius Clemens, because they would not offer sacrifices before his image. He filled the capitol with statues of himself.

He did not trust even those who pledged full loyalty to him, and finally, Will Durant observes, 'The Emperor's fear of conspiracy became almost a madness. He lined with shining stone the walls of the porticoes under which he walked, so that he might see mirrored in them whatever went on behind him.' A word from the most unreliable informer was enough to doom any citizen.

Finally not even his own household felt safe from the fearful emperor. In 96 he ordered the death of his secretary Epaphrodius on the grounds that 27 years earlier he had aided Nero to commit suicide. Other servants felt threatened and plotted to kill Domitian, aided by not only many members of the Senate but also the emperor's wife, Domitia, and almost certainly his successor, Nerva.

Domitian undoubtedly knew his time had come. The night before his murder, he leaped from his bed in fright to resist an imagined attack. The real attack came 24 hours later, the first blow struck by his wife's servant. Four other members of the household joined in the assassination.

The Senate reacted with joy upon hearing of Domitian's murder. Members destroyed all the images of Domitian that had been erected in the chamber, and the Senate decreed that all statues of Domitian throughout the empire as well as all inscriptions bearing his name were to be destroyed. His widow lived well into the next century, much honored.

Further reading: *The Cambridge Ancient History*, Vol. II, Chapters 1 and 4; *A History of the Roman World*, 30 *BC-AD* 138, by E. T. Salmon.

DOUGLAS, William, Eighth Earl of (1425–1452)   One of the Black Douglases, William, eighth earl of Douglas, had lost his lands following accusations of treason against the Scottish crown. Later the earl recovered Wigtown and Galloway by marrying his cousin, Margaret Douglas, the 'Fair Maid of Galloway.'

For a time Douglas stood in relatively high favor with young King James II, but by 1450 the king had forayed the earl's lands while he was away on a pilgrimage to Rome. The king was certain that Douglas had been engaging in treasonable correspondence with England. In 1452 the king offered safe conduct to Douglas to visit him at Stirling Castle. James II entertained Douglas lavishly but then suddenly demanded that Douglas dissolve an alliance he had established with Alexander Lindsay, the 'Tiger,' fourth earl of Crawford. When Douglas refused, the king – safe conduct or no – personally stabbed him to death with the assistance of his courtiers, who held the victim helpless.

DOYLE, William (?–1983)   On January 16, 1983, with shocked Catholic worshipers looking on, Judge William Doyle was murdered as he left St. Bridget's Church in South Belfast, Northern Ireland. Judge Doyle had just opened the door of his car to offer an elderly female parishioner a lift when two young gunmen let loose with handguns at close range. The woman was hit in the stomach and was seriously wounded; the judge was hit several times. Three doctors attending the mass tried to save him with first-aid equipment but failed, and the priest who had celebrated the mass administered the last rites.

The Provisional IRA took responsibility for the assassination, calling Judge Doyle 'a key part in the British Government's repressive occupation machine.' Traditionally a certain number of Catholic judges are appointed in Protestant Northern Ireland, and Judge Doyle, who sat on numerous trials of terrorists, had sent to prison Catholics and Protestants alike. He disliked police protection and insisted on always going to his parish church alone. Judge Doyle was only the latest in a series of murders of judges whom the IRA had long declared legitimate targets.

DRUMMOND, Edward (?–1843) On January 20, 1843, at Charing Cross, London, a mad Scotsman named Daniel McNaughton shot Edward Drummond, private secretary to Sir Robert Peel, the British prime minister. Drummond died of his wounds the following day, and it was assumed that McNaughton had mistaken him for the prime minister.

McNaughton was charged with murder, but his counsel pleaded partial insanity. The chief justice, sitting with two other judges, instructed the jury that the key test was whether McNaughton had been capable of distinguishing right from wrong in respect to his actions at the time. McNaughton was found insane and was sent to a mental institution.

The case drew much attention since it broke new legal ground, and the judges were questioned by the House of Lords. Thus was established for the first time what became known as the McNaughton Rule, whereby the defendant's knowledge of the nature and quality of a crime at the time of commission became the test for criminal responsibility. This defense had been rejected by the courts in 1812 when John Bellingham had assassinated Prime Minister Spencer Perceval, but it was soon adopted in many other nations, especially in the United States, and has been involved in countless cases from 1843 on. (See PERCEVAL, SPENCER.)

DRUSUS, Marcus Livius (?–91 B.C.). In 91 B.C. Marcus Livius Drusus, a newly elected tribune of the people, made what may be called the last nonviolent effort to reform the government of republican Rome. It was a grim period in Roman history – which H. G. Wells characterized in *The Outline of History* as one in which, '. . . the sullen, shapeless discontent of the mass of the people was still seeking some effective outlet. The rich grew richer and the poor poorer.' Every previous effort of extreme democratic leaders such as Saturninus and Glaucia ended in assassination, which hardly altered the social forces in conflict.

Drusus offered colonial and agrarian reform bills, as well as a general enfranchisement of the Italians and a general abolition of debts. The wealthy senators, among them many 'usurers' and 'land-grabbers,' to use Wells's terms, struck back, declaring Drusus's legislation invalid on technicalities. Disturbances increased on the Italian Peninsula. Then Drusus was stabbed to death in his home by an unknown assailant, although the general belief was that an element within the Senate had arranged the assassination.

Assassination was now replaced by desperate insurrection in two years of bitter civil war called the Social War. The fighting ended when the Roman Senate surrendered to the idea of reform 'in principle.' In practice, that body reneged on the reforms as soon as the rebels dispersed. Rome and Italy remained in the hands of the military.

DRUSUS CAESAR (c. 13 B.C.–A.D. 23) The son of the Roman emperor Tiberius, Drusus Caesar became heir to the throne after the death of Tiberius's nephew and adoptive son Germanicus in A.D. 19. Drusus met the common, and almost required, traits of the time – violence and degeneracy – but he proved an excellent representative of all-powerful Rome. He suppressed a mutiny in Pannonia, and later as governor of Illyricum (A.D. 17–20) he maneuvered the downfall of Maroboduus, the king of the German Marcomanni. Made consul for a second time in A.D. 21, he earned the enmity of the powerful Sejanus, adviser to the emperor and commander of the Praetorian Guard.

It is generally conceded that Sejanus's long-range plan was to overthrow Tiberius and take the purple for himself. In that context Drusus loomed as an obstacle. In A.D. 23 Drusus died, most likely having been poisoned, either by Sejanus or by Drusus's wife, Livilla, under Sejanus's influence. At first no suspicion fell upon Sejanus, and he encouraged Tiberius's decision to retire to Capri and leave much of the affairs of Rome in his hands. However, by A.D. 31 suspicions in the death of Drusus came to the fore and Tiberius finally became convinced that Sejanus was guilty and that he Sejanus was plotting to overthrow him. In an example of swift Roman justice, Sejanus was imprisoned, condemned to death and executed on the same day.

DUBS, Adolph (1920–1979) On February 14, 1979, U.S. Ambassador Adolph Dubs was shot to death in Kabul, Afghanistan, after being kidnapped by Afghan Muslim extremists. The 30-year veteran of the diplomatic corps had taken up his post in Afghanistan only the previous year, and he was being driven to the embassy in the city when his car was stopped by four armed men. He was held prisoner in a hotel room while his abductors demanded the release of men they described as Muslim 'religious figures' and the kidnappers threatened to kill Dubs if their demands were not met.

Meanwhile Afghan security men located the hotel and stormed the building, despite pleas from American officials 'to exercise patience and to secure the ambassador's release without recourse to force.' Dubs was shot to death, but it was not clear whether he had been deliberately murdered by his captors or whether he had been hit in the crossfire.

The U.S. government later cut aid to Afghanistan because of a number of factors, according to a White House statement, including 'circumstances surrounding the death of Mr. Dubs.' The United States had also protested the role of Soviet advisers in the storming of the hotel. However, the incident did not deter the United States from later providing military aid over the years to essentially those forces that had kidnapped Ambassador Dubs.

DUCA, Ion G. (1879–1933)   A longtime liberal within the meaning of the term in early 20th-century Romania, Ion G. Duca became premier in November 1933, after having served as an elected member of the parliament in 1907, and holding a number of posts since 1916. He became leader of the Liberal Party in 1930.

An outspoken opponent of Fascism, he immediately undertook the task of destroying the Iron Guard and other similar anti-Semitic groups and those with close sympathies to the Italian Fascists or the German Nazis.

On December 30, 1933, Duca was in a train station in Carpathia when he was shot to death by an Iron Guardist, Radu Constantinescu. Duca had been in office just over six weeks. His assassination marked a period of bloodletting over the next half dozen years. Dozens of political figures and untold others were killed until the future war criminal Marshall Ion Antonescu, a friend of Hitler, came to power in 1940 and soon thereafter brought Romania into the war on Germany's side.

E

EDWARD II, King of England (1284–1327) King of England from 1307 to 1326, Edward II proved to be a less than effectual monarch, troubled from without by Robert the Bruce of Scotland who defeated English forces on the battlefield and by his own barons who constantly threatened his throne. Edward surrounded himself with dubious supporters, especially a frivolous favorite (and possible lover), Piers Gaveston. After the king granted Gaveston the earldom of Cornwall, a 21-member baronial committee drafted what became known as the Ordinances which restricted Edward's powers over appointments and finances.

Pretending to accept the demands, the king sent Gaveston abroad but soon permitted his return. The angered barons seized Gaveston and executed him in June 1312. A foray into Scotland in 1314 proved a disaster as Bruce routed Edward's forces. Back in England Edward was now at the mercy of the barons, and his cousin Thomas of Lancaster, the head of the baronial group, became essentially the ruler of England. A falling out between the barons in 1318 gave Edward the opportunity to regain a modicum of power thanks to two favorites – Hugh le Despenser and his son and namesake. Edward approved a foray into Wales by the young Despenser, and in turn Lancaster took up arms against the Despensers. Edward defeated Lancaster and his barons in 1322, and Lancaster was captured and executed.

Free at last of baronial interference, Edward felt strong enough to revoke the Ordinances. However, his queen, Isabella, for many years disgraced and enraged by Edward's effeminate relationship with the Despensers, took up residence in Paris. There she met Roger Mortimer, an exiled baron, and they became lovers.

By 1326 support for Edward had waned because of the Despensers and Isabella and Mortimer invaded England and hanged the Despensers. Edward was forced to abdicate in favor of his 15-year-old son, Edward III. However, the boy king was kept well away from power and Mortimer ruled if he did not reign.

Mortimer had Edward II kept in relatively gentle confinement at Kenilworth, but the following spring he was transferred to the custody of two knights, Thomas de Gournay and John Maltravers. The deposed king was shifted from one castle to another, ending up at Berkeley. It was clear that the government of Isabella and Mortimer was so fragile that the pair could not allow Edward II to remain alive as a possible rallying cry of opponents. Edward II was subjected to mistreatment in the hope that he would die. In one case Edward was confined to a charnel house but he proved too robust of body to succumb to disease. Finally, his jailers gave up such subtle efforts and simply murdered him in his bed in late September 1327. His dying screams are said to have echoed through the castle.

Every effort was made to make the murder appear to have been natural death, and the killers offered up the body in full view to indicate that to be the case.

By 1330 Edward III, then 18, gathered enough support to arrest Mortimer who was given a show trial and hanged at Tyburn, not even being accorded the dignity of a beheading. Edward III later had a lavish tomb, one of the glories of medieval sculpture and decorative tabernacle work, erected over his tomb at what is now Gloucester Cathedral.

EDWARD V, King of England (1470–1483?) The elder of two young sons of Edward IV, Edward V succeeded to the throne at the age of 12 for a brief reign that ended in a way that has fascinated writers for centuries. On April 30, 1483, three weeks after he had become king, Edward and his younger brother, Richard, were kidnapped while en route to London by their uncle Richard, duke of Gloucester. Gloucester declared himself the young king's protector, and the two young boys were housed in the Tower of London, which at the time was both a prison and a royal residence.

Edward V's short reign ended on June 26 when Gloucester got an assembly of lords and commoners to agree with him that Edward IV's marriage had been invalid and that his children by Queen Elizabeth (Woodville) were bastards. The assembly proclaimed Gloucester to be King Richard III.

The two young princes were never seen alive again. Most likely the princes were assassinated by King Richard's henchmen, but many historians attribute the killings to Henry Stafford, duke of Buckingham, and to King Richard's successor, Henry VII. In 1674, during the reign of the Restoration king Charles II, skeletons of two young boys were exhumed in the Tower of London, almost certainly those of Edward V and Prince Richard.

EID, Guy   See NOEL, CLEO A., JR.

ELAGABALUS, Emperor of Rome (204–222)   When the Roman emperor Caracalla was assassinated in 217, he was replaced by the chief plotter against him, the Praetorian prefect Macrinus. Marius Avitus Bassianus, the young cousin of the murdered Caracalla, was 13 and was at the time living in Emesa, in the eastern empire, where the family of his mother, Julia Soaemias, were the hereditary high priests of the sun god Baal. Young Bassianus's mother and grandmother, Julia Maesa, won the allegiance of nearby troops by convincing them that the boy was the illegitimate son of Caracalla, an argument reinforced by enormous bribes. By the following year most of the Roman armies in the East deserted Macrinus and supported Bassianus.

Accepted by the Senate in 218 as the rightful emperor, Bassianus, because of his priestly functions, became known as Elagabalus (the sun god Baal was worshiped in Emesa as Elah-Gabal – hence Elagabalus). He also comes down to us as Heliogabalus. Whatever his name, it became synonymous with peculiar vices. In today's terms Elagabalus was a transsexual. One of his first royal acts upon becoming emperor at 14 was to seek a sex-change operation. He finally settled for simple castration and actually went through marriage and the necessary honeymoon rites with a male slave named Zoticus.

Elagabalus insisted on being addressed as 'empress' and proclaimed himself the patroness of the prostitutes of Rome. He lectured them knowingly on various acts and perversions they might be called upon to perform, and finally he took to the streets himself, accosting men and offering his services. Once he even entered a brothel, ejected the prostitutes and took their tasks upon himself.

In his spare time Elagabalus stressed religion or, as Will Durant put it, he 'perfumed his lust with piety,' imposing the worship of Baal upon the Romans. Warned by a soothsayer that he would die a violent death, Elagabalus decided to prepare worthy means of suicide – swords of gold, cords of purple silk, and poisons enclosed in sapphires and emeralds. On a more practical level, he executed a large number of dissident generals.

He promoted youths solely on what may be regarded as personal beauty. As royal homosexual orgies became even more blatant, Roman citizens and, perhaps more important, the soldiery became more outraged. Sensing this, Julia Maesa, the real power in the government, sought to ensure the succession and convinced Elagabalus to adopt his docile cousin Alexander Serverus as his son and heir.

Some time later Elagabalus awoke from an orgy and realized that naming Alexander his heir was hardly prudent. In panicked jealousy, he determined to have his cousin killed, but his plans were discovered and the Praetorian Guard mutinied. They invaded the palace and killed the emperor's mother, Soaemias. Elagabalus did not avail himself of his suicide options and was cornered in a latrine and butchered. The guards dragged his corpse through the streets and around the Circus and finally heaved it into the Tiber. The soldiery proclaimed Alexander Severus emperor. (See ALEXANDER SEVERUS, EMPEROR OF ROME.)

Further reading: *A Criminal History of Mankind*, by Colin Wilson; *The Story of Civilization III – Caesar and Christ*, by Will Durant; *History of Twenty Caesars*, by Herodian.

ELIZABETH, Empress of Austria (1837–1898)   The wife of Emperor Franz Joseph, Empress Elizabeth of Austria was hardly the most likely candidate as an assassin's target. Suffering from melancholia much of the time – due to such disheartening events as the suicides of her only son, the tragic Rudolf, at Mayerling, and her cousin Ludwig II of Bavaria – she tended to avoid court as much as possible in favor of travel, a fact that complicated her personal protection.

On September 10, 1898, Elizabeth was visiting Geneva, Switzerland, where lived a young Italian workman and anarchist named Luigi Luccheni, who frequently told coworkers: 'Ah, how I'd like to kill somebody. But it must be somebody important, so it gets in the papers.' Seizing the opportunity when it arose, he stabbed Elizabeth to death with a shoemaker's awl.

ELIZABETH, Grand Duchess (1864–1918)   On July 17, 1918, the day after the assassination of former Czar Nicholas II of Russia and his immediate family, the revolutionary Bolsheviks, in keeping with their policy of killing every member of the Romanov family they could get their hands on, brutally murdered six more, including Grand Duchess Elizabeth, Czarina Alexandra's sister.

Elizabeth, called Ella, was the widow of Grand Duke Sergei, who had been assassinated in 1905. Elizabeth had rejected all offers of either security or escape in revolutionary 1917. In March 1917 the provisional government asked her to leave the abbey she had previously built and retired to several years earlier and take refuge in the Kremlin. Elizabeth refused. In 1918 Kaiser Wilhelm of Germany, who had once been in love with her, sought through the offices of Sweden and later through his ambassador to the Soviet Union, Count von Mirbach, to bring her to safety in his country.

Mirbach's efforts ended on July 6, 1918, when he himself was assassinated. On July 16 the czar and his family were murdered. The next day Elizabeth, being held by the Bolsheviks in the town of Alapayevsk in the Urals, was put on a peasant cart, as were her fellow prisoners: Grand Duke Sergei Mikhailovich; three sons of Grand Duke Constantine, Ivan, Constantine, and Igor; and the son of Grand Duke Paul, Prince Vladimir Paley. They were taken to the mouth of an abandoned mine shaft and thrown in, still alive. Heavy lumber and hand grenades were thrown down the shaft, but apparently this did not conclude the murderous work. After the assassination squad left, a peasant who crept to the edge of the pit heard hymns being sung from below. And when the bodies were later recovered by the White opponents of the Bolsheviks, the head of one of the boys was found to have been carefully bandaged with Elizabeth's handkerchief. (See SERGEI, GRAND DUKE.)

Further reading: *Nicholas and Alexandra*, by Robert K. Massie.

ELIZABETH I, Queen of England (1533–1603) – Attempted Assassinations   Queen Elizabeth I of England had to ward off several assassination plots against her, most done with the purpose of raising to the throne Mary, the Catholic queen of Scots. Literature and histories, depending on their viewpoint, tend to portray Mary as either a tragic and romantic figure or a scheming adulteress and almost certainly a murderess herself. Whether justified or not, Mary is considered by many to have been well aware of the plot, if not the actual instigator, that resulted in the assassination of her husband, Henry Lord Darnley in 1567.

Eventually, in 1568, Mary's political reversals in Scotland forced her to seek refuge in England, which presented Elizabeth with a dilemma. The Scots refused to take her back as queen, and Elizabeth could hardly allow her to proceed abroad, where she most certainly would have raised an army in either France or Spain to try to invade England, since Mary too claimed the throne of England. Indeed, English Catholics felt that Mary was already the proper queen on the grounds that Henry VIII's second marriage – to Anne Boleyn, Elizabeth's mother, after the annulment of his previous marriage to Catherine of Aragon – was unlawful. As it was, following Elizabeth's accession to the throne of England in 1558, Mary was the next in line as the daughter of Henry's sister Margaret.

Elizabeth could not send Mary anywhere, and confinement, genteel in quality, seemed to be the queen's only option. She dared not accept the advice in 1570 of the Protestant reformer John Knox to put Mary to death. That would incur the wrath of the Vatican and of France and Spain. Elizabeth needed many more years of peace to strengthen her realm and to build a navy that would displace the worldwide sea power of Spain. She could but abide Mary.

Mary constantly plotted her escape, always insisting that was her sole aim, but those who plotted with her planned the death of Elizabeth and the installment of Mary in her place. In 1571 Roberto di Ridolfi, a Florentine banker with considerable enterprises in London, became intermediary between Mary, the Spanish ambassador, the bishop of Ross, Philip of Spain, the duke of Alva in the Spanish Netherlands, and Pope Pius V. Ridolfi proposed that Alva should send troops into England while a Catholic army swept in from Scotland, and that the duke of Norfolk should marry Mary, who would mount the throne. Norfolk was informed of the plot, and while he did not clearly agree, he also did not reveal it. Mary gave her tentative consent. The pope was impressed enough to give money to Ridolfi and recommended the plot to Philip, who also approved, provided that Alva agreed. Alva found the plot scatterbrained and it fell through, but not without fatal repercussions.

Letters of Norfolk and Ridolfi were found, and the plotters and a number of Catholic nobles were imprisoned. Norfolk was convicted of treason, and sentenced to death. Elizabeth hesitated on executing so prominent a noble, but her chief adviser, William Cecil, as well as Parliament and the Anglican hierarchy pushed for the execution of Norfolk – and Mary as well. Elizabeth sent Norfolk to the block.

There were many other plots on Elizabeth's life, but they were always stymied by the royal spy system. After each, however, there were repeated public calls for Mary's head, and when, in 1580, Pope Gregory XIII declared it would be no sin to kill the 'heretic' Elizabeth, there were more cries for execution. There followed the French duke of Guise's enterprise in 1582, which also called for the queen's murder, with Mary's complicity. Still Elizabeth hesitated to act, no doubt partially in fear of what the reaction of her Catholic subjects might be.

The queen was greatly shaken by the 1584 assassination of the other great Protestant leader of the world, William the Silent, in the Netherlands at Catholic hands. Finally, the Babington Plot of 1586 galvanized Elizabeth to action.

A Roman Catholic priest named John Ballard convinced a young, rich Catholic, Anthony Babington, to organize a conspiracy to kill the queen with a combined invasion of England by armies from Spain, France and the Low Countries. Babington put the proposal in writing in a letter smuggled to Mary in her place of confinement that told specifically of the plan to kill Elizabeth. Mary approved Babington's proposal, without giving any specific statement on the assassination but promising rewards for the success of the plan – a situation hardly qualifying as 'credible deniability.'

Spies working for Elizabeth's chief spy, Sir Francis Walsingham, unraveled the conspiracy. Babington and Ballard were arrested, and after them some 300 Catholics as well. Ballard and Babington confessed, and Mary's secretary was induced to admit the authenticity of Mary's letter responding to Babington. Thirteen conspirators were executed, and all over England there were celebrations of thanksgiving that Elizabeth had been saved. There were now larger-than-ever demonstrations for Mary's execution. She was tried and found guilty in October 1586, but it took the queen's councillors three months to get her to sign the death warrant.

When she finally did, the council dispatched the warrant immediately to facilitate the execution before the queen had a change of heart. In typical Elizabethan manner, the queen threw a tantrum when informed the execution had been carried out on February 8, 1587, insisting she had never intended this final step. Nevertheless, there was popular rejoicing at the news of the execution, and London church bells were rung for 24 hours.

Further reading: *Mary Queen of Scots*, by Antonia Fraser; *The Story of Civilization VII – The Age of Reason Begins*, by Will and Ariel Durant.

EPHIALTES (?–461 B.C.) Historians have been frustrated that they know so little of Ephialtes, the poor but incorruptible leader of the democratic forces of Athens in the 460s B.C. Elected general soon after 465, Ephialtes opposed the pro-Sparta position of Cimon, the military leader of the aristocrats. In 462, over Ephialtes's opposition, Cimon was given authority to send an Athenian force to assist in putting down a revolt of the Helots in Sparta. Sparta, however, always suspicious of Athenians, refused to use the soldiers. Cimon's men returned to Athens in anger, and Cimon was in disgrace.

Ephialtes adroitly turned the popular anger to his advantage and used the people's sentiment to strip the aristocratic court, the Areopagus, of its political power. He impeached a number of that body's members for malfeasance and had a number executed for their crimes. The oligarchy attempted to regain its hold on power by bribing Ephialtes, but he steadfastly resisted their offers. With Ephialtes quickly consolidating his democratic gains, the desperate aristocrats had him murdered by an unknown assassin. However, they acted too late. By that time Ephialtes had already consolidated the political revolution. Thereafter the leadership of the democrats fell to Pericles, and Athens was launched into the Age of Pericles and the great democratic experiment.

ERZBERGER, Matthias (1875–1921) Thrust into power on the collapse of imperial Germany near the end of World War I, German politician Matthias Erzberger had the courage to sign the armistice in November 1918. A leader of the left wing of the Catholic Center Party, Erzberger had been a rabid annexationist earlier in the war, but by 1917 he had authored the Reichstag Resolution of 1917, which called for a peace of understanding. He favored accepting the Treaty of Versailles, fearing a German rejection would result in the utter destruction of the country.

Within the provisional government at Weimar, Erzberger urged signing, pointing out that the terms could be easily evaded. This did not win any points from the German right, and Erzberger came under severe slanderous attack for alleged questionable financial practices and corruption. Cleared after a lawsuit, Erzberger nevertheless was continually denounced as a manipulator who had undermined Germany's chances of victory. Feeling that his own party had failed to support him in these attacks, Erzberger resigned from the government in June 1920. On August 26, 1921, he was vacationing in the Black Forest when he was assassinated by gunmen of the extreme rightist Ferme group, who also assassinated Foreign Minister Walther Rathenau, the 'Judeo-Democrat,' the following year.

EVERS, Medgar W. (1926–1963) Medgar Evers became an early victim of the black civil rights movement in the 1960s when he was shot in the back and killed just after midnight on June 11, 1963, as he returned to his home in Jackson, Mississippi. The 37-year-old Evers, state field secretary for the NAACP for the past nine years, had just left his car when he was struck down by a bullet fired from ambush. A .30-06 caliber rifle with a telescopic sight was found nearby.

At the time civil rights protests in Jackson and elsewhere in the state were at their height. Governor Ross Barnett, who at the time was deeply involved in trying to prevent a second black student (after James H. Meredith, who had been admitted the previous year) from being allowed to enroll at the University of Mississippi, said of the slaying, 'Apparently it was a dastardly act.'

Black leaders denounced officials in Mississippi and criticized President John F. Kennedy and Attorney General Robert F. Kennedy for not acting forcefully enough in the civil rights crisis.

Ten days after the assassination, Byron de la Beckwith, a 42-year-old fertilizer salesman and member of the Citizens Council of Mississippi, was arrested by FBI agents. FBI Director J. Edgar Hoover said clues leading to the arrest were a telescopic sight and Beckwith's fingerprint on a rifle found near the Evers home after the murder. In Beckwith's hometown of Greenwood, a White Citizens Legal Fund was set up to pay his legal fees and provide legal aid to other whites in rights matters. Despite two trials, no murder conviction was obtained in the case. Evers, who had received two Bronze Stars in World War II, was buried in Arlington National Cemetery.

EWART-BIGGS, Christopher (1921–1976)   Three weeks after he had been appointed British ambassador to the Republic of Ireland, Christopher Ewart-Biggs was killed by a land mine. Ewart-Biggs drove only 180 yards from his official residence on July 21, 1976 to meet with Foreign Minister Garret FitzGerald when his car struck the bomb. Because there were only two ways a car could go from the residence to reach the main roads, a routine inspection of the roads before the ambassador left would have turned

up the mine, which was made up of more than 100 pounds
of explosives and was set off by wire from a wooded hill
about 300 yards from the road. Both the ambassador and
his personal secretary, Judith Cooke, were killed outright.
The chauffeur and another British official were injured.
Three men, two carrying rifles, were seen running from
the area. The assassinations were attributed to the Irish
Republican Army, although it did not claim responsibility
for them.

F

FAISAL IBN AL SAUD, King of Saudi Arabia (1905–1975) On March 25, 1975, at the magnificent palace in Riyadh, King Faisal ibn al Saud, the 69-year-old absolute ruler of Saudi Arabia, celebrated the 1,405th birthday of the Prophet Muhammad with an early morning reception for a visiting Kuwaiti delegation led by that country's oil minister. He greeted the members of a long reception line, among whom was a 27-year-old Saudi prince, Faisal ibn Musad Abdel Azziz. When the prince reached King Faisal, the king recognized him and lowered his head so that the prince, following custom, could kiss the tip of the king's nose. Prince Faisal drew a pistol from under his robe and shot the king three times in the face, killing him instantly. 'Now my brother is avenged!' the royal assassin cried, as palace guards beat him to the ground.

Prince Faisal was the son of Prince Musad, an exiled brother of King Faisal. The prince's brother had been killed several years before by police for taking part in an armed attack on a new television station whose broadcasts of the human image were blasphemous under the raiders' strict interpretation of the Koran.

Despite the brutality of the assassination, there was considerable speculation that Prince Faisal would not be executed. As a member of the royal family, Saudi watchers believed, there was a good chance he would be found insane and simply locked away.

Unfortunately for the prince, his act was found to be not a simple case of vengeance but essentially a political act. Prince Faisal, saddened Saudi religious figures noted, had suffered the evil of too much travel and too much foreign influence. Educated at San Francisco State College, the University of Colorado and at the University of California at Berkeley, he had let his hair grow long, smoked marijuana and sold LSD, for which he had been arrested in Colorado. At Berkeley, the prince had socialized with militant Arab students, the sort who regarded King Faisal and the royal institutions as standing in the way of a progressive Saudi Arabia. Apparently, although Faisal did not believe it possible to end the monarchy entirely, he did hope to see the king succeeded by more moderate royal leadership.

In June Faisal was found guilty of murder by an Islamic religious court. Within hours of the pronouncement of the death sentence, he was taken to the public square in front of Riyadh's Great Mosque and was decapitated there with one stroke of a large, golden-hilted sword.

King Faisal was succeeded by King Khalid, who came to be regarded as a bit more moderate than his predecessor. But Prince Faisal's goal of a more progressive, democratic Saudi Arabia was not achieved.

FAISAL II, King of Iraq (1935–1958) King Faisal II of Iraq, the son of King Ghazi and grandson of Faisal I, succeeded to the throne when he was four years old. He took the royal oath in 1953 on his eighteenth birthday. In early 1958 Faisal agreed to federation with Jordan, which was ruled by his cousin, King Hussein I, but the arrangement was disrupted by a military coup by Iraqi General Qassim.

Army units attacked the palace, meeting spirited resistance by the royal guards. However, Faisal and his family were trapped, and finally Faisal, after winning promises of safe conduct, ordered his men to cease resistance. No sooner had the royal guards laid down their weapons than Qassim's assassins stormed the palace, machine-gunning the king and the entire royal family, including even baby girls.

Qassim established a dictatorship that lasted until February 1963, when he was overthrown and executed.

FLORIAN, Emperor of Rome (232–276) Florian (full Latin name: Marcus Annius Florianus) is generally regarded as a usurper who seized the Roman throne upon the death of his brother, the emperor Tacitus, in 276. Tacitus was considered a worthy emperor but was quite old and reigned for a mere six months, dying on a military campaign in Asia, a task for which he was physically unfit. Florian had a different father than Tacitus but still claimed the purple, and a weak-kneed Senate and the legions in the West offered no serious objections. But the armies in Syria rejected Florian and supported their leader, Marcus Aurelius Probus.

Civil war ensued, and Probus – who, many agree, did not actively covet the purple – clearly bested Florian in a number of battles. When it became clear to Florian's troops that they were not likely to be on the winning side, they apparently murdered Florian, who had ruled only from June to September 276. Probus was recognized as emperor. (See PROBUS, MARCUS AURELIUS, EMPEROR OF ROME.)

FORD, Gerald (1913–) – Attempted Assassination On September 5, 1975, 26-year-old Lynette 'Squeaky' Fromme, a member of the Charles Manson 'murder family,' became probably the first woman to try to kill a president of the United States (if we dismiss what Professor Franklin L. Ford of Harvard called the 'deeply flawed' conviction of Mary Surratt as an accessory in the Lincoln assassination of 1865).

Squeaky pointed a pistol at President Ford at a range of two feet as he was shaking hands with the public near the California Capitol in Sacramento, where he was to address the legislature on violent crime. An alert Secret Service agent, Larry M. Buendorf, leaped forward and grasped the gun before Fromme could fire. Eyewitnesses said the president's face drained of color during the incident. The Secret Service agent's hand was cut when he seized the gun, apparently on the cocked hammer. Fromme was variously quoted as crying as she was subdued, 'Don't get excited! It didn't go off. It didn't go off!' and 'It didn't go off. Can you believe it? It didn't go off.' Later, when shoved against a nearby tree, she shouted over and over, 'He is not a public servant! He is not a public servant!'

Fromme was a follower of Charles M. Manson, leader of a cult convicted of murdering actress Sharon Tate and six others in 1969 and serving a life sentence.

Fromme had a long FBI record, as did all suspected members of the Manson family. She had been arrested several times, on charges ranging from drug possession to murder, but had been convicted only once, getting 90 days in jail in 1971 along with three other family members for trying to keep a witness from testifying in the Tate murder by doctoring a hamburger with the hallucinogenic drug LSD. Fromme was one of Manson's most vocal out-of-court defenders during the trial and had been a spokeswoman for what was left of the group afterward.

Among many others, Professor James W. Clarke of the University of Arizona attributed the 'major dimension' of her behavior to an 'obsessive-compulsive commitment' to Manson.

Her motive in attacking President Ford was not to attract attention to herself or to make anyone else feel guilty for what she had done. Rather she hoped to stand trial so that Manson could be called as a witness in her defense. With the media attention such a trial would command, Fromme reasoned, Manson's message would at long last reach the ears of the world. She viewed him as a Christ figure with a solution for the world's problems.

Fromme's far-out thoughts did not qualify her as insane, and she was sentenced to life imprisonment.

Less than three weeks later Ford was the victim of yet another assassination try, also by a woman, which much of the press labeled a copycat act. The would-be assassin was Sara Jane Moore, 45, whose private life could be described only as 'deprived.' A former suburban matron, she had run through five marriages (two of them to the same man) and had abandoned three of her children with her parents back in West Virginia. Suffering from fears of isolation and needing to win acceptance, she joined a number of left-wing groups. At the same time, her highly impressionable state made her an easy 'turn' target for the FBI, who recruited her as a spy with effusive praise that she was saving the country. Now Moore was accepted on two sides, but in time she suffered pangs of regret and informed some of her unwitting political associates of her FBI role. For this she was shunned by the left, and by the FBI as well. Her isolation thus doubled, and she grew to fear assassination at the hands of the people she had spied on. Moore had a clear need to do penance. There is little doubt that Squeaky Fromme served as an inspiration to her.

About 3:30 P.M. on September 22, 1975, President Ford was leaving the St. Francis Hotel in San Francisco and waved to a crowd of about 3,000 persons who had gathered to catch a glimpse of him. About 40 feet away Sara Jane Moore raised a .38-caliber handgun and aimed at Ford. Oliver Sipple, a 33-year-old former Marine, spotted her and grabbed her arm. The gun went off, and the bullet ricocheted away from the president and struck a cabdriver, who suffered a minor groin injury. The president was hustled into a waiting limousine and taken swiftly to San Francisco International Airport for a fast return to Washington.

In custody, Moore said she would have had to leave the crowd outside the hotel 'to pick up my boy' at school (she still had one child, a nine-year-old boy, living with her) if the president had been any later. She also said, 'If I had had my .44 I would have caught him.'

It turned out that Moore's .44 had been confiscated the day before her act. Moore had in the meantime returned to her informing ways, she had a contact with the local police and also was doing some work for the Federal Bureau of Alcohol, Tobacco and Firearms. However, the police had reason to check Moore on September 21 to see if she had a weapon and found her carrying an unloaded .44 revolver and two boxes of ammunition in her home. She was cited for carrying a concealed weapon, a misdemeanor under state law. The gun was taken from her and she was released. The police notified the Secret Service, and its agents interrogated Moore later the same day. Apparently the fact that she was an informer for the police and a federal agency caused the Secret Service to let her go. The next day Moore tried to kill Ford.

As in the case of Fromme, no assassination conspiracy was discovered, and Moore's act was attributed to an attempt to solve a personal dilemma and relieve a sense of rejection with a startling political act. In that sense her act was closely in tune to those of Samuel Byck (see NIXON, RICHARD M.) and President John F. Kennedy's assassin, Lee Harvey Oswald.

In 1987 Squeaky Fromme, then 39, did manage to escape from the Federal Correctional Institution for Women at Alderson, West Virginia on December 23. Her escape triggered a nationwide alert by law enforcement officials, and the more sensational media saw a threat to former President Ford. Fromme was recaptured some 40 hours later on Christmas Day while walking along a country road, only two miles from the prison.

Further reading: *American Assassins: The Darker Side of Politics,* by James W. Clarke; *Political Murder,* by Franklin L. Ford.

FOX, William (1937–1974) On March 12, 1974, Billy Fox, a popular Protestant senator and member of the Fine Gael Party, was ambushed and shot to death near the Northern Ireland border by 12 masked men. Fox was a caustic critic of the actions of the British army in Northern Ireland. The Ulster Freedom Fighters (UFF), a Protestant extremist group, claimed responsibility for the assassination and claimed that Fox had intimate ties with the IRA. Five men – Sean McGettiaan, 19; George McDermott, 20; James McPhillips, 26; Sean Kinsella, 28; Michael Kinsella, 24 – were caught and in June were sentenced to life imprisonment for the killing.

Remarkably, the Fox assassination was the first political murder recorded in the Republic of Ireland since 1927.

FRANCIS FERDINAND, Archduke (1863–1914) In May 1914 President Woodrow Wilson sent Colonel Edward M. House as his personal representative to Europe to observe conditions and to report on the likelihood of war. What House saw upset him immensely. He reported, 'The situation is extraordinary; it is militarism run stark mad. . . . It only needs a spark to set the whole thing off.'

That 'spark' occurred on June 28, 1914, when the heir to the Austrian throne, Archduke Francis Ferdinand, and his wife, Sophie, were assassinated on the streets of Sarajevo, the capital of Bosnia. It was not an unplanned assassination. There were in fact no less than seven assassins in the crowd that observed the arrival of the archduke. Behind the plot was the Serbian Black Hand, a Pan-Serbian society whose motto was 'Union or Death.' Ironically, the leader of that group was Colonel Dragutin Dimitrievich, who was also the chief of intelligence of the Serbian general staff. Within the Black Hand he was known as Apis.

When Apis heard the archduke was coming to Sarajevo, he determined to have him assassinated. Apis found three secondary school students who were eager would-be assassins, Nedeljiko Cabrinovic, Trifko Grabez and Gavrilo Princip. Apis inducted them into the Black Hand and had them repeat the society's oath: 'By the sun which warms me, by the earth that feeds me, by God, by the blood of my ancestors, by my honor and my life, I swear fidelity to the cause of Serbian nationalism, and to sacrifice my life for it.'

The trio were each given a pistol and a grenade, and later six bombs, four Browning revolvers and doses of cyanide to commit suicide if apprehended. Apis then arranged to have them slipped across the Bosnian border to hide out in the house of Danilo Ilic, a member of the

Black Hand in Sarajevo. Following Apis's instruction, Ilic had also lined up four other assassins. It should be noted here, as historian Robert Ergang states: 'Several members of the Serbian cabinet, including the prime minister, were aware of the plot, and had they wished to do so they could easily have prevented the crime.'

On the morning of June 28 the archduke and his consort, Sophie, arrived in Sarajevo and were escorted through the winding streets of the town. Despite the heavy crowds there were few Austrian soldiers stationed along the route. The military knew that Emperor Francis Joseph disapproved of the pomp and ceremony being accorded the archduke, whom he could not abide. The emperor's nephew had incurred the royal wrath when he married Sophie Chotek, a mere countess. In fact, Francis Joseph had already declared the couple's children morganatic so that they could not accede to the throne themselves.

There were about 120 policemen in the crowd, however, and this was sufficient to thwart several of the seven assassins scattered in the crowd. One assassin found a policeman too near him to try shooting. Another was caught up in the crowd and could not extricate himself in time. A third was reluctant to try for fear of killing Sophie, and a fourth simply lost his nerve. Finally Cabrinovic acted, throwing a bomb, but his aim was poor and it landed under another car in the entourage and exploded, wounding an army officer. (Another version is that the bomb landed on the hood of the archduke's car but that Francis Ferdinand knocked it off.)

Cabrinovic swallowed his poison, but it didn't work, so he threw himself into the River Miljacka; however, the river was nearly dry in the summer heat, and he was captured.

Meanwhile, having heard the explosion, Gavrilo Princip assumed the plot had succeeded and adjourned to a café to celebrate. But the archduke had safely reached the town hall, where he was greeted by the mayor, who delivered a flowery welcoming speech. The archduke delivered a short address and decided to visit in hospital the colonel who had been injured in the bomb attack. This meant the entourage had to retrace its path. On the way the driver of the archduke's car took a wrong turn and ended up on the street where Princip had just emerged from the café. Seeing the archduke, Princip walked briskly toward the car, shooting twice. One bullet hit the archduke high in the collar, smashing through the jugular vein and lodging in the spine. Sophie half arose and got in the way of the second shot, which wounded her fatally. She collapsed, her head in the archduke's lap. The archduke cradled her head and cried, 'Soferl, Soferl, don't die. Live for my children.' She died, and within 15 minutes so did Francis Ferdinand. The assassin Princip swallowed his poison, but it only made him ill. He was captured.

Emperor Francis Joseph buried his nephew and Sophie with restraint, if not disinterest. He marked Sophie's grave with two white gloves, the symbol of a mere lady-in-waiting. The Austrian government, however, chose to make a great deal of the assassination. And while apologies could clearly have stopped the outbreak of war, at least for this particular moment, the Austrians were determined to destroy Serbia and discourage other minority unrest. Germany could not restrain Austria, and Russia mobilized to save its Slav cousins and contain Austria. By August the Great War was raging. It would leave some 20 million dead by late 1918.

Of the conspirators, 16 were found guilty and several were executed, including Ilic. (Apis was later given the death sentence himself.) The three recruited students, including the actual assassin, Princip, were sentenced to 20 years' imprisonment. All three were mistreated behind bars and were dead before the end of the war. Today on the street of the assassination stands the Gavrilo Princip Museum in honor of the assassin whose crime is given credit for having caused World War I.

Further reading: *Europe Since Waterloo*, by Robert Ergang; *The Road to Sarajevo*, by V. Dedijer.

FRASER, Hugh (1918–1984) – Attempted Assassination
Cancer specialist Gordon Hamilton Fairley, in charge of
tumor research at London's St. Bartholomew's Hospital
and a research worker of world repute, was killed on
October 23, 1975 by an IRA bomb blast – a case of
mistaken assassination. The bomb had been planted
under the car of Hugh Fraser, a Conservative member of
Parliament who was outspoken against terrorism. At the
time Caroline Kennedy, the daughter of the assassinated
U.S. president John F. Kennedy, was a Fraser house
guest, and the blast occurred just before the pair were
about to leave the house to enter the car. Professor
Fairley just happened to be passing.

Eventually several members of an IRA unit were
captured and in 1977 several were convicted of murdering
Fairley and eight other persons in various bombings and
shootings in London. Among those given massive prison
sentences were Martin O'Connell, Harry Duggan,
Edward Butler and Hugh Doherty, all in their mid-20s. In
June 1980 Brian Paschal Keenan, regarded as the mastermind behind the IRA attacks and in custody in Ireland,
was convicted of lesser charges of conspiring to cause
explosions to endanger life and plotting to possess firearms. He was sentenced to 18 years' imprisonment.

In the aftermath of the Fairley attack, journalist Ross
McWhirter, coeditor of the *Guinness Book of Records*,
launched a 'Beat the Bombers' campaign against the IRA.
He too was assassinated. (See McWHIRTER, ROSS.)

FRICK, Henry Clay (1849–1919) During the terrible
Homestead Steel Strike of 1892 no man invited more
hatred from the forces of American labor and radicalism
than did Henry Clay Frick, chairman of the Carnegie Steel
Company. Even his senior partner, Andrew Carnegie, did
not gain the enmity that Frick achieved, but then Carnegie
had the foresight to depart for a vacation in Scotland when
the great labor crisis was about to erupt. Carnegie wanted
the strike – called by workers who refused to take a
reduction in wages from a company that offered working

conditions almost universally recognized as abysmal – crushed by any means. No one was more capable or indeed more eager to carry out such a mission than Frick. Frick's steely determination invited trouble and indeed ultimately made an obscure 21-year-old anarchist one of the best-known radicals in American history.

Alexander Berkman followed each development in the strike with mounting anger. Frick recruited a private army of 300 Pinkertons and converted the company's mill at Homestead, Pennsylvania, into a virtual fortress. Then, under cover of night, Frick sent the Pinkertons up the Monogahela River by barge. They opened fire on the strikers without warning, killing several, among them a small boy, and wounding scores more. The strikers countered with dynamite, home-made cannon and burning oil. The fighting ended in stalemate, and Frick turned to the state government for help. The state dispatched 8,000 militiamen to the scene. Despite a rising anger in the country with Frick's tactics, the industrialist continued his antiunion activities.

Alexander Berkman, though a fiery anarchist, was known to friends as extremely gentle and sensitive. He was the lover of another soon-to-be famous anarchist, Emma Goldman. Berkman was outraged at Frick's behavior during the strike and decided he had to assassinate the industrialist as an act of alliance with his shackled steelworker comrades.

Goldman wrote of Berkman: ' "Homestead!" he exclaimed. "I must go to Homestead!" I flung my arms around him, crying out his name. I too would go. . . . I have never heard Sasha [as she called Berkman] so eloquent. He seemed to have grown in stature. He looked strong and defiant, an inner light on his face making him beautiful, as he had never before appeared to me.'

At first Berkman tried to make a bomb, but he lacked the expertise. Emma then went into the streets as a prostitute to raise money so they could buy a gun. Her first client was a kindly older man who guessed her amateur status and sent her home with $10. Berkman had his murder weapon.

On July 23, 1892, Frick was in his private office with his chief aide, John Leishman, planning company strategy when Berkman, representing himself as an agent for a New York employment firm, got permission to enter.

The assassination attempt is graphically described in a contemporary account in *Harper's Weekly*:

Mr. Frick had been sitting with his face half turned from the door, his right leg thrown over the arm of his chair . . . and almost before he had realized the presence of a third party in the room, the man fired at him. The aim had been for the brain, but the sudden turning of the chairman spoiled it, and the bullet ploughed its way into the left side of his neck. The shock staggered Mr. Frick. Mr. Leishman jumped up and faced the assailant. As he did so another shot was fired and a second bullet entered Mr. Frick's neck, but on the left side. Again the aim had been bad. Mr. Leishman, who is a small man, sprang around the desk, and just as the assailant was firing the third time, he seized his hand and threw it upward and back. The bullet embedded itself in the ceiling back of where the man was standing. . . . Mr. Frick recovered almost instantly from the two shots and ran to the assistance of Leishman, who was grappling with the would-be assassin. . . . The exertion made the blood spurt from his wounds and it dyed the clothing of the assailant.

The struggle lasted fully two minutes. Not a word was spoken by any one, and no cry had been uttered. The fast-increasing crowd in the street looked up at it open-mouthed and apparently paralyzed (Frick's upper-floor office could be readily seen into from across the street). There were no calls for the police and no apparent excitement, only spellbound interest. The three men swayed to and fro in struggle, getting all the time nearer to the windows. Once the assailant managed to shake himself loose, but before he could bring his revolver again into play, Mr. Leishman knocked his knees from under him, and the combined weight of himself and Mr. Frick bore the man to the floor. In the fall, he succeeded in loosening one hand and with it he drew an old-fashioned dirk-knife from his pocket and began slashing with it. He held it in his left hand. Mr. Frick was trying to hold him on that side. Again and again, the knife plunged into Mr. Frick until seven distinct wounds had been made, and then Mr. Frick succeeded in catching and holding the arm.

At the first sign of the knife the crowd in the street seemed to recover itself and there were loud calls of 'Police!' 'Fire!' The clerks in the main office recovered from their stupefaction, and rushed pell-mell into the office of their chief. Deputy Sheriff May, who happened to be in the office, was in the lead. He drew a revolver, and was about to use it, when Mr. Frick cried: 'Don't shoot! Don't kill him! The law will punish him.' The deputy's hand was seized and held by one of the clerks, while half a dozen others fell on the prostrate assailant. The police were in the office in a few minutes and took the man away. Fully two thousand people had gathered in the street, and there were cries of 'Shoot him! Lynch him!'

Berkman himself contributed this ending to his unsuccessful attempt: 'Police, clerks, workmen in overalls surround me. An officer pulls my head back by the hair, and my eyes meet Frick's. He stands in front of me, supported by several men. His face is ashen gray; the black beard is streaked with red, and blood is oozing from his neck. For an instant a strange feeling, as of shame, comes over me; but the next moment I am filled with anger at the sentiment, so unworthy of a revolutionist. With defiant hatred I look him full in the face.'

Although wounded nine times, Frick returned to his office within a week. Berkman served 14 years in prison before being pardoned in 1906. As is often true in acts of terrorism, his effort did not help the intended beneficiaries. The strikers generally denounced the attempted killing, though many did so with seemingly little conviction. From 1906 to 1919 Berkman and Goldman were the top spokesmen of American anarchism. In 1919 both were deported to their native Russia, where they were enthusiastically received by the new revolutionary government. However, both soon became disenchanted with the Soviet Union, given the differing tenets of anarchism and communism. Berkman was outspoken in his denunciation of the savage suppression of the Kronstadt Mutiny of 1921 by the Lenin regime. Both Berkman and Goldman were threatened with violence unless they remained silent, and their Soviet hosts were much relieved when both left Russia.

Berkman moved on to Sweden, then to Germany and finally to France. He continued his anarchist writing and edited many of Goldman's works. He eked out a pitiful living by translating and ghostwriting for European and American publishers and on contributions from political supporters. Ill and despondent, Berkman committed suicide in 1936. Of Berkman, H. L. Mencken wrote that he was a 'transparently honest man . . . a shrewder and a braver spirit than had been seen in public among us since the Civil War.'

Further reading: *Living My Life*, by Emma Goldman.

FUENTES MOHR, Alberto (1928–1979)   A former foreign minister and finance minister of Guatemala, Alberto Fuentes Mohr played such a unique role in Guatemalan politics, somewhere between the left and the right, that uncertainty remains about which side was responsible for his 1979 assassination.

In 1970 Fuentes Mohr was taken hostage by left-wing terrorists but later was exchanged for an imprisoned guerrilla. The former finance minister had been dismissed from that post when he angered wealthy landowners with a plan to tax the rich to finance domestic development programs. Becoming foreign minister in 1969, he was soon involved in a dispute with West Germany following the

1970 kidnapping of the West German ambassador, Count Karl von Spreti, by the FAR (Rebel Armed Forces), a left-wing terrorist group that demanded the release of a number of political detainees and a cash ransom of $700,000. Fuentes Mohr was apparently a key figure in the Guatemalan government's discussion to reject any deal, which, it was felt, would threaten the lives of Guatemalan officials and sap government credibility. Von Spreti was murdered.

Later that same year Fuentes Mohr was himself kidnapped, but in this case the Guatemalan government showed no aversion to making a deal, giving up an imprisoned guerrilla for the foreign minister's safe return. Shortly thereafter Fuentes Mohr left office.

After residing in Costa Rica until 1973, he returned and ran for vice president the following year as the candidate of the National Opposition Front. Although generally regarded to have won the election, Fuentes Mohr was denied the post, and a military candidate was placed in office in his stead. Back in exile Fuentes Mohr held a United Nations post until 1977. He returned to Guatemala yet again in 1978 and that year ran successfully for the Senate. As the leader of the Authentic Revolutionary Party in that body, he became a consistent critic of extremists on both the left and the right.

On January 25, 1979, Fuentes Mohr was submachine-gunned to death in Guatemala City. Police attributed the assassination to the Guerrilla Army of the Poor, but independent observers noted that Fuentes Mohr had enjoyed good relations with many leftist groups. In the United States, Senator Edward M. Kennedy described Fuentes Mohr as a 'true patriot,' adding, 'I have little doubt this man of peace and democracy could have played a major role in leading his country to a future of political and economic justice.'

There was a general consensus by independent observers that even if Fuentes Mohr was assassinated by the left, the chief beneficiary of the killing was the right. (See SPRETI, COUNT KARL VON.)

G

GALBA, Emperor of Rome (?3 B.C.–A.D. 69)   The tyrant
Nero was succeeded as emperor by Servius Sulpicius
Galba, a stiff-necked old warrior who commanded the
legions in Spain. In fact, Galba's move to depose Nero by
bribing the Praetorian Guard is what finally turned Nero
to suicide in A.D. 68, when he realized that all his
supporters had deserted him.

Galba was thought by many to be worthy of the purple,
but in the final analysis he was viewed as one 'whom all
men counted fit to rule – had he not ruled.' Certainly
Galba considered himself of noble enough rank, having
traced his lineage on his father's side back to the god
Jupiter, and on his mother's side to Pasiphae, wife of
Minos and the bull.

Marching back to Rome, Galba was hailed on all sides;
yet six months later he would be assassinated. His sins
were as monumental as they were impractical; he shocked
the army by his niggardliness toward it and toward
dispensing public funds. Then Galba ruled that all those
who had received pensions or gifts from Nero had to
return 90 percent of the monies to the treasury. As one
historian put it, 'A thousand new enemies arose, and
Galba's days ran out.'

A Roman senator, Marcus Otho, announced he could
pay his debts only by becoming emperor. That seemed a
reasonable offer to the Praetorians, and in January A.D.
69 they confronted Galba as he was riding in a litter in the
forum. The emperor realized resistance was useless and
surrendered his neck to the guards' swords. The Praetorians cut off his head, his arms and his lips, and one of their
number carried the head to Otho, who was anointed by

the Senate as the new emperor.

Otho ruled for a mere 95 days, until Aulus Vitellius, Rome's commander in Germany, swept down toward the capital to claim the throne for himself. Vitellius easily crushed Otho's forces at Bedriacum in the Lombard plain, and Otho avoided assassination only by committing suicide. The emperor Vitellius was the third of four emperors of Rome in the year A.D. 69, for he was soon to share Galba's fate, but even more ignobly. (See VITELLIUS, EMPEROR OF ROME.)

GALLIENUS, Emperor of Rome (c.218–268) The emperor Gallienus ruled over a Roman empire that was rapidly disintegrating in the third century. At first Gallienus ruled as co-emperor with his father, Valerian, because the Senate had concluded in 253 that no one man could direct the vast military operations needed to deal with foreign invaders from many sides. Gallienus had some military successes but was never as skilled as Valerian. Valerian, however, suffered crushing defeats on the eastern frontiers, was captured by the Persian king, Sapor I, and was ill-treated in captivity until his death. Thus in A.D. 260 Gallienus was serving as sole emperor.

While he struggled with foreign invaders, he suffered the further indignity of having a host of claimants to the throne of the Caesars challenge him. Although by most counts there were no more than 19 of them, these claimants became known as the Thirty Tyrants. The pretenders appeared all over the provinces, snatching power by the rebellion of their soldiers and usually lasting only a few months before being assassinated by rivals, their own troops or unknown elements.

Under the twin threats of attacks by Persian and Goth outsiders and by Roman generals, Gallienus found his empire shrinking to the point that he maintained effective control only of Italy and the Balkans. Then the most serious threat to Gallienus's throne was launched by a general, Aureolus, who led the legions from the Rhine into Italy. The author of many defeats by that time,

Gallienus roused himself for battle with this threat and besieged Aureolus in Milan. But Gallienus was himself doomed. He had broken a tradition of seven centuries by turning over command of the Roman armies from the senators to the professional equestrian officers. More than any emperor before him Gallienus depended on the kindness of his military officers, and the die was cast outside Milan. The military had lost faith in the emperor and decided to assassinate him. He was lured from his wine cups and slain. With his last words the dying Gallienus named his successor, his highly capable cavalry commander Claudius, who succeeded him as Claudius II. Perhaps Gallienus reasoned in his dying moments that at least he was thwarting the plans of his assassins. But, they too had decided on their candidate: ironically, the same Claudius.

GANDHI, Indira (1917–1984) Despite the belief by many that the 1984 assassination of Indian Prime Minister Indira Gandhi was the result of a conspiracy, the Asian subcontinent's most important political murder since that of Mohandas K. Gandhi in 1948 can probably be ascribed to mere miscalculation.

During her years in power – from 1966 to 1984 with a respite of only three years (1977–1980) – Gandhi espoused a fierce dedication to her concept of a united India and consistently placed other interests second to that primary aim. She repeatedly suspended opposition state governments and did not hesitate to use force, as in the Sikh rebellion in the Punjab, whenever the Indian federation appeared threatened.

In the year prior to her murder, Gandhi faced escalating tensions between her country and neighboring Pakistan, dissension in her own party, and above all the continued demands of the Sikhs for autonomy in Punjab state, where they formed the majority. The most divisive action taken by Gandhi's government in this period was the army raid in June on the Golden Temple of Amritsar – the most holy of Sikh shrines – in an effort to crush an uprising based there. In the clash more than 100 soldiers were killed, along with hundreds of militants and pilgrims inside the shrine. Estimates of total deaths were between 600 and 1,000. Among those killed was Sant Jarnail Singh Bhindranwale, the extremist leader.

The raid fueled outrage among Sikhs across India, and in one case Sikh cadets shot an Indian army brigadier soon after word of the attack spread. In July a Sikh guard for a cabinet minister hijacked a domestic airliner to protest the action against the Golden Temple.

Under these circumstances it would appear unthinkable to security experts that among the prime minister's bodyguards were a number of Sikhs. Indeed, senior officials appeared to have ignored intelligence warnings on the peril of using such guards. However, senior aides to Gandhi later testified that after the Sikhs had been removed from the bodyguard unit, the prime minister herself ordered their reinstatement, feeling that such a move would strengthen her image. Weeks before her murder she said, 'I've lived with danger all my life, and it makes no difference whether you die in bed or you die standing up.' And the day before the assassination she told a political gathering: 'If I die today, every drop of my blood will invigorate the nation.'

On the morning of October 31, 1984, Gandhi was riddled with submachine-gun and revolver bullets as she walked from her home to her office for an interview with the British actor Peter Ustinov. The shots were fired by Beant Singh, a member of the special security detail, and Satwant Singh, a Delphi police constable. Other security guards immediately fired on Beant Singh, killing him. Satwant Singh was critically wounded and taken alive.

After a four-year trial, Satwant Singh and a third Sikh, a former government clerk named Kehar Singh, were executed in January 1989. In March 1989 the release of a secret government report indicated that a powerful Gandhi aide, Rajendra Kumar Dhawan, was closely investigated for possible involvement in the assassination plot. Dhawan was ousted from his position by Mrs. Gandhi's son and successor, Rajiv Gandhi, but after completion of the investigation was reinstated. With the official release of the report and the clearing of Dhawan, Home Affairs Minister Buta Singh added mystery to the situation by claiming investigators had uncovered a larger conspiracy in the assassination and saying legal action would soon be taken. Observers concluded this would consist of more generalized charges that 'an unnamed foreign agency' had inspired and trained Sikh terrorists in an effort to destabilize India. The obvious reference was to Pakistan.

GANDHI, Mohandas Karamchand (Mahatma) (1869–1948) Political and spiritual leader Mohandas K. Gandhi, called lovingly *Mahatma*, or 'Great Soul,' was the father of modern India. Gandhi pioneered the use of nonviolent resistance and did more than any other single individual to win India's independence from British rule.

Born in Porbandar, India, in 1869, Gandhi studied law and practiced for some years in India before migrating to South Africa, where he first gained prominence as a pacifist worker for civil rights, especially for the Indian minority in South Africa. In 1915 he returned to India, viewed by the Indians with hope and by the British with trepidation as a spokesman for the nationalist movement to win India's independence. In the teeming hatreds of the subcontinent, Gandhi preached the unity of mankind. In India he perfected his nonviolent techniques, such as fasts, protest marches, general strikes and mass civil disobedience. He opposed the caste system, especially the plight of the untouchables, and child marriages. Jailed many times, he frequently won his freedom by vowing to fast until death. As his following grew, so did British fears.

Gandhi was imprisoned during World War II when he refused to support the British war effort. Released in 1944, he continued battling for independence, which finally came in 1947, but with a plan for partitioning the subcontinent into Muslim Pakistan and Hindu India. Gandhi opposed this, calling for one India with the major groups living in harmony. Mass rioting between Hindus and Muslims broke out and thousands were killed; Gandhi resorted to fasts and visits to troubled areas to personally stop the violence.

He was on one such vigil on January 30, 1948, when a 37-year-old Hindu fanatic named Nathuram Godse approached him at a prayer meeting outside Gandhi's quarters at Birla House in Delphi. Godse, vehemently opposed to Gandhi's tolerance toward Muslims, bowed to Gandhi before pulling a gun from his jacket and shooting the 78-year-old pacifist in the abdomen and chest. The fast-weakened Gandhi, at the time being supported on each side by two nieces, managed to cry out, *'Hai Rama! Hai Rama!'* ('Oh, God! Oh, God!'). Many times Gandhi had said, 'If blood be shed, let it be my blood. Cultivate the quiet courage of dying without killing. For man lives freely only by his readiness to die, if need be, at the hands of his brother, never by killing him.' Before Gandhi collapsed and died, he gave his assassin the sign of forgiveness.

Godse, an editor of a Hindu nationalist newspaper, and seven others were tried for the assassination. In a 92-page handwritten statement to the court, Godse denounced Gandhi as 'a political and ethical impostor' and a 'curse to India, a force for evil' whose actions would create a situation in which Muslims would take over India and destroy Hinduism.

Godse and Narayan Dattatraya Apte, the production manager of his publication, were hanged on February 10, 1949. Over the years there have been charges of a wider conspiracy. Godse and his fellow plotters had originally tried to kill Gandhi 10 days previously, but the plan fell apart in confusion over who among them would carry guns and hand grenades to be used in the attack. One conspirator was apprehended in the abortive attempt, and there were later reports that he had revealed much about his fellow conspirators. Some writers thereafter insisted the police had let the conspirators continue their work to remove the troublesome Gandhi.

Further reading: *The Life and Death of Mahatma Gandhi*, by Robert Payne.

GANDHI, Rajiv (1944–1991) Rajiv Gandhi, who had become prime minister of India in 1984 after the assassination of his mother, Indira Gandhi, was himself murdered by a bomb blast on May 21, 1991. At the time Gandhi, who had been turned out of office by a disillusioned electorate in 1989, was attempting a political comeback and appeared likely to win.

Gandhi was walking from his car to an election rally platform in Sriperumbudur, 25 miles from Madras. He had been surrounded by crowds of supporters and deluged with flower garlands and bouquets. At first it was unclear how the bombing, in which at least 16 other people were also killed, had been carried out. After an analysis of photographs taken at the scene just before the killing, police determined that the assassin was a bespectacled, bewigged female, probably in her mid-thirties, who carried a plastic explosive, riddled with metal pellets, beneath her loose-fitting dress. As she bent over in front of Gandhi, she flipped the switches and detonated the bomb which killed both herself and her intended victim. The explosion decapitated the woman but left her face intact. She remained unidentified.

As news of Gandhi's assassination spread, violence erupted in a number of Indian cities and the national government issued a 'red alert,' closing government offices and schools and colleges throughout the country in an effort to prevent mobs from gathering.

Police suspicions rapidly narrowed to the Liberation Tigers of Tamil Eelam (LTTE), a Sri Lankan separatist group. That group denied any responsibility. In 1987 Gandhi had angered the Tamil separatists by sending in Indian troops to put down upheavals.

Finally, the police zeroed in on a chief suspect in the assassination plot, a Sri Lankan Tamil known as Sivarasan, reportedly the intelligence chief of the LTTE. After a 90-day manhunt Sivarasan (his real name was reported to be Raja Arumainayagam and he was also known as 'One-Eyed Jack') was cornered with six companions in a hideout in Bangalore. At the conclusion of a lengthy gun battle, six of the Tamils committed suicide by taking cyanide pills. Sivarasan shot himself to death.

GAPON, Father Georgii (1870–1906) Father Georgii Gapon was the leader of Russia's notorious Bloody Sunday march in 1905, in which hundreds of working men seeking to petition the czar in St. Petersburg were shot down by soldiers. He was also a police spy.

The idea of creating a workers' organization that could be secretly directed into officially desirable channels by the intelligence services was the brilliant work of Minister of the Interior Vyacheslav K. Plehve. Father Gapon was an inspired choice for front man of such a conspiracy, because his interest in the people was sincere. Gapon felt that mild protests would help the workers by 'immunizing' them from revolutionary diseases and strengthening their support of the monarchy. Under Plehve's direction economic complaints would be guided away from the government and the czar and toward the employers, the budding capitalist class. The latter were placated by the idea that a movement stage-managed by the police was better than one dominated by socialist revolutionaries.

Gapon preached earnestly that his Assembly of Russian Workingmen would in the end uplift the workingman to a sound and benign Christian spirit. Only a few workers suspected Gapon's police ties; the great mass were thankful to have anyone speak for them and to help them voice their grievances. Then on July 28, 1904, Plehve himself was assassinated. Others took on the task of managing Father Gapon, but it is doubtful they did it with the finesse that Plehve had brought to the deception. As labor unrest, fueled by defeats in the war with Japan, increased, a major strike developed in St. Petersburg in January 1905. Gapon was caught up in the fervor, and it is possible that he may have contemplated a complete break with his police masters. On January 22 Father Gapon led a mass march on the Winter Palace to petition the czar, who ironically was not even there. Many of the marchers carried crosses, religious banners, national flags and pictures of the czar. The march was peaceful, yet the soldiers opened fire, killing men, women and children. The official death toll was given as 92 and later 130, but it was probably much higher; and hundreds, perhaps thousands, more were wounded. The day, known as Bloody Sunday, probably caused the final alienation of the Russian people from their czar. Internationally there was a great outcry against Nicholas II.

In the melee Father Gapon disappeared, but he then issued a call from hiding that denounced 'Nicholas Romanov, formerly Tsar and at present soul-murderer of the Russian empire. The innocent blood of workers, their wives and children lies forever between you and the Russian people. . . . May all the blood which must be spilled fall upon you, you Hangman!'

Gapon also called on all the 'socialist parties of Russia to come to an immediate agreement among themselves and begin an armed uprising against Tsarism.' Had Gapon been converted into a true revolutionary? To be on the safe side, the social revolutionaries fell on Gapon in April 1906, murdered him and left his body hanging in an abandoned cottage in Finland.

Further reading: *Nicholas and Alexandra*, by Robert K. Massie; *The Rise and Fall of the Romanovs*, by Anatole G. Majour.

GARCIA MORENO, Gabriel (1821–1875) Gabriel Garcia Moreno was the dictator of Ecuador in the 1860s and 1870s and was in many ways out of step with the politics of most Latin American countries, whose governments at that time tended to be liberal (a situation that would be largely reversed in later decades). Born in Guayaquil on December 21, 1821, he developed a strong conservative philosophy as a law and theological student at the University of Quito. This conservatism became increasingly militant after the young Garcia visited Europe during the bloody liberal revolutions of 1848.

In 1861 at the age of 39 he became president of Ecuador. His term was marked by aggressive development of the country's natural resources and a despotic attitude on religion and education. Those stands, as well as charges of corruption, forced Garcia into retirement before the completion of his presidential term. After an intervening term under a liberal chief executive, Garcia again won election as president by means now generally agreed to have been corrupt. Garcia became more tyrannical than ever, introducing a constitution that established church courts independent of the civil jurisdiction, restored control of education to the clergy and restricted citizenship to Roman Catholics. Fundamentally, Garcia maintained that the clergy owed its authority to the head of state and that the head of state, although ostensibly elected by a national convention, was responsible only to the clergy for his acts. Ecuadoran liberals formed a resistance movement in New Granada. A secret group of assassins drew lots to determine who would kill Garcia.

On August 6, 1875, President Garcia was walking in the corridor of the government palace at Quito, when three men he passed saluted him then felled him. One hacked him with a sabre-length machete and the others shot him with revolvers. Garcia managed to stagger out of the palace before collapsing. Two of the assassins, later identified as Roberto Andrade and Manuel Cornego, made good their escape. The third assassin, Faustinio Rayo, a Colombian, was run through by a palace guard's bayonet.

President Borrero, Garcia's successor, immediately announced a program guaranteeing full political liberty and press freedom. However, in short order conservative generals defeated the government forces in a military insurrection, and the nation endured 25 years of alternate uprisings of liberal and conservative forces.

GARFIELD, James A. (1831–1881) Of all the successful U.S. presidential assassins, Charles J. Guiteau, who killed

Above: Despite a government "assassinations alert", Czar Alexander II was finally killed by revolutionaries after a number of attempts on March 1, 1881.

Below: Cesare Borgia, left, had numerous discussions with Machiavelli, right, on the grand art of assassination, including that of the hapless Alfonso of Aragon.

Castro, shown here during his anti-Batista revolution, later became the target of a bizarre partnership between the CIA and organized crime.

Right: When anarchist Alexander Berkman, shown here, determined to kill industrialist Henry Clay Frick, Emma Goldman wrote, "I flung my arms around him, crying out his name. I too would go. . . He looked strong and defiant, an inner light on his face making him beautiful. . ."

Below: Guiteau ambushed President Garfield in a Washington railroad station as he was accompanied by Secretary of State James Blaine. In New York City bulletins were posted on the fatally wounded president's condition for anxious crowds.

This on-the-spot photo of the attempted assassination of Mayor Gaynor is often called the greatest crime picture ever taken. *Evening World* city editor Charles Chapin exclaimed, "Look, what a wonderful thing! Blood all over him – and exclusive too!"

General Karl Heinrich Stuelpnagel (shown with eye patch in the Nazi People's Court) attempted suicide when the plot against Hitler failed. He survived, although he shot out one eye and severely damaged the other. Treated at a military hospital, he was tried, condemned and, at Hitler's explicit orders, strangled in prison.

Above: A mentally disturbed house painter, Richard Lawrence, became the first man to try to kill a U.S. president, Andrew Jackson. Jackson always believed the attack was masterminded by his Whig opponents.

Left: The murder of the outlaw Jesse James, shown here in death, became an assassination scandal in Missouri that ended the governor's political career. Assassin Bob Ford became infamous as "that dirty rotten coward".

After his arrest a manacled Lee Harvey Oswald defiantly denied killing either President John F. Kennedy or Officer Tippit.

WANTED

FOR

TREASON

THIS MAN is wanted for treasonous activities against the United States:

1. Betraying the Constitution (which he swore to uphold):
   He is turning the sovereignty of the U. S. over to the communist controlled United Nations.
   He is betraying our friends (Cuba, Katanga, Portugal) and befriending our enemies (Russia, Yugoslavia, Poland).
2. He has been WRONG on innumerable issues affecting the security of the U S (United Nations-Berlin wall-Missle removal-Cuba-Wheat deals-Test Ban Treaty, etc.)

3. He has been lax in enforcing Communist Registration laws.
4. He has given support and encouragement to the Communist inspired racial riots.
5. He has illegally invaded a sovereign State with federal troops.
6. He has consistantly appointed Anti-Christians to Federal office:
   Upholds the Supreme Court in its Anti-Christian rulings.
   Aliens and known Communists abound in Federal offices
7. He has been caught in fantastic LIES to the American people (including personal ones like his previous marrage and divorce)

A hate-Kennedy handbill that was circulated in Dallas the day before the president arrived.

President James A. Garfield, was clearly the most deranged. That, however, does not explain why it was so easy for him to kill the chief executive of the United States – a mere 16 years after the assassination of Abraham Lincoln. It is perhaps astounding by today's standards that Guiteau could have gotten as close to the president as he did at the Washington railroad station on the morning of July 2, 1881. Moreover, Guiteau missed on his first shot; today he would never have been given the chance to fire a second.

The president did not die immediately; he lingered two and a half agonizing months through midsummer and died on September 19, 1881. In that sense the Garfield assassination became the first American drama to be experienced vicariously by the entire American population, which was then 50 million. As the *New York Tribune* noted: 'By the everyday miracle of the telegraph and the printing press, the whole mass of the people have been admitted to his bedside.'

'How could anybody be so cold-blooded as to want to kill my baby?' Garfield's mother asked. It was a question Guiteau was eager to answer, and he did so in a rambling memoir in his jail cell. He had had an erratic background as a self-styled lawyer, having been admitted to the bar with the ease then permitted. He became active in Democratic politics, and during Horace Greeley's presidential campaign in 1872 he was a familiar figure at Democratic headquarters in New York. Most others there sought to avoid this nervous little man – 'the Eloquent Chicago Lawyer,' his own handbills proclaimed him – who constantly composed speeches that no one would deliver. Strictly in his own imagination Guiteau became convinced that if Greeley were elected, Guiteau would be named minister to Chile. It was all he talked about with his wife, whom he made sit through long diplomatic speeches; if she were not available, he simply addressed the mirror.

Greeley lost the election; Guiteau was downcast for months. Then he left his wife for a teenage prostitute and the Democrats for the Republicans. For the 1880 elections he composed a speech, 'Garfield vs. Hancock,' which he informed Republican officials would guarantee the Democrats' defeat. He had the speech printed at his own expense and handed out copies to a number of prominent Republicans, almost in self-defense a few of whom allowed that Guiteau had some good ideas. No one delivered the speech, however, except for Guiteau once himself, venturing forth to a Negro rally on New York's Twenty-fifth Street. The audience of six began to leave when they tired of his manic speechifying and Guiteau became too rattled to continue.

Nevertheless, when Garfield won the election Guiteau was convinced that 'Garfield vs. Hancock' had provided the margin of victory, and he set off to claim his spoils – his heart now being set on the ambassadorship to Austria, or perhaps the 'Paris consulship.'

He got neither, even though he wrote to Garfield that Secretary of State James Blaine had approved him for the Paris post. He also wrote to Blaine saying that Garfield had approved him.

Guiteau decided he had been cruelly abused. He bought a .44-caliber pistol and sharpened his shooting skills by using trees along the Potomac as targets. Then he started dogging Garfield. Whenever he was uncertain of the president's schedule on a certain day, he simply sauntered up to the White House doorman and asked. Guiteau once got near enough to Garfield in church to shoot him but decided not to since Mrs. Garfield – 'a dear soul' – was within range.

Then he got his chance at the Baltimore and Potomac railroad station. He was standing behind a bench when Garfield, who was leaving for a brief vacation, and Blaine came walking through. He shot Garfield and was immediately captured. In his left hand he held a note addressed to General William Sherman, asking for troops to protect the jail where he would be taken.

Guiteau was brought to trial two months after the president's death, and during the ten-and-a-half-week trial he subjected the courtroom to venomous outbursts. Witnesses were 'dirty liars,' and the prosecutor was alternately 'a low-livered whelp' and an 'old hog.' At times he was most courteous, though, and after the Christmas and New Year's recesses, he informed the judge he 'had a very happy holiday.'

When confined in his cell, Guiteau strutted back and forth so that visitors and the crowds outside the building could gawk at him. In court he informed the jury that God had told him to kill Garfield. 'Let your verdict be, it was the Deity's act, not mine,' he roared.

When he was found guilty, he shook an angry finger at the jury box and snarled, 'You are all low, consummate jackasses!'

As his execution neared, Guiteau seemed relaxed and unrepentant during his waking hours but suffered nightmares and moaned constantly in his sleep.

On June 30, 1882, Guiteau ate a hearty meal and memorized a long poem he had written to recite on the scaffold. He did so. It stated:

> I am going to the Lordy, I am so glad . . .
> I saved my party and my land; glory, hallelujah.
> But they have murdered me for it, and that is the reason
> I am going to the Lordy. . . .

The hangman waited patiently until Guiteau completed his poetical rendition and then placed the black hood over Guiteau's head and sprang the trap. 'Glory, Glory, Glory . . .' were the last words on Guiteau's lips.

Further reading: *American Assassins*, by James W. Clarke; *Assassination in America*, by James McKinley.

GAYNOR, William Jay (1849–1913) – Attempted Assassination It was often said by his opponents that New York Mayor William Jay Gaynor had a personality that made him a likely candidate for assassination. His opponents included, among a long list, the forces of Tammany and publisher William Randolph Hearst. When an actual attempt was made on the mayor's life, those voices were judiciously stilled.

The son of an Irish farmer, Gaynor lived his childhood in extreme poverty in Oneida County in upstate New York. He was educated for the priesthood, but he abandoned Catholicism and worked as an itinerant teacher. He later took up the study of law and in 1875 was admitted to the bar. He then moved to the village of Flatbush, Long Island, which was ruled by corrupt politicians. He became police commissioner and carried out a number of civic reforms, then returned to law practice, in Brooklyn in 1885. Operating as a one-man crime commission, he exposed large-scale civic corruption and forced city officials to collect tax arrears from the elevated railroads.

Gaynor rejected an offer to run for mayor, and in 1893 he was elected a justice of the state supreme court. From the bench Gaynor feuded with Brooklyn's Democratic leadership, and he sent a number of politicians, including Coney Island boss John Y. McKane, to the penitentiary. In 1904 Tammany Hall denied Gaynor the nomination for governor, using his lapsed Catholicism as an excuse. By 1909, however, Tammany needed an impeccable candidate for mayor and nominated Gaynor, who was elected (beating the Republicans and Hearst), although the rest of the Tammany slate went down to defeat. In office Gaynor ignored Tammany's requests for patronage and launched a reform program that purged no-show jobs from the city payroll, costing the Tiger over 400 positions. He instituted a program to insure city employees worked full eight-hour days. Prickly independent and a child of his day, Gaynor was not averse to creating new enemies. He unblinkingly informed suffragettes that most people aspire 'to that thing which [they] are least fitted for.' But his prime enemies remained Tammany and the vitriolic Hearst.

On August 9, 1910, the mayor boarded the *Kaiser Wilhelm* for a European vacation. On deck he was confronted by a discharged city employee named James Gallagher, who shot him through the neck. A news photographer nearby snapped a picture of the still-erect mayor a second after the shot, creating what has been called the greatest crime photo ever taken. When Charles Chapin, the city editor of the *Evening World* saw the picture, he exclaimed, 'Look, what a wonderful thing! Blood all over him – and exclusive too!'

The mayor was hospitalized for three weeks, and the bullet, which passed through his throat, was never extracted. After the assassination attempt, Gaynor proved more irascible than ever. For the rest of his life he blamed Hearst, whose printed attacks he felt prompted the shooting.

Gaynor's health never fully improved, but he continued his political career, rejecting a race for governor, which he considered an unimportant office. In 1913 Gaynor was eager to run for another term as mayor, this time on a reform coalition ticket, and was considered the likely winner. Before undertaking what would have been an arduous campaign, Gaynor sailed for Europe for a brief vacation. On September 10 he died, ironically aboard ship, found dead in a deck chair. His biographer, Mortimer Smith, ascribed his death to 'the aftermath of the shooting, and the rigors of his office, having finally weakened his heart.'

Further reading: *A Brief History of New York City*, by George J. Lankevich and Howard B. Furer; *William Jay Gaynor*, by Mortimer Smith.

GEMAYEL, Bashir (1947–1982) On September 14, 1982, Bashir Gemayel, who was scheduled to take office as president of Lebanon later in the month, was killed when a bomb blast demolished the headquarters of his Lebanese Christian Party in East Beirut. At the time Gemayel was regarded as the most powerful Christian leader in a country torn by civil strife. He was also known as a ruthless foe to many elements – Muslim, Palestinian and other Christian forces.

Born in 1947, Bashir was the youngest son of Pierre Gemayel, the first leader of the Phalangist Party, and through a period that demonstrated his toughness, ruthlessness and ambition, Bashir became the most powerful of the Phalangist clan leaders. In the civil war of 1975–76, Gemayel led his forces in a bloody battle over a Palestinian refugee camp, an attack that ended in the massacre of the camp's survivors.

Bashir never lacked for enemies, and two previous assassination attempts on him, in 1978 and 1979, were attributed by his supporters to former President Suleiman Franjieh, the leader of another Maronite Christian faction. According to this theory Franjieh was seeking revenge for the murder of his son and 30 family members and supporters in 1978 by Gemayel's militiamen. In one of these attacks, a car bombing, Bashir's 18-month-old daughter was killed.

The successful 1982 bomb attack was carefully planned, the work of skilled professionals who somehow got access to the heavily guarded building and attached over 400 pounds of dynamite to sophisticated timing devices. Christian East Beirut reacted to the assassination in panic, which lifted temporarily when it was erroneously reported that Gemayel had miraculously survived. His crushed body, along with at least eight others, was later pulled from the rubble. Fifty more supporters had been wounded. In the aftermath of the assassination, charges and countercharges flew, with Muslims, Syria and PLO leader Yasir Arafat blaming Israel, with whom Gemayel had recently refused to sign a treaty. Israel in turn blamed the Arabs, and in Lebanon some Christians blamed other Christians. In the deteriorating political climate, Amin Gemayel, Bashir's older brother, who was described by some observers as 'a lightweight,' was selected as president by the parliament. Chaos, civil strife and violence continued.

GEORGE I, King of Greece (1845–1913) The second son of Christian IX of Denmark, Christian George, was put on the Greek throne in 1863 by the joint action of Britain, France and Russia following the overthrow of Otto I, the first king of Greece. He took the name 'George I, King of the Hellenes' to indicate he held authority over all Greeks, even those living in areas not incorporated into Greek territory at the time. Although he was unpopular for the first ten years of his reign, George I, described early on as 'courteous, kingly and physically mature, but intellectually young for his age,' slowly gained hold of the affections of the people, especially with the ouster of Count Sponneck, the adviser provided by his father.

In 1867, George I married Olga, niece of Alexander II of Russia, and his dynastic connections through the marriages of his sisters and other relatives probably enhanced Greece's position in European affairs beyond what the nation would have achieved otherwise. The king's major accomplishments were in the expansion of Greek territory. Britain gave up the Ionian Islands in 1864, and Greece got Thessaly and part of Epirus in 1881. In the early part of the 20th century Crete was all but a part of Greece, and in March 1913 George I went to Salonika to assert his demand for the annexation of Macedonia.

Despite the inflamed political situation, the king thought nothing of walking unattended through city streets. On March 13, just a few days before the 50th anniversary of his accession to the throne, George I was shot to death by a Greek named Schinas. The assassination was regarded as the act of a madman. George was succeeded by his son, the unpopular Constantine I. But the main result of the assassination was that it marked the beginning of constant intervention of the army in Greek politics.

Further reading: *The Web of Modern Greek Politics*, by Jane Perry Clark Carey and Andrew Galbraith Carey.

GERMANICUS CAESAR (15 B.C.–A.D. 19) The death, almost certainly an assassination, of Germanicus Caesar, the handsome and popular nephew of the Roman emperor Tiberius, in A.D. 19 altered the imperial succession. Had Germanicus lived, Rome might well have been spared such disastrous reigns as those of Caligula and Nero.

Tiberius had adopted Germanicus as his own son and made him his likely successor. Indeed, upon the death in A.D. 14 of Tiberius's predecessor, Augustus, there were many Romans who urged Germanicus to claim the empire for himself. Among them were those who still yearned for the republic, and, as Germanicus was a grandson of the republican Marc Antony, they made him a symbol for their cause. However, Germanicus rebuffed all such entreaties and remained totally loyal to Tiberius, even suppressing a mutiny in the legions.

Nevertheless, Tiberius, true to his nature, eventually grew suspicious or at least jealous of Germanicus and transferred him to supreme command of the eastern provinces. In Syria, Germanicus came into conflict with Tiberius's governor, Piso, and when Germanicus suddenly grew fatally ill in A.D. 19, he suspected Piso, through Piso's wife, Plancina, of poisoning him.

The overwhelming feeling in Rome was that Tiberius was behind the death. Piso was brought before the Senate for prosecution, and the tide of the investigation flowed strongly against him. Foreseeing conviction, Piso committed suicide, a process under which the law preserved his property for his family. Tiberius's involvement in the murder of Germanicus was never established. All he had asked the Senate was to give Piso a fair trial. And Germanicus's mother, Antonia, remained faithful to Tiberius. In fact, when the ambitious prefect of the Praetorian Guard, Sejanus, plotted the emperor's assassination in A.D. 31, it was Antonia who saved Tiberius, informing him of the plot at great risk to her own life.

Further reading: *The Story of Civilization III, Caesar and Christ*, by Will Durant.

GETA, Publius Septimius, Co-Emperor of Rome (189–212) When the brutal but efficient Roman emperor Severus died while campaigning in Britain in 211, after a reign of 18 years, he left the throne to both his older son, Caracalla, and his younger son, Geta. His advice to them was to stick together, pay their soldiers well and forget all other elements in the empire. It was advice neither could take. The furious rivalry between the two brothers had been more or less kept from public view as long as Severus lived, but once he died, it exploded into the open.

The brothers hurried back to Rome and formed their own military factions. Civil war threatened, and not even their mother, Julia Domna, the highly respected and trusted consort of Severus, could contain the brothers' mutual hostility. In fact, she could not in the end even prevent Caracalla from breaking into her private apartment in the imperial palace and killing Geta in her arms, the dying youth's blood soaking her garments.

Caracalla, appearing before the Senate to demand and receive its recognition of him as sole emperor ('with the blood of his brother Geta still wet upon his hands,' according to one account), claimed he had had to slay his brother in self-defense. When the highly respected prefect Papinian, whom Severus had entrusted with the civil administration of the empire, declined to provide an official defense for the murder, he paid with his life.

Caracalla then unleashed a wholesale slaughter by putting to death a host of Geta's real and suspected partisans. Estimates of the number killed have been put as high as 20,000. (See CARACALLA, EMPEROR OF ROME.)

Further reading: *History of Rome*, by Dio Cassius.

GHASHMI, Ahmed Hussein al- (1941–1978) On June 24, 1978, North Yemeni President Ahmed Hussein al-Ghashmi received an envoy from hostile South Yemen at the President's office at military headquarters in the capital city of Sana. The envoy, whose identity was not determined, supposedly bore a letter from South Yemeni President Salem Rubaya Ali in a briefcase. As the envoy opened the briefcase, supposedly to get the letter, a bomb went off, killing both President Ghashmi and the unknown envoy.

The assassination was to have a profound impact within pro-Soviet South Yemen's ruling National Liberation Front. As a result of the conflict that developed between rival groups in the front, President Rubaya was deposed and executed on June 26. This followed bloody fighting after President Rubaya attempted to arrest Abdel Fattah Ismail, the extreme pro-Soviet secretary general of the front, on charges that he had engineered the Ghashmi assassination. Ismail countered by moving to strip Rubaya of his office for his alleged involvement in the killing.

The underlying cause of Rubaya's downfall was believed to be his differences with Ismail on a number of points. The president had been in favor of improving relations with both Saudi Arabia and the United States as well as backing off from the close relationship with the Soviet Union, especially by denying the Soviets the use of Aden as a link for armaments and troop airlifts to aid leftist Ethiopia in its conflict with Eritrean rebels. Thus the Ghashmi assassination facilitated the transition of power. Oddly, another theory excluded both the Rubaya and Ismail forces from involvement in the assassination. Some Arab diplomats felt that the real plotters were North Yemeni exiles in South Yemen. A number of these exiles had defected to Aden the previous month, after an unsuccessful mutiny. They were led by Major Abdullah Abdul Alim, who had previously been a member of the Military Command Council under Ghashmi, which took power following the assassination of the previous president, Ibrahim al-Hamidi.

Ismail served as president of South Yemen from late 1978 until June 1980. In 1986 he was killed in fighting while attempting a coup against President Ali Nasser Mohammed. (See HAMIDI, IBRAHIM AL-.)

GODFREY, Sir Edmund Berri (1621–1678) A justice of the peace for the City of Westminster, Edmund Berri Godfrey was knighted in 1666 for services rendered during the Great Plague of London in 1664–65. In 1678 Godfrey was murdered, a crime that gave great initial impetus for belief in the fabricated 'Popish Plot,' in which English Roman Catholics were accused of seeking to assassinate Charles II and elevate his Roman Catholic brother,

James, the Duke of York, to the throne.

In September 1678 the conspirator Titus Oates, a renegade Anglican priest, and two others laid out before Godfrey what they purported to be evidence of a Jesuit plan to kill the king. Then on the morning of October 12, 1678, Godfrey disappeared under unexplained circumstances. On October 17 his corpse was found in a ditch about three miles from Westminster. He had been run through with his own sword, most likely after death. His neck was dislocated and there were strangulation marks around the throat, as well as many bruises to the chest.

Immediately, there was deep public outrage, and the anti-Court faction in England blamed the killing on the Catholics. Author Maurice Petherick writes that the Godfrey murder 'set all England ablaze and let loose a fury of anti-Catholic feeling in which fear and hatred struggled for predominance. Nervous citizens bought themselves pistols and side arms. The train bands were called out in London and barriers placed across the streets. Large rewards were offered for the discovery of Godfrey's assassins, and scores of prominent Roman Catholics, especially priests, were arrested and flung into noisome gaols. The fierce laws against the Catholics, for long indulgently disregarded by the government, were rigidly enforced.'

At this stage two men stepped forward with 'evidence.' One was William Bedloe, to be judged by history as great a rogue as Titus Oates. Bedloe offered the first real allegations that the killing was a Catholic act. Then another unsavory witness, a Catholic silversmith named Miles Prance, confessed that he had witnessed hirelings kill Godfrey in the presence of Catholic priests. Prance, who was confined in freezing Newgate prison in the depths of a bitter winter, somehow found the inspiration to name as principals or accomplices in the deed the following: Father Dominick Kelly; Girald (or Fitzgerald) an Irish priest; Robert Green, a cushionlayer in Somerset House Chapel; Lawrence Hill, a servant of the reverend Doctor Thomas Godden (whose actual name was Tylden); Phillibert Vernatti; and Henry Berry, a porter at Somerset House and, incidentally, a Protestant. Girald-Fitzgerald, Vernatti and Kelly fled – Kelly was known to have gone to France – but Green, Berry and Hill (all lesser figures in the case) were tried and convicted and in 1679 were hanged, drawn and quartered.

An effort was made by the anti-Catholics to involve Samuel Pepys, a close friend of the Duke of York, in the supposed plot, but this failed. Later Miles Prance confessed he had lied about having knowledge of the murder and had condemned three innocent men. The Godfrey assassination was relegated to the unsolved category, but as a part of the Popish Plot it was a factor in a movement in Parliament to deny the Duke of York the succession. York did eventually become James II, but he was finally forced to flee and died in exile.

Further reading: *Restoration Rogues*, by Maurice Petherick.

GOEBEL, William (1856–1900) In 1900, assassination for the first time involved a major candidate in the political struggle between the Republican and Democratic parties in the United States. The victim was William Goebel, the Democratic candidate for governor of Kentucky in the election of 1899. Of Goebel, one historian said, 'He probably inspired a greater amount of loyalty in his supporters and of personal hatred on the part of his opponents than any other figure in Kentucky politics.' A reformer, he had earned the enmity of powerful forces in the state, and especially that of the Louisville & Nashville Railroad, because of his activities in the state senate that pushed through taxes and regulation of railroads. He was a master of hardball politics and had won the nomination for governor at the Democratic convention with a series of cunning political moves that added more names to his list of enemies.

The election turned out to be one of the closest and most exciting in Kentucky history. His Republican opponent, William S. Taylor, was at first declared the winner by the barest majority. However, Goebel charged fraud, and the contest was thrown into the Democrat-dominated legislature. While the contest was in limbo, Goebel was shot by a man named Yountsey on January 30, 1900, who was ultimately sentenced to life imprisonment. Meanwhile the legislature ruled in Goebel's favor and he was sworn in on his deathbed. He died on February 3, and the state teetered on the edge of open hostilities. However, Goebel's successor, Lieutenant Governor J.C.W. Beckham, restored calm.

A number of Republican officials were also convicted of taking part in the assassination conspiracy; however, most of these convictions were overturned on appeal. One Republican whose conviction was upheld was Caleb Powers, the Republican secretary of state, who was sentenced to eight years' imprisonment. That blot on Powers's record did not prevent him from later being elected to several terms in Congress.

Further reading: *Famous Kentucky Tragedies and Trials*, by L.F. Johnson; *That Kentucky Campaign*, by R.E. Hughes, F.W. Schaefer and L.E. Williams.

GORDIAN III, Emperor of Rome (225–244)   Gordian III became emperor of Rome in August 238 after no less than five Roman emperors were crowned and assassinated during the prior year. He was only 13 years old at the time. His grandfather Gordian I and his uncle Gordian II were among the luckless quintet of assassinated emperors.

The government was first controlled by Gordian III's mother and then by his father-in-law, Mistheus (or Timeistheus), his tutor, and who was also the Praetorian prefect. In 242 Gordian III and Mistheus launched a highly successful campaign across the Euphrates against the Persians, but in 243 the competent Mistheus died of an illness and was replaced by the crafty Philip the Arabian as prefect. Philip the Arabian lost little time supplanting Gordian III in the soldiers' affection. When Philip felt sure of his position, he had his henchmen murder Gordian III, and the troops hailed him on the faraway banks of the

Euphrates as the new emperor of Rome.

Philip the Arabian ruled until 249, when he either fell in combat or was executed immediately after the battle at Verona. His conqueror, Decius, was the commander of the Roman legions on the lower Danube, who demanded that Decius take the throne from Philip. Most historians agree that Decius had not sought power, but the uncontrollable soldiers had offered him the choice of empire or instant assassination. Under those circumstances, Decius opted for deposing Philip. (See MAXIMINUS, EMPEROR OF ROME.)

GOW, Ian (1937–1990)   It was hardly a surprise when Ian Gow's name turned up on a Provisional Irish Republican Army assassination list which surfaced in December 1988. Gow was a hard-line Conservative Member of Parliament on Northern Ireland matters, a close personal friend and adviser of Prime Minister Margaret Thatcher, and was often described as 'more Thatcherite than Mrs. Thatcher.' Despite police warnings that his life was in danger, Gow insisted on living openly in his home village of Hankham, East Sussex, his home telephone number and address listed in the local telephone directory.

At 8:30 on the morning of July 31, the 53-year-old MP stepped into his car when a bomb planted under the driver's side exploded. Gow's wife heard the blast and rushed out of the house to try to aid her husband. Gow died while an ambulance crew was treating him at the scene.

Prime Minister Thatcher went to the murder site later in the day and turned away, having briefly viewed the bombed car where her close friend had died.

Gow had been in Parliament since 1974 and was an ardent supporter of Mrs. Thatcher as her first private parliamentary secretary from 1979 to 1983. He broke briefly with Mrs. Thatcher in 1985, resigning his post as a deputy treasury minister to protest the signing of the British–Irish agreement between London and Dublin which gave the Irish government a consultative role in

Northern Ireland affairs. Gow insisted that this would only 'prolong and not diminish the agony' of the province.

During the week before his assassination, Gow appeared on television to condemn the IRA bitterly for an attack that had killed a Roman Catholic nun and three policemen. 'These murders are as odious as they are futile,' he said. 'Once again wives have been turned into widows and children into orphans. And for what purpose?' He added such tactics will 'never never win.'

Officials speculated that such verbal onslaughts against terrorism raised Gow to the head of the hit list. The day after the Gow murder the IRA issued a statement in Dublin taking responsibility for the 'execution' and vowing 'to strike whenever and wherever the opportunity arises' until Britain agreed to a united Ireland.

GREGORY V, Pope See OTTO III, HOLY ROMAN EMPEROR.

GUEVARA, Ernesto 'Che' (1928–1967) In the 1960s Ernesto 'Che' Guevara, top aide to Cuba's Fidel Castro, was as repugnant to the United States and some Latin American governments as the Cuban leader himself. Some viewed Guevara, born to a wealthy Spanish-Irish family, more dedicated a revolutionary than Castro, and a romantic (but small) following gathered around him. Guevara disappeared from public view in Cuba in early 1965, rumored to have had a falling out with Castro. In October he renounced his Cuban citizenship and declared he was embarking on new revolutionary activities. After that he was reported to be in several countries in South America, as well as in the Dominican Republic, Algeria and Vietnam. At various times he was reported captured or killed in many countries.

Sometime in 1966 Guevara turned up in Bolivia, which he wrongly assessed as ripe for revolution. While Guevara's movements and activities were clouded in mystery and later distorted by Bolivian government reports, it is doubtful he ever enjoyed the complete support of Bolivian rebels, who viewed him as an outsider who did not condone their overt terrorism. It could also be that the Bolivian peasants looked upon Guevara not as a savior but as an adventurer more likely to bring down the wrath of a brutal government upon them.

For well over a year Guevara slogged through the Bolivian backcountry, surviving on hawk meat and barely escaping one government ambush after another. Suffering from chronic asthma and arthritis and frequently incapacitated, Guevara was reported to have been attempting to escape the Bolivian wilds and leave the country, but the government's U.S.-backed anti-insurgency campaign blocked his efforts.

The final confrontation between Guevara's small band of guerrillas and the government's much larger force occurred on October 8, 1967. According to the report of General Alfredo Ovando Candia, the commander of the Bolivian armed forces, the wounded Guevara revealed his identity before dying, telling his captors: 'I am Che Guevara, and I have failed.'

According to official reports Guevara lingered until the next day before expiring, but later medical examinations indicated that it would have been impossible for him to have survived 24 hours with his wounds and that he had been summarily killed by the Bolivian army. On October 12 the government put an effective end to the debate by cremating the body and scattering the ashes to the wind. In Havana Fidel Castro announced that the news of Guevara's death was 'sadly true.' (See ZENTENO ANAYA, JOAQUIN.)

GUISE, Henry, Duke of (1550–1588) Henry I de Lorraine, the third duke of Guise, played a key role in the religious conflicts of 16th-century France and was the acknowledged chief of the Catholic Party and the Holy League. He was one of the planners of the Massacre of St. Bartholomew, although his interests in it may be said to have been more limited to personal assassination than in the mass killing of Huguenots.

His father, Francois of Guise, had been one of the military leaders in the fight against the Protestants until he was cut down by a Huguenot assassin in 1563, when Henry was 13. The young Henry vowed vengeance for his father's death and held the Huguenot leader, Admiral Gaspard de Coligny, personally responsible for the assassination. Most historians regard this theory as inaccurate, but it represented a distortion not uncommon in the extreme partisanship of the day. In 1566 Henry left France seeking to do battle with the Turks to gain military experience, but the conflict ended before his arrival. He returned home to take part in a number of religious conflicts, gaining huge popularity in Paris with his acts of derring-do.

In 1572 Catherine de' Medici, the queen mother and regent, turned to the House of Guise for aid in getting rid of Admiral Coligny, who was exercising considerable influence upon the young king Charles IX. At last Henry of Guise had his opportunity for revenge. An attempted assassination of Coligny resulted in the admiral being wounded but not killed by gunfire. The following day, August 23, Henry attended a secret meeting with Catherine and, most probably, her son, the future Henry III, at which details of the Massacre of St. Bartholomew were worked out. The first priority had to be the murder of the wounded Coligny, which would signal the massacre of thousands of Huguenots in Paris.

The following day, a band of assassins under Henry of Guise stormed Coligny's home, stabbed him to death and dragged the body out into the street and hacked it to pieces. Coligny's head was said to have been later sent to Pope Gregory XIII.

His father's death properly avenged by his standards, Henry of Guise, by some accounts, took no further part in the ensuing bloodbath; in fact he may even have harbored about 100 Huguenots in his home.

In the following years, Guise became perhaps the most powerful man in France, with more influence than either Catherine or Henry III, who became king in 1574. During the War of the Three Henrys, Guise ruled the capital as a sort of 'King of Paris' when Henry III was forced to flee. The king eventually feigned peace with Henry of Guise, appointing him lieutenant general of the kingdom. Secretly Henry III was determined to destroy Guise. On December 23, 1588, when the latter left a council meeting to answer a royal summons, the king's bodyguard fell on him and stabbed him to death. The following day Henry of Guise's brother, Louis, cardinal of Lorraine, who had played a bloody role in the religious conflicts, was also assassinated. The two bodies were burned and the ashes thrown into the Loire.

The assassination string was not broken. Within the year, King Henry III would fall to a Catholic assassin. (See COLIGNY, ADMIRAL GASPARD DE; HENRY III, KING OF FRANCE.)

Further reading: *The Story of Civilization VII – The Age of Reason Begins*, by Will and Ariel Durant.

GUITERREZ DE CASTRO, S. Guitterez (?–1869) It has been called the most dramatic assassination in Spanish history, and the Spaniards have a special phrase to describe it: *matar alevosamente*, meaning to destroy with treachery and guile. The crime is known as the Burgos Cathedral Murder, and this sobriquet is better known than the name of the actual victim, S. Guitterez Guiterrez de Castro, who in 1869 was the civil governor of Burgos.

In the 1860s Burgos was the center of myriad conspiracies seeking to reduce the power of the church and replace Queen Isabella II with a nominee of the Bourbons. However, although Isabella was forced to flee abroad, she maintained the strong support of the clerical party. Late in January 1869, the governor, noted for his opposition to church influence in state matters, went to mass at the beautiful 13th-century cathedral at Burgos. As he prayed, several priests pulled knives from under their cassocks and brutally stabbed him to death.

The cathedral murder shocked the country and produced a wave of anticlericalism. Riots took place in several cities, especially in Madrid, where mobs surged through the streets, crying, 'Death to the Papal Nuncio.' Rioters tore the pope's coat of arms from the door of the papal consulate and ceremoniously burned it in the street.

Several priests at Burgos were condemned, and in the end one was executed for the governor's assassination. In 1870 Isabella formally abdicated.

Further reading: *The History of Assassination*, by Brian McConnell.

GUSTAV III, King of Sweden (1746–1792) As king of Sweden from 1771 to 1792, Gustav III restored the royal prerogatives over the Riksdag (parliament) during a reign that became known as the Gustavian Enlightenment. The royal house had been weakened during the previous half century by parliamentary rules. In the process of attacking the Riksdag Gustav launched a number of reforms, such as freedom of the press, amendment of the poor law, increased free trade and a much-strengthened navy, which was to prove fortuitous in his war with Russia.

By amiability of character, Gustav gained the affection of the people, and he was continuously able to counter the nobility seeking to win renewed dominance in the Riksdag. In 1788 Gustav launched a highly unpopular war with Russia over territory. The Swedish army fared poorly, but the navy scored a brilliant victory at Svensksund in July 1790. Swedish patriotism revived the king's popularity, but aristocratic conspiracies continued to mount. By 1792 the conspirators could count on 100 nobles as active participants in the plot against the king.

On March 16, 1792, Gustav received a letter urging him to avoid a masquerade ball to be held that night in the French Theater. Since he would be masked, the king decided to ignore the warning. However, a leader in the conspiracy, Jacob Johan Anckarstrom, was able to identify him, and shot and mortally wounded the king.

Gustav was borne back to the palace in his coach. Within hours Anckarstrom was apprehended, as were several others ringleaders in the plot, and crowds outside the palace called for their execution. Gustav, lingering on his deathbed, counseled clemency, and only Anckarstrom was scourged, beheaded and quartered. The king died 10 days after the shooting. The royal line continued under Gustav III's son, Gustav IV, until 1809, when a coup by liberal officials and army officers forced him into exile in Switzerland, his heirs forever barred from the succession.

H

HACHED, Farhat (1913–1952) The murder of Farhat Hached, secretary general of the Tunisian Labor Federation, on December 5, 1952, was to have far-reaching effects throughout French North Africa, marking the beginning of the end for French colonial rule in much of the area. Hached was machine-gunned to death outside Tunis. Tunisian nationalist leaders attributed the killing to members of a secret society of French colonials known as the Red Hand.

The assassination of the popular Hached led to rioting and violence throughout much of North Africa; and while the French would try to maintain control of Algeria into the 1960s, they soon realized they could not resist the tide of nationalism and history in Tunisia. By 1955 French and Tunisian negotiators had reached an agreement on independence for the colony, which became effective on March 20, 1956.

HAIG, General Alexander (1924–) – Attempted Assassination As supreme commander of NATO, U.S. General Alexander Haig narrowly survived an attempted bomb assassination in 1979. As he drove to SHAPE headquarters in Belgium on June 25, a land mine of more than 100 pounds of explosives was command-detonated from a bridge about 1,000 yards away. The would-be killers were so far away that they mistimed the blast, and although the general's armored Mercedes-Benz took heavy damage, Haig escaped unharmed. The West German Red Army Faction claimed responsibility for the bombing.

When Haig became secretary of state in 1981, black-masked youths handed out leaflets featuring photos of

Haig's badly damaged car with a caption reading ONLY 2.7 SECONDS TOO LATE.

HAJARI, Cadi Abdullah al- (1912–1977) While sitting in a car near his London hotel, former Premier Cadi Abdullah al-Hajari was shot to death on April 10, 1977. Killed in the same gunfire were his companions in the vehicle – his wife Fatimah and Abdullah Ali al-Hammami, a diplomat attached to the North Yemeni embassy. Hajari had served as premier of North Yemen from December 1972 to February 1974. At the time of his assassination he was deputy chief of the nation's supreme court.

As premier, Hajari, a royalist with strong ties to Saudi Arabia, led the conservative elements that opposed the proposed unification with Marxist-dominated South Yemen. During his premiership, Hajari imprisoned thousands of pro-unification republicans and executed 50 alleged enemies of the state. At the time of Hajari's assassination, unification was again under consideration, and although the assassins were never apprehended, the supposition was that Hajari had been removed to help effect the merger. The union was not accomplished, however, and when in 1977 North Yemen's president Ibrahim al-Hamidi was also assassinated, charges were made that his killing was also a plot to forestall unification. (See also HAMIDI, IBRAHIM AL-.)

HAMIDI, Colonel Abdullah Mohammed al- See HAMIDI, IBRAHIM AL-.

HAMIDI, Ibrahim al- (1943–1977) On October 10, 1977, President Ibrahim al-Hamidi was visiting the home of his brother Colonel Abdullah Mohammed al-Hamidi, when unidentified assassins broke into the house and started shooting. Killed along with the president and his brother was Colonel Ali Kannas Zahra, head of North Yemen's armed forces.

The assassinations occurred before President Hamidi's planned visit to Marxist-dominated South Yemen, and the

South Yemenis charged that the assassinations were the work of antiunification forces within North Yemen that were inspired by outside influences. These influences were presumed to include Saudi Arabia and by extension the United States. (See HAJARI, CADI ABDULLAH AL-.)

HAMMAMI, Abdullah Ali al-   See HAJARI, CADI ABDULLAH AL-.

HAMMARSKJOLD, Dag (1905–1961) On September 18, 1961, a DC-6B airliner crashed in the African jungle near Ndola, in what is today Zambia. Among the 16 on board was Dag Hammarskjold, the 56-year-old Swedish secretary-general of the United Nations. To this day speculation that Hammarskjold's death had been an assassination has not been quenched. Former U.S. President Harry S Truman said, 'Dag Hammarskjold was on the point of getting something done when they killed him. Notice that I said "when they killed him." '

During his tenure as secretary-general, Hammarskjold had frequently come under attack from both the left and right. Hammarskjold had skillfully insisted on many independent actions clearly designed to demonstrate that the U.N. would not be totally dominated by the chief source of its military and financial sustenance, the United States. Still, he continued to come under strong criticism by the Communist bloc, and in September 1960 the Soviet Union demanded his resignation. Hammarskjold was specifically criticized by the Soviets for having sent a U.N. force to the Congo to suppress civil strife after it had become an independent republic the previous June. The Soviet Union demanded that the office of secretary-general be abolished and replaced by a three-man board, or troika, which would give representation to the Western, Communist, and neutral, or Third-World, nations. Hammarskjold rejected the proposal.

In September 1961 the secretary-general was on a peace mission to President Moise Tshombe in the Congo when his plane crashed. Of those aboard – a six-man crew,

Hammarskjold and his staff of eight men and a woman – only Hammarskjold and one aide, thrown clear of the wreckage, survived impact.

Although the plane was several hours overdue and a police official had called the airport to describe a mysterious flash, no search was launched until 10:00 the following morning. The wreckage was found at 3:00 that afternoon. Hammarskjold had died during the night, but the aide, Sergeant Harold Julien, lived for five days, raving about 'explosions' and 'sparks in the sky.'

Examination of the other dead revealed that two were riddled with bullets. The official finding was that this was caused by a box of ammunition that exploded on impact and that the cause of the crash was 'pilot error.' However, considering the tense political situation at the time in the Congo, the rumors of assassination cropped up and have continued for years.

In any event, Dag Hammarskjold was posthumously awarded the 1961 Nobel Peace Prize.

HAMMER, Michael (1938–1981) On January 3, 1981, two American agricultural advisers and the head of El Salvador's agrarian reform program were sitting in the coffee shop of the Sheraton Hotel in San Salvador when two gunmen approached and shot them to death. Witnesses at the scene said the gunmen – and a boy who stood guard while the shooting occurred – had 'calmly tucked their pistols into the waist of their trousers and very calmly left' through the main entrance.

What was remarkable about this was that the hotel had long been heavily guarded and that members of the hotel security force who had been seen moments before the shooting had suddenly disappeared. President Jose Napoleon Duarte said, 'In my opinion, it was almost certainly an action by the extreme Right.' He promised full cooperation in an investigation.

The victims were Michael P. Hammer, Mark David Pearlman and Jose Rodolfo Viera. Hammer and Pearlman were representatives of the U.S.-based American

Institute for Free Labor Development, the international arm of the AFL-CIO. They were advising Viera, who was the founder of the Salvadoran Communal Union, the country's largest organization of rural farmers, and director of the country's agrarian reform project.

Salvador's right wing was violently opposed to land redistribution to poor farm families. The investigation led to the arrest of a wealthy Salvadoran landowner who was soon freed by the courts for insufficient evidence. If there was difficulty in finding the spiritual fathers of the assassinations, then it was far easier to find and convict the actual gunmen (although this took until 1986, following charges from U.S. labor interests that there was considerable foot-dragging in the investigation). The two gunmen, Jose Dimas Valle Acevedo and Santiago Gomez Gonzalez, both former members of the National Guard, confessed the killings and said they had been carried out under orders of military superiors and business interests. The two triggermen were given consecutive sentences of 12 years in prison for each murder, but the law limited the total sentence to 30 years. No one else was charged in the crimes because under Salvadoran law testimony of persons accused of a crime was not admissible.

HASSAN II, King of Morocco (1929–) – Attempted Assassination The attempted assassination of King Hassan II of Morocco in 1972 was remarkable for the sheer persistence of the effort, as well as the resourcefulness of the intended victim. The previous year Hassan had successfully suppressed an attempted coup. On August 16 he was flying back to Morocco after a visit to France and Spain, when his royal Boeing 727 was met by five Moroccan Air Force jets. As Hassan's airliner entered Moroccan air space three of the escorts opened fire, badly damaging the craft. A radio appeal from the airliner, supposedly from a mechanic, asked that the shooting stop since the king was 'mortally wounded' and there was no need to kill others on board. The jets broke off the attack. In actuality the voice was later said to have been that of the uninjured King Hassan himself.

When the airliner landed at Rabat Airport, the king coolly proceeded with scheduled welcoming ceremonies, but as he spoke, approximately eight air force jets launched another attack, killing eight persons and wounding at least 47 others including four government ministers. Hassan saved himself by diving for cover into a grove of trees. Later, as he was being driven to the city, jets attacked the guest house adjoining the royal palace, where Hassan was believed to have taken refuge.

Most of the attacking jets returned to Kenitra air base, which had been taken over by forces under Defense Minister General Mohamed Oufkir, who had long been regarded as one of Hassan's most loyal supporters. The next day Oufkir committed suicide after two officers involved in the assassination plot identified him as the mastermind behind the conspiracy. Oufkir had planned to rule the country as regent for Hassan's 9-year-old son, Crown Prince Sidi Mohamed.

Eleven air force officers were sentenced to death for the attempted assassination, and 32 other defendants got prison terms of 3 to 20 years. Ironically, General Oufkir had directed his earlier assassination efforts on behalf of the throne. He had been found guilty in absentia by a French court for directing the abduction and murder of Moroccan opposition leader Mehdi Ben Barka in 1965.

HELIOGABALUS See ELAGABALUS, EMPEROR OF ROME.

HENRY III, King of France (1551–1589) Since he was the son of the cunning Catherine de' Medici and lived during the worst period of France's religious wars, it should not be too surprising that the career of Henry III of France was marked with assassinations before, during and at the conclusion of his reign.

Having been made a lieutenant general of the royal armies by his regent mother, the young Henry helped lead those forces to victory over the Protestant Huguenot troops in several key battles in 1569. Yet, like his mother, Henry often tried to play – rather unsuccessfully – a middle role between Catholics and Huguenots. There is little reason to doubt that Henry took part in the conspiracy of Catherine and the House of Guise to assassinate the gifted Admiral Gaspard de Coligny in 1572, the first killing that launched the Massacre of St. Bartholomew, in which thousands of French Huguenots – men, women and children – were slaughtered.

Succeeding to the throne on the death of his brother, Charles IX, in 1574, Henry III tried to take a more moderate course for a time, but he was not the most cunning of manipulators, a deficiency enhanced by a reputation as what one historical account describes as 'a youthful degenerate who wore earrings and a pearl necklace and consorted with a group of wastrels who could give even the king lessons in degeneracy.'

In any event, Henry III was constantly caught up in the power struggle between the House of Guise and the Huguenots under Henry of Navarre. In the War of the Three Henrys, the king was the least competent player and his power eroded to the extent that he was forced to maneuver for a time seeking Catholic protection, and at other times Huguenot protection. In 1588 Henry III sought to correct this demeaning situation by effecting the assassination of the duke of Guise. Henry invited Guise to a private conference, and as the noble approached, nine assailants stabbed him to death. Opening a door, the king gazed in excited satisfaction upon his desired aim. Henry then ordered the death of the Duke's brother, Louis, Cardinal of Lorraine. These killings enraged the Catholics of the Holy League, and they rose up and drove the king from Paris.

Forced into an alliance with Henry of Navarre, the king besieged his capital city with a Huguenot army. Inside the isolated city a fanatic Dominican monk, Jacques Clement, became fired up by denunciations of Henry III as an assassin. Urged on further by the tears and beauty of

Catherine, duchess of Montpensier, the sister of the murdered Guises, the monk secured a dagger slipped through the siege lines and gained admission to the king's presence, saying he bore important intelligence. He fatally stabbed the king in the stomach before being killed by guards. Clement died confident of having achieved paradise, and within the city delirium broke out among the supporters of the league, as the besieging army melted away. Some churches placed the monk's picture on the altar, and his act was hailed as the noblest of God's doings since the Incarnation of Jesus Christ. The monk's mother was imported from the provinces and was hailed by a sacred chant: 'Blessed be the womb that bore thee, and the paps that gave thee suck.' (See COLIGNY, ADMIRAL GASPARD DE; GUISE, HENRY, DUKE OF.)

Further reading: *The Century of the Renaissance*, by Louis Batiffol; *The Later Years of Catherine de' Medici*, by Edith Sichel; *The Story of Civilization VII – The Age of Reason Begins*, by Will and Ariel Durant.

HENRY IV (HENRY OF NAVARRE), King of France (1553–1610) Henry of Navarre was raised as a Protestant, but he renounced his faith and adopted Catholicism to save himself from the St. Bartholomew Day Massacre of the Huguenots, of whom he was the nominal head, in 1572. Four years later he returned to Protestantism and thereafter found his life imperiled by religious turmoil.

Henry became the first Bourbon monarch of France in 1589 after the assassination of Henry III by a fanatic Catholic monk, Jacques Clement. However, even after his defeat of the Catholic League at Arques in 1589 and at Ivry in 1590, Henry IV could not enter Paris, which remained in control of the Catholic forces aided by Spain. However, in 1593 Henry won by vows what he could not gain by force. For a second time he abjured Protestantism, allegedly remarking, 'Paris is well worth a Mass.' He entered the city in 1594 and soon won the support of most of the French people with his conciliatory actions. He restored peace to the country by 1598 and that year issued the Edict of Nantes, which while confirming Roman Catholicism as the official religion of the nation, nevertheless granted the Huguenots considerable religious freedom, the right to hold government office and the right to maintain military forces in several fortified cities.

Much of the remainder of Henry IV's reign was devoted to restoring order, industry and trade. However, he also maneuvered to align himself with the Protestant princes of Germany against the Catholic Hapsburgs and the more fanatic French Catholic elements became convinced that Henry planned war against the papacy. Rumors began to circulate that Henry would be killed.

On May 14, 1610, he was. That day he set out in an open coach to visit the ailing duke of Sully. To avoid notice the king dismissed his guards but was accompanied by seven members of his court. In the Rue de la Ferronnerie his coach was blocked by a hay wagon, and Francois Ravaillac, a 32-year-old visionary fanatic, seized the opportunity to spring at the king, who was reading a dispatch. Ravaillac stabbed the king just above the heart, severing the aorta. The assassination caused profound grief throughout France, even among many Catholics.

Francois Ravaillac of Angouleme was an unstable individual who had previously been arrested for a crime he had not committed. In his cell he had a vision, and he studied theological tracts and tracts defending tyrannicide, eventually becoming convinced it was his duty to save France from the horror of Protestantism. Several times after his release he tried to reach the king, to ask him if he was planning to war on the pope, and if the Huguenots were about to massacre the Catholics. He tried to join the Jesuits but was rejected. For a time he went back home, then returned to Paris and murdered the king.

Texts on torture to this day spend considerable time detailing Ravaillac's interrogation and torture. A metal boot was placed on one of his legs, and then three screws were turned down slowly, crushing his joints. He finally lapsed into unconsciousness, revealing no names. For his execution Ravaillac was first taken in a cart to the main portal of Notre Dame to make a confession, but the howls of the bloodthirsty crowd kept anyone from hearing his words. He was then transported to the scaffold on the Place de Greve, where he screamed out for forgiveness (although he still maintained God would forgive his act due to the justice of his cause). Ravaillac's arm, the one used in committing the regicide, was plunged into burning sulfur, and red-hot pincers were used to tear out pieces of his chest, arms, thighs and calves. Molten lead, resin, boiling oil, wax and sulfur were then used to cauterize the wounds to keep him alive for the next phase of punishment. After an hour, Ravaillac's limbs were ripped off by four horses. Then another horse was used to crack the condemned man's thighbone, and his trunk was set ablaze. In all it took Ravaillac 90 minutes to die.

Ravaillac's property was seized by the crowd. The house where he was born was destroyed, and no future building was permitted on the site. His parents were given two weeks to leave the country on pain of death if they ever returned. His other relatives were henceforth forbidden to use the name Ravaillac.

Ravaillac's punishment, however, was but a minor episode in what the Paris *Parlement* called 'the most wicked, abominable and detestable parricide committed on the person of our late King Henry the Fourth.' Many, especially at the Sorbonne, accused the Jesuits of having inflamed the assassin's mind. They cited the writings especially of Juan de Mariana, certainly the greatest historian among the Jesuits and perhaps in all Europe at the time, for advocating 'honorable' tyrannicide against a heretical king in his 1599 work, *De rege et regis institutione (On the King and His Education)*. The Jesuits protested that in 1599 Claudio Aquaviva, the general of the Society of Jesus, had ordered that *De rege* be 'corrected' and that the work had been explicitly condemned by a Jesuit assembly in Paris in 1606. However, *De rege* had been sold openly in Paris shops, and the Sorbonne judged the Jesuits guilty of 'dangerous doctrines.' Mariana's book was officially burned.

Two months after the assassination of Henry IV, Aquaviva condemned Mariana's teaching on tyrannicide and ordered it not to be propagated in Jesuit teaching thereafter. By that time Mariana was imprisoned in Spain, not for *De rege* but for publishing *De monetae mutatione*, in which he condemned the Spanish king Philip II's debasement of the coinage and warned of the evils of inflation. (See also HENRY III, KING OF FRANCE.)

Further reading: *The Assassination of Henry IV*, by Roland Mousnier.

HERRHAUSEN, Alfred (1930–1989) On November 30, 1989, Alfred Herrhausen, the head of the Deutsche Bank, the largest in West Germany, was being driven from his home through Bad Homburg, a fashionable suburb of Frankfurt. Herrhausen, often described as the most powerful person in the West German economy, was riding in the center car of a three-car convoy as it passed near a bicycle on a tree-lined street. The bicycle camouflaged a bomb that could be triggered by a light beam some 660 feet away from it. Evidently the light beam was not switched on until the lead car passed. Then Herrhausen's armored Mercedes-Benz triggered the bomb, and the vehicle was thrown several yards in the air, its windows obliterated and its doors, hood and trunk blown open. The car burst into flames. Herrhausen died instantly, and his driver was severely injured.

A note found near the scene bore the symbol of the Red Army Faction, a West German terrorist group, who took responsibility for the attack. It was signed, the Wolfgang Beer Commando, named for a member of the Red Army Faction who died with another suspected terrorist in an auto crash near Stuttgart in 1980. In the late 1980s antiterrorist precautions had become a way of life for board members of large West German companies. Most executives traveled in cars equipped with armor plating and bulletproof glass and had drivers trained in antiterrorist tactics.

Although the Herrhausen murder was the first successful assassination since 1986, it was a harsh reminder that the Red Army Faction, founded by Andreas Baader and Ulrike Meinhof in the 1960s, was still flourishing, despite the belief of the West German police that the group had been severely crippled in recent years by the arrests of many of its leading members. It was further proof that even if such terrorist attacks failed to alter the social direction of a nation, it remained virtually impossible to eliminate terrorist groups since only a few activities were necessary to carry out assassination plots. Authorities labeled the Herrhausen attack a complicated one, planned weeks in advance and executed with precision.

HEUREAUX, Ulises (1845–1899) Ulises Heureaux was perhaps, even considering Rafael Trujillo, the sternest dictator in the history of the Dominican Republic. He was also the man who allowed the major part of his country's economy to fall under U.S. domination.

Heureaux proved a brave fighter in the Dominican Republic's battle for independence, and he became a steadily more important military figure in the nation's civil wars. In 1882 he assumed the presidency and immediately tightened his control by exiling many of his former comrades. Stepping down in 1884 because of the constitutional barrier against reelection, Heureaux handpicked the next two presidents but maintained actual power himself. In 1887 he again became president after altering the constitution, and he continued in office until his death.

It may be said that Heureaux imposed order on the Dominican Republic, doing so by the simple expedient of executing anyone who opposed him in any way. He imported a huge amount of capital from the United States to build up transportation and agriculture, especially the growing of sugar, but his improvident financial dealings bankrupted what was already an impoverished land.

On July 26, 1899, a group of political enemies led by Ramon Caceres, a member of a wealthy family, shot him to death in governmental office. In the ensuing years, U.S. interference in Dominican affairs became more pronounced. After some years of political chaos, Caceres himself became president in 1906. Caceres reformed the constitution and brought about a public works system. He proved popular with the people but faced a number of plots against him. And finally, on November 19, 1911, Caceres too was shot to death, setting the stage for direct U.S. military intervention in the country for several years.

HEYDRICH, Reinhard Tristan (1904–1942) In the eyes of rabid Hitlerites, Reinhard Heydrich was the beau idéal of Nazism. In fact, Adolf Hitler saw the charismatic, icy-eyed, ambitious Reinhard Heydrich as his possible successor. At 14 Heydrich joined a Free Corps band in which he was schooled in street-fighting and terrorism. He joined the navy in 1922, rising in rank to first lieutenant, but he was forced to resign in 1931 because of some sexual indiscretions. Thenceforth he applied all his waking hours to the Nazi cause. In 1933 shortly after Hitler came to power, Heydrich was made chief of the political department of the Munich police, which included control of the notorious Dachau concentration camp.

In 1934 he moved on to the post of SS chief for Berlin and later was made deputy chief of the SS under Heinrich Himmler. Together with Joseph Goebbels, he labored diligently to provide the pretext for – and to carry out – Hitler's purge of the Brownshirts during the 1934 'Night of the Long Knives.'

Heydrich was put in charge of police matters in Austria following the Anschluss in 1938. He played a key role in fabricating Polish 'atrocities' against Germans to justify the invasion of Poland. In 1941 he was made *Reichsprotektor* of Bohemia-Moravia. Within five weeks of his arrival in Prague he ordered the execution of 300 Czechs. Thereafter, while maintaining this post, he was assigned to Norway, Holland and occupied France to put down outbreaks of sabotage and terrorism. His visits were always marked by mass executions, and he became notorious as 'Hangman Heydrich.' He also took charge of the establishment and operation of the extermination camps to liquidate millions of Jews and other 'undesirables.'

Personally, Heydrich was a man of considerable accomplishments, which included violin playing and fencing. Personally brave, he reveled in flying volunteer sorties with Luftwaffe fighter pilots and was shot down over the Russian Front and wounded, managing to force-land in German-held territory. Such stunts, some of his contemporaries were convinced, were part of a plan to undermine Himmler and replace him as one of Hitler's top advisers. Walter Schellenberg, the Nazi intelligence ace, says of Heydrich in his memoirs: 'This man was the hidden pivot around which the Nazi regime revolved. The development of a whole nation was guided indirectly by his forceful character.' Historians have long speculated on Heydrich's role during the balance of the Nazi years had he not been assassinated.

On the morning of May 27, 1942, Heydrich was riding in an open touring car when he was fatally wounded in a grenade attack by two Czechs. The car was blown apart and Heydrich's spine shattered. The attackers, Jan Kubis and Josef Gabeik of the free Czechoslovak army in England, had been parachuted into the country by the Royal Air Force. The attack was carried out with precision, and the assassins made good their escape under cover of a smoke screen. They were given sanctuary by priests of the Karl Borromaeus Church, but were betrayed by Karel Curda and were among 120 members of the resistance wiped out to the last man by attacking SS troops. (Curda himself was later killed by the underground.)

In retaliation for the killing of Heydrich, the entire village of Lidice, in Czechoslovakia was destroyed, and all men 16 years and older – 172 in all – were executed, as were some of the women. The remaining females, who numbered 195, were shipped to concentration camps, where at least 52 died. Four of the women who were about to give birth were shipped to a maternity hospital in Prague, where the newborns were murdered, after which the mothers were shipped to a concentration camp. Many of the 70 children of Lidice were also murdered while others were brought up as Germans, if they passed muster by the SS 'racial experts.' In addition, on the day of the bombing Goebbels had 500 of the few Jews still at large in Berlin rounded up, and when Heydrich died of his wounds eight days later, 152 were executed. Some 3,000 Jews from the so-called privileged ghetto of Theresienstadt were also deported to the east for extermination.

The question remains of why Heydrich was assassinated and whether the price was worth paying. The Czechs seemed to be acting under British orders, and for years one theory was that Heydrich was silenced because he knew too much about the treasonable activities of the duke of Windsor. However, in his book *The Killing of SS Obergruppenfuhrer Reinhard Heydrich*, Callum MacDonald argues persuasively that the act was a desperate gamble by Eduard Benes, the head of the Czechoslovak government in exile, (1) to prove to England and Russia that the Czech underground was a viable force; (2) to gain prestige to the detriment of the Czechoslovak Communists; and (3) to ensure that the Czechoslovak people would not make a compromise peace with the Nazis. If this thesis is viable, there could be no doubt that both Benes and the allies realized a great amount of blood would be spilled in consequence.

Further reading: *Hitler's Secret Service*, by Walter Schellenberg; *The Killing of SS Obergruppenfuhrer Reinhard Heydrich*, by Callum MacDonald; *The Rise and Fall of the Third Reich*, by William L. Shirer.

HITLER, Adolf (1889–1945) – Attempted Assassinations While there were many plots to kill Hitler, only two reached the overt stage: one on November 8, 1939 and one on July 20, 1944.

Every November 8, the anniversary of the Munich *putsch* in 1923, Adolf Hitler delivered a speech in the beer cellar where the attempted coup had originated. Hitler's speech in 1939 was much shorter than usual, and he did not follow his custom of lingering with some of his top aides to reminisce with old beer-drinking party comrades. Twelve minutes after the Hitler entourage left, a bomb planted in a pillar directly behind the speaker's platform exploded, killing seven Nazis and wounding 63 others.

Hitler firmly believed that the British secret service, inspired by Neville Chamberlain, had tried to kill him. Others at the time thought it to be another Nazi fabrication; journalist William L. Shirer wrote in his diary that the event 'smells of another Reichstag fire.' Even Walter Schellenberg, head of the SS foreign intelligence service, suspected the hand of Heinrich Himmler and Reinhard Heydrich in the management of the affair. However, after investigating the bombing, Schellenberg determined it to be a real assassination attempt, but one that did not involve any of the Third Reich's military foes.

The attempt had been carried out by a 36-year-old Swabian cabinetmaker, electrician and all-around tinkerer named Johann Georg Elser, who was arrested trying to cross the Swiss border right after the attack. Under intense questioning Elser confessed that he had built an explosive mechanism into one of the wooden pillars in the beer cellar, using an ingenious timing device that could run three days. At first Elser said he had performed the entire operation alone well in advance of Hitler's appearance there. Later, however, he claimed to have two co-conspirators, whose names he claimed not to know, who had promised him a refuge abroad afterward.

Gestapo torture, drugs and hypnosis failed to get Elser to alter his story. He was outraged when interrogators doubted he had the expertise to carry out the plot on his own, and Elser insisted on being given access to a carpenter's shop, in which he reconstructed the bomb. In the end Himmler, Heydrich and Schellenberg were satisfied that Elser was a fanatic with an abnormal need for recognition. However, none of this satisfied Hitler, who insisted that Elser be kept alive in a concentration camp and questioned further. Five and a half years later, when all hope for Germany was clearly lost, Elser was murdered by the Gestapo at Dachau under cover of an Allied air raid on April 9, 1945. Elser's intended victim outlived him by only three weeks.

The attempt on July 20, 1944, was perhaps one of the most important unsuccessful assassinations in history. Ironically, some historians now argue that it was fortuitous that Hitler was not killed in this attempt. By then it was clear that Germany would lose the war, and, so goes the theory, if Hitler were killed, it would have led to a replay of the post-World War I chaos when extremists and especially Hitler had argued that Germany had lost the war only through betrayal. The thesis is that it was better that World War II continued, even with its further loss of life, than that the seeds of militarism and nationalism be planted anew in Germany.

However, this was not the thinking of most of the planners of the 1944 attempt. They had lost faith in Hitler, and, realizing that Germany was beaten, they sought to bring the conflict to its climax by killing the Fuhrer, an act they hoped would open the way for a negotiated agreement with the Allies that might save Germany from destruction and maintain the integrity of German territory or, for some at least, the integrity of the army.

Plans were laid to kill Hitler and seize control of the government, imprison or kill the other leading Nazis, and sue for peace. Bombs were placed on Hitler's plane but failed to go off. In another try, three young officers who were modeling the latest Nazi uniforms volunteered to carry bombs under their coats and blow themselves and Hitler up at the same time. Unfortunately, Hitler departed too early. A bomb was smuggled inside a briefcase into a high-level conference, but Hitler canceled his appearance. Another time Hitler was to be killed while visiting an art gallery, but he left early and the bomb carrier had to flee with his deadly device. By design Hitler was an elusive target, failing to follow a prearranged schedule precisely to thwart attempts on his life.

But the plotters would not give up. The next try was to be made by Lieutenant Colonel Klaus Schenk von Stauffenberg. A capable staff officer who had long exhibited a hatred for Hitler, Stauffenberg as early as 1936 referred to Hitler as 'the buffoon' and 'the enemy of the world' in private conversations. Within the officer corps he was about as liberal as any to be found. In fact, his own peace program called for naming a socialist leader, Julius Leber, to be minister of the interior after the coup. It may also be that Stauffenberg, or at least some of his fellow officers, believed the rumors that after Hitler's victory in the war there would be a wave of executions of the German aristocracy.

In short, many officers had different motivations for joining the conspiracy, and many more kept silent to see first how the tide would flow. General Erwin Rommel, the 'Desert Fox,' was implicated to some extent but did not join the plot, seeking instead to protect his flanks by insisting that Hitler be taken alive and put on trial. Most of the plotters dismissed this as fantasy.

In June 1944 Stauffenberg was made chief of staff to General Friedrich Fromm, the head of the reserve army, which gave him access to Hitler's headquarters. Plans were laid more than once for Stauffenberg, who because of war injuries went through much lighter security checks when coming in contact with Hitler, to detonate a bomb that would kill the Fuhrer, Goering and Himmler at the same time. That happy set of circumstances always slipped away, and finally it was decided by the plotters to go after Hitler alone if necessary.

On July 20, 1944, Stauffenberg attended a staff conference at Rastenburg, Hitler's 'wolf lair' headquarters in East Prussia. Before entering a wooden hut for the meeting, Stauffenberg activated an acid detonator on a bomb in his briefcase, which he placed under a table around which a number of military men and Hitler were going over maps and reports. The briefcase was set near Hitler, and then Stauffenberg stepped out of the conference room, supposedly to make an important telephone call. He walked out into the fresh air and kept going for quite a distance and then waited.

The explosion was enormous, and Stauffenberg was

sure Hitler could not have survived. But Hitler had, for two reasons. First, the meeting place had been changed at the last moment from a concrete bunker to the wood-constructed enclosure. This allowed much of the force of the explosion to dissipate rather than be contained inside. Even more important, after Stauffenberg left the meeting, another officer leaning over the table found the briefcase in his way and moved it to the other side of a huge oak table support that now separated the bomb from Hitler. In the explosion four were killed and several badly hurt. Hitler himself suffered shock, minor burns and injury to his eardrums, but was otherwise unscathed.

Meanwhile, as soon as the explosion occurred, Stauffenberg had a fellow conspirator telephone the information back to Berlin so that the plotters could move to take over the government. Then he and his adjutant with considerable bravado bluffed their way past two road-blocks outside the headquarters and made for the airport.

When Stauffenberg arrived in Berlin, he found his colleagues had not proceeded as far as he hoped. Most had insisted on learning with absolute certainty that Hitler had indeed perished. This probably reflected the ambivalence that afflicted many of the plotters about taking part in an assassination. Stauffenberg tried to rouse them by claiming to have seen Hitler's corpse, but the plotters could not convince General Fromm, for one, to act. Fromm had been one who had no intention of joining the plot until victory was assured. When there was some indication out of Rastenberg that Hitler had survived, Fromm tried to arrest a number of the plotters but was himself made a prisoner. When, however, it became apparent that Hitler was alive and loyal Nazi troops in the capital were on the attack, Fromm took over. Stauffenberg and several others were instantly court-martialed and sentenced to death. The former chief of the general staff, Ludwig Beck, was given the choice of suicide or execution and chose the former. Stauffenberg and the others were led to the courtyard wall and executed by firing squad.

In the ensuing weeks and months there were numerous

arrests; one estimate is 7,000, with 2,000 death sentences handed down by the Nazi People's Courts. None of the defendants were given the right to present any evidence on their own behalf. Hitler ordered that a number of the conspirators be hanged 'like cattle.' Eight condemned officers were herded into a small room at Ploetzensee prison in which eight meathooks hung from the ceiling. One by one, stripped to the waist, they were strung up by a noose of piano wire attached to the meathooks. A film was made of their death throes; their trousers fell as they struggled, leaving them naked in their final agonies. The film was rushed to Hitler for viewing in his personal projection room. It was said that Joseph Goebbels kept himself from fainting during the ghastly showing by covering his eyes with his hands.

Hitler's vengeance continued, and Rommel, whose complicity was less than others, was offered the choice of taking poison or facing a great show trial. He was told that if he took poison, his death would be announced to have been a tragic accident and he would receive the full honors of a German hero and his family would go unscathed. Otherwise, they too would face the grim consequences. Rommel killed himself. In any event there probably would have been no trial. He most likely would have been killed and the same announcement made.

One of the last to die in the purge was General Fromm, who was executed in March 1945 for cowardice during the coup attempt, even though he had executed some of the leading plotters, although more to protect himself than the Fuhrer.

Further reading: *The Rise and Fall of the Third Reich*, by William L. Shirer; *Hitler's Secret Service*, by Walter Schellenberg.

HORMIZD IV, King of Persia (?–590) Father of the great Persian king Khosrow (or Chosroe) II, Hormizd IV reigned from 578 or 579 until 590. According to sketchy historic records, he protected the common people and maintained strict discipline over the priests, army and courtiers. He rebuffed the priests, who called for persecution of the Christians, declaring that the welfare of the throne and the very government required the loyalty of both leading religions in the area. If that meant Hormizd IV faced strong ecclesiastical opposition, it may have been insignificant compared to that of the military, then headed by the general Bahram.

Bahram had successfully repelled an invasion by the Turks but in 589 was defeated in a major battle by the Romans. Hormizd IV was not a monarch who rewarded failure, and he heaped abuse upon the still-powerful general. The following year the courtiers launched a palace coup headed by two of the king's brothers-in-law. Bahram withdrew the army's support from the king and took over the revolt in his own right. Hormizd IV was assassinated, and Bahram placed the dead king's young son, Khosrow II, on the throne, with himself as the real power. Khosrow II was soon forced to flee the country to avoid assassination by Bahram, and the general declared himself king as Bahram VI Chubin. (See BAHRAM VI CHUBIN, KING OF PERSIA; KHOSROW II, KING OF PERSIA.)

HUMBERT I, King　See UMBERTO I, KING OF ITALY.

HUSSEIN AVNI PASHA　See ABDUL-AZIZ, OTTOMAN SULTAN; MIDHAT PASA.

I

INUKAI TSUYOSHI (1855–1932) Of samurai origins, Inukai Tsuyoshi was one of Japan's leading democratic leaders since the turn of the 20th century. He finally became prime minister in 1931. His assassination the following year by hawkish ultranationalists marked the effective end of party participation in the government in the decade preceding World War II.

In 1890 Inukai became a Conservative Party member of the first House of Representatives in the Imperial Diet, and in 1898 became minister of education and formed the Constitutional National Party. In 1913 he started a popular movement that finally ousted the autocratic and unpopular government of ex-army general Katsura Taro. Thereafter Inukai opposed most militarist policies of the ultranationalists. Becoming prime minister in late 1931, Inukai faced an army that claimed the right of autonomous command in occupying the Chinese provinces of Manchuria. Inukai strove to prevent the military from usurping the policy-making functions of the cabinet and even prepared to send a representative to China to halt any further military activities.

Inukai's efforts infuriated the armed forces, and on May 15, 1932, nine young naval officers invaded the prime minister's home and shot him in the stomach and neck. It was clear that Inukai's killers sought to give more power to the military, and that direction was set thereafter. Inukai's assassins were caught, tried and convicted, but did not serve any prison terms.

ITO HIROBUMI, Prince of Japan (1841–1909) Prince Ito Hirobumi, a Japanese elder statesman who served as premier four times from 1885 to 1901, was one of the architects of modern Japan. A protege of such important Japanese political figures as Kido Takayoshi and Okubo Toshimichi, Ito succeeded Okubo, the most important man in the government, as minister of home affairs when the latter was assassinated in 1878. Ito framed the country's new constitution and led the Sino–Japanese War of 1894–5. He also played a key role in the Russo–Japanese War of 1904–5 and thereafter helped consolidate Japanese influence in Korea and Manchuria.

Unlike many other strong-willed leaders of Japan in this period, Ito was a compromiser, and his efforts frequently kept opposing factions in relative harmony. Ito's style as resident general in Korea, however, proved a failure, as he was unsuccessful in gaining the trust of the Koreans, even though his rule was by most standards sympathetic and moderate. But the political forces in Japan were against him, and those who favored annexing Korea gained the upper hand against Ito's less imperialist efforts.

In October 1909 Ito was on a visit to Harbin in North China when he was shot to death by An Chung-gun, an activist in the Korean independence movement. Realizing he was the victim of a political assassination, Ito exclaimed, as he was dying: '*Baka na yatsu ja!*' – 'He is a fool!' All the Korean resistance had accomplished was the removal of the one Japanese official who advocated an evenhanded Korean policy.

J

JACKSON, Andrew (1767–1845) – Attempted Assassination   On January 30, 1835, Richard Lawrence, a house painter, became the first man to attempt a kill a president of the United States, Andrew Jackson. Lawrence attacked Jackson on the rotunda of the Capitol after the president had just attended funeral services for Warren R. Davis, a South Carolina congressman. Lawrence had patiently waited behind a pillar on the east portico for Jackson to appear, and when the president did so, he pulled out a pistol and pulled the trigger with Jackson no more than eight feet away. The pistol misfired, only the cap exploding noisily. Startled a moment but feeling no pain, Jackson rushed at his assailant, cane upraised. Lawrence produced a second pistol and once more pulled the trigger. Incredibly, the result was the same. Apparently in both cases the powder and lead balls with which the pistols had been loaded had fallen out in Lawrence's pockets. Clearly, as an assassin, Lawrence was a much better house painter.

President Jackson, however, took Lawrence very seriously. Held back by a number of onlookers while others wrestled Lawrence to the ground, Jackson flailed his cane shouting, 'Let me alone! Let me alone! I know where this came from.'

To his dying day Jackson would remain convinced Lawrence was but a small cog in an intricate Whig conspiracy to assassinate him. His political foes would by contrast insist it had all been a ruse managed by Jackson himself to gain public sympathy. Almost certainly neither theory was accurate, but the claims and counterclaims established early in American history that presidential assassination, successful or otherwise, would frequently be forced into a grand conspiracy mosaic, with or without confirming facts.

Independent authorities soon readily accepted the opinion that Lawrence was mentally afflicted, in a way that would today be diagnosed as paranoid schizophrenia. Born in England in 1800 or 1801, Lawrence came to the United States with his family when he was about 12 years old. He was described later by relatives and acquaintances as 'a remarkably fine boy' and one 'reserved in his manner, but industrious and of good moral habits.' If that were so, by his thirties he did exhibit some strange peccadilloes. He was subject to fits of rage and wild laughter, making claims that the United States owed him money for confiscating his property in 1802 – when he was a babe in England. He saw threats in many, and he made threats to others, warning, 'I will put a ball through your head.' He particularly saw Jackson as an enemy, presumably one who disputed his claim to being the rightful heir to the English throne.

At his trial after the attempted assassination, Lawrence really looked down his nose at the jury, declaring, 'It is for me, gentlemen, to pass upon you, and not you upon me.'

The evidence of his bizarre past and present behavior was so overwhelming that the jury readily concluded, with even the prosecutor, national anthem composer Francis Scott Key, in agreement, that Lawrence was not criminally responsible for his act. On his acquittal, Lawrence was confined for the rest of his life to mental hospitals, where he died in June 1861.

While it has become common for some authorities and many popular writers habitually to refer to all successful or unsuccessful assassins of American presidents as 'madmen,' the description most readily fitted Lawrence. It should be noted, however, that the madman defense has worked for would-be assassins, but never for a successful one who has been convicted and sentenced to death.

Further reading: *American Assassins: The Darker Side*

of Politics, by James W. Clarke; *Assassination in America*, by James McKinley.

JAMES, Jesse (1847–1882) Jesse James was an outlaw. There was no question of that. And when he was killed, shot in the back for the reward money, public opinion thought otherwise, calling it an assassination. In fact, the killing of Jesse James did have a profound effect on politics and actually destroyed the promising political career of Missouri Governor Thomas T. Crittenden.

Crittenden was governor of Missouri during the final years of the James gang's reign. He clearly conspired with the Ford brothers, Bob and Charles, to murder the notorious outlaw. By 1882 the James gang was in disarray, most of its original members dead or imprisoned, and Jesse and Frank James were forced to rely on criminals they considered untrustworthy, among them Dick Little and the Ford brothers. Since late 1881 Little was secretly negotiating to surrender, and either through him or others the Fords had begun dickering with Crittenden about the $10,000 reward offered for Jesse James, dead or alive. They eventually met with Crittenden, and it later became common belief that the governor actually gave them a written guarantee that they would be pardoned and get the reward if they killed James. No such document was ever found, but when on April 3, 1882, Bob Ford shot Jesse in the back – in Jesse's home on the outskirts of St. Joseph, where he lived under the name of Howard – Crittenden did grant the Fords pardons and the reward.

Crittenden expected to win accolades and political rewards himself for ridding Missouri of Jesse James. He certainly was not ready for the maudlin support given the murdered outlaw. 'GOODBYE JESSE!' sobbed the *Kansas City Journal*. 'JESSE BY JEHOVAH,' mourned the *St. Joseph Gazette*. Clearly having failed to accurately gauge public reaction, the governor proceeded to shoot himself in the foot by his pronouncements to the *St. Louis Republican*: 'I have no excuse to make, no apologies to render to any living man for the part I have played in this bloody drama . . . I am not regretful of his death and have no censure for the boys who removed him. They deserve credit, in my candid, solemn opinion. Why should these boys be so abused?' And abused they were. Charley Ford was denounced as having one of 'the blackest hearts in Creation,' and when he was found dead in a Richmond, Missouri hotel room in 1884, it was labeled a suicide by the coroner and an act of remorse by the press and public. As for Bob Ford, he was immortalized in ballad folklore as the 'dirty rotten coward who shot Mr. Howard.' In 1892 he was shot to death in a saloon and gambling tent he was running in Creede, Colorado by a man named Edward O'Kelly, who was very distant kin to Jesse James. There was some speculation that O'Kelly did it to avenge Jesse, but it was far more likely he had been paid by a Ford business rival. O'Kelly was sentenced to 20 years, but apparently there was no way that the killer of Jesse James's assassin would have to do that kind of time, and he was pardoned after just two years.

Governor Crittenden's political life didn't survive Jesse James's murder. When shortly after Jesse's death Frank James strutted into the Governor's office, unstrapped his guns and declared it was the first time he had done that since his days riding with Quantrill in the Civil War, the governor probably had an inkling that things had gone wrong. Mobs cheered Frank James as he stood on train platforms on his way back to trial in Clay County. Crittenden was booed.

Crittenden's political plans had been simple: Win another term as governor and then pick up the mantle of the illustrious George Vest in the U.S. Senate. After that the White House would not be far beyond reach? However, the Missouri 'James vote' was strong enough that his Crittenden's party refused to renominate him for governor, and his political career was in shambles. Assassination – real or perceived – simply was not a good platform in 19th-century America.

Further reading: *Pictorial History of the Wild West*, by James D. Horan and Paul Sann.

JAMES I, King of England (1566–1625) – Attempted Assassination Guy Fawkes Day (November 5) is one of England's most raucous holidays, including fireworks, masked children begging for pennies, and the burning of 'guys,' little effigies of one of the nation's most infamous conspirators.

Fawkes was a participant in the 1605 'Gunpowder Plot,' aimed at blowing up the English Houses of Parliament while King James I and his top ministers were present. Fawkes, from a prominent Yorkshire family, had converted to Roman Catholicism and was, like his coconspirators, angered by the increasing oppression of Roman Catholics in England.

Fawkes had left England in 1593 to fight with the Spanish in the Protestant Netherlands, and he gained a considerable reputation as a brave and resourceful soldier. In 1604 a small group of Catholic plotters under Robert Catesby concocted the plan to destroy Parliament and, in need of a military man to carry it out, enlisted Fawkes through emissaries sent to the Netherlands.

Together with other conspirators disguised as coal men, Fawkes smuggled 36 barrels of gunpowder into the cellars beneath the Parliament chambers. Unknown to Fawkes, however, one of the other conspirators decided to send an anonymous letter to Lord Monteagle, a Catholic peer, to stay away from the opening of Parliament set for November 5: 'Retire to the country, for though there may be no appearance of any stir, yet I say they shall receive a terrible blow this Parliament, yet shall they not see who hurt them.'

Monteagle did not obey the warning but instead informed the authorities. A search of Parliament turned up nothing untoward, but, dissatisfied, Monteagle decided to make a further personal search. Shortly before midnight on November 4, Fawkes was apprehended in the cellar. He insisted he was merely a servant looking for his master, but Monteagle noticed that the coal and faggot pile seemed out of proportion. The gunpowder barrels were uncovered.

Fawkes was subjected to brutal tortures under the direct orders of James I: 'The gentler tortours are to be first usid unto him, *et sic per gradus ad ima tenditur* [and by degrees into hell].' Only after enduring extreme agony on the rack did Fawkes make a confession and name his accomplices.

Found guilty by a special commission, Guy Fawkes was hanged, drawn and quartered in front of the Parliament building on January 31, 1606.

JAMES I, King of Scotland (1394–1437) The son of Robert III, the future James I of Scotland was sent to France when he was 12 to keep him out of the reach of the king's brother, the powerful and cunning Robert Stuart, the duke of Albany. However, James was captured by the English and kept in genteel imprisonment until after the Scots signed the Perpetual Peace in 1423, renouncing all future cooperation with France. During James's captivity, Albany served as regent, Robert III having died soon after the boy's seizure. Albany had no inclination to ransom James and ruled until his own death in 1420, when the regency passed to his son Murdac.

In 1424 young James was ransomed by a group of Scottish nobles and restored to the throne. James I proved to be an energetic if vindictive ruler. He pursued harsh measures to weaken the power and independence of the Scottish nobility. He arrested a number of nobles and executed several, including Murdac and other members of his family. The quick-tempered James was capable of violence, but he also had a more genteel side, for instance, writing allegorical poems of surprising merit. He won popular support by demonstrating his superb abilities as a rider, runner, wrestler, archer, spearman, craftsman and musician. He eliminated graft in great measure, penalizing dishonest trade and negligent husbandry. He improved the administration of justice for the common people, built hospitals, cut drunkenness by closing taverns at 9 P.M., demanded ecclesiastical discipline and sought to keep revenues from being sent to the pope in Rome.

James raised monies needed for his administration by confiscating the estates of his enemies. He sought to lessen the power of the highland lords as well and called to the Parliament the lairds – the owners of lesser estates – thus establishing them as a middle-class counter to the clergy and the nobles. Despite his general popularity, a group of conspirators thought they could provoke a general uprising by assassinating the king. The deed was carried out by a group of nobles headed by Walter, earl of Atholl, who sought the crown for himself. Walter garnered no mass support after the murder, and the king's widow ordered the conspirators brought to justice and executed. The king's only surviving son, James II, became monarch at the age of 6.

Further reading: *James I, King of Scots*, by E.W.M. Balfour-Melville.

JAMES III, King of Scotland (1452–1488) A weak monarch, James III of Scotland 'paid the penalty,' according to Will Durant in *The Story of Civilization*, 'of his father's lawlessness.' James II had earned the enmity of many Scottish nobles for his harsh and often devious treatment. James II's assassination by his own hand of William, earl of Douglas, in 1452 after granting him 'safe conduct' was an example of the throne's deceit. As a result, James III was forced, after a long minority, to fight many ferocious battles with noble clans, and, unlike James I and James II, he proved unable to restore strong central government. More interested in the arts than the martial arts, James III offended many of his nobles by taking artists as his favorites.

In 1479 James III arrested his brothers, Alexander, duke of Albany, and John, earl of Mar, on suspicion of treason. Albany escaped to England and returned in 1482 with English troops and regained his domain. During the conflict, rankled Scottish nobles took the opportunity to hang James's court favorites.

The following year, however, James drove Albany out once again. But he was beset by a number of other revolts, and two great border families, the Hepburns and the Homes, reached a secret agreement with the king's 15-year-old son to remove the monarch. The defeated James III was captured after the Battle of Sauchieburn on June 11, 1488, and was summarily murdered. His son, James IV, succeeded to the throne. (See DOUGLAS, WILLIAM, EIGHTH EARL OF.)

JAURES, Jean Leon (1859–1914)   French socialist leader and historian Jean Leon Jaures was before his assassination regarded as the most articulate and respected socialist in his country before World War I. Already an accomplished writer before entering the chamber of deputies at the age of 25, Jaures was defeated for reelection and returned to teaching and writing, authoring a number of philosophical tracts. He returned as a deputy in 1893, and 11 years later became a founder and editor of *L'Humanite*.

Seeing what he regarded as clear preparations for war, Jaures condemned a military buildup and advocated arbitration to settle growing disputes between France and Germany. On July 31, 1914, Jaures was dining in a cafe in Paris when he was assassinated by a right-wing patriot, Raoul Villain. The assassination removed a leading voice for peace from the political scene. Twenty-two years later leftists finally avenged Jaures's assassination by killing Villain in Spain.

JOHN PAUL I, Pope (1912–1978) – Alleged Assassination
At 10 P.M. on September 28, 1978, the newly elected Pope John Paul I retired in his Vatican apartment in the Apostolic Palace. He did not appear for morning mass, and at 5:30 A.M. an aide entered the pope's private chambers. The light was burning and a book, *The Imitation of Christ* by Thomas a Kempis, was open beside him. The pope was dead.

Three doctors examined the body and certified that death had occurred about 11 P.M. due to cardiac arrest. He had been in office only 33 days, the shortest reign as pope since Leo XI ruled for only 18 days in 1605. Immediately there were rumors that the Pope had been murdered, presumably poisoned. Although never proven, the rumors have never been completely stilled.

In 1984 a controversial book, *In God's Name: An Investigation into the Murder of Pope John Paul I* by David A. Yallop was published in the United States and five other countries. It charged that several persons had strong motives to kill the pope. The author specifically identified Licio Gelli, the fugitive grandmaster of the outlawed Italian masonic lodge Propaganda Due, as being 'at the heart of the conspiracy' to commit murder.

The Vatican flatly rejected the thesis of the book, but conspiracy theorists continued to cling to the murder theory and argued that without active support by Vatican officials for an investigation, a coverup would result. The fact remained that *In God's Name* had little impact other than on the already convinced. It should be noted that long reigns have always been rarer than short reigns in papal history, since spiritual leaders were generally elected late in life.

JOHN PAUL II, Pope (1920–) – Attempted Assassination
On May 13, 1981, Pope John Paul II was being driven though the great piazza in front of St. Peter's Basilica when 23-year-old Mehmet Ali Agca opened fire, hitting the pope twice, as well as two onlookers. John Paul II was badly wounded, underwent surgery and finally recovered. Ali Agca was convicted of attempted murder and sentenced to life imprisonment.

That hardly marked the end of the case. At first it was generally accepted that Agca was an Islamic fanatic who viewed the pope as 'the Commander of the Crusaders,' the foe of Islam. However, charges soon surfaced that there might be a rather more startling secular motivation behind Agca's crime. In an article in the September 1982 issue of *Reader's Digest*, longtime American foreign correspondent Claire Sterling charged that Agca was a tool of the Communists, and that Agca had been manipulated by the Bulgarian state-security police (DS), acting on orders of the Russian KGB.

There were many observers, as well as the Italian government, who agreed with her thesis, which is stated in a book Sterling wrote on the case, *The Time of the Assassins*. She says: 'What was seen, photographed and reported worldwide from St. Peter's Square – the instant image of the gunman, the conspicuous rightwing tracks he'd laid from Istanbul straight across Europe – led to the seemingly inescapable conclusion that this was a right-wing terrorist hit. In reality, it was not a terrorist hit at all, rightist or leftist, however artfully it was mounted to make it seem so. The now familiar pattern of international terrorism was merely used to camouflage an old-fashioned state-planned assassination, using secret police to elimi-nate a public figure regarded as an intolerable threat to that state's security.'

However, there were many observers who did not subscribe to the Sterling thesis, including, in large mea-sure, the intelligence operatives of the CIA. These experts had been unimpressed with many of Sterling's previous charges against the Soviet Union, including those in her book *The Terror Network* and an adaptation of it that appeared in *The New York Times Magazine*, highlighting her claim of Soviet involvement in international terrorism. Sterling posited a 'Guerrilla International,' with Cubans, KGB instructors, Palestinians and Red Brigades inter-twined in the plots, holding secret meetings at a number of training camps. Sterling made three case studies of Turkish terrorists, the IRA in Northern Ireland, and the Italian Red Brigades and tied them all directly to the KGB.

Langley's experts did not buy the story. As Bob Wood-ward noted in his book *Veil: The Secret Wars of the CIA 1981–1987*: 'The covert operators argued that Sterling's method was preposterous. Her verdict followed from flawed reasoning – a kind of McCarthyist "linkmanship." In her three case studies, Turkey, Northern Ireland and Italy became, by some leap of logic, "target nations" of the Soviets. In each section, the KGB was mentioned once.'

There was also an ironic twist to the story. It turned out that some of the material about the Red Brigades used by Sterling was from an Italian press story actually planted by the CIA in a covert propaganda operation. Within the CIA in that period the one Sterling supporter was the director, William Casey. He upbraided his staff with demands that they 'read Claire Sterling's book. . . . I paid $13.95 for this and it told me more than you bastards whom I pay $50,000 a year.' In time, though, Casey accepted the less enthusiastic evaluation of Sterling. On the matter of the attempted assassination of Pope John Paul II, Casey was at first inclined to agree with Sterling, but here too he later switched.

The Italian government did not switch. Although Agca had already been convicted for attempted murder, he was retried along with three Turks, mostly with right-wing affiliations, and three Bulgarians, regarded as the key connections to Bulgarian intelligence. One, Sergei I. Antonov, was a minor functionary with the Bulgarian national airline and travel office, and the others were service officers with the embassy in Rome. Of the three only Antonov was present for trial, the others having hurriedly left for Sofia, where they were safe from extradition.

The trial itself was a shambles, with Agca interrupting the proceedings with frequent outbursts, with declarations such as, 'I am Jesus Christ. In the name of the omnipotent God, I announce the end of the world. No one, neither the Americans nor the Soviets, will be saved. There will be destruction.' More important, Agca frequently altered his testimony. Almost in desperation, the prosecutor had to defend Agca by saying, 'I do not believe he's crazy. When he begins to talk about facts, he is extremely reliable.'

The court could hardly find so, and only Agca himself and one of the Turks were found guilty of just smuggling the assassination weapon into Italy. Even the prosecutor,

Antonio Marini, had called for acquittals of the three Bulgarians, the heart of the conspiracy case.

Quite naturally the Soviet Union and Bulgaria hailed the verdict. The Soviet press agency, Tass, said, 'The so-called Bulgarian connection charge crumbled to nothing.' The Bulgarians insisted the idea of Bulgarian involvement 'existed solely in the writings of professional anticommunists, disinformants, political provocateurs and experts in subversion and psychological warfare.'

The verdict was not that clear-cut. Under Italian law, the ruling 'lack of proof' implied that the evidence in the case was too ambiguous to allow a simple verdict of guilt or innocence. For most this meant the case would likely remain unresolved. Certainly though, the Sterling thesis was unproved. With the upheavals of 1989 in Eastern Europe, reformers in several countries took custody of probably billions of secret documents. It was possible that an opening of files in Sofia could shed light on any possible Bulgarian and Soviet involvement in the John Paul II assassination attempt.

Further reading: *The Time of the Assassins*, by Claire Sterling; *Veil: The Secret Wars of the CIA 1981–1987*, by Bob Woodward.

JOHN THE FEARLESS, Second Duke of Burgundy (1371–1419) To many students of French history, John the Fearless comes down as a villain, traitor and assassin. Under him, the importance of ducal Burgundy loomed even larger than during the 41-year reign of his father, Philip the Bold. John was a master of constructing webs of alliances and intrigues to make Burgundy preeminent over France and the duke of Burgundy more important than the king of France himself, who at the time was the deranged Charles VI. To fill the vacuum Charles's younger brother, Louis, duke of Orleans, sought to protect the monarchy first against Philip the Bold and then against John the Fearless.

In 1407 John the Fearless eliminated Louis's opposition by having his henchmen lure the duke into a fatal ambush in Paris. Afterward, the rivalry against Burgundy was taken up by Bernard VII of Armagnac, whose daughter married Orleans's son. Control of Paris shifted back and forth between the Burgundy and Armagnac parties in a civil war. During this period, while feigning opposition to England, John the Fearless entered into intermittent negotiations with England's Henry V, but never firmed up a true alliance. After being forced out of Paris for a time, John once more took control and held sway over the hapless king, forcing the Dauphin, the future Charles VII, into exile with the Armagnacs.

At this point the ever-devious John the Fearless determined to betray his English friends and opened negotiations with the Dauphin in 1419. The two princes, with 10 companions each, met on the bridge of Montereau, about 50 miles outside Paris. As the parley started, the Armagnacs provoked an almost certainly premeditated dispute, and John the Fearless, too rash for once, was stabbed to death. The Armagnacs had little doubt that had they not struck first, John the Fearless would at some future time have sought thereafter to eliminate the Dauphin.

JOSEPH I, King of Portugal (1715–1777) – Attempted Assassination It has been said that an unsuccessful regicide may well strengthen a ruler. In the case of Joseph I of Portugal it solidified the enormous power of the greatest and most terrible minister who ever governed that country, the marquis of Pombal. In 1755 Pombal, already the favorite of the weak King Joseph I, was engaged in a fierce struggle against powerful elements of the nobility and the Jesuits, whom he saw as encouraging Indian resistance to Portuguese colonial policies in South America. As much as Joseph was under Pombal's influence, it is doubtful that he would have dared go along with his minister's plans to eject the Jesuits from the country had there not been an attempt on the king's life.

On September 3, 1758 two attacks were made on the king's coach as he was returning late at night to the palace from a romantic rendezvous. First, three masked men fired into the coach, but no shots hit the target. The coach continued on and met a second ambush. This time the coachman was wounded, as was the king, who was hit in his right shoulder and arm. Later a court of inquiry assembled by Pombal determined that a third ambush had awaited, this one allegedly manned by members of the Tavora family, bitter opponents of Pombal. However, the king had unwittingly avoided this third and perhaps fatal attack by ordering the coach to leave the main road and drive directly to the house of the royal surgeon.

Now the king was ready to follow Pombal's lead, and the minister used the unsuccessful assassination as a pretext to strike at all his enemies, especially the duke of Aveiro and the House of Tavora. Several members of the Aveiro and Tavora families were arrested, as well as all their servants and a number of other nobles.

On the same day all Jesuit colleges were surrounded by soldiers, and 13 leading Jesuits were incarcerated. Operating under a special royal decree, Pombal was permitted to use torture to elicit confessions, a practice against Portuguese custom. Needless to say, many of the 50 prisoners confessed and implicated others. One Tavora who did not break under torture was the older marquis. Pombal personally took part in the examining of witnesses and prisoners. Guilty verdicts were rammed through even though many of those charged could offer alibis for the night of the attempt, and on January 13, 1759, nine executions were carried out in the public square of Belem. The first to die was the old marchioness of Tavora. She was forced to gaze on the instruments of torture – hammer, wheel and faggots – by which her husband and sons were to die, after which she was beheaded. In a slow procession eight others, including the duke of Aveiro and the Tavoras, were broken on the wheel and finally strangled. Some of the others were burned alive.

With his aristocratic foes disposed of, Pombal turned his attention to the Jesuits, and scores were imprisoned. Fearing a total rupture between Portugal and the papacy, Pope Clement XIII accepted the trial of a number of

Jesuits in secular courts. The pope even appealed to the king for mercy for the Jesuits and said he hoped that all Portuguese Jesuits would not be punished for the errors of a few. The papal appeal fell on deaf ears and on the first anniversary of the attempted assassination, all Jesuits were expelled from the country.

Now Pombal became virtual dictator of the country, and he continued his use of terror by charging still more priests and nobles with that plot, and yet new ones, against the throne. In September 1761 Pombal ordered the Jesuit hero of Brazil, Father Gabriel Malagrida, strangled and burned at the stake on charges that he had been involved in the original conspiracy. It was not a popular act, since the 72-year-old Father Malagrida was by then clearly senile.

Pombal wasn't seeking to destroy the church in Portugal, merely to make it subject to the will of the king – and of himself. In 1770 Pope Clement XIV agreed to allow the state to nominate bishops, and Pombal made peace with the Vatican. The pope even granted a cardinal's hat to Pombal's brother.

However, as Joseph I neared death, Pombal realized that his own power was also nearing an end. When the king died on February 24, 1777, Pombal abruptly fell from grace. Under the new queen, Maria I, political prisoners were freed; Pombal, now 80, was charged with abuse of powers and was subjected to severe interrogation. He pleaded to the queen for mercy, and it was granted since her father's signature appeared on every edict by which Pombal conducted policy. The queen established a new court of inquiry, confirmed the guilt of Aveiro and several of his servants, but cleared the rest of the accused. The House of Tavora was restored to full honors and the property remitted to the survivors.

As for the Jesuits, there was no doubt that as a group they had opposed Pombal's policy. Father Malagrida and some others had predicted the fall of Pombal and the early death of the king, and several Jesuits had often conferred with the minister's aristocratic enemies. However, even unsympathetic historians have concluded that there is no positive evidence against the Jesuits in this matter.

Happily for the queen, who remained under pressure to punish Pombal, the ex-minister died in May 1782. Forty-five years later a passing group of Jesuits visited Pombal's grave and, as one historian put it, 'recited a requiem, in triumph and pity, for the repose of his soul.'

Further reading: *Dictator of Portugal: A Life of the Marquis of Pombal*, by Marcus Cheke.

JUMBLAT, Kamal (1917–1977) While it may be said that political violence has been a hallmark of Lebanese life since the civil strife of the 1970s, few families could match the history of the Jumblat family. In fact, the assassination of the clan's leader, Kamal Jumblat, led as much as any single event to the bloody renewal of the civil war in 1977.

Jumblat's father was assassinated in the political violence of the 1920s, and his sister, Linda Atrash, was murdered in Beirut in May 1975. Jumblat himself was the hereditary chief of the Jumblatist Druse clan and ruled the group since 1940. Later he was elected to the Lebanese parliament and founded the Progressive Socialist Party. Jumblat exercised considerable political power and made and unmade a number of Lebanese presidents. While he was accorded the Lenin Peace Prize in 1973 and was a socialist friendly to the Soviet Union, he could not be considered a Communist, and the Russians were unable to count on his support for their position in Lebanon.

On March 16 the Muslim leader was assassinated by machine-gunners outside the mountain village of Baaklin, about 18 miles from Beirut. Also killed were his bodyguard and driver. It was assumed that Jumblat's killers were Christians, and in the three-day period from March 16 to March 18 more than 200 Christians were murdered by Muslims in retaliation.

K

KAHANE, Rabbi Meir (1932–1990) On November 5, 1990, Rabbi Meir Kahane, the extremist founder of the Jewish Defense League in the United States and the anti-Arab Kach party in Israel, had just concluded a speech to about 70 people in the conference room of a midtown New York hotel when he was shot. In the speech Kahane expounded on his program to 'transfer' or expel Arabs from Israel and the occupied territories. As Kahane finished talking, he was shot in the neck by a fatal bullet which then exited through his cheek.

Arrested and charged with the crime was 34-year-old El Sayyid A. Nosair, an Egyptian immigrant who had become a U.S. citizen in 1989 and worked for a city agency. According to the police, the gunman shot and wounded an elderly bystander as he fled the room and on the street commandeered a cab at gunpoint. About a block further the gunman jumped out of the cab and was confronted by an on-duty U.S. Postal Service policeman, Carlos Acosta. Police said the gunman fired a shot which was deflected by the officer's bulletproof vest and wounded the officer in the arm. Acosta returned the fire and his bullet struck Nosair in the neck and lodged in his chin.

Nosair was hospitalized in a serious condition. On November 20 Nosair was charged with second-degree murder, second-degree attempted murder, aggravated assault of a police officer, second-degree assault, three counts of criminal possession of a weapon, reckless endangerment and coercion. Meanwhile, federal officials warned six prominent New York City Jews that their names appeared on a list kept by Nosair, a devout

Moslem. However, authorities could find no ties to Palestinian groups or international terrorism.

As it developed, authorities were in for a rough time trying to tie Nosair to the assassination, despite what they regarded as an overwhelming case. On December 21, 1991 Nosair was acquitted of the most serious charges against him – the murder of Kahane and the shooting of the post office policeman, Acosta. He was convicted only of gun possession, assault on a police officer, assault on the man who had tried to prevent him from fleeing the meeting room and coercion for ordering a taxi driver to run a red light in order to get him away from the scene.

After the verdict, a juror and an alternate juror told the press that they felt the prosecution had not provided sufficient evidence to prove that Nosair had shot Kahane, and that no one testified to having seen him do so. (One witness testified to seeing Nosair pointing a gun at Kahane moments after the shooting.) The jurors also said the state had failed to prove that the gun found in the street near Nosair was the one that had been used to kill Kahane.

For the defense, noted attorney William M. Kunstler had claimed that Kahane had been killed by a dissident member of the JDL in a financial dispute. But after the verdict several newspaper accounts noted that Kunstler seemed rather stunned that he had basically won his case.

KAHR, Gustav von (?–1934) Gustav von Kahr, general commissioner of the state of Bavaria during Adolf Hitler's rise to power, in 1923 played a fatal role – for himself in due course – in the bizarre event known as the Beer Hall Putsch. Even when threatened, along with two others, at pistol point by Hitler personally, von Kahr refused to join the putsch until he was awed by the presence of General Erich Ludendorff and finally agreed. However, a short time later, with Hitler absent, von Kahr regained his nerve, escaped the plotters and suppressed the Munich putsch. Hitler never forgot this betrayal.

When Hitler embarked on his purge of the Brownshirts

under the notorious Ernst Roehm in 1934 ('the Night of the Long Knives'), he decided it was the perfect time to even old scores as well. Von Kahr was long retired from politics, but this did not save him from disappearing during the reign of terror. His mutilated body was found later in a swamp near Dachau. He had apparently been pickaxed to death.

Further reading: *The Rise and Fall of the Third Reich*, by William L. Shirer.

KARAMI, Rashid See MOAWAD, RENE.

KARUME, Sheik Abeid Amani (1926–1972) Sheik Abeid Amani Karume, vice president of Tanzania and chairman of the governing Revolutionary Council, was mortally wounded on April 7, 1972, when four assassins broke into the headquarters of the Afro-Shirazi Party, where Karume was playing cards with political allies. Karume had seized power in Zanzibar in a violent coup in 1964 and then joined his island nation with mainland Tanganyika to form the union of Tanzania. However, Karume continued to maintain an ironfisted socialist-oriented rule over Zanzibar.

In the assassination, Karume's bodyguards shot and killed one of the attackers, who were described as three black Africans and an Arab, but the others escaped temporarily. One assassin later killed himself in the Stone House area of Zanzibar town when his capture was imminent, and security forces cornered and shot to death the remaining pair at Bumbwini, 16 miles away.

With all the assassins dead there was no certain way to explain the motivation behind the deed. In any event, Julius K. Nyere, the president of Tanzania, appointed a successor to Karume, who maintained the Karume's political and economic policies.

KATKOV, Arkady (?–1985) In the first known incident in which Soviet citizens were abducted in Lebanon, three Soviet diplomats and a doctor were kidnapped September

30, 1985, in West Beirut by a group of Sunni Muslims. The abducted men were identified as Oleg Spirin and Valery Mirkov, both embassy attaches; Arkady Katkov, a consular secretary; and Dr. Nikolai Svirsky, the embassy physician.

The day after the kidnapping a communique was issued by a previously unknown group called the Islamic Liberation Organization (ILO) who claimed responsibility for the abduction. The communique was accompanied by photographs of the four Soviets with pistols held to their heads. On October 2, the body of Katkov was discovered after a telephone tip in an empty West Beirut lot. He had been shot in the head at close range.

The caller said the ILO had executed the Russian and intended to execute the rest of the hostages 'one after another if the atheistic campaign against Islamic Tripoli does not stop.' At the time Syria was engaged in a bloody military offensive against the Islamic fundamentalist Tawheed militia in Tripoli.

Immediately after the kidnappings the Soviet Union had labeled the acts a 'heinous crime' by 'bandits' from an 'arch-reactionary ultra-right-wing organization.' Some of the blame was also heaped on Israel, who the Russians said had incited strife in Lebanon. After Katkov's body was found the Russians warned it was 'an atrocity that cannot be pardoned.' The Soviet government exerted massive pressure throughout the Middle East, and especially on Syria, to win the freedom of the hostages.

On October 30, one month after the abductions, the captive trio was released unharmed and dropped off a few blocks from their embassy. The trio said they had been blindfolded and incommunicado the entire 30 days and had been unaware that their colleague had been executed. The ILO described the release as a gesture of 'goodwill.' Other Lebanese sources said the Sunni extremists had realized the search net was closing in on them.

Sometime later a London newspaper, the *Daily Mail*, citing intelligence sources from an unidentified country (thought to be the CIA), published a report that agents of the KGB had abducted 12 Muslim extremists and killed one of them in retaliation for the slaying of the Soviet hostage, and then had threatened to kill the rest of the extremists, including a brother of one of the Sunni kidnappers, one at a time unless the surviving trio was freed.

KENNEDY, Caroline See FRASER, HUGH.

KENNEDY, John F. (1917–1963) Without doubt the most publicized assassination of the 20th century, with a profound impact on public opinion throughout the world, was that of U.S. President John F. Kennedy. Kennedy was shot to death in Dallas, Texas, at 12:30 P.M., on November 22, 1963, with a rifle belonging to Lee Harvey Oswald. Oswald was an employee of the Texas School Book Depository, and as such he had access to a sixth-floor window that provided a perfect vantage for the sniping. As the motorcade passed, Oswald fired two or three times (according to differing scenarios), killing Kennedy and seriously wounding Texas Governor John B. Connally, who was sitting directly in front of the president in the executive limousine.

Of the event a story by Philip Shenon in the *New York Times* in 1988 stated: 'A quarter-century after gunshots echoed across Dealey Plaza in Dallas and left the President mortally wounded, investigators, scientists and the public seem no closer to a consensus about the circumstances of John F. Kennedy's assassination.

'For many students of the events of Nov. 22, 1963, all that really seems clear is their ignorance. They know they may never understand exactly what happened that day, or why.'

However, many other observers do not share that ambivalence about the facts; they believe that Oswald was a disturbed assassin acting alone. They tend to accept in large measure the findings of the Warren Commission, set up after Kennedy's assassination, and especially the reconstruction of events, including the commission's declaration that a single bullet hit both Kennedy and Connally.

After the shooting Oswald concealed his rifle among some crates and casually departed the building. He went home, secured a pistol and went out again. When stopped by Dallas policeman J. D. Tippit, Oswald shot the officer four times, killing him. He took refuge in a movie house without purchasing a ticket and was apprehended there by police officers. When approached by police, he attempted to resist by pointing his gun at them, but it misfired.

Oswald consistently denied having killed either the president or Tippit, although several witnesses identified him as Tippit's killer and his palm print was found on the weapon used to kill Kennedy.

Investigation of Oswald's background produced a picture of a misfit and an apparent on-again, off-again believer in communism. He had received a hardship discharge from the Marines in 1959 because of an injury his mother had suffered, but he did not stay home long to help her. Instead, he traveled to the Soviet Union, where he attempted to give up his American citizenship. When he was notified that his visa would expire and that he had to leave Moscow in two hours, Oswald responded with an apparent suicide attempt. He was finally allowed to remain in the country, got a job and met a Russian woman, Marina, whom he married after a short courtship. After two and a half years Oswald tired of the drabness of Soviet life and decided to move back to America with his wife and young daughter. He secured a loan from the U.S. State Department and returned to New Orleans, where he appeared to have divided his political affiliations among such diverse groups as the right-wing China Lobby, the left-wing Fair Play for Cuba, the Communist Party and that organization's hated foe, the Trotskyite Socialist Workers Party. He also had links with persons who were known conduits for arms and money from the CIA to counterinsurgency forces. Thus Oswald could have been a Soviet agent, a CIA agent or plant, or just a kook.

Oswald was to offer no answers as to why he had killed Kennedy. Two days after his apprehension he was shot to death by Jack Ruby, a Dallas nightclub operator, as police were transferring him to the county jail. The murder was recorded live on television, as the media covered Oswald's movements. That such a valuable prisoner could be so easily assassinated was shocking and led to a bitter denunciation of Dallas law-enforcement officials. In fact, over time many observers found it impossible to believe that the Dallas police could have been so inept and concluded that they had been involved either in the assassination itself or in a subsequent cover-up. Almost immediately a number of conspiracy theorists, or 'assass-inologists,' as some prefer to call themselves, found what they regarded as evidence of a second gunman – a film of the assassination made by Abraham Zapruder on his home movie camera.

According to their analysis it was not possible for Kennedy and Governor Connally to have been hit by separate bullets fired from the book depository because Oswald could not have fired the rifle fast enough. The Warren Commission had under the circumstances con-cluded that the bullet that had hit Kennedy in the neck had also struck Connally. Some could not accept this theory, claiming the bullet's path could not have permit-ted this. Connally himself agreed, insisting he was hit by a separate bullet. (In that regard some seasoned crime authorities and reporters took little stock in Connally's statement, regarding a victim's recollections in such a traumatic event to be the least reliable. For instance, when Leon Trotsky was fatally struck from behind by an ice ax wielded by a Kremlin assassin, he staggered from his study and gasped to colleagues: 'Jacson shot me with a revolver. . . .')

Still Connally's view assisted the conspiracy theorists' claim that a second gunman had fired at the presidential limousine from 'the grassy knoll,' an area ahead of and to the right of the president's motorcade on Elm Street; Oswald was on the right, but behind the motorcade.

All this led to a torrent of theories as to who Oswald's accomplices or 'masters' were. Some said the conspiracy was run by the KGB, others by pro-Castro agents; by anti-Castro agents; by supporters of Teamsters Union head Jimmy Hoffa, who hated Attorney General Robert F. Kennedy and determined that the removal of John Kennedy would strip the president's brother of his power to prosecute them; by the Mafia – with or without the support of the Hoffa forces – by right-wing extremists typified by conservative oilman H. L. Hunt; by the CIA; by the FBI; and by varying combinations of some or most of the above.

Some assassinologists were so convinced of a web of conspiracy that they claimed that between the time of the shipping of Kennedy's body from Dallas and its arrival in the autopsy room in Washington, members of the conspiracy managed to remove the body from the casket and surgically alter the wounds so they appeared to have come from the back instead of the front, while at the same time other conspirators planted a bullet from Oswald's rifle near Governor Connally's stretcher in Parkland Memorial Hospital back in Dallas.

By the mid-1970s the steady drumbeat of criticism of the Warren Commission led to the establishment of the House Select Committee on Assassinations, headed (after a long period of internal dissension) by Ohio Democrat Louis Stokes. The committee's mandate was to reinvestigate not only the presidential assassination but that of Martin Luther King, Jr. as well. By this time the country had become increasingly conspiracy conscious and assassinologists were labeling not only those two killings but also that of Robert Kennedy in 1968 as criminal plots burdened with enormous cover-ups.

Although the House panel would eventually issue findings contradicting the Warren Commission, it appeared for much of the time to be confirming that body's basic conclusions. To the chagrin of many conspiracy advocates, the panel agreed that Oswald had killed Tippit and that he had not been framed for that murder. Medical experts confirmed that the bullet that passed through Kennedy's neck also struck Connally and caused all of his wounds. Neutron-activation analysis tests performed on bullet fragments taken from Connally's wrist and the virtually whole bullet that fell off his stretcher corroborated the Warren Commission's single-bullet thesis.

However, the panel also received new evidence not revealed to the Warren probers, namely that the CIA and members of the Mafia were involved in plots to assassinate Cuba's Fidel Castro. This made a field day for the conspiracy theorists: Now the CIA, it was charged, could have been involved in a cover-up to prevent this embarrassing information from becoming public. The Mafia could be involved in a cover-up. Castro could be involved as a suspect acting in revenge. And through Castro the Soviet Union could be involved.

Eventually the panel dismissed any involvement by Castro in the killing and by the CIA in a cover-up. Representative Stokes journeyed to Cuba as part of the committee's investigation and met Castro. 'I asked him directly whether he was involved in the assassination. And he told me, "Listen, I would have to be crazy to kill the president of the United States. They would wipe my little country off the face of the earth." ' Stokes added, 'I believed him, Castro is too intelligent to be involved.'

The committee heard some additional evidence that linked Jack Ruby and Oswald himself to underworld elements, who had some involvement with organized crime. But the panel was prepared to confirm the Warren findings in large measure, having come up with no real evidence to back a conspiracy scenario.

This changed dramatically when only two weeks of the committee's mandate remained. Supposed acoustic evidence from a Dictabelt recording of one of two police radio channels produced indications of gunshots on the tapes that were not audible to the ordinary listener. An acoustic expert claimed to detect the unique oscillating wave patterns indicative of gunshots – and stated a 50–50 possibility that there was a second gunman who fired from the grassy knoll. The panel did not feel this constituted sufficient proof of a conspiracy theory, and work continued on the final report stating no indication of a plot.

Then in the final two-week period two other acoustic experts declared a 95% certainty that the oscillating waves indicated the presence of a second gunman firing from the grassy knoll.

On that basis the majority of the panel switched to a conspiracy theory and declared that although Oswald had shot Kennedy, there had been a second gunman, almost certainly a mob hit man. The report suggested that the most logical culprits in a Mafia conspiracy were Carlos Marcello, the mob boss of New Orleans; Santo Traffi-cante, the top Florida mobster; Jimmy Hoffa; and perhaps others. A minority of the panel dissented in the findings, feeling there had been a rush to judgment on the acoustic evidence. Congressman Robert Edgar bemoaned 'our own limitations of time and familiarity with the science.'

The wisdom of the speedy flip-flop was later put further in doubt by the findings of a new panel that became known as the Committee of Ballistic Acoustics of the National Research Council and was funded by a grant from the National Science Foundation. The panel was chaired by Norman F. Ramsey, Higgins Professor of Physics at Harvard. Also on the panel were Ph.Ds from MIT, the University of California, Columbia and Prince-ton, as well as from research centers of Bell Telephone Laboratories, Xerox, IBM and Trisolar Corporation, and an expert from the Firearms National Laboratory Center of the Department of the Treasury. The experts produced unanimous findings: There was 'no acoustic basis for the claim of a 95% probability of such a shot. The acoustic analyses impulses attributed to gunshots were recorded about one minute after the president had been shot and the motorcade had been instructed to go to the hospital.'

Some of the conspiracy theorists accepted the new evidence, but many continued to dispute the single-bullet theory. In 1987 the Justice Department at last closed its own inquiry, aligning itself behind the Warren Report, a situation that invited further cries of cover-up.

Most new conspiracy claims continue to revolve around the Mafia, a theory backed by G. Robert Blakey, chief counsel to the House panel, in a book, *The Plot to Kill the President*, written with Richard N. Billings, he started immediately after the issuance of the committee's report at the end of 1978. The book appeared before the latest acoustic finding, but Blakey, a law professor at the University of Notre Dame, has continued to hold for the second gunman theory – that this other assassin had fired but missed.

The Mafia theory continued to grow throughout the 1980s culminating in two 1988–89 books: *Contract on America*, by David E. Schiem; and *Mafia Kingfish: Carlos Marcello and the Assassination of John F. Kennedy*, by John H. Davis, a generalist biographer of the Kennedys, the Bouviers and the Guggenheims. Both writers made new and controversial disclosures and enjoyed wide readership. Less attention was paid to James Reston, Jr., whose book *The Great Expectations of John Connally*, published about the same time, resurrected the thesis that Oswald had not been gunning for JFK but rather the governor of Texas in a personal vendetta.

Also in late 1988 David W. Belin, counsel to the Warren Commission, published *Final Disclosure: The Full Truth About the Assassination of President Kennedy*, in which he stated that, despite some minor defects, 'fifty years hence, historians will agree the Warren Commission was right.'

Belin attacks eight authors of other books on the assassination for ignoring crucial facts, for taking quotations out of context and for concocting specious arguments. Though he is quite critical of Blakey of the House panel, he is particularly vehement toward 'assassination sensationalists,' 'the assassination scam' and 'the continuing deception of the American people about what took place.'

It soon becomes apparent to the independent researcher that the conspiracy theorists have not had their work subjected to the withering analyses made of the Warren Report. This would be a monumental task and probably require a Warren-type inquiry of its own. Scheim's work alone bears several thousand footnotes and source references. Of Scheim, a manager of computerized information at the National Institutes of Health, *Time* magazine has said: 'He seems to have amassed every reference ever printed about the JFK assassination figures and mobsters, then woven these threads to fit a Mafia-hit theory.'

Would the Mafia really attempt to murder the president of the United States? One who doesn't think so is informer Jimmy 'the Weasel' Fratianno, who in *The Last Mafioso* says, 'It's against the fucking rules to kill a cop, so now we're going to kill the president.'

Since the establishment of the national syndicate in the early 1930s it has been Mafia policy not to kill police officers, FBI men, prosecutors, high public officials and, for that matter, reporters and writers. (For a striking demonstration of this rule, see SCHULTZ, DUTCH.) When for instance a mafioso in New York killed a police officer he mistook for a criminal rival, the mob immediately ordered him to surrender. Given that . . . kill the *president*?

Thus, if the Mafia killed President Kennedy, it would stand out as the most atypical mob hit of all time. True, the assassinologists offer some intriguing and portentous underworld quotations:

'Kennedy's not going to make it to the [1964] election – he's going to be hit.' – Santo Trafficante, the Tampa Mafia boss, in conversation with an FBI informer.

'You know what they say in Sicily: If you want to kill a dog, you don't cut off the tail, you cut off the head.' – Carlos Marcello, the Mafia boss in New Orleans, to an acquaintance about the same time as the Trafficante statement, explaining why John Kennedy and not Attorney General Robert Kennedy would be killed.

However, it seems unlikely that men of such stature could say such things, not to other mafiosi but to outsiders, if they were meant seriously. In the true Mafia hit, a complete curtain of silence is lowered in advance. Yet here are top bosses blabbing in a way that would call for the death sentence for lower echelon mobsters.

Furthermore, it is argued by crime reporters that despite the claims of assassinologists, neither Trafficante nor Marcello or for that matter even Chicago's Sam Giancana had enough stature in mob circles to pull off such an assassination without the full approval of the Mafia's national commission, which in reality meant the okay of Carlo Gambino, the last Mafia de facto 'boss of bosses.' As a New York crime reporter with well over three decades of experience says, 'It's inconceivable that a cautious don like Gambino would have ever approved such a plan, but if he had, and if he had heard of the indiscretions of Trafficante and Marcello – and he would have – he would have sent a half hundred hit men to New Orleans and Tampa to make sure such errant bosses were never able to utter a wrong word again.'

Similarly, the assassinologists make much of Jack Ruby's frequent use of the telephone in the period before the assassination. They insist that Ruby was a committed mobster and involved in the conspiracy. At hit time, crime reporters know, unsafe phones are never used because they can leave not only a paper trail but a wiretap invitation as well. On the other hand, when they find a dearth of telephone calls, these same conspiracy theorists declare it is because Marcello had aides use telephones that couldn't be traced.

In all the conspiracy theories there is a patsy selected by the conspirators to 'take the fall' and cover up the conspiracy. Thus, Oswald is a patsy, Sirhan Sirhan is a patsy, James Earl Ray is a patsy. And as there are 'doubles' abounding – a double Oswald, a double Ruby, and there is always a 'second gunman.' For JFK there is a gunman on the grassy knoll, for Robert Kennedy there is a second gunman in that fatal hotel pantry in Los Angeles, in Memphis there is a second gunman near the motel where Martin Luther King, Jr. is shot. And even in the early 1930s when Zangara is shooting at either Roosevelt or Mayor Cermak there is a second killer who takes advantage of the scene to blaze away as well. Remarkably, all these second gunmen fire bullets that are never found or identified.

Unless the Mafia theorists can summon vivid new arguments, inevitably attention will refocus on Oswald as a lone, emotionally distressed killer. For example, there is extensive evidence that Oswald attempted to assassinate ultraconservative Major General Edwin Walker by firing through a window of his Dallas home in April 1963. Walker moved at the last moment, and the bullet barely missed. There is the grudging admission by Marina Oswald that her husband had revealed his act to her immediately after it occurred. (She at first concealed her knowledge for fear she'd be prosecuted for failing to reveal it at the time.) Oswald left a note written in Russian that indicated he planned some major act. And Oswald had taken photographs of General Walker's house.

Stalking Walker and then shooting Kennedy, two characters widely separated on the political spectrum, brings Oswald in line with the disturbed assassin Zangara, who by his own admission would have just as likely killed Calvin Coolidge or Herbert Hoover; John W. Hinckley, who first stalked then-President Jimmy Carter and then shot President Ronald Reagan; or Arthur Herman Bremer, who journeyed to Canada after Richard Nixon but was unable to get near enough to him and later shot George Wallace.

What emerges is not Oswald, the man of a thousand plots, but a figure frustrated with the idea that he was a failure and was sexually at odds with his wife, alternately beating her and begging her forgiveness, and in turn being taunted and rejected by her. The night before the assassination Oswald went to bed first, and Marina followed him without speaking to him, although she thought he was awake. The next morning Oswald left before anyone else arose, leaving his wedding ring in a cup on the dresser and $170 in cash in a wallet in a drawer. He was off to kill the president of the United States. It is difficult to dispute Professor James W. Clarke in *American Assassins: The Darker Side of Politics*, in which he describes Oswald as 'a mercurial, anxiety-ridden young man who, the facts suggest, could have been turned away from his deadly assignment with a kind word and loving embrace.'

KENNEDY, Robert F. (1925–1968) On June 5, 1968, almost five years after the assassination of his brother, President John F. Kennedy, Senator Robert Kennedy had reached a moment of personal and political triumph. He had just won the California presidential primary, defeating Senator Eugene McCarthy and becoming the most likely winner of the Democratic nomination.

Kennedy delivered a victory speech in his Los Angeles campaign headquarters in the Ambassador Hotel, and afterward was led by bodyguards through a jubilant crowd on an apparently unplanned route through a service pantry to escape the crush. As Kennedy made for the exit shortly after midnight a 24-year-old Palestinian, Sirhan Bishara Sirhan, approached. He held a Kennedy campaign poster and behind that a .22-caliber eight-shot Iver Johnson pistol. He snarled, 'Kennedy, you son of a bitch.' He fired several shots at Kennedy, two of which hit the target in the armpit and would not have been fatal. A third shot entered the side of Kennedy's head behind the right ear. Kennedy collapsed, mortally wounded, while his assailant was wrestled into submission by the senator's bodyguards, including former athletic stars Rosey Grier and Rafer Johnson. As they did so, Sirhan wildly emptied his weapon into the crowd, wounding a number of bystanders.

Robert Kennedy died at 1:44 the next morning. Sirhan exhibited unrestrained pride for his deed. He joked with his police guards and then somberly spoke of the sorry state of society and the violence that permeated it. He found the acts of the Boston Strangler to be simply terrible. Meanwhile reports started building that more than eight shots had been fired, leading to speculation that Sirhan had not acted alone – that there had to have been a second gunman. Some witnesses insisted that Sirhan had not gotten closer than two or three feet of Kennedy, yet there were powder burns around the fatal wound, indicating a weapon had been placed directly on the victim. A number of explanations were offered for this, ranging from mistaken eyewitness testimony to the possibility that Kennedy's body had been twisted by the impact of the shots and been thrown against Sirhan's gun. As for charges that there were more than eight shots fired, many authorities felt this was easily explained by bullets richocheting around the room, thus creating more bullet tracks than eight bullets would normally allow. In any event no bullets from a second weapon were found.

This hardly limited conspiracy speculators, who in some cases named the alleged 'second gunman': one of the security guards, a man named Thane Eugene Cesar, who according to witnesses, had drawn his gun and fired it. However, Cesar's service revolver was a .38-caliber weapon, prompting some conspiracy theorists to suggest he could have carried a .22-caliber weapon in his sock, drawn and fired that one himself, and then passed it off to a confederate. Cesar, of course, was never charged.

Other suspects were investigated. During Kennedy's speech, Sandy Serrano stepped out onto a hotel balcony to escape the heat and have a smoke. Two men and a young woman in a white polka-dot dress went by her into the building. Later, after the shooting, the trio rushed out, nearly bowling Serrano over. The woman wearing the polka-dot dress shouted, 'We shot him!' Serrano asked whom they had shot, and the woman allegedly replied, 'We shot Kennedy!'

The police in time turned up a woman named Cathy Fulmer, but Serrano failed to identify her as the woman in the polka-dot dress. Some days after Sirhan was convicted of the assassination, Fulmer was found dead in a motel room.

Sirhan freely confessed his act and was sentenced to death, a fate from which he was saved when the Supreme Court abolished capital punishment in 1972. In the streets of Arab cities around the Middle East posters hailed SIRHAN BISHARA SIRHAN, A COMMANDO, NOT AN ASSAS-

SIN, and 'commando sources' said that in shooting
Kennedy, Sirhan was acting on behalf of all dispossessed
Palestinians by striking at a supporter of Israel. Today
Sirhan remains imprisoned, with parole denied thus far.

In the years since the killing, books and movies outlining various conspiracy theories have appeared. Many of
these hold the Mafia responsible for the murder. In a
sense this is entirely logical. Since the basic theory of
Mafia involvement in the death of President Kennedy was
that the mob sought to silence Attorney General Robert
Kennedy by killing his brother and thus effectively ending
his campaign against organized crime, it was almost
incumbent on the Mafia conspiracy advocates to require
that Robert Kennedy be likewise the victim of a Mafia hit
to prevent him from becoming president and resuming the
fight against the mob. However, despite considerable
effort, tying Sirhan to organized crime figures proved
more tenuous than in the case of Jack Ruby and Lee
Harvey Oswald.

Perhaps the most detailed recent effort to tie Sirhan and
the Robert Kennedy killing to the Mafia was made by
John H. Davis, a leading Mafia assassinologist (see
KENNEDY, JOHN F.), in his 1989 book, *Mafia Kingfish*. It
offers an excellent opportunity to gauge Davis's method-
ology and credibility. Davis had stated that New Orleans
crime boss Carlos Marcello was the guiding light behind
the assassination of John Kennedy and offers Marcello for
a logical role in the Los Angeles murder as well. Acting as
the California agent in the plot, according to Davis, is the
notorious racketeer Mickey Cohen. Davis declared Marcello 'had remained on friendly terms with West Coast
mobster Mickey Cohen since the days he and Cohen had
sat together at the witness table during one of the McClel-
lan Committee hearings on organized crime in 1959. That
day both Marcello and Cohen had encountered Robert
Kennedy face-to-face for the first time.' Marcello and
Cohen came to hate Robert Kennedy.

Without attributing any sources Davis goes on to say
that Cohen figured to lose big if Robert Kennedy became

president. 'Kennedy had singled out Cohen for intensive investigation and eventual prosecution back in 1961 but had to abandon his campaign against him after his brother's assassination. Kennedy had been particularly revolted by reports he had received of Cohen's practice of getting his henchmen to sexually compromise movie stars, then blackmailing them. Chances were that President Robert F. Kennedy would have his attorney general make the pursuit of Cohen a top Justice Department priority.' Davis also says, 'By 1968 Cohen had become king of the rackets in Los Angeles, particularly gambling. He controlled the Santa Anita and Del Mar racetracks.'

How does Sirhan Sirhan connect with this kingpin Jewish mobster? 'It was at the Santa Anita track that Robert Kennedy's convicted killer, Sirhan Sirhan, had worked as a groom and exercise boy while piling up debts playing the horses in his spare time.' And further: 'Racetrack gamblers like Mickey Cohen were always on the alert for hard-up gamblers, big and small, who had to cover their debts. They were useful when he had to find someone to do some nasty job. Given Cohen's near-absolute control of the Los Angeles track, and track betting, and his almost daily presence at either Santa Anita or Del Mar, it is not unreasonable to assume that one of his guys at the track might have alerted him to the existence of this Arab exercise boy who had piled up a stack of debts. As a Jew, Cohen might be more aware than most of the possibilities of exploiting the young Palestinian's smoldering hatred of Israel to further his designs.'

A review of the facts of the case seem to make the Cohen–Sirhan conspiracy theory less plausible. In 1956, Sirhan, age 12, came to the United States with most of his family. In 1961 Mickey Cohen was convicted on income tax charges and was sentenced to prison for 15 years. He was sent to the federal penitentiary in Atlanta in 1962.

In 1963 Sirhan graduated from John Muir High School in Pasadena, California. About that time Cohen was sitting in a prison TV room when another convict hit him over the head with a lead pipe. Cohen was in a coma for two weeks. He later was transferred to the federal facility at Springfield, Missouri. He was partially paralyzed and, according to the criminal grapevine, possibly no longer in full possession of his faculties.

Meanwhile Sirhan had entered Pasadena City College but in 1964 was dismissed for poor grades. Since his injury Cohen had his own woes, none of them involving Robert Kennedy, but rather fighting off homosexual advances by a prison guard while he was paralyzed.

After leaving college, Sirhan worked for a time in a gas station and later as a gardener. Late in 1965 he got a job as a stable boy and hot walker at Santa Anita (Cohen's racetrack, according to Davis). It was here apparently, according to Davis, that Cohen became aware of him. In 1966 Sirhan left Santa Anita for a job as an exercise boy at the Granja Vista Del Rio Ranch in Corona, California. His ambition was to become a jockey. About that time Cohen's main ambition was probably to be mobile with the use of a walker.

In 1966 Sirhan took a bad spill from a horse and found his jockey ambitions cut short. In 1967 he filed for workman's compensation. 'In 1968,' Davis says, 'Cohen had become king of the rackets in Los Angeles.' He did at least become mobile by then with his walker, still in prison. In 1968 Sirhan collected $2,000 on his claim, and in March quit his $2-an-hour job at a health food store.

In June Sirhan Sirhan killed Robert Kennedy. Cohen, hardly anymore a major underworld figure at this point was released from prison in 1972 and announced his intention to go straight. In 1974 he attracted attention by campaigning for prison reform and later by stating he had been in touch with people who knew the whereabouts of kidnap victim Patricia Hearst. He published his biography in 1975 and died the following year. He was never accused of assassinating Robert Kennedy.

Thus, the student of the two Kennedy and King assassinations must approach Mafia conspiracy theories with extreme caution. While some conspiracy writers insist

Sirhan was not interested in Arab affairs, the opposite was true, fully reflected by his library card record: He checked out many books on the Middle East. His personal discussions indicated fierce hatred of Jews and Israel. Since Kennedy supported the shipment of more bombers to Israel, Sirhan clearly saw his election as president as the end of hope for the Palestinian Arabs. His mission clearly was to stop Kennedy and thus Israel. (See KENNEDY, JOHN F.)

Further reading: *American Assassins*, by James W. Clarke; *Assassination in America*, by James McKinley.

KHOSROW (OR CHOSROE) II, King of Persia (?–628)
Khosrow II, who ruled Persia from 590 or 591 to 628, took the empire early in his reign to its greatest heights since Xerxes by conquering much Byzantine territory. He also presided over the empire's mighty fall, typified by his demeaning assassination. Assassinations marked much of Khosrow II's career. His father, Hormizd IV, died by such means, carried out by the king's own general, Bahram, and the king's brothers-in-law, Bostam and Bindoe.

Although Khosrow II was the rightful heir to the throne, he was forced to flee by the cunning Bahram, who seized the monarchy for himself as Bahram VI Chubin. Restored to power with Byzantine military support, Khosrow II carried out a reign of vengeance against his father's killers. Key among his victims was his uncle, Bindoe, who had plotted against Hormizd IV but then had used his military acumen to save the fleeing Khosrow II from death at the hands of Bahram. Once Khosrow II solidified his position, he had no more need of Bindoe – Bahram having been forced to seek refuge in Turkistan – and he had his father's brother-in-law killed. Khosrow's revenge was not completed until his agents had also assassinated Bahram.

As a price for his aid, the Greek emperor Maurice secured a promise from Khosrow II that he would cede Armenia back to Byzantium. However, when Phocas usurped the Byzantine throne from Maurice, Khosrow II seized the excuse to hold Armenia and even declare war.

The Persian armies took Dara, Amida, Hierapolis, Edessa, Apamea, Aleppo and Damascus. In 614 Khosrow II sacked Jerusalem, massacring 90,000 Christians. In 616 the Persians took Alexandria and within three years all of Egypt. The Persians also triumphed in much of Asia Minor.

Eventually Khosrow II turned over the warring to his generals and took up his residence in the luxurious palace at Dastagird, devoting his attention to art and love. He attracted architects, sculptors and painters, the last two especially to fashion likenesses of Shirin, a Christian and the fairest and most loved of his 3,000 wives. Khosrow, under Shirin's influence, even permitted the building of many Christian churches and monasteries. Overall, Persia prospered, perhaps as never before.

However, over a decade, the power of Byzantium was restored under Heraclius, who struck at Persia anew. Time after time the Persian forces were defeated. Khosrow II heaped insults on his generals, and so the military joined forces with the Persian nobles to depose Khosrow II and make peace.

Khosrow II was imprisoned and fed only bread and water. He suffered the grief of watching 18 of his sons murdered before his eyes. Then his son Sheroye, a member of the conspiracy against him, personally slew Khosrow and ascended the throne as Kavadh (Qobad) II. (See BAHRAM VI CHUBIN; HORMIZD IV, KING OF PERSIA.)

KING, Martin Luther, Jr. (1929–1968) In April 1968 the Reverend Martin Luther King, Jr., the acknowledged leader of the black civil rights movement in America and an advocate of Gandhian principles of nonviolent resistance, came to Memphis, Tennessee, in support of a strike by the city's sanitation workers. On the evening of April 4 he was on the balcony of his room at the Lorraine Motel when a bullet from a 30.06-caliber rifle struck the right side of his jaw, entered his neck and severed his spinal cord. The force of the bullet ripped his necktie completely from his shirt.

The assassin was quickly identified, although it was some time before he was apprehended. As he was leaving the boarding-house room he had rented because of its view of the motel, he saw a police car and instinctively discarded a bedspread in which he had wrapped the murder weapon and a number of personal belongings, then fled the scene. The recovered possessions were traced to cities as far away as Atlanta and Los Angeles, and their owner was identified as a white man named James Earl Ray, a minor habitual criminal whose previous offenses included stealing a typewriter, robbing a cab driver, stealing money orders and robbing a supermarket. Sentenced to 20 years for that last offense, Ray, after unsuccessful escape attempts in 1960 and 1966, had finally gotten away in April 1967, concealed in a bread truck.

After the murder Ray fled to Canada and the following month to London with a Canadian passport, thus displaying a sophistication in avoiding detection that he had never exhibited before. It is known that he later made a trip to Lisbon, although the purpose of this was never established. He was finally captured at London's Heathrow airport and returned to the United States.

The King case was to remain controversial, with a number of details indicating the existence of a broad plot to kill the civil rights leader. There were even charges that the FBI was involved in his death and that Ray was merely a scapegoat. Nothing of the kind was ever proved, but there was no doubt that some elements within the agency did not regret King's demise. A retired FBI man who had worked in the agency's Atlanta office at the time of the assassination reported a deep anti-King feeling prevalent there and told how one agent literally leaped for joy when he learned that King had been killed. The FBI reluctantly admitted that it had wiretapped King's home and sent his wife, Coretta King, letters implying her husband was sexually involved with several other women. When King was awarded the Nobel Peace Prize in 1964, FBI director J. Edgar Hoover was beside himself. The FBI even went so far as to send King a letter intimating he should commit suicide before the award was given. It read in part: 'King – there is only one thing left for you to do. You know what it is. You have just 34 days in which to do it. It has definite practical significance. You are done. There is but one way out. . . .'

Hoover had authorized the investigation of King's sex life, had ordered many of the illegal harassments used against him and had called King 'the most notorious liar in the country.' He had even inspired a news story of possible violence that had led to King's switching from his initial choice of a white-owned hotel to the Lorraine Motel, where Ray shot him.

The most troubling aspect of the case was that James Earl Ray appeared too much of a misfit to be involved in so monumental a matter as the King assassination. A 10th-grade dropout, he was later discharged from the army for 'ineptness and lack of adaptability to military service.' His crime record was bush-league; when he escaped from the Missouri State Prison in 1967, the reward posted for him was $50. When Ray was being hunted for the King killing, his father was quoted as saying that if James Earl had committed the crime, 'he couldn't have planned it alone; he wasn't smart enough for that.'

Ray pleaded guilty to the murder and was sentenced to 99 years. Within 24 hours he attempted to reverse his plea and insisted on dropping his original attorney, the famous Percy Foreman, and obtaining new counsel. Ray now maintained he was innocent and that 'Raoul,' a shadowy individual apparently known only to Ray, had sent him to Memphis for a gun-smuggling caper and had passed him money and orders. He insisted he didn't know who had killed King.

When the House Select Committee on Assassinations held hearings on the King case in 1978, a St. Louis man, Russell Byers said he had been offered $50,000 to arrange King's death. He said the offer came from two men, John Kauffmann and John Sutherland, acting on behalf of a group of businessmen. The offer, Byers said, had taken place in the Confederate-flag-decked den of Sutherland, a well-to-do attorney, and that Sutherland had greeted him in the uniform of a Confederate officer, complete with a colonel's hat.

Both Kauffmann and Sutherland were by that time dead, of natural causes, and their widows denied that their husbands would have taken part in such a plot. Indeed, the FBI had known of Byers's charges in 1973, but the information was never passed to agents investigating the King assassination. A spokesman for the bureau called the handling of the information a 'violation of established rules and procedures,' but the FBI claimed it to be a simple case of 'administrative error' (that is, misfiling). The agent handling the material had since retired.

Byers told House investigators he suspected that Sutherland and Kauffmann were really seeking to recruit him as a dupe to take the blame for the murder but not to actually carry it out. This prompted an investigation trying to link Byers or Sutherland or Kauffmann to Ray's escape from the penitentiary in 1967. The committee received testimony that Ray committed the murder in the hope of getting a $50,000 bounty, and in December 1978 it concluded there was a 'likelihood' of a conspiracy. The panel cleared all federal, state and local government agencies of involvement in the assassination of King, but it called the Domestic Intelligence Division of the FBI guilty of 'gross' abuse of its legal authority in its surveillance of King, and it stated that the Justice Department had 'failed to supervise adequately' that division.

After all the investigations James Earl Ray remained the only person convicted in the King assassination, and he was behind bars continually since 1969 except for a three-day escape in 1977. During his brief freedom he exhibited none of the adept planning and generous financing that marked his flight after the King killing, and he was quickly apprehended.

Further reading: *American Assassins*, by James W. Clarke; *He Slew the Dreamer*, by William Bradford Huie; *The Making of an Assassin*, by George McMillan.

KIROV, Sergei M. (1886–1934)   Popular opinion holds that the most important assassination of the 20th century was that of Archduke Francis Ferdinand and his wife Sophie, at Sarajevo in 1914. However, if one takes a more determinist approach to history and believes that those killings were more 'sparks' than 'causes' of World War I, then the most meaningful assassination may well have been that of Sergei Kirov, the Communist Party leader, in Leningrad on December 1, 1934.

Kirov was shot down in his office in the Smolny (a former girls' school converted to the party's regional headquarters) by Leonid Nikolayev. There never was any doubt of Nikolayev's guilt, and steady inquiry over the years has well established the fact that his crime had been stage-managed by the Russian secret police, the NKVD, on the direct orders of Joseph Stalin.

Nikolayev was a disgruntled, unbalanced Communist worker who acted out of purely personal motives, bearing a grudge against the authorities. The question that arose was how he had managed to penetrate the Smolny so easily without being seized by guards. In fact, he had been planning to kill Kirov for some time. In the previous few months he had been arrested twice in Kirov's vicinity while carrying a revolver. Unaccountably, he was released by the usually over-vigilant NKVD, on the express orders of the deputy head in Leningrad, Ivan Zaporozhets.

There is little doubt of Stalin's motives for having Kirov assassinated. By 1934 Kirov was the second most powerful figure in the Communist Party and had started to diverge from Stalin's views on a number of policies. Until that time Kirov had been a hard-line supporter of Stalin, but now he felt it was time to effect some reconciliation within the party and with the Soviet people at large. By Stalinist standards he might be judged to have become a moderate. There was even an abortive attempt within the party to demote Stalin to a lesser post and raise Kirov to the position of general secretary. It was hardly an offer that Stalin would soon forget. It called for vengeance not only against Kirov but against all those who supported him as well as those who might stray from his side in the future.

In the definitive study of the assassination, the veteran Sovietologist Robert Conquest, in his 1989 book *Stalin and the Kirov Murder*, traces the chilling details of the crime and convincingly illustrates Stalin's method in the assignment of the task to Genrikh Yagoda, the feared head of NKVD, who in turn passed the operation to his aide, Zaporozhets. Apparently the NKVD informed the gunman that his act would be interrupted at the last moment and thus he would be protesting against and helping to destroy the bureaucratic wall that was being built up within the party.

Naturally Nikolayev was not interrupted, and he carried out the murder. When questioned later by Stalin on why he had committed the crime, the assassin pointed boldly at the NKVD men present and told Stalin he should ask them that question. As Conquest reports, 'He was thereupon silenced and removed.'

Stalin made a dramatic show out of Kirov's funeral, even kissing the corpse. Then he started laying the groundwork for the terrible purges of 1937–1938, in which Communists of the left, right, and center died. In fact, even Yagoda and the other NKVD men involved in the plot were executed. Stalin blamed the crime on the long-deported Leon Trotsky, and on old Bolsheviks like Grigory Zinoviev, Lev Kamenev, and Nikolay Bukharin. All were executed, many after 'confessing' various crimes, including many in which it would have been physically impossible for them to have taken part, and to the Kirov assassination in particular. Thousands died in Stalin's terror, and forced-labor camps were filled as never before. Stalin was now supreme.

As Nicholas V. Riasanovsky states in *A History of Russia*, 'When the Eighteenth All-Union Party Congress gathered in 1939, Old Bolsheviks composed only about 20% of its membership compared to 80% at the Seventeenth Congress in 1934. Moreover, except for a few lieutenants of Stalin, such as Viacheslav Molotov, born Skriabin, almost no leaders of any prominence were left.

For example, with the exception of Stalin himself and of Trotsky, who was murdered in 1940, Lenin's entire Politburo had been wiped out.'

An investigation by Khrushchev produced some 200 volumes of documents concerning the Kirov murder. It was never made public, and Khrushchev himself never openly blamed Stalin, but he clearly hinted at it. Why then had Khrushchev not made the documents public? By that time the Soviet leader was in decline, soon to be overwhelmed by a return of the hardliners.

In 1987 and 1988, in the era of glasnost, the Supreme Court of the Soviet Union reversed the convictions of Zinoviev, Kamenev and Bukharin and rehabilitated them posthumously. And some favorable comments even started to appear in the Soviet press about the great ogre, Trotsky.

In November 1987 Mikhail Gorbachev set up a new commission of inquiry into Stalin's crimes, and it was announced that Kirov's assassination was one of the cases to be investigated. Considering the contributions of Conquest, and despite the contentions of the revisionists now questioning Stalin's role not only in the Kirov murder but in the great purges as well (which some observers call akin to the revisionist idea that Hitler knew nothing of the Holocaust), confirmation of Stalin's guilt is now considered by most experts to be inevitable.

Further reading: *Stalin and the Kirov Murder*, by Robert Conquest.

KRIM, Belkacem (1922–1970) On October 20, 1970, the body of Belkacem Krim, a former leader of the Algerian Front for National Liberation (FLN), was found in a Frankfurt, Germany, hotel room. He had been strangled and had been dead for at least two days.

Once a close ally of Ahmed Ben Bella, who became Algeria's first president, Krim had been living in exile in France. Krim had been active in the Algerian nationalist movement since the 1940s and had been sentenced to death at least three times by the French. In 1958 he served as vice president and armed forces minister in the Algerian provisional revolutionary government. During the 1962 talks with France that brought Algerian independence, Krim functioned as minister of foreign affairs. However, shortly thereafter Krim and Ben Bella had a political falling out and Krim left the government to oppose Ben Bella and his successor, Houari Boumedienne. Fleeing to France, Krim in 1967 established an exile group opposed to the Algerian government. In 1969 an Algerian court sentenced him to death in absentia.

Both West German and French intelligence officials had little doubt that Krim's assassination was the work of agents of the Algerian government, and West German police named two Moroccans and an Algerian who had registered at the Frankfurt hotel as suspects in the investigation. No solution to the Krim assassination was ever officially reached.

KUMAR, Major General B. N. (?–1988) On November 7, 1988, gunmen presumed to be Sikhs machine-gunned to death Major General B. N. Kumar, the highest ranking Indian army officer to be killed by terrorists in six years of violence in the Punjab. In recent years Sikh extremists had been held responsible for the assassination of Prime Minister Indira Gandhi in 1984 and General Arun Vaidya, the retired army chief, in 1986.

The major long-standing Sikh demand had been the establishment of an autonomous Punjab state, and the main focus of Sikh anger since 1984 had been the Indian army's raid on the holiest of Sikh shrines, the Golden Temple in Amritsar, in which hundreds of Sikh militants and pilgrims were killed. Since then violence against army officers such as General Vaidya, held responsible for planning the attack, had been extremely bloody. General Kumar's murder and the wounding of two of his aides was carried out by two gunmen who fired automatic weapons at him as he left his home in Chandigarh, the Punjabi capital. The gunmen escaped in a van.

The assassination occurred after a week of stepped-up

killings in the Punjab in which more than 40 persons died in three separate bombing attacks carried out by extremists. The hostility against General Kumar was heightened by criticism of his handling of a flood crisis in the Punjab the previous September. General Kumar was then chairman of the Bhakra Beas Management Board, which supervised the operations of a dam providing irrigation for a vast area of the Punjab. During the flooding, water was released from the overfilled reservoir, worsening the disaster. More than 600 were killed in the flooding, and tens of thousands more were displaced, with crops, cattle and farm machinery worth millions of dollars lost. General Kumar denied he had taken any improper action. (See VAIDYA, GENERAL ARUN.)

L

LAGO, General Victor (1919–1982) The war between Spain and Basque nationalists seeking their independence has been marked since the 1960s by bloody acts of terrorism. The accession to the throne of King Juan Carlos and his enlightened rule following the death of dictator Francisco Franco in 1975 did not end the struggle, despite the king's concessions, including legalizing the political arm of the ETA (Basque Homeland and Liberation) movement, easing of anti-terrorist legislation and reforming of the security forces, whose treatment of Basque nationalists had been brutal.

The continuing ETA violence was directed largely against the Spanish armed forces, and especially at those elements who in the past had supported France or had taken part in retributions against the Basques.

On November 4, 1982, General Victor Lago, commander of Spain's crack Brunete armored division, was motoring to his headquarters in an army car. As the vehicle neared the Arch of Triumph on the western outskirts of Madrid, two ETA motorcyclists drew up alongside the army car and raked it with submachine guns. Lago died within minutes; his driver was wounded but recovered. Lago had long been associated with Franco, having fought in the civil war in the 1930s. He had also been an enthusiastic member of the Spanish Blue Division, which had served in Russia alongside Nazi troops in World War II.

Lago was the 29th Spanish army officer to be killed by terrorists between 1977 and 1982. Eight of them were generals.

LAMBRAKIS, Gregory (1917–1963) Gregory Lambrakis, a left-wing deputy of the Greek parliament and a leading nuclear arms foe, was struck and killed by a motorcycle in Athens on May 22, 1963. His death caused considerable turmoil both inside and outside Greece, and in 1969 it provided the inspiration for Costa-Gavras's much-acclaimed motion picture *Z*.

Right after the death of Lambrakis, Greek leftist political figures charged the government with moral responsibility. Later it was established to the satisfaction of most unaligned individuals that the Lambrakis murder was carried out with both the knowledge and the sanction of the police. When then-King Paul and Queen Frederika, accompanied by Premier Psnyotis Pipinelis, visited England the following July, they were met by mass demonstrations in London demanding nuclear disarmament and condemning the Lambrakis murder.

The Lambrakis affair did much to strengthen the left in Greece temporarily and led to the establishment of the Democratic Youth Lambrakis by the Communists in 1963. By 1966 the organization had at least 60,000 members in about 4,500 Lambrakis clubs operating even in the smallest villages. Under the composer Mikis Theodorakis the clubs became a thorn in the side of the right-wing Greek government.

Further reading: *The Web of Modern Greek Politics*, by Jane Oerry Clark Carey and Andrew Galbraith Carey.

LAPORTE, Pierre (1921–1970) In two related kidnappings in October 1970 that shocked Canada and marked the apex of terrorism by French separatists of the Front de Liberation du Quebec (FLQ), British trade commissioner James R. Cross and Quebec Labor Minister Pierre Laporte were both seized and threatened with death.

Cross was abducted first, being taken from his home in Montreal on October 5 and driven off in a taxi by four armed men. The kidnappers issued terms for Cross's life, including the release of 23 imprisoned separatists, a ransom of $500,000 in gold, and safe passage to Cuba or

Algeria for the kidnappers. There were a number of other demands, including one for the identification of a police informer who the FLQ believed was operating within their ranks.

The government rejected the demands but then acceded to one minor one, authorizing the Canadian Broadcasting Corporation to read the FLQ manifesto on television. Thwarted, the FLQ issued a 'final' deadline of 6 P.M. October 10, at which time Cross would be killed. Instead, minutes before the deadline two masked men armed with submachine guns seized Laporte in his home and drove off with him. The separatists threatened to execute him by 10 P.M. if the earlier demands were not met in full. A written message from Laporte pleaded with Quebec Premier Robert Bourassa to meet the demands: 'You have the power to decide on my life or my death. We are in the presence of a well-organized escalation. . . . After me there will be a third and a fourth and a fifth.'

At 9:55 P.M., five minutes before the deadline, Bourassa went on television to say the provincial government could not meet the terrorist demands before it was sure that the two captives would be released. Further jockeying continued for several days. On October 15 Bourassa rejected the demand for the release of the 23 separatists and instead offered to free five and give the kidnappers safe passage out of the country, terming this the government's 'final offer.'

The next day the federal government issued for the first time in its peacetime history the War Measure Act to declare a state of potential insurrection in the province, allowing the government to do whatever necessary to maintain national security. At least 250 persons were detained in Quebec Province in a wave of early-morning arrests. On October 17 the government accompanied this stern action with a conciliatory gesture: a detailed plan to provide the kidnappers with safe conduct. They were offered immunity if they brought themselves and their hostages to a site of Expo '67, which would be declared an extension of the Cuban consulate in Montreal. The two hostages would be held by Cuban consular officials until the kidnappers arrived in Cuba.

The offer came too late. On October 18, after a call to a Montreal radio station, Laporte's bloodied body was found in the same car by which he had originally been kidnapped. He had been garroted.

While the body of Laporte, the father of two, lay in state in the Montreal Palais de Justice, the police issued a bulletin for the arrest of Paul Rose, 27, and Marc Carbonneau, 37, in connection with the kidnappings. The hunt went on for Cross, and finally, on December 2 the police surrounded the house in Montreal where they had learned the British official was being held. At this point the kidnappers agreed to negotiate the release of their captive. An agreement was reached whereby the kidnappers left the booby-trapped house and traveled in a booby-trapped car with their relatives and Cross to the Expo '67 site, where they turned over their prisoner to Cuban officials. The Cuban government issued a statement that it was involving itself in the affair for humanitarian reasons following a request by the Canadian government. The kidnappers were then flown to Cuba. The seven on the plane were identified as Carbonneau, a Montreal taxi driver; Jacques Lanctot, 25; his wife, Suzanne, and a child; Pierre Seguin, another alleged kidnapper; Jacques Cossette-Trudel and Louise Cossette-Trudel. Several other accused kidnappers did not leave the country and were arrested and convicted. Paul Rose and Francis Simard, 23, were given life imprisonment, and a third man, Bernard Lortie, drew a 20-year sentence.

In 1974 it was discovered that the three kidnappers given passage to Cuba had entered France from Czechoslovakia, in what the French described as a 'security error.' However, unnamed authorities indicated that a Canadian request for their extradition would not be honored, and Prime Minister Trudeau declared that as part of the 1970 agreement the three separatists were immune from Canadian legal reprisal unless they set foot in Canada.

LA TORRE, Pio (1927–1982) Pio La Torre, leader of the Communist Party in Sicily, was a tireless foe of the Mafia, which had made Palermo, Sicily, a key transit point in the worldwide heroin trade. As a member of the Italian parliament's Anti-Mafia Commission, he sponsored a bill that would give police sweeping powers to suppress the criminal organization, including access to private banking records and the right to tap telephone conversations. The 'La Torre law' had not made it into the statute books when La Torre and his driver were shot to death on April 30, 1982 near the Communist Party headquarters in Palermo.

La Torre was the first member of the parliament to be slain since the 1978 assassination of former-Premier Aldo Moro by the ultraleft Red Brigades. After the La Torre killing, Communist Party national leader Enrico Berlinguer called for a 'mass campaign against terrorism in all its forms,' arguing that terrorism threatened the existence of the democratic state as never before.

Shortly thereafter General Alberto Dalla Chiesa, the policeman who did much to defeat the Red Brigades, was appointed prefect of Palermo. Dalla Chiesa had vigorously backed the proposed law, which had foundered in parliamentary debate. On September 3, 1982, Dalla Chiesa, his young wife and his police escort were ambushed and killed. This assassination finally triggered the passage of the La Torre law and caused the papacy to launch a strenuous attack on the Italian Mafia. Mass arrests led to a crackdown, and the successful prosecutions of scores of alleged Mafia figures followed – if not the final resolution of the La Torre and Dalla Chiesa assassinations.

LENIN, Vladimir Ilyich (1870–1924) – Attempted Assassination Vladimir Ilyich Lenin, the Russian revolutionary, founder of Bolshevism, and the major force behind the 1917 revolution, eschewed political assassination as a revolutionary method, not on moral grounds but on the belief that it was ineffective. This put the Bolsheviks in opposition to the Social Revolutionaries, who practiced assassination as a way to alter society. It may explain why Lenin himself was almost assassinated on August 30, 1918, since his would-be assassin, a woman, was thought to be a member of the Social Revolutionary Party.

There is some doubt whether Fanya Kaplan and her sister Dora were Social Revolutionary members at all, but they had long been active in the radical movement against the czarist regime. Fanya had been convicted of attempting to kill a czarist official and had only recently returned from a long sentence in Siberia after the February revolution.

On August 30 Lenin made a long speech to the workers at the Michelson factory in Moscow, and outside while approaching his car and chauffeur, he paused to answer eager questions from a crowd that had gathered. Two of his questioners were Fanya and Dora Kaplan. Suddenly Fanya pulled a revolver from under her clothing and shot the short, balding leader in the neck and shoulder. The crowd pursued the Kaplan sisters, apprehending Fanya quickly and later nabbing Dora.

Fearing the hospitals, where he might be attended by a doctor or nurse with czarist, capitalist, Kerensky or Social Revolutionary sympathies, Lenin instructed his driver to take him home. Several trusted doctors were summoned, and in time Lenin recovered, although never fully. Neither bullet was removed, and his lung was permanently damaged. Chances are the assassination attempt considerably shortened Lenin's life.

From his sickbed Lenin ordered that his would-be assassins be imprisoned for life so that they might be allowed to witness the success of the Soviet state. This was done in the case of Dora Kaplan (who was reported to have died in 1958), but not with Fanya, whose questioning soon convinced the Soviets that the woman was demented. When asked, for instance, 'Why did you shoot Comrade Lenin?' she replied, 'Why do you have to know?' It was learned that in her confinement at hard labor she suffered continuous headaches and suffered the loss of her eyesight for long periods. Once it seemed clear that Fanya was incompetent and would hardly benefit from watching the U.S.S.R. prosper, she was simply shot without a trial.

The fact that Fanya never offered any information about any accomplices did not prevent the Soviets from launching a reign of terror in which hundreds were killed. Many were Social Revolutionaries and many more Czarist officials and capitalists imprisoned for a long time and with no record of any resistance at all to the Bolsheviks.

Lenin lived until just short of his 54th birthday in January 1924. Officially he was said to have died of a series of strokes, often attributed to the earlier assassination attempt. There has also been suspicion that Lenin was poisoned on orders from Joseph Stalin, who was ready to begin his own quest for dictatorial power. In her 1956 book, *Face of a Victim*, Elisabeth Lermolo tells of Lenin on his deathbed writing a note and handing it to an aide, saying, 'I've been poisoned.' The note itself, according to Lermolo, repeated the charge that he was being poisoned and ordered anyone reading it to 'tell Trotsky.'

After a period during which a quadrumvirate of Trotsky, Stalin, Grigory Zinoviev and Lev Kamenev ran the party and the country, Trotsky was forced into exile in 1929, and Zinoviev and Kamenev were executed in the great purge of the 1930s. In 1940 Trotsky was assassinated in Mexico, clearly on Stalin's orders.

Further reading: *The Bolsheviks*, by Adam B. Ulam; *The History of Assassination*, by Brian McConnell.

LEO V, Byzantine Emperor (?–820) Leo the Armenian, the future Leo V, was a Byzantine general who distinguished himself during the reigns of Nicephorus I and Michael I. He was a credible fighter against the Bulgars in 813, and when Michael I foolishly rejected reasonable peace terms, his troops revolted and elected Leo as the new emperor. Michael was allowed to go into exile with his family, but to secure Leo's reign, Michael I's male offspring were emasculated.

Leo made peace with Omortag, the Bulgarian khan, and inaugurated the second iconoclast period (that is, opposition to religious images on the grounds that they led to idolatry). He was regarded by many to be a heretic – he deposed the Orthodox patriarch Nicephorus and reimposed the decrees of the iconoclast Synod of Hieria of 754 – but his reign from 814 to 820, in the words of Harvard historian Romilly Jenkins, 'passed in one of those very rare ages when the eastern empire enjoyed profound peace.'

Leo V's problems were personal ones. For years he had been close friends with Michael the Amorian, his count of the tent (or aide-de-camp) during the war years in the early 800s. After Leo became emperor the relationship slowly began to deteriorate. Michael was driven by jealousy and became more and more notorious for his public criticism of the emperor. At first Leo suffered the criticisms, but finally he issued a warning for Michael to be silent. Michael ignored the warning, and Leo ordered that he be watched closely. Finally evidence was found that Michael was planning treason.

On Christmas Eve 820 Leo sentenced his former friend to death by burning in the palace furnace. If Leo had carried out the punishment without delay, his own life might have been spared. However, Empress Theodosia begged him to postpone the execution since the following day was Christmas, and Leo ordered Michael be put in irons until after the holiday.

On Christmas Day, the Emperor attended dawn service at St. Stephen's Chapel, where it was his custom to conduct the singing of the chorus. Lurking among the choristers were a number of Michael's allies. As Leo sang from his favorite hymn, 'In their love of the Almighty they despised the things of this world,' the conspirators charged forward, surrounding him. Leo did not die easily. He seized the ceremonial cross and successfully defended himself until one attacker severed his arm with a mighty blow. Leo fell to the floor, where he was finished off.

Michael was freed from the dungeon, but since a

blacksmith could not be found at that hour, he was seated on the imperial throne with his legs still shackled. He became Michael II, the new 'master of the world.'

Further reading: *Byzantium: The Imperial Centuries A.D. 610–1071*, by Romilly Jenkins.

LEO X, Pope (1475–1521) – Alleged Attempted Assassination Few assassination attempts, real or fanciful, redounded as badly on the alleged target than did that against Pope Leo X, Giovanni de' Medici, in 1517. To this day there is considerable dispute whether there had been a conspiracy at all to kill the pope. In any event Leo professed to having learned of such a plot by several cardinals. It was said the leader of the conspiracy, the young cardinal Alfonso Petrucci of Siena, arranged to bribe a doctor who was to inject Leo with poison while treating him for a boil on the buttocks.

Arrests were made, alleged informers tortured and a number of cardinals questioned. Although safe in Siena, Petrucci, as well as a number of other suspect cardinals, came willingly to Rome under guarantees of safe conduct. However, Pope Leo's record concerning safe conduct was less than wholesome, and, true to form, Petrucci and the others were imprisoned. Subjected to severe grilling, many made incriminating statements and confessions. The revelations shocked Rome, especially when Cardinal Petrucci pleaded, or was forced to plead, guilty. Petrucci was sentenced to death and was strangled with the appropriate red silk noose; the execution was carried out by a Moor because protocol made it impossible for a prince of the Church to die at the hands of a Christian.

There were no other executions since the remaining cardinals, all very rich, saw the wisdom of pleading guilty and then accepting pardons on the payment of huge fines. Cardinal Raffaele Riario bought his life for a staggering 150,000 ducats.

The entire Petrucci affair was considered so outlandish and unbelievable that popular opinion held that the pope had merely concocted the plot himself to raise the huge fines. Leo X is often described as the most profligate of all who sat on the papal throne, needing great sums for ceremony, family aggrandizement, wars and lavish expenditures on art in many forms. To finance his life-style Leo raised the sale of church offices to new highs, to the point where they increased the papacy's annual revenues more than sixfold – and still there was not enough money. Leo increased the sale of indulgences to a level of inventiveness no pope before had ever attempted through the activities of his agent, Johann Tetzel. Pope Leo could hardly be called the cause of the Protestant Reformation, but it is not surprising that Martin Luther would nail his 95 theses on the church door at Wittenberg during Leo's reign. In that context the Petrucci affair came to be viewed as the greatest scandal of the age.

Ironically, states historian Barbara Tuchman, 'Recent investigation in Vatican archives suggests that the plot may in fact have been real, but what counts is the impression made at the time.' That was best indicated by the low estate of the papacy upon Leo's death in 1521. Romans in the street, Tuchman notes, 'hissed the cardinals going to the conclave to choose his successor.'

Further reading: *The March of Folly*, by Barbara W. Tuchman; *Rome in the High Renaissance*: *The Age of Leo X*, by Bonner Mitchell.

LETELIER, Orlando (1932–1976) In an event that shocked the Washington diplomatic corps, Orlando Letelier, the foreign minister of Chile during the presidency of Salvador Allende, was killed on Embassy Row when a bomb in his car exploded on September 21, 1976. The bombing also killed 25-year-old Ronni Moffitt, an American associate of Letelier in his position with the Institute for Policy Studies, a liberal research group in Washington. Letelier had been Chile's ambassador to the United States, from 1970 to 1973, until Allende's overthrow and death. Since that time Letelier had been outspoken in his opposition to Chilean dictator General Augusto Pinochet.

The Letelier assassination was laid to the operations of

DINA, the Chilean national intelligence agency, and for a time, at least it led to severely strained relations between the United States and Chile. In 1978 a DINA agent, American-born Michael V. Townley, confessed he had planted the bomb. He pleaded guilty to conspiracy to murder a foreign official and served 62 months in prison.

In 1980 the Federal District Court in Washington concluded that the government of Chile and its agents were responsible for the deaths of Letelier and Moffitt and awarded their families more than $5 million in damages, which they were unable to collect. In 1987 another former DINA agent, Armando Fernandez, voluntarily returned to the United States from Chile, remorsefully declaring in court that he too had played a role in the assassination preparations. He said that at one time he had been held in detention in a military hospital for 14 months after the murders and was ordered by General Pinochet not to attempt to return to the United States. The U.S. Department of Justice agreed to provide Fernandez with a new identity.

In 1988 the Reagan administration presented a bill for $12 million to the government of Chile. The sum reflected the claims on behalf of the relatives of Letelier and Moffitt as well as the costs incurred in investigating the killings. The Pinochet government refused to pay. In May 1990 the democratically elected government of President Patricio Aylwin reversed the Pinochet decision and agreed to pay compensation. A commission was to set the amounts of payment but was not to investigate the question of who was responsible for the killings. While no longer president, General Pinochet remained commander of the army under the Aylwin government.

LIAQUAT Ali Khan (1895–1951) The division of the Indian subcontinent into the independent states of Hindu India and Muslim Pakistan did not end the friction between the two peoples, and moderating voices in the conflict were often stilled by assassination. Such was the case of Liaquat Ali Khan, Pakistan's first prime minister.

Born in Karnal, East Punjab, now a part of India, Liaquat Ali studied law at Oxford University then returned to India, where he spent most of his life in politics. Joining the Moslem League in 1923, he served as top aide to Mohammed Ali Jinnah. Upon the establishment of an independent Pakistan in 1947, Liaquat Ali gave up family estates in the United Provinces to relocate in Pakistan, where he became prime minister. Upon the death of Jinnah in 1948, Liaquat Ali assumed responsibility for running the country. Despite their political differences, Liaquat Ali was a close friend of India's Jawaharlal Nehru, which brought him criticism from Muslims.

The most pressing problem Liaquat Ali faced was the territorial dispute with India over Kashmir. Liaquat Ali firmly resisted pressure to go to war over the issue and maintained a restraining influence on Muslim extremists in Pakistan.

On October 16, 1951, Liaquat Ali began an address at a public meeting in Rawalpindi, West Punjab Province, near the Kashmir frontier. A Muslim fanatic shot him several times, and the premier died in a nearby hospital. The assassin, Syed Azbar Khan, was identified as a fanatic from Afghanistan, which had been demanding the creation of a new free state of Pushtunistan on the Afghan–Pakistan frontier. The murderer was mobbed and killed on the spot by the audience.

LIEBKNECHT, Karl   See LUXEMBURG, ROSA.

LINCOLN, Abraham (1809–1865)   Had his assassination plot gone according to plan, actor-turned-assassin John Wilkes Booth would have killed not only the president, Abraham Lincoln, but a future president as well, General Ulysses S. Grant. The Lincolns and Grants were supposed to go together to Washington's Ford's Theater on the night of April 14, 1865, to attend a performance of a mediocre comedy, *Our American Cousin*. However, Mrs. Grant had become annoyed with the now rather frequent hysterical outbursts of Mary Lincoln and had canceled. As a substitute, the daughter of Senator Ira Harris and her fiance, Major Henry Rathbone, joined the presidential couple.

Although Lee had surrendered, there was still a clear danger to Lincoln, and under the circumstances his protection at the theater was limited, one might even say negligent. Earlier in the day the president had asked the War Department to provide a special guard, but, strangely, the request was refused, a matter of some puzzlement to historians. The only presidential bodyguard that night was a shiftless member of the Washington police force who after the start of the performance, incredibly, deserted his post outside the flag-draped presidential box to adjourn to a nearby tavern.

While there he may well have shared the bar with another imbiber, John Wilkes Booth, who had been drinking steadily that day, having decided that evening he would assassinate Lincoln. At age 26, Booth was a reasonable success as a Shakespearean actor, having come from a famed Maryland acting family, but he certainly never achieved the stature of his noted brother, Edwin. John, unlike the rest of the Booth family, who supported the Union, was a rabid Southern sympathizer. It was almost unimaginable that the War Department did not hear of his drunken boasting for weeks or months about a plot to kidnap Lincoln and drag him off in chains to Richmond, where he would be held until the North agreed to an armistice or to a massive return of Confederate prisoners. As a matter of fact, Booth and a small group of conspirators had waited in ambush about three weeks earlier to seize Lincoln's carriage outside the city limits but were frustrated by a change of presidential plans.

After that failure and then the fall of Richmond, Booth realized the war was lost and that only revenge and assassination were now possible. Booth's plan called for him to kill Lincoln (and Grant) while other members of the group simultaneously attacked Vice President Johnson and various Cabinet members.

At 10:00 Booth left the bar and headed for the theater,

pausing to get a chaw of tobacco from a ticket taker he knew. An actress, Jennie Gourlay, saw Booth in the foyer and later said he seemed ill and distraught, with 'a wild look in his eyes.'

Without the slightest interference, Booth walked into Lincoln's unguarded box, placed his one-shot Derringer behind the unaware Lincoln's left ear and pulled the trigger. As Lincoln slumped Booth shouted, '*Sic semper tyrannis!*' ('Ever thus to tyrants!'), dropped the gun and pulled out a dagger to stop Major Rathbone, who lunged at him. He slashed the officer and then hurdled the rail of the box to the stage, crying, 'The South is avenged!' However, his leap was broken when his spur caught in the flag outside the box, causing him to almost fall on his face. Miraculously, he kept his footing, and, limping across the stage on a fractured left leg, he made it out of the theater to the street, mounted his horse and rode off.

If his injury had not slowed him, Booth might have made a quick escape across the Potomac and lost himself among the soldiers being demobilized following Lee's surrender. The pain slowed Booth, who finally lined up with another conspirator, David Herold, who while Booth was shooting the president was botching up an attempt to kill Secretary of State William Seward. The pair located Dr. Samuel Mudd, a Maryland physician, who set Booth's leg. Booth and Herold left the doctor's home and made it to the river, awaiting an opportunity to get across to Virginia.

Meanwhile the hunt for the assassins was on, according to many, with incredible ineptness. It was not until April 26 that the pair were finally run to ground in a tobacco shed on a farm outside Port Royal, Virginia. The commander of the Union troops ordered the pair to surrender or they would be burned out, to which Booth called out: 'Let us have a little time to consider it.'

A few minutes later Booth shouted: 'Captain, I know you to be a brave man, and I believe you to be honorable; I am a cripple. I have got but one leg; if you withdraw your men in one line one hundred yards from the door, I will come out and fight you.'

The officer, actually a Lieutenant, rejected the terms and Booth replied, 'Well, my brave boys, prepare a stretcher for me.'

The troops then heard loud voices from the shed and Booth's voice rose: 'You damned coward, will you leave me now? Go, go; I would not have you stay with me.' Then he yelled out, 'There's a man in here who wants to come out.'

Herold emerged, shaking.

The wood structure was set aflame, and a dark figure could be seen hobbling about. Then there was a shot. Perhaps it was fired by Booth, perhaps by an erratic Union soldier named Boston Corbett – and Booth fell. Soldiers rushed in and pulled him out of the flaming structure.

Booth was dying. His last whispered words were, 'Tell Mother I die for my country.'

Even before Booth's death the government had named nine persons involved in various phases of the assassination – Booth, Herold, George A. Atzerodt (who was supposed to kill Vice President Johnson but got drunk instead), Lewis Paine (assigned to Seward along with Herold), Mary E. Surratt, her son John H. Surratt, Edward Spangler, Dr. Mudd and Michael O'Laughlin. All except Booth, of course, and John Surratt, who eluded capture, were tried before a military commission, on the ground that Lincoln was the commander in chief and had died 'in actual service in time of war.'

The trial lasted from May 9 to June 30 and could hardly be held up as an example of a fair and impartial hearing. Amid the postwar hysteria the defendants were linked to the deeds of the Confederate government and even to the brutal conditions at the notorious Andersonville Prison and the plot to burn New York City. Many witnesses who should have been called were not, including John F. Parker, the officer who left the Lincoln box unguarded (he was not even reprimanded by the Washington police force). Above all there was very little evidence to implicate Mary Surratt, the only information about her coming from a notorious liar and drunkard. In fact, the only thing that could definitely be said against her was that she owned the rooming house where much of the plotting had occurred.

Despite this, Surratt was sentenced to hang along with Paine, Herold and Atzerodt. O'Laughlin, Herold and Mudd received life sentences, and Spangler drew a six-year term.

The condemned were hanged on a sweltering day, July 7, 1865. The prisoners' heads were thoughtfully shielded from the sun by umbrellas as they stood on the gallows. Up to the last moment it was assumed by many that Mary Surratt would be pardoned. Paine told the executioner: 'If I had two lives to give, I'd give one gladly to save Mrs. Surratt. I know she is innocent, and would never die in this way if I hadn't been found at her house. She knew nothing about the conspiracy at all.' The trap was sprung on all four at the same moment.

The luckiest of all the suspects was John Surratt, who escaped to Europe. He was finally run to earth in Italy serving in the Swiss Guard. By the time he came back for trial in 1867, a greater sense of justice pervaded the country and the courts, and Surratt went free when the jury could not agree on his guilt. It was also now evident that the men being held in prison had had only the weakest of cases made against them. By March 1869 President Johnson had granted all of them pardons except for O'Laughlin, who had died in prison in 1867.

Until the assassination of John F. Kennedy, the Lincoln murder had more advocates of various conspiracy theories than any other in U.S. history. A favorite villain was Secretary of War Edwin Stanton. One of the most controversial conspiracy accounts is the 1977 book *The Lincoln Conspiracy*, by David Balsiger and Charles E. Sellier. They insist that Booth was not merely laboring for the Confederacy but was in the pay of a group of Northern cotton and gold speculators and a number of radical

Republicans, including Stanton, who, they said, removed 18 incriminating pages from a Booth diary with key facts on the broad conspiracy. The authors claimed to have located the pages. They also said that after Booth bungled three kidnap attempts in early 1865, he was fired by the conspirators and replaced by James William Boyd, a captured Confederate spy supposedly released from prison to take on the assignment. This galvanized Booth to assassinate the president before Boyd got to Lincoln first. And, falling in line with other conspiracy experts who insisted that Booth had not been killed at Port Royal, Balsiger and Sellier insisted the man who died there was actually Boyd.

Further reading: *Assassination in America*, by James McKinley; *The Day Lincoln Was Shot*, by Jim Bishop.

LIN PIAO (1907–1971)   Since 1972 there has been much speculation in the West whether Chinese Communist military leader Lin Piao, once considered the logical successor of Mao Zedong, was the victim of an assassination.

Lin Piao was originally a protege of Chou En-lai and served under Mao in the Red Army since the late 1920s, accompanying Mao on the famous Long March. After the successful conclusion of the civil war, Lin continued to rise in both the Communist Party and the military, and in 1959 he was named minister of defense. As the power of the military grew, Lin replaced Liu Shao-ch'i as the number two man in the party.

Lin Piao was reported to have been killed in a plane crash in 1971 under circumstances never fully explained. He was charged with having tried to overthrow, and perhaps even to assassinate, Mao. Then, his plot having failed, or so the accusations went, Lin tried to escape to the Soviet Union. There was no official announcement of Lin Piao's death until July 1972, a fact that indicated to many China watchers that his death was a political killing. Also reported as dying in the plane crash was Lin's wife, Yeh Chun, and seven close supporters. Reports from the

Soviet Union – politically estranged from the Red Chinese government – indicated that the bodies of the victims were riddled with bullet wounds.

LONG, Huey P. (1893–1935) He was the Kingfish of Louisiana politics. Serving as governor from 1928 to 1931, flamboyant Huey P. Long used ruthless and demagogic methods to establish dictatorial power and to push his program of social and economic reform. In 1930 he was elected to the U.S. Senate, but he continued to control the Louisiana state government from Washington through his handpicked successor Oscar O. K. Allen, as governor. With the United States mired in the Depression, Long sought and gained considerable popular support with his Share the Wealth program. He was considered likely to play a significant role in the 1936 presidential election, most probably as a candidate but possibly as a kingmaker imposing his positions in large measure on Franklin D. Roosevelt, who detested him.

Huey Long was, depending on what segment of American society one talked to, among the most-beloved and most-hated men in his state and the nation. His supporters hailed him as 'the one friend the poor has,' while foes saw him as a 'demagogue,' a 'madman,' and the 'destroyer of constitutional government.' Among the important groups solidly behind Long was organized crime, with whom he could always reach accommodation. When Mayor Fiorello La Guardia of New York attacked the syndicate's slot machine empire, Long invited Mafia kingpin Frank Costello to set up operations in Louisiana. The underworld shipped in one-armed bandits by the thousands, making New Orleans and the state the illegal slot machine center of the country. Crime syndicate payoffs in the millions contributed a significant amount of the grease that kept the Long machine running.

Long was assassinated on September 8, 1935. The facts are muddy other than that Long was shot to death while attending a special session of the state house of representatives in Baton Rouge. The standard version is that as he marched down one of the capitol corridors with five bodyguards in attendance, a 29-year-old man, Carl Weiss, regarded as a brilliant medical doctor, stepped out from behind a pillar and shot Long with a .32-caliber automatic. Long cried out in pain and, clutching his side, ran down the hall. His bodyguards threw Weiss to the floor, shooting him twice. As he continued to struggle, a fusillade of 61 shots turned his white linen suit bloody crimson. Weiss died immediately, while Long lingered for 30 hours as doctors struggled to save his life.

What was Weiss's motive for the crime? The traditional consensus has been that either he and his family thoroughly hated the Kingfish or that he was demented. A second theory is quite different. According to this view, Weiss never intended to kill Long. Instead, he had approached Long and punched him in the mouth, cutting his lip (a fact not well explained in the standard version). This so angered Long's bodyguards that they pulled their guns and started shooting wildly, and actually one of their bullets fatally wounded their master. Then after killing Weiss, they found his gun and fired it. Since the bullet that hit Long passed through his body, it was impossible to tell which of the many shots was the fatal one. This theory comes in a different version as well: that Weiss had indeed intended to kill Long but had been laid low without ever having fired a shot. In either case, the story went, Long's aides and bodyguards had no choice but to put the blame on Weiss to absolve themselves.

Long was buried on the landscaped grounds of the capitol he built, amid much mourning by the faithful. Many on the Long fringe had little doubt that the assassination of their hero had been engineered by President Roosevelt to keep him out of the 1936 election. A novel based on Long's career, *All the King's Men*, by Robert Penn Warren, won the 1947 Pulitzer Prize and the movie version garnered an Academy Award in 1949.

For further reading for widely diverging theories: *The Day Huey Long Was Shot*, by David Zinman; *The Huey Long Murder Case*, by Hermann B. Deutsch.

LONGOWAL, Harchand Singh (1928–1985) The assassination of Harchand Singh Longowal, the leader of the Akali Dal, India's mainstream Sikh political party, on August 20, 1985, once more illustrated the deep divisions remaining among the various ethnic and religious groups on the subcontinent. Shortly before his assassination, Longowal, noted as a disciple of Mahatma Gandhi's policy of nonviolent civil disobedience, had signed an accord with Indian Prime Minister Rajiv Gandhi to end the violence that had raged in the Sikh-dominated Punjab state for three years. The accord allowed for some Sikh autonomy but was considered a sellout by Sikh extremists.

Longowal was shot and killed as he addressed a Punjab rally of his supporters. Two young Sikhs, identified as Malvinder Singh and Gian Singh, were arrested following the shooting. Although the assassination was the work of Sikhs, opposition Indian politicians placed the blame on Prime Minister Gandhi's Congress Party, claiming their Congress's decision to hold new elections the following September had galvanized the extremists to action. Longowal himself had favored elections in early 1986 instead to 'allow the dust to settle' following the government's crackdown on recent violence. Longowal's assassination signaled further Sikh–Hindu violence ahead. (See DASS, ARJUN.)

LOUIS, Duke of Orleans See JOHN THE FEARLESS, SECOND DUKE OF BURGUNDY.

LOUIS XV, King of France (1710–1774) – Attempted Assassination In 1756 the disputes within Catholicism were at fever pitch between orthodox Catholics and the Jansenists, who were often described as Calvinistic Catholics. The Jansenists stressed predestination, greater personal holiness and the discouragement of frequent communion. Christophe de Beaumont, archbishop of Paris, aggravated the conflict by ordering clergy under his rule to administer the sacraments only to worshipers who had confessed to a non-Jansenist priest. The Jansenist dominated Parlement of Paris, which was composed mostly of rich lawyers and which functioned as a sort of appellant court, refused to accept the restrictions and ordered the clergy not to obey the edict.

The government of Louis XV vacillated in the dispute and finally banished the archbishop to Conflans in eastern France. Then in a reversal 10 days later, needing loan from the clergy to pursue the Seven Years' War, the government ordered the Parlement to accept a papal bull against the Jansenists.

The dispute grew more heated, and on January 5, 1757, the king was on a Versailles street when he was stabbed with a large penknife by 41-year-old Robert Francois Damiens. Damiens made no attempt to flee, and the king ordered his bodyguard, 'Secure him, but let no one do him any harm.'

Louis was not seriously hurt, and Damiens later claimed, 'I had no intention to kill the king. I might have done this had I been so inclined. I did it only that God might touch the king's heart, and work on him to restore things to their former footing.' He insisted that 'the archbishop of Paris is the cause of all the disturbances about the sacraments, by having refused them.'

The grand chamber of the Parlement tried and convicted Damiens and placed his parents and sister in perpetual banishment. Damiens was punished with the tortures required of regicides, with his flesh torn out by red-hot pincers, his body covered with boiling lead, and his limbs torn from his torso by four horses. The ladies of court paid outrageous fees to gain vantage points to view the grisly procedure. The king himself was disgusted with the tortures and sent pensions to the banished family.

The unpopular king won some sympathy for the attempted assassination and his treatment of Damiens's family, but that soon dissipated as terror set in on the ruler and he issued an edict making it a capital offense to write or print 'any works intended to attack religion, to assail the royal authority or to disturb the order and tranquillity of the realm.'

Now the atheistic philosophers followed Diderot and turned against the monarchy. Louis's later banishment of the Jesuits turned many Catholics against him, as well. The cry for representative government was heard, presaging the French Revolution of 1789. Louis's inability to offer necessary economic and political reforms – which inspired Damiens's attack – led directly to the coming 'deluge.'

Further reading: *Competition for Empire*, by Walter L. Dorn; *Works, XVIa*, by Francois-Marie Arouet Voltaire.

LOUIS (GUISE), Cardinal of Lorraine See GUISE, HENRY, DUKE OF.

LOUIS PHILIPPE (1773–1850) – Attempted Assassination According to some counts at least 21 European rulers were singled out for assassination attacks in the course of the 19th century. Louis Philippe, the 'Citizen King' of France (1830–1848), was subjected to more than one, hardly surprising since he became increasingly unpopular with both the right and left. None of the attacks succeeded, but Philippe has the distinction of being the target of the most spectacular attempt.

On July 28, 1835, the Corsican conspirator for independence Giuseppe Maria Fieschi tried to kill Philippe by firing at him from an upper window in a building on the Boulevard du Temple, through which a parade honoring the July revolution was to march. Fieschi rigged up an infernal machine consisting of 24 gun barrels designed to shoot simultaneously. Remarkably the king was not hit, but 18 others were killed, and Fieschi himself was severely wounded when the bizarre weapon blew up as he triggered it.

Fieschi and two confederates died on the guillotine on February 19, 1836.

LUMUMBA, Patrice (1926–1961) The cable read in part: 'Removal must be an urgent and prime objective and . . . under existing conditions this should be a high priority of our covert action.' The cable was sent August 25, 1960 by then-CIA Director Allen Dulles to the station chief in Zaire (formerly the Congo) outlining plans for the assassination of Congolese nationalist leader Patrice Lumumba. Later it would be claimed that before the CIA plan could be put into effect, Lumumba was actually murdered by others.

The firebrand Lumumba had many enemies. Named the first prime minister of the Congo republic upon its gaining independence on June 30, 1960, Lumumba immediately faced problems, especially when mineral-rich Katanga province seceded under Moise Tshombe, who had the support of Belgian troops. Lumumba appealed to the United Nations for aid in evicting the Belgian forces, and failing that turned to the Soviet Union for help. Russian and Czech 'technicians' began pouring into the country, much to the distress of the United States.

A few weeks after the Dulles cable, Congolese army leader Colonel Joseph Mobutu seized power. He in turn reached an agreement with President Kasavubu, who a few days earlier had dismissed Lumumba. Lumumba was contesting his removal, and both groups now claimed to be the legitimate government. In November Lumumba tried to travel from Leopoldville, where the United Nations had provided him protection, to Stanleyville, which was held by his supporters. He was captured by the Kasavubu forces on December 2. Some six weeks later he and two aides were placed aboard a plane and turned over to Katanga, on January 17, 1961. It is believed that he and his aides were brutally beaten by guards on the plane and never disembarked alive.

Officially, however, Katanga insisted that the three men were delivered to it and held captive in a remote villa but had escaped on February 10. Two days later, the version went, the trio 'died in the bush,' killed by villagers for the 3,000 pound reward. It was said that the bodies had been buried immediately after death, with no postmortem examination. And unfortunately there were no photographs of the bodies. The authorities also said the village where the alleged killings took place could not be named since it would then become a mecca for Lumumba followers. The story got little credence, and the general assumption was that Lumumba had died on January 17.

In November 1975 the Senate Select Committee on Intelligence Activities made public a document saying that U.S. officials had ordered the assassinations of Fidel Castro of Cuba and Lumumba and had been involved in assassination plans against three other foreign officials, Rafael Trujillo of the Dominican Republic, Ngo Dinh Diem of South Vietnam and General Rene Schneider of Chile. The report of the committee concluded that although four of the five men had been killed, none of them had died as the direct result of the assassination plans initiated by U.S. officials. Many were nevertheless skeptical.

LUWUM, Janani (1925–1977) On February 16, 1977, Janani Luwum, the Anglican archbishop of Uganda, Rwanda, Burundi and Boga-Zaire, was arrested by Ugandan police on charges of taking part in a coup attempt against dictator Idi Amin Dada. Several hours later, according to a government statement made the following day, the archbishop was killed in an automobile crash that also took the lives of two senior government officials – Lieutenant Colonel Erenaya Oryema, minister of land and water resources, and A.C.K. Oboth-Ofumbi, internal affairs minister.

The overwhelming opinion throughout Africa was that the trio were murdered under orders of President Amin. Andrew Young, U.S. ambassador to the United Nations, denounced the deaths as 'assassination,' and he compared the official report to government reports of detainee deaths in South Africa, which were listed as suicides. President Jimmy Carter backed Young's accusations.

Idi Amin reacted angrily to the charge and ordered all U.S. nationals in Uganda to meet with him in Kampala on February 28, before which they would not be allowed to leave the country. In a long telegram to President Carter,

Amin attacked Carter's statements about events in Uganda and further accused the U.S. Central Intelligence Agency of seeking to overthrow him. A few days later Amin retreated, called off the meeting with U.S. nationals and lifted the ban on their travel.

In the ensuing period there was one or more attempts on Amin's life. And 15 persons were executed on September 9, on charges of plotting to assassinate him. Until his ouster in 1979 it was estimated that Idi Amin orchestrated the political murders of at least 100,000 of his countrymen.

LUXEMBURG, Rosa (1870–1919) On January 15, 1919, German revolutionary leaders Rosa Luxemburg and Karl Liebknecht (1871–1919) were murdered. The official version was that the pair had been arrested, and while Liebknecht was being transferred under military escort to a Berlin prison by car, an unknown assailant had dealt him a heavy blow to the head. The car then developed engine trouble and Liebknecht, bleeding profusely and staggering, was ordered to continue by foot. Instead he tried to escape and was shot.

Something similar was alleged to have happened to Rosa Luxemburg. She was attacked by a mob at the Hotel Eden, where she was first taken under arrest, but her military escort rescued her and put her, unconscious, into a car. As the car drove off, another unknown assailant jumped on the running board and fired a pistol at her. The car drove on until a crowd near the Landwehr Canal stopped it and dragged her away, screaming, 'This is Rosa!' Her body was not found at the time.

The truth bore little resemblance to these concoctions. Luxemburg, a leading theoretician of the Marxist movement, and Liebknecht, the leader of the left wing of the Socialists, who had opposed the war and in 1916 was expelled from the Social Democratic Party and later imprisoned, were since the end of the war leading the 'Spartacus' revolt in Germany. With the capital paralyzed by a general strike, they were preparing to establish a soviet republic under the newly proclaimed Communist Party of Germany.

This move was violently opposed by Friedrich Ebert, the Social Democratic leader of the provisional government (all other political forces having collapsed) and the army under Generals Paul von Hindenburg and Wilhelm Groener. Although it did not become known for some years, Ebert (who said of social revolution, 'I hate it like sin') and Groener reached a secret agreement whereby Ebert would put down anarchy and Bolshevism. The army, in return for its continued existence with all its traditions, would collaborate in the effort.

That to the army obviously meant the assassination of Luxemburg and Liebknecht and any of their associates that were captured. The pair were caught through information given by a police spy, brought to the Hotel Eden and separated. Immediately, Captain Waldemar Pabst made plans to send them to their deaths. Liebknecht was rifle-butted in the head twice. He asked for a bandage but was ignored. Later he was taken from the hotel, allegedly for prison, rifle-butted again and dumped into a car. In the Tiergarten he was hauled semiconscious from the vehicle for a short distance and shot several times. The corpse was dumped back in the car and transported to the mortuary, identified as 'an unknown man found dead in the Tiergarten.'

Meanwhile Red Rosa was also mistreated in the hotel and later dragged to a car for her arranged death. Of that, Luxemburg biographer Elzbieta Ettinger said, 'The manner of death chosen for the offenders, was, it seems, in keeping with their station. Liebknecht was to be shot – he was a German. The mob murder was reserved for Luxemburg – she, a Jew, should perish in a pogrom.'

Unfortunately the mob failed to materialize. As she was led out of the hotel by Lieutenant Kurt Vogel, a trooper named Otto Runge struck her on the head with the butt of his carbine. Her skull was smashed by two blows, and she was dumped half-dead into a car and taken away by Vogel and some other officers. She was beaten on the head with the butt of a revolver and then Vogel shot her in the head at point-blank range. The car drove onto the Liechtenstein Bridge, and her corpse was hurled into the canal, not to be recovered until May.

Even the government could not long maintain the fiction of the official version of the murders, and a trial had to be held for the perpetrators. The magistrate for the prosecution, Paul Jorns, stated that Vogel and Runge had 'severely mistreated' the prisoners. But Jorns saw 'extenuating circumstances' – they had excellent war records, and Runge's 'fury' at the very sight of Luxemburg and Liebknecht was 'hardly surprising.' In the end Vogel was sentenced to 28 months' imprisonment for committing a misdemeanor while on guard duty, illegally disposing of a corpse and filing an inaccurate report. Runge got just over two years for 'attempted manslaughter.'

In 1928 a court agreed that Jorns had abetted the assassins, but that hardly mattered. He was at the time a public prosecutor for the Supreme Court of the Weimar Republic and in the Third Reich would serve in the infamous Nazi People's Court. The Nazis later compensated Jorns for his ordeal. In 1933 Runge also requested compensation for being so unfairly punished: 'My noble Fuhrer, the People's Chancellor, Adolf Hitler has also paid for his ideals with prison.' The German government awarded Runge a lump sum payment of 6,000 marks.

In the 1960s students in Cologne named the local university after Rosa Luxemburg, but in 1962 the German Federal Republic declared the assassination had been 'executions in accordance with martial law' (although there had been no charges and no trial). By the 1970s the Federal Republic had altered its position so far as to issue a postage stamp with Rosa Luxemburg's likeness. Some Germans were outraged that such an honor could be accorded to someone who was politely referred to as 'the foreigner,' and they burned the stamps.

Further reading: *Rosa Luxemburg*, by Paul Frolich; *Rosa Luxemburg: A Life*, by Elzbieta Ettinger.

M

MCKINLEY, William (1843–1901) It was an eager and excited crowd at the Temple of Music at the Pan-American exposition in Buffalo, New York, that queued up to meet and shake hands with President William McKinley on September 6, 1901. Waiting patiently in the long line was a 28-year-old man of slight stature. His name was Leon Czolgosz. His right hand was swathed in a phony bandage. When Czolgosz neared the front of the line, he lowered his head in order that he not be recognized by local police at the scene. He had lived in nearby West Seneca for some time and had been regarded by the authorities as a dangerous anarchist.

Czolgosz stopped a few feet short of the portly, tuxedoed president, and McKinley stepped toward him, smiling. Suddenly, Czolgosz whipped a pistol from under the bandage and fired. His shot hit a button and bounced away harmlessly, but Czolgosz's second shot struck the president in the abdomen. The president did not lose consciousness as soldiers and guards pounced on the gunman.

'I done my duty!' Czolgosz cried. An enraged guard smashed his fist into Czolgosz's face.

The president stopped the assault by murmuring weakly, 'Be easy with him, boys.'

Eight days later on September 14, the president died of gangrene of the pancreas. Today it is said his death was caused as much by his botched emergency surgery, hampered by inadequate surgical instruments and poor lighting in the operating room as by the assassin's bullet. The surgeons were unable to locate the fatal bullet in the operation, and in fact could not even find it during the autopsy, a situation they blamed on McKinley's obesity.

The law wasted no time bringing Czolgosz to trial, nine days after the president's death. The trial lasted only eight hours, with Czolgosz ignoring his court-appointed lawyers and refusing to take the stand. He showed no reaction when the guilty verdict was announced.

The press made much of Czolgosz's radical beliefs and suggested the possibility of a wide-ranging conspiracy. However, it developed that an anarchist publication, *Free Society*, had warned other anarchists to stay away from him, its editor, Abe Isaak, being convinced that Czolgosz was at best a dangerous crank and more likely a spy or a police agent. In the fall of 1897 Czolgosz had apparently suffered an emotional and physical breakdown following the Lattimer Mines massacre, in which a large number of Slavic miners staging a peaceful protest were murdered in one of the most brutal and shameful instances of labor violence in America.

For a long time thereafter Czolgosz was morose and hardly spoke to anyone. He did not go back to work, and in July 1900 he became greatly excited by the assassination of King Umberto I of Italy by an Italian-American anarchist named Gaetano Bresci, who had saved up the money to travel to Europe to commit regicide. Czolgosz was impressed that Bresci had received much praise in anarchist publications around the world. Shortly thereafter Czolgosz traveled to Chicago to join the anarchist circles active there, but he soon alienated these radicals by his bizarre behavior.

When the denunciation of him appeared in *Free Society* Czolgosz fled Chicago and went on to kill the president of the United States. The noted anarchist Emma Goldman was later to speculate that the charges in the anarchist press may have provoked Czolgosz into the assassination as a way to demonstrate his fidelity to the cause.

Czolgosz was executed with considerable speed on October 29, 1901. As he was strapped into the electric chair at Auburn prison in New York, according to witnesses, Czolgosz was 'calm and . . . self-possessed, his head erect . . . his face bore an expression of defiant determination.' He said, 'I killed the president because he was the enemy of the good people – the good working people. I am not sorry for my crime. I am sorry I could not see my father.'

Czolgosz's brother tried to claim the body for burial, but prison authorities refused the request. Instead, Czolgosz was buried in a prison grave and 'six barrels of quicklime and a carboy of sulfuric acid' poured on his body. It was estimated that the body decomposed in 12 hours.

With the third assassination of U.S. president in 36 years, the new chief executive, Theodore Roosevelt, assigned the Secret Service full responsibility for safeguarding all chief executives thereafter.

Further reading: *American Assassins*, by James W. Clarke; *Assassination in America*, by James McKinley; *The Man Who Shot McKinley*, by A. Wesley Johns.

McWHIRTER, Ross (1925–1975) In 1975 Ross McWhirter, coeditor, with his twin brother, Norris, of the *Guinness Book of Records*, earned the undying enmity of the Irish Republican Army when he posted a $100,000 reward for the capture of a terrorist death squad then ravaging England. McWhirter's efforts, which he dubbed 'Beat the Bombers,' followed the chance murder of Gordon Hamilton Fairley, a world-noted cancer specialist, by a car bomb intended for his neighbor Hugh Fraser, a Conservative member of Parliament. Fairley had been walking by when the explosion occurred.

In addition to the Beat the Bombers campaign, McWhirter, who harbored political ambitions, also headed Self-Help, an organization calling for the reinstitution of the death penalty in Britain by making terrorism a treasonable offense. He also had proposed requiring all southern Irish nationals residing in Britain to register. McWhirter hardly underestimated the danger he faced. 'I live . . . in constant fear of my life,' he stated. 'I know the IRA have got me on their death list.'

The IRA did. On November 27, 1975, two gunmen hid themselves in McWhirter's garden in Village Lane, Enfield. When McWhirter opened his front door to greet his wife, leaving himself silhouetted against the light, the assassins opened fire. McWhirter was shot in the head and elsewhere and died minutes after being taken to the hospital. His wife escaped unharmed.

Early the following month London police captured four IRA members after a shootout and a six-day siege. The four – Martin O'Connell, Harry Duggan, Edward Butler and Hugh Doherty, all in their 20s – were convicted of the murder of nine persons (including Fairley) and the wounding of 200 others in their bomb and shooting campaign. (See FRASER, HUGH.)

MADERO, Francisco Indalecio (1873–1913) Today Francisco Madero stands as a martyr of the Mexican Revolution that started in 1910 and swept out the dictatorial Diaz regime that had ruled the country for 35 years, always in the interests of the few at the expense of the many. From a wealthy family, a vegetarian and a teetotaler, Madero was also a dedicated democrat and social reformer – or in the view of some critics an ineffectual idealist and dreamer.

Madero succeeded Porfiro Diaz as president in 1911 but proved unable to placate the contending forces in Mexican politics, including the adherents to the old regime, the military and the other revolutionists such as Zapata, who demanded complete and immediate land reform for the benefit of the peasants. Madero also had to contend with a hostile conservative press, as well as the harassment of Henry Lane Wilson, the U.S. ambassador. By early 1913 Madero had been obliged to jail a number of military leaders who had helped him rise to power, but two generals, Felix Diaz and Bernardo Reyes, continued their plots from behind bars. In February Madero was forced to release them, and Diaz and Reyes immediately organized an attack on the National Palace. During the 10 days of fighting Reyes was shot to death. Madero relied on another general, Victoriano Huerta, to stop the rebels, but Huerta had already secretly joined with Diaz and Reyes. Under Huerta there was a good deal of cannonading of the attackers, during what historians have called Mexico's Ten Tragic Days, but the bombardment wounded more innocent people than combatants.

Finally General Huerta demanded that Madero resign, and when he refused, both the president and Vice President Pino Suarez were arrested on February 17. On the same day Madero's brother, Gustavo Madero, was seized; his eyes were mutilated and he was then brutally murdered. Mrs. Francisco Madero, anxious for her husband, who was being held in the National Palace, appealed to Huerta for mercy. On February 20, Madero and Suarez officially resigned, having been given assurances they would be permitted to go into exile. On February 22, Washington's Birthday, a meeting was held at the U.S. embassy, chaired by Ambassador Wilson. According to historian Samuel H. Mayo, 'Huerta . . . turned to Ambassador Wilson and asked what should be done with the imprisoned Madero. Should we commit him to an insane asylum or exile him? Wilson responded, "Do what is best for the peace of the country." '

Later that evening, Madero and Suarez were put into automobiles and driven toward the railway station, but when the vehicles did not stop there, the men realized their fate was not to be exiled. About 11 P.M. the party reached the penitentiary of Calle Lecumberri. The pair were shoved from the cars as the drivers and guards hurled obscenities at them. One of the escorts, Major Francisco Cardenas, pulled a gun and shot Madero in the back of the head. He then turned the weapon on the stunned Suarez and dispatched him in similar fashion. The official account was that the pair were killed attempting to escape.

According to Professor Mayo, 'Victoriano Huerta and Ambassador Henry Lane Wilson truly believed that the fall of the Madero government would usher in an era of peace and prosperity in Mexico.' Actually, the Revolution of 1910 had many bloody years yet to run, and Huerta himself would be forced to abandon his violent and corrupt dictatorship in 1914 and flee the country.

Further reading: *A History of Mexico*, by Samuel H. Mayo.

MAHER PASHA, Ahmed (?–1945) On February 24, 1945, Premier Ahmed Maher Pasha of Egypt was shot fatally on the floor of parliament just after reading a royal declaration of war on Germany and Japan. The gunman, a 28-year-old lawyer named Mahmoud Essawy, had long espoused support for the Axis powers as a way to rid Egypt of British rule. Essawy was quickly tried by the Supreme Military Court, found guilty and hanged the following September.

MAHMUD, Mir (1697–1725) After more than 200 years of Persian occupation of a large portion of Afghanistan, the Afghans under Mir Vais drove out the occupiers in 1708. Vais's son Mir Mahmud later invaded Persia and in 1722 deposed the Safavid ruler Husein and declared himself shah of Persia. To solidify his rule Mahmud summarily executed 3,000 of Husein's bodyguards, some 300 nobles and about 200 children who might be expected to resent the murders of their fathers. Three years later Mahmud ordered the slaughter of all members of the royal family save Husein and two of his younger children.

Some two months after this bloodletting Mahmud went insane and was killed by his cousin Ashraf, who proclaimed himself the new shah. It was a murder that did not go unapproved by either Afghans or Persians. However, the seeds of Ashraf's fall were already sown with the survival of Husein's son Tahmasp. Tahmasp rallied to his support of an obscure fighter named Nadir Kali, who was destined to be the greatest conqueror since Timur, and in due course to ascend the throne himself as Nadir Shah. (See NADIR SHAH.)

Further reading: *History of Persia*, by Sir Percy Sykes.

MAKEN, Lalit See DASS, ARJUN.

MALCOLM X (1925–1965) Within much of the black American community there is today as much controversy about the official findings in the 1965 assassination of the charismatic Black Muslim leader Malcolm X as there is among the general population concerning the murder of President John F. Kennedy. Many blacks insist that although three men were convicted and imprisoned for life, the police investigation was at best superficial and that one or more of the convicted men were unjustly charged. There are many who do not believe the assassination was the work of the Black Muslims or at least not of that group alone.

Born Malcolm Little in Omaha, Nebraska, Malcolm moved to Boston to live with a half-sister after the death of his father, a Baptist minister and organizer in the Marcus Garvey Back To Africa movement. Later he moved on to New York and in both cities gained the reputation in the black ghetto as a hustler. When he was 18 he went to prison for burglary, and there he discovered the teachings of Black Muslim leader Elijah Muhammad and changed his name to Malcolm X. Released from prison in 1952, he settled in Detroit and became assistant minister of Muslim Temple No. 1. He was put in charge of the Muslims' New York temple two years later, and by 1963 he was the Muslims' first 'national minister' and the second most powerful figure in the Nation of Islam, then the name for the movement.

Malcolm X clearly represented a threat to Elijah Muhammad and to his presumptive successor and son-in-law, Raymond Sharrief. In 1964 the relationship between Elijah Mohammad and Malcolm X deteriorated, and Malcolm X was suspended from his post. He then split away and formed his own group, the Organization of Afro-American Unity.

Earlier in his career Malcolm X had called himself 'the angriest black man in America,' and his call for self-defense appealed to many blacks irritated with the nonviolent integrationist strategy of the civil rights movement. It also frightened many whites. However, now outside the

Nation of Islam, Malcolm X altered many of his positions. During a five-week trip to Mecca and Africa he wrote his much-publicized *Letter from Mecca*, in which he reflected favorably on his experiences with caucasian Muslims, and he began to reevaluate his positions on whites and how they might help in a fight against racism in America.

By 1965 he had moved closer to the civil rights move= ment and had stopped calling black integrationists 'Uncle Toms.' In early February 1965 he visited Selma, Alabama, during the voter registration drive there and told Coretta Scott King that his own militant reputation would scare whites into supporting her husband's campaign.

During this period tension escalated between Malcolm X's supporters and those of the Nation of Islam. Shortly after Malcolm X's return from Selma, his home was firebombed.

The next Sunday, February 21, Malcolm X took the podium to address an audience of 400 at a mosque in Harlem. A disturbance broke out near the front rows and a voice cried out: 'Get your hands off my pockets! – Don't be messin' with my pockets!' Malcolm X tried to calm matters, saying 'Now, brothers, be cool.' Four of at least six bodyguards moved toward the disturbance, which was clearly an arranged distraction. At that moment another argument erupted further back in the audience. As heads turned, a smoke bomb was ignited. In the turmoil a black man with a sawed-off shotgun dashed toward the stage and loosed a blast into Malcolm X's chest. Quickly two other blacks rushed forward with handguns and fired several bullets into Malcolm's X prone body.

As is usual in moments of sudden violence, the audience and most of Malcolm X's bodyguards froze as the killers sought to escape. One fast-thinking bodyguard shot one of the attackers in the thigh. As he dropped at the front stairway exit to the ballroom, members of the audience, coming out of their lethargy, surrounded him and pummeled him until he was pulled to safety by police officers.

The general opinion of the police, the press and Malcolm X's supporters was that the act had been carried out by the Black Muslims. A Muslim mosque was burned in retaliation. However, the assailant captured at the scene, 22-year-old Talmadge Hayer, a married man with two children, could not be linked to the Black Muslims. Two other men arrested later and tried with Hayer were Black Muslims. Hayer admitted his part in the assassination and said he had three accomplices, but would not name them. He claimed neither of his codefendants, Norman 3X Butler, 27, and Thomas 15X Johnson, 30, were involved. All three were convicted.

In time public opinion in the black community agreed that Butler and Johnson were innocent. It was pointed out that both were well-known Black Muslims and would have found it very difficult to get through the security at the mosque. In addition, Butler had been treated at a Bronx hospital on the morning of the murder for thrombophlebitis, his right leg had been bandaged and he had been given medication, making him an unlikely assassin. Oddly, several of those present at the mosque, including three of Malcolm's X's lieutenants and bodyguards, disappeared afterward.

Further reading: *Autobiography of Malcolm X*, by Alex Haley; *The Last Year of Malcolm X*, by George Breitman.

MARAT, Jean-Paul (1743–1793) Early in July 1793 a 24-year-old woman named Charlotte Corday set out from her home in Caen in Normandy for Paris. She was a woman with a mission – to save France. Normandy was a stronghold of anti-Jacobin sentiments, and in Caen the impressionable Corday heard a leading Girondist, Jeanne Pierre Brissot, denounce the Jacobins in control of revolutionary Paris and especially one of their leaders, Jean-Paul Marat: 'This monster is unfeeling, violent and cruel. Three hundred thousand heads must be struck off before liberty is established. That will be until this man Marat, whose soul is kneaded in blood and dirt, and is a disgrace to humanity and to the revolution, is dead.'

Charlotte Corday determined to kill Marat.

The 50-year-old Marat was a doctor-scientist turned journalist-revolutionary. Since 1789 he had published a radical newspaper, *The Friend of the People*, which eventually called for a 'reign of terror' to protect the revolution. In July 1790 he told his readers: 'Five or six hundred heads cut off would have assured your repose, freedom and happiness. A false humanity has held your arms and suspended your blows; because of this millions of your brothers will lose their lives.'

Marat raged not only against the nobility but even against more moderate revolutionary leaders such as Lafayette, Mirabeau and Jean-Sylvain Bailly. In time he determined that the monarchy had to be totally abolished. He approved of the September 1892 massacres of jailed 'enemies of the Revolution' in which 1,000 to 1,500 men, women and children were slaughtered. Marat saw the episode as a necessary price for success and determined that the guillotine must be kept busy thereafter to keep the mob fired up. Thus innocent and guilty alike went to their death. It was Marat who demanded the establishment of the committee of surveillance, an office of suspicion, to aid in his rooting out of antirevolutionaries. He composed death lists. More than any other leader he demanded that the king be tried and then executed.

It was in the tumult of revolutionary Paris that Charlotte Corday arrived. On the afternoon of July 13 she appeared at Marat's apartment asking for an interview with him so that she might 'put him in a condition to render a great service to France.' Instead two female aides of Marat ejected her.

Corday returned that evening and again demanded to see Marat. The protective women once more barred her, but Marat, hearing the disturbance in the anteroom, called out to admit her. Corday was ushered into a room where Marat sat in a large metal tub soaking his disease-wracked body in a medicinal bath. Marat was forced to take such baths regularly to relieve a festering skin disease he had supposedly contracted by hiding out so often in the sewers of Paris. (Today it is theorized he probably suffered from an intense case of herpes.)

Marat carried on his revolutionary activities in his bath, writing on a wooden plank positioned across the tub. Corday waited until the female attendants left the chamber and then told Marat of some alleged insurrectionist plans being concocted by the Girondists in Caen. Enthusiastically Marat scribbled the names Corday ticked off. 'I shall send them all to the guillotine in a few days,' he fairly shouted.

With that Corday pulled from the bosom of her white muslin dress a 6-inch butcher knife she had purchased the day before for two francs. She plunged it into Marat's body, piercing the lung and severing the aorta. As blood quickly crimsoned the bathwater, Marat lived only long enough to call out, '*A moi, ma chere amie.*' ('*To me, my dear friend.*')

Marat's women aides rushed in and struggled with the assassin until help arrived. A porter knocked her down with a chair, then tied her hands behind her back. Put on trial quickly, Corday mocked the Revolutionary Tribunal as courageously as any prisoner. When asked if she had anything to say, she replied, 'Nothing, except that I have succeeded.' When her lawyer tried to plead insanity, she brushed the contention aside, saying she had committed an act of assassination. 'That is the only defense worthy of me.'

The last two days of Charlotte Corday's life were filled. She posed for Jean-Jacques Hauer to paint her portrait, a work now in the museum at Versailles. She wrote back to Caen saying, 'I long to be with Brutus in Elysian fields.'

On July 17, just four days after killing Marat, the 'Angel of the Assassination' was guillotined.

Corday's act triggered many more executions of royalists and Girondists alike, and there is much to be said for the contention by some students of the French Revolution that as a result of her action, many more thousands perished than even Marat himself would have ever doomed.

Further reading: *Jean-Paul Marat: A Study in Radical-*

ism, by Louis Reichenthal Gottschalk.

MARCEL, Etienne (c.1316–1358) Etienne Marcel, a 14th-century bourgeois leader, clothier and provost of the merchants of Paris, was the leading spirit in the Paris revolution of 1355–58 and for a time, while King John II was a prisoner in England, was the most powerful man in France. Had Marcel's rebellion been successful and not cut short by his assassination, the French Revolution would have occurred centuries earlier.

In 1355 the king called the States-General to collect taxes to finance the continuation of the Hundred Years' War (1337–1453), only to have Marcel counter by proposing that the assembly administer the revenue. After John was defeated and captured by the English at Poitiers in September 1356, Marcel was the leader of an assembly that essentially established a merchants' government that ruled Paris. The assembly passed the Great Ordinance of 1357, which sought to remove John's corrupt officials, ordered judges to speed up their calendars (often 20 years behind) by starting their sessions at sunrise and forbade nobles to leave the country or wage private war. Essentially, what Marcel sought was to make the aristocracy subject to the communes and the nobles subject to the business class. Royalty was to be required to obey the chosen representatives of the people. In short, this would have established a constitutional and parliamentary government.

With the king out of the way, Marcel and his allies forced the Dauphin, Charles of Valois (the future Charles V), to sign the ordinance. Immediately after signing, the Dauphin set about evading its requirements. However, Charles was without money to finance the war and to raise ransom for the king, and under those circumstances was forced to reassemble the States-General. To demonstrate his power, Marcel stormed the royal palace with a band of armed men hooded in the city's official colors of blue and red and rebuked Charles for seeking to thwart the will of the merchants. When Charles refused to pledge obedience to the instructions of the States-General, Marcel's men killed two chamberlains guarding the Dauphin.

Under Marcel's lead, the new States-General decreed that only it could enact laws for France and that the king in the future could act on important matters only with its approval. The Dauphin and many nobles fled Paris, leaving the city to complete merchant rule. The Dauphin set about raising an army with the aid of the nobles in Picardy and demanded that the people of Paris surrender the revolt's leaders. Marcel answered by ringing the city with new massive walls and moving his government into the Louvre itself.

Meanwhile the French peasantry rose against the nobles, and Marcel sent hundreds of agents into the countryside to foment their revolt. The Dauphin and the nobles finally succeeded in crushing the peasants, killing tens of thousands, and they then turned their attention back to Paris. The city's food supply was cut off, and Marcel's position steadily deteriorated. He sought help from the Flemish and even the English, and finally in desperation he sought to save himself by offering the French throne to Charles the Bad of Navarre.

Even some of Marcel's most ardent followers took this as treason, and his longtime friend and aide Jean Maillart entered into secret negotiations with the Dauphin. An agreement was reached on Marcel's assassination, which was carried out July 31, 1358, when Maillart and others slew their leader with an ax. Clearly, the merchants and bourgeois proved not yet powerful enough to establish republican rule. Instead the monarchy survived the revolt stronger than ever, with a docile States-General under its thumb.

Further reading: *Chronicles*, by Sir John Froissart; *The Story of Civilization VI – The Reformation*, by Will Durant.

MARKOV, Georgi (1929–1978) Six months before he was murdered in bizarre fashion in September 1978, Georgi Markov, a Bulgarian defector broadcasting in London for the BBC and the U.S.-backed Radio Free

Europe, had been tipped off by an anonymous compatriot that he was slated for assassination. According to the story, the Communists planned to make his death look natural, the result of a flu- or virus-induced high fever.

Markov took the warning seriously. He knew there were many reasons the Bulgarians wanted him dead. In the late 1960s he angered high Bulgarian officials by writing a play about a plot to murder an important general. Markov left Bulgaria to work in Italy and then moved on to England, where he was granted political asylum in 1969. Among his recent broadcasts that had irritated his former country was one that highlighted details of Bulgarian leaders' sex habits.

On September 7, 1978, about 6:30 P.M., the 49-year-old broadcaster was walking from his car to his night job as a BBC commentator when he felt a sharp sting to the back of his right thigh. Markov turned to see a stranger in a bus line holding a closed umbrella. 'I'm sorry,' the man said in a heavy accent and, getting out of line, disappeared into a taxi.

For the next several hours Markov felt fine, but back home he developed a fever and started vomiting. His leg had stiffened badly. Taken to the hospital, he told doctors, 'I've been poisoned. The umbrella man could have been an assassin.' Four days later Markov died.

British intelligence took Markov's dying opinion seriously. It was clear he had suffered blood poisoning. Microbiological warfare experts tested the skin tissue from the victim's thigh and found a minuscule platinum-iridium pellet, smaller than the head of a pin. The pellet contained a deadly poison, eventually identified as ricin, a derivative of the castor-oil plant that Eastern European scientists had researched extensively. The experts tested ricin on a pig, and the animal died in 25 hours. Doctors said that even if they had known Markov had been poisoned with ricin, there would have been nothing to be done for him since there was no known antidote.

It turned out it was not the first pellet attack on a Bulgarian defector. The previous August Vladimir

Kostov, who had been French correspondent for the Bulgarian radio network before defecting, was mysteriously hit in the back while on an escalator in a Paris subway station. Kostov became desperately ill but recovered. After Markov's death, Kostov was X-rayed and a tiny pellet was extracted from his back. Shipped to London, it was found to be the same as the Markov pellet. Doctors theorized that Kostov had survived because his pellet had not contained a lethal dose of the poison.

It was obvious to investigators that the attack had been the work of the Bulgarian secret service and had been carried out with the permission of the Soviet KGB. When the poisoned umbrella story broke, the Bulgarian government reacted angrily, at first denouncing the story as James Bondian nonsense. Later the Bulgars charged the Markov murder had been a plot, by some emigre group in league with a Western intelligence agency to embarrass Bulgaria by killing an expendable defector and putting the blame on Sofia. While this claim was dismissed, there were experts in the West who doubted Bulgarian involvement on the ground that country's intelligence lacked the scientific expertise needed for such a plot. These intelligence experts felt only SMERSH, the KGB section charged with carrying out international murders could have carried it out.

It has never been clear whether there were any other assassinations carried out in the same manner as that of Markov. U.S. intelligence figures privately indicated there had been other suspicious attacks and at least two deaths involving other exiles, not only Bulgarian but Croatian as well.

Further reading: *Encyclopedia of Modern Murder*, by Colin Wilson and Donald Seaman.

MATTEOTTI, Giacomo (1885–1924) The murder of Socialist leader Giacomo Matteotti by Italian Fascists in 1924 should have, with more astute handling, brought down the fledgling regime of Benito Mussolini, perhaps altering the history of World War II. A lawyer, Matteotti had joined the Italian Socialist Party in his teens and entered the Chamber of Deputies in 1919, and a few years later he became secretary general of his party.

In the meantime Mussolini had taken power and was conducting terrorist attacks on the left, with Matteotti standing as a bulwark against him, making ringing attacks on the Duce in the Chamber. On June 10, 1924, a Fascist terror flying squad kidnapped Matteotti in Rome, brutally murdered him and burned his body. The case shocked not only Italy but the entire world. Italian public opinion turned violently against the Fascists, who stopped wearing their party badges. Mussolini became a pariah, and his government offices were devoid of visitors.

The opposition then committed a major blunder in what became known as the Aventine secession, withdrawing from the Chamber to condemn the murder and to call for the overthrow of Mussolini. Out of office, however, the opposition was unable to keep public opinion at the boiling point, just as similarly they had been unable to prevent Mussolini's rise to power in 1922. After several months during which it appeared the government would actually topple, Mussolini shook off his personal funk and daringly acknowledged the guilt of his party for the Matteotti murder. Although he remained silent on whether he had ordered the assassination, Mussolini challenged the opposition to have him prosecuted.

The opposition lacked the strength for this, and in a prolonged judicial investigation, six individuals charged with the murder were freed. Having weakened the opposition, Mussolini then moved rapidly to establish a full dictatorship, suppressed the opposition press, purged all non-Fascist ministers and set up a secret police force.

At the end of World War II, the new Italian government launched an investigation of the Matteotti case, and the three assassins still alive were given 30-year terms.

MAXIMINUS, Emperor of Rome (?–238) A former shepherd and a brilliant soldier, a Thracian named Gaius Julius Maximus was the first military man to rise from the ranks to become Roman emperor, achieving that exalted position in 235 when Emperor Alexander Severus was assassinated by his own troops along the German border. The mutineers decided that the new emperor should be the giant Maximinus – some Roman historians say he was 8 feet tall – whose enormous strength and powers of endurance had first attracted the attention of Emperor Severus 30 years earlier. Maximinus's idea of ruling was to avenge himself on every man whose character, ability or ambition he feared or by whom he believed himself to have been slighted in the past. All over the empire Maximinus robbed cities of their public funds and stripped their temples of treasures. His response to any resistance was ruthless massacre.

Finally, the Roman upper classes revolted against Maximinus. They scorned him as a man with no education; he berated education but actually was envious of it. He was a butcher, they said, but many Roman emperors had been butchers and did not produce the class warfare that Maximinus inspired. The real reason was economic. To appease his troops and finance his military campaigns, the emperor levied huge taxes on the well-to-do. Said the contemporary historian Herodian, 'Every day one could see the richest of men of yesterday turned beggars today.'

The Senate, fired up to an extent not witnessed in decades, decreed that Maximinus was a public enemy and accepted as new co-emperors the elderly Gordian and his reluctant son Gordian II. However, an army commander in Mauretania fell upon the two Gordians and slew them. The panicked Senate, realizing that Maximinus, heading for Rome from the northern frontier, would offer it no mercy, named two of their members, Balbinus and Maximus, to rule jointly.

In the meantime Maximinus passed the Alps and, in need of supplies for his troops, stopped at Aquilea. When the citizens would not admit or feed him, Maximinus laid siege to the city. The deposed emperor thought to starve the city out, but his own troops starved as well. Their hunger led them to mutiny, and they murdered Maximinus in his tent.

Left with little recourse, the soldiers accepted the orders of the Senate and pledged their support to the two co-emperors. Unfortunately, Balbinus and Maximus thought their Senatorial revolution was now secure and proposed new disciplines for the army. Once more the soldiery revolted and slew the two emperors. The army then decided, and a frightened Senate concurred, that the new emperor would be the 13-year-old Gordian III. The level of bloodletting by assassination had driven all elements to exhaustion. In a period of 12 months in 237–38, five emperors of Rome had been murdered. It was time for a brief pause. (See ALEXANDER SEVERUS, EMPEROR OF ROME; GORDIAN III, EMPEROR OF ROME.)

Further reading: *History of Twenty Caesars*, by Herodian.

MAXIMUS, Emperor of Rome See VALENTINIAN III, EMPEROR OF ROME.

MBOYA, Thomas (1930–1969) The assassination of 38-year-old Tom Mboya, Kenyan political leader and minister of economic affairs, on a Nairobi street on July 5, 1969, let loose a period of tribal and political unrest. As soon as the news spread of Mboya's death, violent clashes between the Luo and Kikuyu tribes broke out. Mboya, a Luo, was secretary-general of the ruling Kenya African National Union headed by President Jomo Kenyatta, a Kikuyu.

Kenyatta declared a week of national mourning, but this did not prevent stones from being hurled at the president's car at the funeral. It was the first time the *mzee* ('old man') of Kenyan politics was jeered by the public. Kenyatta did not attend the burial.

Before his murder Mboya had been considered a leading presidential candidate in the upcoming elections, and the government claimed the assassination was a 'political execution.' Vice President Arap Moi denied Communist charges that Western powers were behind the killing. At the time the Soviets were offering considerable economic assistance in Luo areas.

On July 21 Nahashon Isaac Njenga Njoroge, a Kikuyu tribesman, was charged with the Mboya murder. In the meantime the *New York Times* reported that Mboya had expressed his fear of assassination to American friends, saying Kenyatta's plans to hold a general election later in the year increased the danger to him. He thought his enemies would try to keep him from exercising a leading role in the elections.

When a preliminary hearing for Njoroge was held, police testified that during the search of his house the defendant said to an officer: 'Oh man, do not go against me. If it is 5,000 or 10,000, I will give it to you.' When a gun was found and he was asked if it was the murder weapon, Njoroge was alleged to have replied: 'Why don't you go and get some big man? We did what we were told.' Njoroge would not answer when asked who the 'big man' was.

The gun was indeed the murder weapon, and the 32-year-old defendant was found guilty and hanged secretly in November after being denied clemency by President Kenyatta.

In the elections held on December 6, Kenyatta's party suffered huge losses (although Kenyatta had been re-elected two weeks earlier in a special uncontested election), and Luo parliament members who were associated with Kenyatta were replaced by others with no such identification.

MEDICI, Alessandro de' (1511–1538) In 1530 republican Florence was defeated by the forces of the Holy Roman Empire, and the papacy once more came under control of the Medici family. Ippolito de' Medici had been destined since childhood to become the head of the state of Florence, but he had been driven out by the republican uprising of 1527. Pope Clement VII, the nephew of Lorenzo the Magnificent, maneuvered to keep Ippolito from his post by replacing him with Alessandro de' Medici, reputedly the pope's illegitimate son, as the hereditary duke of Florence. Ippolito was forced to become a cardinal and was kept out of the way by being sent by the pope on church missions to other countries.

Alessandro brought to Florence a rapacity and cruelty of almost grotesque proportions. Hundreds of those who had supported the republic were tortured, exiled or executed. In desperation some Florentine exiles sought to have Alessandro removed by the Holy Roman emperor, Charles V. They selected Ippolito as their spokesman, but as Ippolito prepared to sail to Tunis, where the emperor was on an expedition, he was poisoned by Giovanni Andrea, at Alessandro's behest. Andrea escaped to Florence and Alessandro's protection, but later Andrea unwisely made a visit to his native town of Borgo San Sepolcro and was stoned to death by the populace.

This hardly weakened Alessandro's hold on Florence, and his tyrannical rule continued. Death, it was said, could be expected by any citizen at any moment. Even the artist Michelangelo feared for his life under Alessandro, and in 1534 he took the opportunity to flee to Rome. Alessandro continued his cruel ways and took as his closest friend, Lorenzino de' Medici, a distant relative. Lorenzino became Alessandro's partner in debauchery, and they frequented brothels together and violated private homes and convents.

On January 5, 1537, the pair came to Lorenzino's dwelling after a day of hectic activities and Alessandro fell asleep on the couch while Lorenzino went forth, ostensibly to secure for the duke a married woman he desired. Instead Lorenzino returned with an assassin named Scoronconcolo, and the two fell on their sleeping victim. Alessandro awakened with the first blade blows and fought desperately for his life before finally expiring.

Lorenzino expected the Florentines to rise up against the tyrannical government, but when that failed to occur, he fled to Bologna to await the exiles' attack on Florence. This attack was defeated, and Lorenzino continued on to

Turkey. Despite his propensity for personal excesses, Lorenzino was a writer of effective elegance. He defended his action in an *Apologia*, presenting himself with lofty eloquence as another Brutus who had played the role of friend and courtier solely out of love for liberty. Most historians regard Lorenzino's writings as no more than self-serving, and for evidence point to his later life, that which continued its devious path until Lorenzino was murdered in Venice in 1548.

Further reading: *The Medici*, by G. F. Young.

MEDICI, Ippolito de' See MEDICI, ALESSANDRO DE'.

MEDICI, Lorenzino de' See MEDICI, ALESSANDRO DE'.

MEDICI, Lorenzo de' (1445–1492) – Attempted Assassination An incredible exercise in assassination began a few days before Easter in 1478, when a group of conspirators arrived in Florence determined to murder Lorenzo de' Medici, 'Il Magnifico.' Involved actively in the plot were Francesco Salviati, the archbishop of Pisa; two leading Florentine bankers, Bernardo Baroncelli and Francesco de' Pazzi; and to the satisfaction of most historians, Pope Sixtus IV, although some believe he stopped just short of sanctioning assassination.

The motivation for the assassination plot, known as the Pazzi Conspiracy, was a treacherous economic war in which the Pazzi bank of Florence lured the business affairs of the papacy away from the Medici bankers. Friction grew between the pope and Lorenzo, the ruler of Florence, and when the latter sought to keep the papacy from extending its temporal power, the conspiracy began with the idea of installing the Pazzis as the rulers of Florence.

It was decided that Lorenzo the Magnificent's younger brother Giuliano should be killed with him. The murders would be followed the next day by arrival of mercenary armies at the gates of Florence. The first plan called for the two Medicis to be murdered at a banquet by a professional assassin named Montesecco. But when

Giuliano took to bed with a damaged knee, the plot was canceled. It was then decided to kill the pair when they attended mass on Easter Sunday in the Duomo. However, Montesecco developed qualms over this, feeling he could not kill men as they knelt at mass. He would not be swayed even when the archbishop assured him that the pope would grant absolution. The plotters then turned to two Duomo priests, Stefano de Bagnone and Antonio Maffei, who suffered no similar moral pangs about committing murder within their own church.

Lorenzo arrived at the cathedral before his brother, and when Giuliano entered, one of the Pazzis embraced him, actually checking to see if he carried a dagger. Giuliano was unarmed, and on signal Baroncelli and one of the priests and several Pazzis fell on him, stabbing him a total of 19 times. Lorenzo was more alert than his ailing brother, and he turned quickly as the priest Maffei lashed out at him with a dagger, receiving only a neck wound. As several of the assassins charged at him, Lorenzo, surrounded by friends, rushed into the sacristy and shut the bronze doors. The assassins battered at the doors but finally were forced to retreat.

Meanwhile Jacopo Pazzi, the head of the family, rode his horse through the streets, waving his sword and proclaiming, 'Liberty and the republic!' As word spread of the killing of Giuliano, the Florentine crowds turned angry and shouted at Pazzi, 'Balls!' – a reference to the Medici coat of arms. Realizing that the citizenry was siding with the Medicis, Jacopo beat a hasty retreat to his country estate.

In the meantime, Archbishop Salviati, carrying out his part in the conspiracy, had hastened to the Signoria Palace, to proclaim to the town councillors that he was taking control of the government. However, he was separated in the courtyard from his armed escort, which was locked outside, and he was taken prisoner. Meanwhile angry crowds converged on the palace and massacred the archbishop's men. Francesco was caught and brought to the palace. Many of the conspirators were hurled out of windows, then Francesco de Pazzi and the archbishop were hanged by ropes from an upper window, the churchman gnawing desperately at Francesco de' Pazzi's shoulder in his dying agony.

In the square others suspected of being involved in the plot were mercilessly hacked to death. Only when Lorenzo appeared at the window and urged the crowds to disperse did the killings stop. Within two days Lorenzo's vengeance was complete. Jacopo Pazzi was tortured, hanged and dragged naked through the streets. Renato Pazzi, who had no part in the conspiracy and in fact opposed it, was also killed. The two priests involved were found in hiding, their noses and ears were cut off and then they were hanged. The original assassin, Montesecco, having made a confession that implicated Pope Sixtus IV, was permitted to die by the sword.

Pope Sixtus retaliated by charging Lorenzo with the killing of an archbishop and demanded that Florence hand Lorenzo over to him. When the city and its clergy rejected the demand, the pope excommunicated the entire city.

It is possible the pope's edict might have prevailed as long as he maintained the support of Ferdinand I, king of Naples. With a true master stroke, Lorenzo went alone to Naples and presented himself to Ferdinand, certainly one of the cruelest rulers of the age. Lorenzo's very boldness, however, apparently disconcerted the ruler, and they concluded a treaty of peace. The pope, isolated, was forced to accept the new reality, and Lorenzo de' Medici emerged from the conspiracy as the firm ruler of Florence and went on to be a great patron of arts and letters and certainly the most brilliant of the Medicis.

Further reading: *A Criminal History of Mankind*, by Colin Wilson; *The Medici* by G. F. Young; *The Story of Civilization V – The Renaissance*, by Will Durant.

MEIN, John Gordon (1913–1968) The 1960s in Guatemala were marked by open guerrilla warfare in which the army suffered high losses at the hands of left-wing terrorists. By 1967 right-wing paramilitary groups, armed with

U.S.-supplied weapons, struck back, and thereafter American diplomatic and military advisers themselves came under attack from the FAR (Rebel Armed Forces) Communist group. In fact, the entire foreign diplomatic corps in Guatemala City felt threatened and demanded increased protection.

In January 1968 two American military aides, Colonel John D. Webber, the head of the U.S. military mission, and Lieutenant Commander Ernest A. Munro, the chief of the U.S. embassy naval section, were shot dead as they drove to the embassy. FAR announced it had carried out the assassinations in retaliation for the murder by rightists of Miss Guatemala of 1950, who was suspected of being a FAR sympathizer.

On August 28, 1968, FAR struck again. U.S. Ambassador John Gordon Mein, a 21-year veteran of the foreign service, was being driven to work when two carloads of FAR terrorists ambushed his car, apparently intending to kidnap him. Mein tried to escape and was machine-gunned to death. His chauffeur was unharmed. Mein was the first U.S. ambassador to be assassinated on active duty.

Two years later West German Ambassador Count Karl von Spreti was kidnapped by FAR, which demanded money and the release of 17 leftist prisoners for his safe return. The Guatemalan government refused and von Spreti was murdered. The West German government expressed bitterness at the turn of events – it was willing to pay the ransom for von Spreti – but the Guatemalan government insisted it could not have released the leftists since four of the 17 named in the proposed exchange deal had confessed to having taken part in the Mein assassination. (See SPRETI, COUNT KARL VON.)

MICHAEL, Grand Duke (1878–1918) When Czar Nicholas II abdicated on March 15, 1917 for both himself and his only son, Alexis, he left the mantle to his brother, Grand Duke Michael. Michael in turn abdicated the next day, leaving the field open for what would prove to be the weak Kerensky government. After the Bolshevik Revolution of October, the grand duke was exiled to Perm in the Ural region. However, his eventual fate was clearly to be determined by whatever the Bolsheviks decided to do with the former czar and his family, who were held elsewhere. The decision was reached in early July, and on or about July 13, the grand duke and his English secretary were assassinated by a secret police contingent headed by the Cheka leader Miasnikov.

The assassins of the grand duke did a much better job of concealing their act than those who killed Nicholas II and his family shortly thereafter. The bodies of Michael and his secretary were never found, apparently having been burned. (See NICHOLAS II, CZAR OF RUSSIA.)

MICHAEL III, Byzantine Emperor (838–867) Michael III became Byzantine emperor in 842 on the death of his father, Theophilus. Although Michael's reign inaugurated a long period of greatness and expansion of the Middle Byzantine Empire, it was no thanks to the young monarch destined to be known as Michael the Drunkard. In the first years of his reign power was exercised by the dowager empress, the shrewd Theodora, and her devoted foreign minister, Theoctistus. In this period, which lasted until 856, Orthodox image-worship was reestablished, but perhaps the most important accomplishment was keeping the youthful emperor under tight control.

However, when Michael neared 15 he came under the influence of Theodora's brilliant brother, Bardas, who had long felt slighted by the powerful Theoctistus. Eager to be a ruler in his own right, Michael agreed to hatch a conspiracy with his uncle. Bardas maneuvered the minister into insulting him and then had him seized and carried from the palace. Theoctistus was then murdered at the young emperor's personal command.

Theodora was shunted to the background, and within a short time tonsured and sent with her daughters to a nunnery. Nothing much changed for Michael. Bardas became chief magistrate and commander in chief of the armed forces and for 10 years ruled as emperor in all but name.

By 865, Michael had come under the influence of Basil the Macedonian, a peasant who had once toiled as a stable hand. He tamed a horse for Michael, and the impressionable monarch took him into the palace service, where he rose in time to the post of lord chamberlain. Basil proved valuable to Michael in his sexual affairs, going so far as to divorce his own peasant wife and marry the emperor's mistress, Eudocia, so that she could conveniently continue her services to the emperor. Apparently Basil himself served as the emperor's bedfellow as well.

Basil was a man of unbounded ambition, and he succeeded in convincing Michael that Bardas was plotting to depose him. With Michael watching, Basil struck down Bardas and strangled him with his powerful peasant hands.

On May 26, 866, the ecstatic Michael had Basil crowned co-emperor. Michael himself was to live just four more months. Some historians doubt that Basil planned to kill Michael but that he would have been content to exercise the same power Bardas had had. But now at age 27 Michael felt he was truly ruler and needed not listen to the murderous ally who had risen from so lowly an estate. Some biographers insist that Michael was not nearly as bad as a monarch as contemporary scribes made out – that they were seeking to clothe in extenuating circumstances the murder of Michael by Basil and his supporters. However, there is little doubt that in these last few months Michael had degenerated into a complete sot. No one around him, Basil included, could feel themselves safe from his taunts and threats. Basil was most likely correct in believing that he himself would soon go the way of Bardas. Basil arranged for a band of his cutthroats to finish off the reeling Michael.

Whatever the crimes of Basil, he launched the grand era of the Macedonian dynasty which was to bring glories to the Byzantine throne and last until the death of Basil's great-great-great-granddaughter Theodora in 1056. Basil himself ruled for 19 years, efficiently but not without great cruelty, until he died in a hunting accident. Some said he was murdered by the friends of his son Leo. This was never proved, but as Harvard historian Romilly Jenkins notes: 'If it were so, the wheel had come full circle. Michael, dangerously mad, was murdered by his adopted son, Basil. Basil, dangerously mad, was murdered by his son Leo. And who shall say that the middle ages were wrong in reposing their trust in the Divine Justice and Retribution?'

Further reading: *Byzantium: The Imperial Centuries A.D. 610–1071*, by Romilly Jenkins.

MIDHAT PASA (1822–1883) Midhat Pasa was a reformer who was largely responsible for the overthrow of Turkish Sultan Abdul-Aziz in 1876 and perhaps for the ex-sultan's subsequent assassination. The son of a judge, Midhat had moved rapidly up the Turkish governmental apparatus, making a considerable number of enemies along the way. In 1872 he attacked the Ottoman grand vizier Mahmud Nedim's political policies, and the sultan, impressed by his boldness, raised Midhat to the post. However, Midhat held the position for only three months before being dropped by the sultan for showing too much independence.

In 1876 Midhat, relegated to lesser posts, joined in a conspiracy with army leader Hussein Avni Pasha to oust the sultan. This proved successful, and a few days after the conspirators seized power it was announced that the former sultan had committed suicide. But the rebels' control of the government was tenuous. Abdul-Aziz was replaced by his nephew Murad V, but because of his insanity he had to be dropped in favor of his brother, who became Abdul-Hamid II.

In the meantime Hussein Avni Pasha was assassinated by a Turkish soldier along with several others, as they took part in a cabinet meeting. For a time Midhat remained as grand vizier, but in February of the following year Abdul-Hamid II had Midhat accused of conspiracy and exiled.

Abdul-Hamid II was to become known as the Great Assassin because of the many persons he had killed to maintain his power and Abdul the Damned because it was believed he was sure to be overthrown and most likely assassinated. To protect himself the sultan had Constantinople's Yildiz palace heavily guarded. His private rooms were fitted with alarm systems, trap doors and mirrors set at angles to reveal intruders. Life-sized wax dummies of the sultan were placed on chairs or reclined on lounges and set near windows in hopes of drawing an assassin's fire.

The sultan's paranoia about possible assassination led to considerable ambivalence toward Midhat Pasa. After a year in exile, Midhat was recalled and named governor of Smyrna. But in May 1881 he was once more stripped of his powers and ordered arrested by the sultan on charges of having caused the death of Sultan Abdul-Aziz. Midhat, highly popular with a number of European countries, managed to escape the country and appealed to the European powers to intervene on his behalf. Shortly thereafter he returned to Turkey and surrendered.

Midhat was tried on the assassination charge and sentenced to death. The sultan relented on the extreme sentence because of British intercession and commuted the penalty to life banishment. It appears the sultan's reaction had been another example of his ambivalence, for on May 8, 1883, Midhat was murdered in his place of confinement at at-Ta'if, Arabia.

As for Abdul-Hamid II, he managed to avoid assassination himself, but under increasing pressure of the Young Turk dissident movement, he was finally deposed in 1909, forced into exile and died in 1918. (See ABDUL-AZIZ, OTTOMAN SULTAN.)

MILK, Harvey (1930–1978) The double assassination of San Francisco Mayor George Moscone and Supervisor Harvey Milk shook the California city; ironically, the killing of the lower-ranking Milk had the greater impact, since Milk was an avowed homosexual and a hero to the city's gay community.

The killings were the work of a 32-year-old former policeman and fireman, Dan White, who had been elected supervisor until he resigned because he found his salary of $9,600 insufficient to support his wife and young child. Under pressure from some of his constituents, White changed his mind and asked the mayor to reappoint him. At first Moscone agreed, but later he too changed his mind, opting for a new appointee. Distraught, White went to Moscone's office and shot him four times. Then he walked to the supervisors' chambers on the other side of City Hall and killed Harvey Milk, who had stated a firm opposition to White's return to the board.

White offered no resistance when arrested. At his trial, the defense contended that White had committed the murders while suffering from diminished mental capacity due to personal and financial pressure and being 'high on junk food.' On May 22, 1979, the jury convicted White of manslaughter rather than of premeditated murder. The verdict shocked much of San Francisco's citizenry, but especially the gay community. Thousand of homosexuals rioted in the streets. It was their contention that the alleged leniency would have never been shown White had Supervisor Milk not been an admitted homosexual. Mob violence aimed at homosexuals had occurred not infrequently in American history, but this was a rare instance in which gays had rioted.

White drew a sentence of seven years and eight months in prison, the maximum term permitted by the jury's verdict. He was paroled in 1984 and committed suicide in 1985.

MIN, Queen of Korea (1851–1895) Queen Min of Korea became consort to King Kojong of the Yi monarchy in 1866, when she was 15 years old. Almost immediately she became a power to be reckoned with and insinuated her clan into important positions in the government bureaucracy. In time, the Min clan became the most powerful faction at court, and she quarreled constantly with the king's father, the *taewon'-gun*, or 'grand prince.'

The Min clan was responsible for opening Korea to foreign commerce and trade in 1871. In 1882 an army revolt to restore the grand prince to power failed. Queen Min was frequently criticized for her notorious immoral behavior as well as the corruption of her relatives. Nevertheless, by shrewdly playing off one enemy against another, the queen maintained her position. Internationally, she obtained the friendship of China to counter the growing menace of Japan. When Japan defeated China in 1894, Queen Min's position was badly threatened. She also faced new revolts over charges of corruption as well as political reforms attempting to limit her powers.

Nevertheless, Min remained a solid roadblock to Japanese domination of the country, and in 1895 Japanese officials plotted her assassination. On October 8, 1895, a group of Koreans and Japanese acting under orders of the Japanese consul, General Goro Miura, broke into the palace and brutally murdered the queen, burning her corpse. The assassination loosed a storm of international protest and disgust, and General Miura was returned to Japan and tried for conspiracy to murder the queen. Although he was found guilty, the general was not sentenced to prison. The queen's assassination had achieved its purpose. Min power vanished from Yi politics.

Further reading: *Encyclopedia of Asian History*.

MIRBACH, Count Wilhelm von (?–1918) Just as the assassination of the Archduke Ferdinand of Austria brought on World War I in 1914, the assassination of Count Wilhelm von Mirbach, the German ambassador to Soviet Russia, was an attempt four years later to restart the conflict between Germany and Russia.

Mirbach was appointed ambassador to Russia following the Brest Litovsk peace treaty, and on his arrival in Moscow he was greeted with disdain by the Left Socialist Revolutionaries, the radical terrorists who favored renewed war with Germany. They expected the assassination of Mirbach to provoke this result, and apparently a vote to effect the murder was taken on June 24, 1918, at the meeting of the central committee of the Socialist Revolutionaries.

There is reason to believe that the Bolsheviks, or at least some of them, became aware of these machinations, but failed to warn the Germans. The Bolsheviks were in a difficult position. True, they did not wish to provoke Germany, but if Mirbach were killed, the Bolsheviks would have an ideal opportunity to crush the Socialist Revolutionary movement.

This is precisely what happened. On July 6, 19-year-old Jacob Blyumkin, a member of the Cheka and an SR, entered the German embassy to confer with the ambassador ostensibly as part of his assignment to guard foreign representatives. With such cover it was relatively easy for Blyumkin not only to kill Count Mirbach but also to manage to escape.

Germany did not go to war. The SRs actually attempted a coup, seizing Cheka boss Felix Dzerzhinsky and staging revolts in several provincial towns. SR generals declared war on both the Bolsheviks and the Germans, but the efforts were all rather inept and easily crushed by the Bolsheviks, who could now move to suppress the Socialist Revolutionaries on charges they were in league with monarchists and Anglo-French capitalists. Many SRs were arrested and by 1922 they were eliminated from the political scene.

Interestingly the assassin Blyumkin, who had vanished, returned a year later, was pardoned, and permitted to join the Communist Party. Blyumkin remained in favor until the Stalin period when he achieved the distinction of being the very first Communist to be shot on charges of Trotskyism.

Further reading: *The Bolsheviks*, by Adam B. Ulam.

MITRIONE, Daniel A. (1920–1970) Few assassinations have been more debated in the media than that of Dan

Mitrione, a U.S. police adviser charged by critics with having been dispatched to Latin America as part of the U.S. government's attempt to maintain totalitarian puppet-allies. Officially Mitrione advised local officials on traffic safety, a somewhat unusual task for a man who had been police chief of Richmond, Indiana, and then a member of the FBI. In 1960 he went to Brazil under the aegis of the State Department's International Cooperation Agency. During Mitrione's seven-year stint in Brazil torture was widely used against foes of the military government, and the police, many of whom received direct training under Mitrione, formed notorious death squads that murdered scores of 'undesirables' without the niceties of arrest or trial.

On August 1, 1970, Mitrione was kidnapped by the Tupamaros (MLN), a revolutionary Marxist group. The kidnappers demanded the release of a large number of political prisoners in exchange for Mitrione's life. The group also released a large number of documents revealing Mitrione's police and FBI status, charges that became a cause celebre in the Uruguayan press and Senate and produced an international reaction. The Uruguayan government refused to accede to the MLN's demands, and Mitrione was murdered.

The U.S. government portrayed Mitrione as a 'defenseless human being,' and Frank Sinatra and Jerry Lewis put on a show in Mitrione's memory. Overall, the world press viewed Mitrione as a do-gooder, although the 1973 film *State of Siege*, directed by Costa-Gavras, later altered this image. The United States determined to crush the Tupamaros and did so by sending FBI and CIA agents, eventually following up with Green Beret advisers.

Today most of the Tupamaros are dead or in prison, but, as Christopher Dobson and Ronald Payne note in *The Terrorists*, 'the repressive measures that the military government took are so harsh that ordinary democratic life has ceased in Uruguay. Freedom of the press and all political traditional rights have been suspended.' The writers posed the possibility the Tupamaros may have 'a posthumous success, the one that terrorists always argue should be achieved: a revolution provoked by the repressive measures taken to contain terrorism. But there is no sign of this at present.'

MOAWAD, Rene (1925–1989) On November 22, 1989, Lebanese President Rene Moawad was killed when a huge 400-pound bomb blew up his armored Mercedes-Benz, leaving it little more than a mass of twisted metal. Moawad had been in office only 17 days. The president's motorcade was returning from a Lebanese independence day ceremony in Muslim West Beirut when the bomb, concealed in a roadside shack along the convoy route, was detonated, apparently by remote control. It left a 30-foot-wide crater about 6 feet deep and killed at least 23 others, including 10 presidential bodyguards. In the aftermath of the explosion, panicky Lebanese and Syrian soldiers ran about firing rifles and rocket launchers in the air, and screaming and bleeding civilians raced in every direction, many begging passing cars to rush them to the American University Hospital, where finally the emergency room door had to be barred because of the crush.

The Moawad killing seemed to put off even further any hope of ending the 14-year religious civil war that had enveloped Lebanon. Who had committed the atrocity? Although General Michel Aoun's Christian forces were a likely candidate, there was actually no dearth of suspects, including Syria, Iran and Israel.

Whoever instigated it, the assassination followed a well-established pattern of murdering Lebanese leaders of whatever persuasion as soon as they showed signs of tempering their partisan positions by even hinting at the need for national reconciliation. Other victims of that pattern were Kamal Jumblat, the Druse leader killed in 1977; Christian President-elect Bashir Gemayel; and Sunni Muslim Prime Minister Rashid Karami, killed by a bomb in 1987.

MONTIGNY, Florent de Montmorency, Baron of (1527–

1570) While history and legend have long branded Philip II of Spain a regal assassin, being deeply involved in the plot to kill Elizabeth and William the Silent (William of Orange) of the Netherlands, it was the murder of the Flemish rebel, Baron Montigny, that perhaps best shows the Spanish king's artful use of murder for reasons of state.

Montigny had been sent by the rebels in the Spanish Netherlands to plead their case to Philip, and for political reasons the king received the baron handsomely and consented to the abolition of the episcopal Inquisition in the Netherlands.

Then Philip sent the notorious duke of Alva to the Netherlands to ferret out all heresy and rebellion in that troubled country. When Alva decided in 1568 to imprison leaders of the revolt, he sent a message that Baron Montigny should not be allowed to return to the Netherlands.

Finally even Pope Pius V, who had formerly rejoiced at Alva's victories, agreed with the Dutch Catholic clergy that Alva's severity was to be deplored. The pope urged that a general amnesty be granted all repentant rebels and heretics, terms to which Philip agreed in early 1569. However, in concert with Alva, the amnesty was not proclaimed until well into 1570. Meanwhile, Baron Montigny, in prison charged with high treason, presented a real problem for Philip. Rather than turn him free, Philip devised a cunning solution and had him garroted in his prison cell. Philip then announced that Montigny had died of fever and gave him a handsome burial with 700 royal masses for the repose of his soul.

Further reading: *The Story of Civilization VII – The Age of Reason Begins*, by Will and Ariel Durant.

MOORE, George C. See NOEL, CLEO A., JR.

MORO, Aldo (1918–1978) The kidnapping of Aldo Moro by the urban guerrilla group the Red Brigades in 1978 demonstrated the terrorists' power in Italy at the time. It also demonstrated what experts Christopher Dobson and Ronald Payne called in *The Terrorists* 'the impotence of security and police forces, who for weeks on end were unable to track down the terrorist hideout where Moro was being held.'

Moro, five-time premier of Italy and one of the nation's leading politicians, was head of the ruling Christian Democratic Party and the architect of the government accords between his party and first the Socialists and then the Communist Party. He was expected to be named the next president of Italy.

Moro was being driven through Rome under heavy escort on March 16, 1978, when he was ambushed by a squad of 11 Red Brigade terrorists dressed in stolen Alitalia airline uniforms. The ambush site had been well prepared by the terrorists, who the day before had slashed all four tires of a florist's pickup truck usually parked at the intersection during business hours. By sabotaging the truck in its nighttime parking area, the abductors eliminated that possible encumbrance from the kidnap site. They drove out of a side street, blocking the oncoming Moro convoy, and opened fire with automatic weapons. Moro's five bodyguards were killed, and he was dragged away unscathed.

At the time 14 of the Red Brigades' leaders were among the defendants in a mass trial of terrorists under way in Turin, and telephone messages were received demanding their release. A total of 15,000 police and 6,000 troops were deployed in a manhunt centering on Rome. They were unsuccessful.

Moro's kidnappers released photographs of Moro being held captive and announced he would be tried by their own 'people's court.' Moro of course was subjected to continual psychological harassment by his captors and wrote letters pleading for his life and later urging the government to accede to the terrorists' demands because he was afraid he might betray state secrets under torture. On April 4 a letter from Moro was sent to newspapers in which he called on Premier Guilio Andreotti and other

Christian Democratic leaders for quick action and said he felt 'a little abandoned by all of you.' Andreotti, at the time of delivery of the letter, was announcing in parliament a hard-line position against any negotiations with the kidnappers. Clearly the kidnappers were seeking to produce chaos and friction with the ruling coalition and to increase pressure on the government by the distraught Moro family and friends.

The manhunt was complicated by numerous hoax telephone calls announcing Moro's execution, and on April 18 the Red Brigades issued a letter with a photograph to prove that Moro was still alive by having him pose with a newspaper dated the day before. The letter added that the government had 48 hours to release the prisoners or Moro would die. Despite fissures within the government, no deal was struck. On May 5 the terrorists sent a message saying they were carrying out Moro's execution because of the government's refusal to negotiate. On May 7 Moro sent a farewell letter to his wife saying, 'They have told me they are going to kill me in a little while.' Despite this, the public was shocked when on May 9 Moro's body, riddled with 11 bullets, was found in a car – parked, with political symbolism, a short distance between the Christian Democratic and Communist parties' headquarters.

Needless to say, political chaos persisted thereafter in Italy, and it would take some five years for the capture and conviction of the terrorists. In the meantime it had become apparent that there had been a split among the Red Brigades, with many wishing to free Moro on the grounds that returning him unharmed would have simply added to the embarrassment of the ruling political parties. In addition a dissident faction criticized the leadership for focusing efforts on the attacks against eminent individuals instead of trying to broaden the base of the support for radical social change.

Thirty-two Red Brigade terrorists were jailed for life in January 1983 for their part in the Moro assassination. Among them were the accused executioner, 33-year-old Prospero Gallinari, and nine women. The defendants had been betrayed by a few of their comrades who got off with lesser sentences in exchange for their cooperation. One of those sentenced to life, Laura Braghetti, named as Moro's keeper in his captivity, screamed abuse at an informer-terrorist, Antonio Savasta, confined in a separate cage, 'You bastard, you would even sell your mother!'

Later, a document smuggled out of the prison where many of the Red Brigades were confined reached the newspaper *La Republica*. Headlined 'THE ARMED STRUGGLE IS OVER,' the document stated, 'The phase of revolutionary struggle which started in the early 1970s . . . is substantially finished.' The document added that the armed struggle was 'short-circuited' and advised their comrades to 'seek new means of revolution.'

The Red Brigades had recognized a central fact about assassination: that it is of limited value in bringing down the establishment.

Further reading: *Combating the Terrorists*, edited by H. H. Tucker; *Contemporary Terrorism*, edited by William Gutteridge; *The Encyclopedia of Modern Murder*, by Colin Wilson.

MOSCONE, George See MILK, HARVEY.

MOUNTBATTEN, Louis, Earl of Burma (1900–1979) Earl Mountbatten of Burma, the great World War II hero and cousin of Queen Elizabeth, spent all his summers at Cassiebawn Castle in Mullaghmore in County Sligo, Ireland. Since 1969, when the IRA reinstituted its terrorism against Britain in an attempt to alter that country's Irish policy, Lord Mountbatten eschewed the maximum security protection offered him. In time he also asked the Sligo police to withdraw the discreet watch they kept on the castle, arguing it was not needed and was a waste of public funds. 'What would they want with an old man like me?' he asked.

On August 27, 1979, Lord Mountbatten, with several members of his family, set out in his fishing yacht *Shadow V* to pick up lobster pots he had dropped earlier. Unbeknownst to Lord Mountbatten a radio fuse bomb was planted in the craft's engine room, and beach goers heard a tremendous roar as the *Shadow V* was turned to matchwood. The radio signal that exploded the bomb came from the cliff top over the bay. Killed along with Lord Mountbatten were his 14-year-old grandson, Nicholas Knatchbull, and 15-year-old Paul Maxwell, a local boat boy. Four others were badly injured: Lady Brabourne, Mountbatten's daughter; her husband, Lord Brabourne; Timothy Knatchbull, young Nicholas's twin brother; and the dowager Lady Brabourne, Lord Brabourne's mother, who died the next day.

The queen was immediately notified of the murders, and the public was horrified in Britain and also in India, where Lord Mountbatten, as the last viceroy, had presided over the negotiations leading to independence for the subcontinent. On the same day as the Mountbatten assassination the IRA killed 18 British soldiers and a vacationing Englishman in an ambush in Northern Ireland.

Three days after the assassination the Provisional IRA announced that the 'bombing was a discriminate act to bring to the attention of the English people the continuing occupation of our country.' The statement declared that the British army had acknowledged that it could not defeat the IRA, 'but yet it continues with the oppression of our people and the torture of our comrades in H Block [the group of prison cells where IRA members were being held].' And 'for this we will tear out their sentimental imperialist hearts.'

Arrests were made in the Mountbatten killing within hours. An alert Irish police officer stopped a car on a routine check, and, becoming suspicious of the driver and passenger, who were extremely nervous, took them into custody on suspicion of being members of the IRA. The driver, a 24-year-old farmer named Francis McGirl, was eventually acquitted, but his passenger, Thomas McMahon, a member of the Provos, was convicted of the assassination based on forensic evidence. Experts found traces of nitroglycerine on his clothing, and sand on his boots was identified as coming from the slipway at Mullaghmore, where Mountbatten's boat had been moored. In addition, flakes of green paint on his boots matched that of the hull of the *Shadow V*. Dubbed 'Bomber' McMahon, the Provo was sentenced to life imprisonment with no appeal.

Additional investigation indicated that Provos had set up an assassination team including McMahon, who settled on Mountbatten as a target to one-up a rival splinter group, the Irish National Liberation Army (INLA), which had assassinated British Tory Member of Parliament Airey Neave the previous March, gaining considerable publicity and for the first time recognition outside the Republic of Ireland. Mountbatten thus became a sacrifice to terrorist rivalries. (See NEAVE, AIREY.)

Further reading: *Encyclopedia of Modern Murder*, by Colin Wilson and Donald Seaman.

MUJIBUR RAHMAN, Sheik (1920–1975) On August 15, 1975, a bloody army coup d'état overthrew the government of Sheik Mujibur Rahman, the founding president of the nation of Bangladesh. Assassinated along with Mujibur, who was killed in a clash outside his home in the capital city of Dacca, were more than 20 members of his family and political associates. The plotters concentrated their lightning attack on three residences where the victims lived. Among those slain were Mujibur's wife, their two children, two politically active nephews, Flood Control Minister Abdul Rab Sernayabat, his wife and their children.

After the assassinations, the officers who led the coup went to the home of Commerce Minister Khadakar Mushtaque Ahmed and offered him the presidency, saying they would put aside their own leadership claims in preference for civilian rule. This attitude did not prove lasting, however, and in November Mushtaque was forced to resign, being replaced by Major General Ziaur Rahman, who had been dismissed by Mushtaque at the start of a power struggle four days earlier on November 3. On that day the soon-to-be new military rulers had put to death former Prime Ministers Tajuddin Ahmed and Mansoor Ali, former Vice President Syed Nasrul Islam and former Commerce Minister A. H. N. Kamuruzzamn, all of whom had been in jail since the original coup against Sheik Mujibur. A number of political refugees, including military officers who escaped to Thailand, said the slaying of the four prisoners were carried out 'because they were the only possible civilian challengers to the new military rulers. They're out to destroy all possible civilian leaders.'

General Zia was to remain in power until 1981, when he too was assassinated. (See ZIAUR RAHMAN, GENERAL.)

MUNRO, Ernest A. See MEIN, JOHN GORDON.

MUSSOLINI, Benito (1883–1945) In April 1945 Benito Mussolini, the strutting Duce who led Fascist Italy for over two decades, was on the run from the Allies and Italian partisans, as German and Italian Fascist resistance crumbled. Mussolini, little more than a wan shadow of his former flamboyant self, tried to escape in a convoy of retreating Germans by hiding in the back of a truck and wearing a German soldier's uniform. In the entourage were his longtime mistress, Clara Petacci, and about 15 political supporters and many members of their families.

Partisans intercepted the convoy on April 24 as it moved from Como toward Switzerland, and a startled partisan commissar recognized Mussolini. Mussolini and Petacci were imprisoned in a three-story farmhouse on the outskirts of the village of Bonzanigo and were given earnest assurances they would not be harmed. This was certainly the intent of the local partisan group, but a decision was reached at partisan headquarters in Milan that Mussolini and his mistress were to be killed. The secret order was issued by Palmiro Togliatti, head of the Italian Communist Party. Togliatti had decided that Mussolini was to be kept out of Allied hands since a war crimes trial would entwine the Allies endlessly in postwar Italian affairs. It was decided to send a dedicated Communist, Walter Audisio, whose *nom de guerre* was Colonel Valerio, to carry out the assassinations.

When Valerio arrived, his mission was strenuously opposed by partisans, many of whom were non-Communist. By threats, Valerio and his companions won out.

About 4:00 in the afternoon of April 28, Valerio charged into the bedroom where Mussolini and the woman were confined and announced, 'Hurry, I have come to rescue you.'

'Really?' Mussolini replied sardonically.

The pair were hustled to a car and taken through the village with two partisans on the running board, and out toward Azzano, where the vehicle stopped before the gate to a villa. Valerio told them to hide in the bushes while he went ahead to see if the coast was clear. Mussolini was hesitant but went to the gate. There was a moment of silence. Then Valerio announced, 'By order of the general headquarters of the Volunteers for Freedom Corps I am required to render justice to the Italian people!' Mussolini stood still but the hysterical Clara threw her arms around his neck, pleading for his life.

'Move away if you don't want to die too,' Valerio told her.

Clara stepped to Mussolini's right. Valerio aimed his machine pistol and pulled the trigger. The weapon did not fire. He then took his pistol and pressed the trigger. It also jammed. Then Valerio took a Mas 7.65 machine pistol from a companion. This one worked, and Mussolini fell under a burst of five shots. Then Valerio turned the gun on Clara Petacci.

That night the corpses were thrown in a van with the bodies of 15 other executed Fascists and taken to Milan, where they were dumped in front of a partly built garage in the Piazzle Loreto, a spot where the previous year 15 hostages had been killed by the Nazis. The corpses were left in a pile, but the next morning they were arranged in a row. Mussolini was positioned so his head rested on Clara's breasts.

Crowds formed and the bodies were kicked and mutilated. Finally Mussolini's corpse was strung up by his feet from a girder. Clara was hanged in similar fashion next to him. In a bow to public modesty, a woman finally climbed up on a box and tucked the Duce's mistress's skirt between her roped legs.

On May Day Mussolini and Petacci were buried in paupers' graves in the Cimitero Maggiore. The macabre humiliation of the Duce marked the passing of Italian Fascism into history.

Further reading: *The Last 100 Days*, by John Toland.

N

NADIR SHAH (1686–1747) An obscure young sheep-
herder, Nadir Kali, the future Nadir Shah of Persia,
achieved in a few short years a military career that was
more brilliant and bloody than any since the time of
Timur. Rising first to the head of his family, then to chief
of a bandit band and finally to head of a movement to
drive the conquering Afghans out of Persia, he deserved
full credit for restoring to the throne in 1730 Tahmasp, the
son of Husein, the ruler who had been toppled by the
invaders. Tahmasp gratefully made Nadir Kali sultan of a
number of territories.

Nadir then set off to drive out the Turks as well, and
thus extend the boundaries of Persia to include Iraq and
Azerbaijan. He then headed for Khurasan to put down a
rebellion. However, during his absence the incompetent
Tahmasp took to the field himself and lost all the lands
that Nadir had won, and then signed an ignoble treaty
with the Turks. Nadir hurried back from the East,
deposed Tahmasp, casting him into prison and raising
Tahmasp's six-month-old son to the throne as Shah Abbas
III, with himself as regent. From 1733 to 1735 Nadir
administered military defeat to the Turks and then threatened Russia, forcing that country to withdraw from Der-
bent and Baku.

When Abbas III died in 1736, Nadir named himself
Nadir Shah. As great a military genius as he was, Nadir
Shah was much less effective in the political arena. Even
when he made what he considered a shrewd political
move, he failed to understand the forces of opposition he
unleashed. Ascribing the many wars between Turkey and
Persia to religious differences, he declared that henceforth

Persia would accept the orthodoxy of Turkey's Sunni Islam over that of the Shi'a sect. This brought considerable resistance from religionists in Persia, which Nadir sought to thwart by the expedient of having the head of the Shi'a sect strangled as quietly as possible. Nadir further antagonized the religious forces by confiscating church endowments to meet the needs of his vast armies. Nadir considered the loyalty of the army his main objective, and when he conquered Kandahar in 1738 he treated its defenders so leniently that a troop of Afghans enlisted under his banner and served him loyally in his campaigns to the day he died.

Nadir looted much of India, capturing even the famous Peacock Throne as tribute. Nadir was now recognized as the greatest conqueror in the East since Timur. But war now became a matter of necessity for Nadir. If he disbanded his warriors, they might become a force for havoc or even insurrection. Thus, he was forced to feed and equip his troops and to provide wars to occupy them. Despite the fruits of conquest, this meant even more taxes on the Persians. He was faced with many plots against him, and suspecting his son, Riza Kuli, of planning to depose him, Nadir had Riza's eyes put out. When the religionists continued to struggle against him, Nadir answered with wholesale executions and ordered pyramids built from the skulls of his victims. Yet opposition to him only increased. Then on June 20, 1747, four of his own bodyguards entered his tent intent on assassinating him. Nadir fought back and killed two of them before being cut down himself. 'All Persia,' report the Durants, 'breathed a sigh of relief.' (See MAHMUD, MIR.)

Further reading: *History of Persia*, by Sir Percy Sykes; *The Story of Civilization – X, Rousseau and Revolution*, by Will and Ariel Durant.

NAPOLEON BONAPARTE (1769–1821) – Attempted Assassination It is not known how many attempts were made to assassinate Napoleon Bonaparte, because he apparently concealed the facts or doctored them to suit his aims. In December 1800 First Consul Bonaparte was subjected to a bomb attempt on his life on a Paris street between the Opera and the Louvre. Thirteen persons in the area were killed, but Bonaparte escaped serious harm. Minister of Police Joseph Fouche soon gathered proof that the attack had been made by fanatic royalists. Bonaparte had little interest in the facts, however, and instead took advantage of the situation to purge the survivors of the old radical left of the Revolution. About 130 of those whom Bonaparte called 'the general staff of the Jacobins' were deported to the penal colony in Guiana. When Fouche rounded up the real assassins, Bonaparte had them sent to the guillotine but refused to pardon the Jacobins, saying they were banished 'for all they have done and all they still might do.'

In 1809 Emperor Napoleon was attacked in Vienna by an 18-year-old Austrian youth, Friedrich Staps, who tried to stab him just after Napoleon's victory at Wagram. The emperor saw no need to have the assassination attempt publicized since it might provoke others, and it did not become known for some years. Staps, nevertheless, suffered a military execution. Some historians suspect that other attempts were made on Napoleon's life but that the news was suppressed, leaving an incomplete record.

There has been a theory that Napoleon was poisoned by royalists in 1821 during his exile on St. Helena. The theory was advanced in 1961 by a Swedish toxicologist, Sten Forshufvud. The most recent version of Forshufvud's theory was made by writers Ben Weider and David Hapgood in a 1982 book, *The Murder of Napoleon*, after tests on Napoleon's hair revealed traces of arsenic. Because arsenic is a preservative, this was thought to explain why Napoleon's body was found to be remarkably well preserved when it was transferred to Paris for reburial in 1840.

Not many experts have embraced the idea that Napoleon was poisoned in an assassination, or even that arsenic really killed him. Professor Franklin L. Ford of Harvard sums up the objections to the theory:

An obvious difficulty lies in the fact that the subject's symptoms of physical decline – growing obesity, fits of lethargy, unnatural pallor – had been remarked by contemporaries with increasing frequency beginning before his coronation in 1804. A further weakness in the case is that it assumes the presence of arsenic in hair and body tissue to be evidence of only one thing: purposeful homicide. In fact, the powdered mineral was widely used in the nineteenth century as a specific for various complaints, notably for dyspepsia, from which Napoleon was known to be a chronic sufferer. Arsenic may have contributed to his death in any number of ways, but from that possibility one can scarcely conclude that it was the sole or even the principal cause, let alone that it could only have been administered with intent to kill, imputed to a shadow assassin whose motives are never clearly spelled out.

Further reading: *The Murder of Napoleon*, by Ben Weider and David Hapgood; *Political Murder*, by Franklin L. Ford.

NEAVE, Airey (1916–1979) In what was to prove to be a bizarre example of 'assassination one-upmanship,' Airey Neave, a leading Conservative member of Britain's Parliament, was killed on March 30, 1979 by a highly sophisticated car bomb activated by a mercury-tilt detonator. Neave was the first M.P. to be assassinated since 1812. At first it was feared that Neave's killers had penetrated House of Commons security when the bomb exploded just as his car cleared an inclined exit ramp of the House of Commons underground car park. However, later investigation showed that the bomb had a double firing system with a timing apparatus that permitted the bomb planters to be miles away before it was detonated. For the bomb to go off it had to be at a certain angle of tilt together with an acceleration of the vehicle. The bombers undoubtedly knew the car-park ramp would get the job done.

A World War II hero and one of the few prisoners of

war to escape from Colditz Castle in Germany, Neave had been a member of the British prosecution team at the Nuremberg trials. Elected to the House of Commons in 1953, he became a leading supporter of Margaret Thatcher and was in the 1970s her chief adviser on Ireland. It was assumed that if Thatcher gained power – as happened later in 1979 – Neave would become secretary of Northern Ireland. Neave was a strong advocate of a continued British military presence in Northern Ireland, and he also pushed for the reintroduction of the death penalty for some terrorist crimes. Most observers in Northern Ireland, as well as both Protestant and Catholic elements there, assumed Neave's appointment would herald tougher security measures and crackdowns.

The 63-year-old Neave was trapped in the car wreckage for 30 minutes after the explosion, as rescue and medical workers fought to save him. He died within a few minutes of reaching a hospital, just before his wife arrived at his bedside. The first inclination was to put the blame on the IRA or its Provisional wing, who accused the Official IRA of having 'gone soft' on the British while seeking a political solution to the Irish problem. Just days before the Neave murder, the Provos had struck in The Hague, shooting to death Sir Richard Sykes, the British ambassador to the Netherlands.

However, it developed that neither IRA faction was involved in the Neave killing, but rather the Irish National Liberation Army (INLA), the militant arm of the Irish Republican Socialist Party, itself a splinter group of the Official Sinn Fein. The Irish Republican Socialist Party's political and philosophical clashes with Roman Catholicism had long tended to limit its influence within the republican cause. But the Neave assassination put the INLA on the international maps, although the killing hardly lessened British influence in Ireland. Of the assassins Margaret Thatcher said, 'They must never, never, never be allowed to triumph, they must never prevail.' Certainly, after becoming prime minister, Mrs. Thatcher never retreated from Neave's positions.

However, the Neave assassination did have an enormous impact within the Irish terrorist movement. The INLA was regarded as having beaten the Provos to the punch by killing Neave, and it was felt that this required a dramatic response on the Provos' part. That was achieved the following August when the Provos assassinated Earl Mountbatten, the British war hero and cousin of Queen Elizabeth.

NGO DINH DIEM (1901–1963) The despotic ruler of South Vietnam, first as premier in 1954 and later the same year as president, Ngo Dinh Diem lasted almost a decade in power, a remarkable feat considering the enmity he incurred among major elements of Vietnamese society – the Buddhists, the military, the peasantry and the intelligentsia – as well as the United States. Diem was regarded as a bigot, a despot and an incompetent. With the growing guerrilla movement in the countryside, he disregarded calls for land reform, ignored governmental corruption and ordered a savage crackdown on critics of his regime.

There were a number of attempts to oust Diem from power. In 1960 elements of the air force and paratroopers attempted to seize the presidential palace but were repelled. In 1962 fighter planes strafed the palace. Diem became increasingly isolated but still maintained his hold on the government, aided greatly by his brother, Ngo Dinh Nhu, who headed the secret police. Since Diem was unmarried, Madame Nhu, his sister-in-law, acted as the official first lady of South Vietnam. A woman noted for harsh views and callous remarks, Madame Nhu was dubbed 'the Dragon Lady' by American reporters. One of her more infamous statements, which provoked outrage worldwide, was her accusation that Buddhist monks who burned themselves to death to protest the Diem government were staging 'a barbecue with imported gasoline.'

By 1963 the Diem regime was tottering, with an almost unfathomable crosscurrent of intrigues. Leading Vietnamese generals conferred on how to oust Diem and his brother. In an effort to retain power, Diem and Nhu evidently concocted a purge of anti-Diem forces within the government. They would fake a coup, flee Saigon to a spot where loyal troops were waiting and after 24 hours return and crush the dissidents, leaving them with no opposition.

Supposedly in on the plot was General Duong Van Minh ('Big Minh' to the Americans). Minh, undoubtedly in contact with American officials, decided the scheme provided the perfect timing for a real coup. Key in the revolt was General Ton That Dinh, who was in charge of martial law in Saigon. Dinh, an opportunist determined to be on the winning side, did not commit himself to the Minh cause until the last possible moment.

In the presidential palace on November 1, 1963, Diem and Nhu at first assumed their plans were on course, but when they could not get any telephone response from General Dinh, they realized things had gone awry. They stuffed a suitcase full of U.S. money, left the palace through an elaborate maze of tunnels and reached the house of a Chinese businessman. The next morning the brothers made it to a Catholic church, from which they called Dinh and offered to surrender.

Troops arrived shortly, and the brothers, their hands tied behind their back, were led to a car, accompanied in the backseat by a man later identified as a tank corps major. The major and Nhu exchanged harsh words, and the major drew a bayonet and stabbed Nhu repeatedly. The officer then drew his revolver and shot Diem in the back of the head before putting a bullet in Nhu's head, as well.

At staff headquarters, Dinh and his fellow officers expressed shock at the deaths but insisted both men had died by their own hand – later this was amended to 'accidentally.'

The brothers were buried in unmarked graves in a prison cemetery. At the time Madame Nhu was on a speaking tour in the United States, and she hurried to exile in Paris, accusing America of engineering the downfall of Diem and her husband. 'All the devils in hell are against us, but we shall triumph,' she said.

Not much more was heard of the actual assassin, although an unconfirmed story circulated that he had wanted to kill Nhu for some time, ever since the execution of a dear friend. Minh established a junta for a short time, but he too fell from power, and in succeeding years events in South Vietnam proceeded to their tragic conclusion.

NGOUABI, Marien (1938–1977) President Marien Ngouabi of the Congo Republic was assassinated on March 18, 1977, by a four-man murder squad reportedly led by former army Captain Barthelemy Kikadidi, who reportedly escaped after the murder. The government linked Kikadidi to former President Alphonse Massamba-Debat, who had been deposed by a leftist coup in September 1968.

Ngouabi, an avowed Marxist, had become president of the Congo on January 1, 1969, and established close ties to other Communist countries. His assassination was clearly part of a failed coup attempt. He was succeeded by Colonel Joachim Yombi Opango, a member of the Congolese Labor Party, the only legal party in the country.

However, the bloodletting did not stop with the assassination of Ngouabi. On March 22, 1977, four days later, Emile Cardinal Biayenda, the Roman Catholic archbishop of Brazzaville, was kidnapped and killed. The following day Congolese radio reported the Biayenda killing had been carried out by the members of the Ngouabi family.

On March 25, ex-President Massamba-Debat was executed for plotting Ngouabi's assassination. The following day six others charged with the Ngouabi and Biayenda killings were executed.

The next month Ngouabi's successor, President Opango, regarded to be a political moderate, suspended the nation's four-year constitution and dissolved the national assembly. In June 1977 the United States and the Congo Republic resumed diplomatic relations after a 12-year break.

NHU, Ngo Dinh   See NGO DINH DIEM.

NICEPHORUS II PHOCAS, Byzantine Emperor (912–969)   One of the great military emperors in history, Nicephorus II Phocas is celebrated in the epic poetry of the 10th-century Christian frontier and venerated by the Greek monks of the Byzantine Empire. The inscription on his sarcophagus sums up at least in part the cause of his demise by assassination: 'You conquered all but a woman.'

That woman was Theophano, a Greek girl, who married the young emperor Romanus II. The record is not clear on Theophano's doings in this period, although she is suspected of poisoning her father-in-law, Constantine VII, and then hastening the death of Romanus as well. This was to leave the 20-year-old empress as acting regent for the legitimate emperors, Basil and Constantine, aged six and three respectively. Actual control of the affairs of state was left under Romanus II's will to the eunuch Joseph Bringas.

Theophano was unhappy with Bringas's rule and seduced the aristocrat Nicephorus, who as head of the Byzantine armies had driven the Muslims from Aleppo and Crete and otherwise defeated many enemies on the frontier. Meanwhile Theophano, with the aid of Basil the chamberlain, undermined the Bringas government, with false charges, fueling a revolt against the eunuch. The imperial army, through the activities of John Tzimisces, Nicephorus's faithful lieutenant, overthrew the government and suffered Nicephorus to take the throne as Nicephorus II Phocas. On September 20, 963, about a month after becoming emperor, he married Theophano, whose hold on the throne now seemed secure.

However, Nicephorus proved less successful as a civil ruler. His taxes and coinage debasement to feed his military needs proved unpopular, and the church objected to his efforts to curb the enrichment of the monasteries. As his domestic problems multiplied, Nicephorus became more withdrawn and dependent on the advice of his brother Leo Phocas, whose obvious self-interest and money-grasping made him unpopular with the people of Constantinople. Theophano feared Leo Phocas's ambitions as well, foreseeing a time when he would seek to remove her children from the succession.

It was time for Theophano to seek a new alliance and protector. She found her man in John Tzimisces, in whom she fired an ambition for the throne. Nicephorus meanwhile had become more mistrustful of all around him, had dismissed minister after minister and finally had moved to the palace of Boukoleion, which he had fortified for his personal safety.

During the night of December 10, 969, a group of former Nicephorus supporters led by Tzimisces and advised of the route by Theophano, slipped into the palace and murdered the emperor; the empress held the victim's severed head out the window for the soldiers below to see. John Tzimisces ascended the throne.

This was to prove to be the final assassination plotted by Theophano. According to some historians John I Tzimisces became remorseful over the betrayal of his former leader, and he repudiated Theophano and exiled her to a convent. Others say he exiled Theophano only reluctantly, after being forced to do so as penance by the patriarch Polyeuctus before he gained ecclesiastical concurrence to his receiving the imperial crown.

Further reading: *The Cambridge Medieval History*, new ed., vol. 4, pt. 1, pp. 147–156.

NICHOLAS II, Czar of Russia (1868–1918) On March 15, 1917, after the February Revolution but before the Bolshevik Revolution the following October, Czar Nicholas II abdicated which brought to eventual power the weak Kerensky government. The immediate problem arose of what to do with the czar. Until that time it had been assumed that a successful coup would be impossible without killing the czar, but he was merely arrested and held prisoner with the rest of the royal family. Following the October Revolution the Bolsheviks inherited the royal prisoners.

Lenin probably was unhappy to be saddled with the problem. Even before the Bolsheviks took power Lenin complained that the English and French revolutions executed their monarchs, but the Russian revolution was being very backward about following suit.

Leon Trotsky, by contrast, was more eager to accept the situation, and suggested to Lenin that the czar be put on trial with Trotsky as the public prosecutor. Lenin rejected the idea for lack of time. 'But,' says Professor Adam B. Ulam of Harvard, 'no doubt he would have refused in any case: There was other business to be attended to in this summer of 1918 and Trotsky's proposal smacked of theatricality, which was entirely alien to his nature. Most of all, he must have realized (and how strange that Trotsky did not) that from the Communist point of view Nicholas II would have made a very poor prisoner in the dock; his very lack of intelligence combined with his dignity and Christian resignation would have made him an object of pity rather than of popular indignation. Indeed, the former emperor, an abject failure while on the throne, displayed while prisoner the kind of fortitude and equanimity that moved even his jailers.'

Trotsky later justified the killing of the Romanovs: 'The execution of the tsar's family was needed not only to frighten, horrify and dishearten the enemy, but also to shake up our own ranks to show them that there was no turning back, that ahead lay either complete victory or ruin. . . . The masses of workers and soldiers had not a minute's doubt. They would not have understood and would not have accepted any other decision. This Lenin sensed well.'

Again, not all historians agree, feeling that Lenin, ever more cautious than Trotsky, would not have gone ahead had he not been forced by the military situation with anti-Bolshevik White forces approaching Ekaterinburg, in the Urals, the royal family's ultimate holding place. Actually, nobody loved the former czar, and even monarchists fighting the Bolsheviks were casting off other members of the Romanov family. Says Ulam, 'Not even the most reactionary White movement during the Civil War made an effort to appeal to monarchist sentiment. If anything, the physical presence of the ex-Emperor in the Whites' camp would have been an embarrassment to them and a political asset to the Bolsheviks.'

On the other hand, Lenin could hardly have allowed the monumental propaganda defeat that would have been involved in the loss of the Romanovs.

The die was cast. The murder of the Romanovs has been told often, with a number of conflicting details. On July 16, 1918, Czar Nicholas II, Czarina Alexandra, their son Alexis, and their four daughters, Olga, Tatiana, Marie, and Anastasia, as well as members of their household staff, were led to the cellar and shot by a firing squad headed by Jakob Yurosky. After the volley, it was found that Anastasia had not been hit, having fainted just before the shots were fired. She was finished off by bayonets and rifle butts, but her temporary survival is probably what gave impetus to the ludicrous tale that Anastasia escaped. The bodies were heaved into a mine shaft, which was then dynamited. (See MICHAEL, GRAND DUKE.)

Further reading: *The Bolsheviks*, by Adam B. Ulam; *Nicholas and Alexandra*, by Robert K. Massie.

NIXON, Richard M. (1913–) – Attempted Assassination
He called it 'Operation Pandora's Box,' and had it been successful Samuel J. Byck, an unemployed 44-year-old Philadelphia salesman, would stand as having pulled off perhaps the most spectacular presidential assassination in American history. Instead, he is little remembered even though two fatalities resulted from his attempt.

Byck's target on February 22, 1974 was President Richard M. Nixon, and his plan called for the hijacking of a commercial jetliner at Baltimore-Washington International Airport, forcing the crew to fly toward the White House, at which point he would shoot the pilot, take the controls and guide the plane directly into the executive mansion, killing Nixon and countless others, as well as himself and all aboard the aircraft.

Byck left a string of rambling letters and tape recordings, which he mailed to various public figures – including Jack Anderson, Jonas Salk, Leonard Bernstein and Senator Abraham Ribicoff – just hours before his hijack attempt.

Byck has been compared in temperament to Lee Harvey Oswald, who killed John F. Kennedy, and to Sara Jane Moore, who tried to shoot Gerald Ford. They all had what has been described as neurotic political personalities and sought to act at personal motives in the name of some larger public interest. Most such neurotic personalities suffer denial or rejection by a spouse, their children, a parent or parents, or other loved ones, and have a generally low self-esteem because of personal failure. Samuel Byck, as revealed in his tapes, suffered severe feelings of rejection. Byck's income as a tire salesman was only marginal, and he resented his younger brother's success in the same business and another brother's career as a dentist. Byck's wife divorced him, taking the children, and he even felt betrayed when his mother, with whom he was living, went to Florida. In his tapes he predicted his mother would return 'in a damn hurry.'

On February 20, two days before Byck's action, he made an unfiled last will in which he left everything to his only friend, a man at the tire store. He added to the document: 'I will each of my children . . . the sum of one dollar each. They have each other and they deserve each other.' The tapes also made clear he held the political establishment's 'corruption' and 'oppression' as the cause of his ever-mounting personal problems.

Byck had first come to the attention of the Secret Service in 1972, when he was alleged to have threatened Nixon's life. Byck denied it, and a psychiatrist who had treated Byck for emotional problems had told the Secret Service Byck was not a threat to himself or others, but merely 'a big talker who makes verbal threats and never acts on them.'

As a result the U.S. attorney's office in Philadelphia declined to prosecute when Byck was committed to a local hospital for mental observation. In the fall of 1973 Byck was arrested twice for parading in front of the White House without a permit, but the charges were dismissed.

On February 22, 1974, Byck's behavior passed from the benign to the deadly. The night before he drove from Philadelphia to the airport, with his gas gauge practically on empty, and dictated to his tapes: 'Wouldn't that be something if the so-called would-be assassin ran out of gas. Some people would have their lives to congratulate for the energy crisis, including my life.'

Just after 7 A.M. Byck went to the line awaiting to board Delta Flight 523 for Atlanta. Suddenly Byck stepped up behind the security guard and pulled a .22-caliber pistol from under his raincoat and fired two shots into the man's back. One severed the main aorta and killed the guard instantly. Amid screams, Byck bolted for the boarding ramp and stormed aboard the plane.

He confronted the crew in the cockpit and ordered an immediate takeoff, firing a shot upward. When he ordered the flight attendants to close the door, they used the chance to run from the plane. Byck fired a shot after them. Again Byck ordered an immediate takeoff, to which the pilot replied he could not until the wheel blocks were removed. Byck went into a rage and pumped a shot into the copilot's stomach. 'The next one will be in the head,' he said.

Byck seized a woman passenger and shoved her into the cockpit, telling her: 'Help this man fly this plane.'

Hearing shots from outside the plane, Byck shoved the woman back to her seat and fired two more shots at the pilots, hitting the wounded copilot in the left eye and the pilot in the shoulder. The pilot, radioing to try to get another pilot to the plane, lost consciousness. The copilot was probably already dead by this point.

Byck reloaded his weapon and seized another woman passenger by the hair and forced her into the cockpit, where he again shot both pilots, who were heaped over the controls. Suddenly, the glass of the cabin door window was splattered by sniper fire from outside the aircraft. Byck, reacting to his hostage's pleas for mercy, let her go, telling her to return to her seat. There were two more shots, and Byck was hit in the stomach and chest. Byck staggered and dropped to the floor. He picked up his gun, placed the barrel to his right temple and pulled the trigger. His attempt to kill the president of the United States had never gotten off the ground.

Further reading: *American Assassins: The Darker Side of Politics*, by James W. Clarke.

NOEL, Cleo A., Jr. (1919–1973) On March 1, 1973, Arab terrorists riding in a Land Rover smashed into the Saudi Arabian embassy in Khartoum, Sudan, seizing control of a reception to honor departing U.S. charge d'affaires George C. Moore. Some diplomats from various countries got away by scaling the embassy wall, while others concealed themselves and escaped later. U.S. Ambassador Cleo A. Noel, Jr. was shot in the ankle and Guy Eid, Belgian charge d'affaires, in the leg. Noel, Eid and Moore were tied up and beaten. The Saudi ambassador, his wife, his four children and the Jordanian charge d'affaires were also held. The terrorists identified themselves as belonging to Black September, but the Land Rover they drove bore diplomatic plates that were later identified as belonging to Al Fatah, the Palestinian group led by Yasser Arafat.

The terrorists announced they would kill six of their hostages unless their demands were met, which included the release of Abu Daoud and other Fatah members imprisoned in Jordan, all Arab women detained in Israel and members of the West German Baader-Meinhof urban guerrilla group, which supported the Palestinian cause. From the United States they demanded the release of Sirhan Sirhan, the convicted assassin of U.S. Senator Robert F. Kennedy.

In negotiations the terrorists withdrew the demands about the Arab women prisoners in Israel and the freeing of the Baader-Meinhof gang (the West German ambassador having left the reception before the attack), but they held onto other demands.

At a press conference on March 21, President Richard Nixon said the United States would 'do everything we can' to have the hostages released but would 'not pay blackmail.' Similarly, the Jordanians refused to release their prisoners.

Sudanese troops ringed the embassy, and the terrorists wired explosives to the embassy floor, warning that the building would be blown up if it were stormed. Ambassador Noel was permitted to call the U.S. embassy and was told an American representative would be arriving that evening. Noel replied, 'That will be too late.'

Later, the captive Saudi ambassador Sheik Abdullah el Malhouk would say, 'We all knew that the two Americans and the Belgian were going to be shot, and they themselves were well aware of it. The guerrillas gave them papers and pen, untied them and told them to write their last letter to their wives and families. It was a terrifying moment. All were extremely brave. They faced the situation with extreme courage.'

On March 3, the Sudanese government reported the three diplomats had been taken down to the basement of the embassy and shot repeatedly at about 9:30 P.M. on March 2.

The terrorists later said they would not hand over the bodies until they got safe conduct. The Sudanese responded by giving them until dawn to surrender. The terrorists caved in and did so. One of the terrorists reportedly confessed that the attack had not been directed by Black September but had been planned at Al Fatah headquarters in Beirut.

On September 24 all eight terrorists, having been found guilty of murder, were sentenced to life imprisonment. However, President Mohammed Gaafar el-Nimeiry immediately commuted their sentences and said they would be sent to Yasser Arafat (who denied complicity). The following day they were released to the PLO and flown to Cairo. There were no details on what punishment they later received, if any. The Al Fatah terrorist Abu Daoud was freed under a general amnesty proclaimed in Jordan a half year later.

NOKRASHY PASHA, Mahmoud Fahmy (1888–1948)
On December 28, 1948, Egyptian Premier Mahmoud Fahmy Nokrashy Pasha was confronted by his killer, 21-year-old veterinary student Abdel Hamid Ahmed Hassan, in a corridor of the interior ministry building in Cairo. Ahmed Hassan fired five bullets into the official, killing him. He intended to use the final bullet on himself but he was overpowered by the premier's bodyguards before he could join his victim in death.

Ahmed Hassan was a member of the Moslem Brotherhood, which Nokrashy Pasha had outlawed some three weeks earlier. The assassin said he had killed the premier because he and the Brotherhood could not tolerate his failure to produce a military victory over the new state of Israel established in Palestine.

A onetime teacher, Nokrashy Pasha became a minor government official in the 1920s and progressed slowly but steadily. He never acquired a personal fortune and was regarded as incorruptible. In 1945 he became president of the Saadist Party and upon the February 24 assassination of then Premier Ahmed Maher Pasha, he assumed that high office. Forced out of office February 15, 1946 he returned to power in December and established himself as a firm advocate of the elimination of the Jewish state. He also vigorously opposed the presence of the British in the Anglo-Egyptian Sudan. In the aftermath of the assassination, the killer was executed and hundreds of members of the Moslem Brotherhood arrested.

NUMERIAN, Co-Emperor of Rome (?–284) Numerian, together with his brother Carinus, succeeded his father, Carus, as co-emperor of Rome in 283. The following year Numerian died in what has been regarded as a certain assassination by Arrius Aper, Numerian's father-in-law and his Praetorian prefect. On withdrawal from a Persian campaign, Numerian fell ill and was confined to a sickbed in his tent, rarely seen by anyone other than Aper. Eventually all communication and business emanated from Aper, until finally some soldiers entered the imperial pavilion and found not a sick ruler but a corpse.

Aper had been maneuvering for the throne, but his plan was faulty. The soldiers instead hailed Gaius Aurelius Valerius Diocletianus (Diocletian), commander of the imperial guard, as the logical successor.

At the solemn inaugural parade for his reign, Diocletian announced his own innocence in the murder of Numerian, and, turning to Aper standing at his side, in front of the astonished troops, he drew his sword and killed Aper.

Further reading: *Illustrated World History. Vol. 2*, edited by Sir John Hammerton and Dr. Harry Elmer Barnes.

O

OBREGON, Alvaro (1880–1928) One of the most successful generals during the Mexican Revolution of 1910–1920 – in the shifting sands of the conflict he at various times defeated the forces of Huerta, Zapata and Villa – Alvaro Obregon was a man of simple background and little formal education. Not active in the 1910–11 revolt by Francisco Madero, which ousted the reactionary Porfirio Diaz, Obregon joined the movement in 1912, supporting Madero. After Madero's assassination by General Victoriano Huerta, Obregon joined the diverse groups of Venustiano Carranza, Emiliano Zapata and Pancho Villa.

With Huerta defeated, Obregon aligned himself with the more conservative Carranza against Zapata and Villa. His relations with Villa were exceedingly stormy, with genuine hatred and equally genuine expressions of affection exchanged toward one another at various times. Each at certain moments plotted the other's assassination, and in one three-day period Villa ordered Obregon's killing at least four times, only to change his mind. In the military struggles, Obregon proved his superiority to Zapata and especially to Villa, whom he defeated in 1915 at Celaya and Leon, after which Villa ceased to be a major power in Mexican military campaigns.

Obregon, compared to Carranza at least, was a radical. For instance, during his military campaigns against Villa he defanged his opponent politically by instituting harsh anticlerical policies and adopting prolabor stances. Obregon dominated the Mexican constitutional convention of 1917, and he pushed through programs that Carranza, who became constitutional president, found odious.

After the convention and short-term service in the

cabinet, Obregon retired to farming life, ignoring politics for two years. By 1920, however, disillusioned by Carranza's increasingly reactionary policies, abrogation of the constitution and attempt to install a puppet successor, Obregon led an uprising against the president. Carranza was assassinated and Obregon succeeded him.

Overall Obregon's term brought considerable prosperity and peace to the country, and he advanced the economic condition of both peasants and laborers. His regime was considered too radical by the United States, which refused to recognize his government until 1923, when Obregon agreed not to expropriate American oil companies. That year, as his nonrenewable term neared its end, Obregon was obsessed with the choice of a successor. Obregon favored Plutarco Elias Calles but worried that Pancho Villa might interfere with the election process. Villa was then living in retirement, and whether he was capable of launching a full-scale insurrection was greatly in question. Nevertheless Obregon decided on his elimination.

Villa's assassination was clearly ordered by Obregon and was organized by Congressman Jesus Salas Barrazas, who was later convicted of the crime but served only six months of a 20-year sentence. Obregon raised the assassination plotter to the rank of colonel in the army, and Calles became the new president.

In 1928 Obregon sought again to become president, insisting the one-term limitation applied only to immediate succession. A constitutional amendment was passed to back this position, and Obregon won the election overwhelmingly. On July 15 Obregon attended a small victory banquet in a restaurant called *La Bombilla* – the 'little bomb.' Present was a cartoonist, Jose de Leon Toral, who sketched the president-elect. Toral was an ardent Catholic who resented the anticlerical acts of both Obregon and Calles. As he approached to show his sketches to Obregon, he drew a pistol and shot Obregon three times at point-blank range. Obregon was killed instantly, probably unaware of what had happened. (See CARRANZA, VENUS-

TIANO; VILLA, PANCHO; ZAPATA, EMILIANO.)

Further reading: *Heroic Mexico*, by William Weber Johnson; *History of Mexico*, by Samuel H. Mayo.

O'HIGGINS, Kevin (1882–1927) Few assassinations in world history can be said to match the hatred that marked the killings in Ireland just before and after the creation of the Irish Free State in 1922. Former friends and fighting comrades turned on each other in disputes over how to bring about the complete independence of all Ireland, a goal not achieved to this day. When Michael Collins, one of the great nationalist heroes of the Anglo-Irish War of 1919–1921, fell an assassination victim in the civil war that followed, much of his work had to be picked up by Kevin O'Higgins, who saw his duty as primarily the preservation of the Free State and the suppression of the unreconciled republicans determined to gain Northern Ireland as well.

O'Higgins, a law student when he joined the Sinn Fein movement, had been imprisoned in 1918 and while behind bars was elected to Parliament. O'Higgins supported the creation of the Irish Free State in 1921 and was propelled to the front leadership ranks with Collins's death. While he was tormented, much as Collins had been, by having to battle former comrades in arms against the British, O'Higgins played out his tragic role. In November 1922 he was a leader in the decision to execute Robert Erskine Childers, the great Irish writer and republican leader, for the offense of possessing an unauthorized pistol.

O'Higgins later concurred that firm action had to be taken after the republicans shot two Free State deputies in December 1922. At the time the government held more than 100 republicans in prison, including four members of the then republican executive. In retribution, although the four had been confined for some time and were in no way connected with the recent killings, it was decided that the quartet were to be shot. O'Higgins agonized longer than any other member of the cabinet about the drastic action, but he finally voted with the rest. Among those executed without trial was Rory O'Connor, who in better days had been best man at O'Higgins's wedding.

All told, in barely over its first six months the new Free State executed 77 republicans, more than three times the number executed by the British during the two and a half years of the Anglo-Irish War. In the continuing civil war another victim was O'Higgins's father, murdered by the republicans. O'Higgins himself remained alive until Sunday, July 10, 1927, when he was walking home alone from mass near Dublin. A man stepped out of a car and fired at O'Higgins at point-blank range. Wounded, O'Higgins tried to run for cover, but he was set upon by two more gunmen, who emptied their revolvers into him as his life ebbed away. O'Higgins became yet another victim in the nationalist cause. His killers were never identified. (See COLLINS, MICHAEL.)

Further reading: *The Green Flag* by Robert Kee.

OKUBO TOSHIMICHI (1830–1878) One of the great samurai political leaders of the 19th century, Okubo Toshimichi was instrumental in the 1868 overthrow of the Tokugawa family, which had ruled Japan for over two and one-half centuries, and in the restoration of the government of the emperor. Okubo became a dominant member of the government and pushed for rapid economic development.

In 1873 a split developed within Okubo's samurai clan when another powerful leader, Saigo Takamori, pushed for the conquest of Korea. Okubo insisted Japan should concentrate on its own industrialization and internal reform. Okubo won the resultant power struggle, and Saigo was forced out of the government. The disaffected Saigo led what was called the Satsuma Rebellion, but his army of samurai warriors was defeated in 1877. Following his defeat Saigo ordered one of his own men to stab him to death with a sword.

Okubo's triumph proved short-lived. On May 14, 1878, six unreconciled Saigo samurai assassinated Okubo in Tokyo. Okubo's political ideas outlived him another 16 years until 1894, when Japan started down the road of external warfare. (See ITO HIROBUMI, PRINCE OF JAPAN.)

OLYMPIO, Sylvanus (1902–1963) A nationalist politician and the first president of Togo, Sylvanus Olympio was the first presidential assassination victim in a rash of African military coups that marked the 1960s. As president of the first territorial assembly after World War II, Olympio was in open but nonviolent opposition to French colonial administration. His longtime dream was to unite the Ewe people living on both sides of the border separating British and French Togoland. For a time his hopes dimmed when British Togoland voted by plebiscite to join the Gold Coast, which was to become independent Ghana in 1957.

When Togo won limited self-government in 1956, Olympio failed to win office, but in U.N.-supervised elections in 1958 his party won a huge victory; he became prime minister and led Togo to independence in 1960. Elected Togo's first president, he held extensive powers and Togo became a one-party state.

Fissures soon appeared, although Olympio seemed secure. Western-educated Togolese resented the authoritarianism of the government, and the northern Togolanders felt ignored. Youthful members of the ruling party wanted Olympio to show more independence of the French and their financial aid. Olympio responded with a massive crackdown in 1962. In January 1963 he was assassinated in the first successful army coup to hit the new African nations.

The Togolese people were left with the dubious distinction of being one of the few modern nations ruled by an acknowledged assassin, as President Eyadema, Olympio's successor, openly claimed to have fired the fatal bullets that had struck down Olympio.

OTHO See GALBA, EMPEROR OF ROME; VITELLIUS, EMPEROR OF ROME.

OTTO III, Holy Roman Emperor (980–1002) Otto III,

the son of Holy Roman Emperor Otto II, sought to reestablish the glory and power of the ancient Roman Empire in a universal Christian state that would be ruled from Rome and whose emperor would be superior to the pope not only in secular matters but in religious affairs as well.

Crowned in A.D. 983, Otto III ruled through the regency of first his mother and on her death that of his grandmother. In 994, the 14-year-old Otto III came of age and started to rule in his own name. As much as Otto longed for a restored Roman Empire, the nobles and commoners of Rome and Lombardy sought to establish a Rome republic instead. In 996 Otto III sought to fill the vacancy in the papacy by naming his 23-year-old cousin Bruno as Gregory V, the first German pope. He put down the republican forces, then pardoned their leader, Crescentius. However, as soon as Otto left Rome, Crescentius in 997 reestablished the republic and deposed Gregory. Gregory excommunicated Crescentius, who simply laughed and dictated the election of John XVI as pope.

Otto hurried back to Rome, brought down John, gouged out his eyes, cut off his nose and tongue, and had him paraded backward through the streets of the city on an ass. Crescentius and 12 other republican leaders went to the chopping block, and their corpses were hung from the battlements of St. Angelo. Gregory was restored to the papal throne but died in 999, most likely through poison. In Gregory's place Otto named his old tutor Gerbert as Pope Sylvester II.

In the meantime love had come to the young emperor, in the form, ironically, of Stephania, the widow of Crescentius. Stephania became Otto's mistress – and also his poisoner. In 1001 Rome revolted against Otto, and he was forced to flee to the monastery of St. Apollinaris near Ravenna. In January 1002 Otto was at the castle of Paterno trying to organize military operations against Rome when he fell deathly ill. As one historical account put it: 'The young king, feeling death in his veins, became a weeping penitent, and died . . . at the age of twenty-two.'

In 1003 Pope Sylvester II also died, poisoned, so went the Roman rumor, by the same Stephania who had dispatched Otto III.

OVERBURY, Sir Thomas (1581–1613) The mysterious death of Sir Thomas Overbury in 1613 was so sensationally interlaced in English-court political intrigue, romantic jealousy and what Professor Joseph H. Marshburn called 'a king's abnormal affection for his favorite' that it could be considered an assassination that had to happen. However, it remains one in which the full facts were never elicited.

The English poet and essayist Overbury was educated at Oxford and became an intimate adviser to Robert Carr (or Ker), who was a particular favorite of King James I and the first Scotsman the king seated in the House of Lords, as the earl of Somerset. Overbury was knighted in 1608, even though the king was known to have become extremely jealous of Carr's affection for Overbury.

In 1611 Carr became romantically involved with Frances Howard, the wife of the earl of Essex, with whom she'd had an arranged childhood marriage. Lady Essex was determined to marry Carr. Overbury, fearful that his relationship with Carr would be upset, advised strongly against such a match. When Carr would not listen, Overbury circulated a poem at court entitled 'A Wife,' which portrayed the virtues that a young man should seek of a woman. Needless to say Lady Essex did not seem to fill that bill and the poem was taken as an obvious attack on Lady Essex.

The king was outraged by the growing scandal, and Lady Essex and her relatives plotted Overbury's doom. On April 26, 1613, the royal court was stunned when Overbury was seized and thrown into the Tower of London. He was to die in September, after a period of more than 100 days in which he was fed a daily diet of arsenic, nitric acid, hemlock, ground diamonds and mercury. Remarkably he lived through it all. Finally his guards were made to dispatch him with an injection of a powerful corrosive. Overbury was buried the same day in the Tower church. On December 26 of the same year Carr and Frances Howard were married, the lady's annulment of marriage having been granted over the dissent of the archbishop of Canterbury and other dignitaries.

The open publication of 'A Wife' in 1614 and continuing rumors forced the authorities to investigate Overbury's death, and the guards and others involved were convicted and hanged. Carr and his wife were also tried and convicted in 1616. Lady Frances was pardoned by James I, resulting in a situation in which, says one account, 'people were so enraged against her that they attacked a coach in which the Queen and other ladies had come privately to town, thinking that Lady Somerset was in the conveyance.'

Undeterred by public reaction, the king stayed Carr's execution a number of times, and he was finally set free in 1621. Needless to say Carr and his wife remained in disgrace. And James I did not escape the Overbury assassination with undisputedly clean hands. Typical were published charges in later years, as Marshburn summarizes in *Murder & Witchcraft in England, 1550–1640*, 'that Ker [Carr] held a trump card which the King did not want played. This fatal secret might have involved the death of Prince Henry, but it more probably related to the secret practices of the King himself.'

P

PALME, Olof (1927–1986) On February 28, 1986, Swedish Prime Minister Olof Palme, and his wife, Lisbeth, were walking home from a movie at Stockholm's Grand Theater. They had no guards, such precautions seeming unnecessary in Sweden. As the couple turned off a dark main street, two .357-caliber bullets killed Palme and grazed his wife. The impact on the Swedish public was wrenching. Swedes have always regarded theirs as a rational society, largely immune from the random violence that afflicts other nations.

The assassination may have been even worse for the official investigators, whose inquiry was at times charitably referred to by the press as 'a shambles.' Stockholm's chief of police resigned after being removed as the key investigator, insisting his successors were disorganized and not up to the task. Desperate officials ran newspaper ads worldwide offering cash rewards that escalated to 50 million Swedish kronor – over $8 million – for information that would solve the murder.

The first suspect in the case was a right-wing Swedish schoolteacher who had heckled Palme, a Social Democrat, at political rallies. However, after seven days he was released for lack of evidence. Early in 1987 a group of left-wing Kurdish immigrants were rounded up, and three were charged as accessories in the assassination. Officials theorized that the Kurdish extremists had been hired by Iran to kill Palme because he had stopped Swedish arms shipments to that country. However, the case against the Kurds was so weak that they were released the same day they were arrested.

After numerous false starts over a long period, the

authorities settled on a new suspect – 'the bayonet man.' Under Swedish press regulations, a person held by the police or even brought to trial may not be identified in print. The bayonet man was a criminal who had spent much of his adult life either in prison or undergoing compulsory psychiatric treatment. He also had a history of drug and alcohol abuse, as well as one of violent crime. In 1970 he killed a youth with a bayonet and served three years imprisonment with psychiatric care under the country's liberal jail policies. In 1975 he got 14 months for assault with a bayonet, and in 1978 he was imprisoned for five years for attempted murder, once again with a bayonet.

The bayonet man, identified by the foreign press as 42-year-old Carl Gustav Christer Pettersson, an unemployed laborer, was brought to trial in 1989. Just before the trial an opinion poll indicated only 18 percent of the public believed him guilty while 42 percent thought him innocent. The case was tried before a panel of two judges and six jurors called lay assessors. Including an undertaker, a retired schoolteacher, a postman and a social worker, they had been culled from a pool of 707 jurors selected along political party lines. Three were Social Democrats like Palme, and three were members of rival conservative parties.

The prosecution presented almost no forensic evidence, offered no murder weapon and provided no clear motive. Mrs. Palme identified Pettersson 'beyond any doubt' as the man she saw a few feet away from her dying husband an instant after the shooting. But she had not actually seen Pettersson fire a gun or even have a gun in his possession. Pettersson denied all guilt.

The verdict was split, with the two professional jurists voting for acquittal and all six lay assessors voting for conviction. The two judges pointed out in their findings that Palme's widow had not identified the defendant on a videotaped police lineup until December 14, 1988, almost two years after the crime.

Pettersson was sentenced to life imprisonment. Immediately after the trial, Swedish television carried a number of interviews with various legal experts as well as the general public that indicated the pretrial polls still held. The general opinion was that the verdict had not settled the key question of whether Pettersson or some other individuals with political purposes had assassinated the 59-year-old Palme.

In October 1989 the appeals court made up of four professional jurists and three lay assessors reversed the original verdict by a vote of 7-0, the court president declaring: 'Our present judgment is that the investigation into the case is insufficient for a conviction.' Pettersson was released from jail the same day. Police officials said they would immediately renew the investigation, with every indication that the hunt would once again become a field day for the conspiracy set.

PARK CHUNG HEE (1917–1979) On August 15, 1974, South Korean President Park Chung Hee survived an assassination attempt in Seoul. His wife, however, was hit by a stray bullet and killed. Five years later Park Chung Hee himself was assassinated. The 1974 attempt was generally attributed to North Korean intelligence. By contrast the 1979 assassination was the work of Park's own South Korean intelligence force; specifically, it was masterminded by Kim Jae Kyu, the head of the Korean Central Intelligence Agency (KCIA).

The murders of Park, his chief bodyguard, Cha Chi Chol, and five others occurred October 26, 1979, in KCIA headquarters in Seoul. The killings were attributed to a coup attempt by Kim Jae Kyu, who feared he might be dismissed from his post. The murders of Park and Cha occurred in the agency's dining room, where they were discussing intelligence matters with Kim. A violent argument broke out between Kim and Cha over student riots that had occurred in Pusan. Kim had generally come to blame Cha for his loss of standing with President Park.

After the argument, Kim walked out and told two of his

aides: 'I am going to finish them off today, so when you hear gunshots in the dining room, you fellows finish off the security agents outside.' After obtaining a pistol, Kim returned to the dining room. He came out again to check on his agents' readiness to carry out the plan and once more reentered the room.

According to the testimony of two hostesses who had been serving the meal, Kim referred to Cha as 'an insect' and produced his weapon and opened fire. Cha, unarmed, was only slightly wounded and fled to a nearby toilet. Kim's second shot caught President Park in the chest. Kim found Cha hiding behind some furniture and shot him in the stomach and then shot Park in the head, killing them both.

A subsequent South Korean government report stated, 'With gunshots as the signal,' five of Kim's men 'split into two teams. One team shot and killed three security guards waiting inside the nearby kitchen,' while the other team shot and killed the deputy presidential security chief and another security agent in another room.

However, the coup did not develop as Kim had hoped, when it failed to win army support. In the ensuing chaos the United States placed its troops in the country on full alert and warned the North Korean government not to attempt to exploit the situation.

On May 24, 1980, Kim and four members of the KCIA were hanged for the murders. Kim Kae Won, President Park's chief of staff, had also been sentenced to death for his part in the plot, but the Martial Law Command commuted his sentence to life imprisonment. (See PARK CHUNG HEE, MADAME.)

PARK CHUNG HEE, Madame (1926–1974)   On August 15, 1974, an attempt to assassinate President Park Chung Hee backfired and his wife was fatally wounded instead. Park was delivering a Liberation Day address to 1,500 people at the National Theater in Seoul when an assailant charged down the center aisle firing a pistol. Park was uninjured as his bulletproof podium deflected some of the shots. Meanwhile one of the bullets struck in the head Yook Young Soo, Madame Park, who was sitting on the stage behind her husband. Additionally, a 17-year-old girl participating in the program was slain by another stray bullet.

The assassin, wounded by return fire from security guards, was seized. After the turmoil subsided, Park resumed his speech and afterward went to the hospital where his wife had been rushed. Madame Park died six hours after being shot.

The assassin was identified as Mun Se Kwang, a 22-year-old Korean residing in Osaka, Japan, who had entered South Korea on a false Japanese passport. Mun had been a member of the Korean Youth League, a Japan based anti-Park organization. At his trial in October Mun stated that he had attempted the assassination of Park on orders of two North Korean agents operating in Japan. He met one aboard a North Korean cargo ship in Osaka and said he was told by the agent that North Korean President Kim II Sung had personally ordered the assassination. Mun was convicted of the murder of Madame Park and on December 20, 1974, was executed. (See PARK CHUNG HEE.)

PAUL I, Czar of Russia (1754–1801) The son of Catherine the Great, Paul was much neglected by his mother, who never allowed him to participate in government affairs, and in fact she apparently intended to name Paul's son Alexander to succeed her. However, this did not happen and Paul came to the throne in 1796 at the age of 42.

Ruling in a tyrannical and capricious manner, Paul did much to counter his mother's works and even went so far as seeking to dim her memory by destroying statues, coins and paintings done in her honor. Politically he reversed Catherine's policies seeking to strengthen the autocracy. He restored the centralized administrative agencies that Catherine had abolished two decades earlier and tried to limit the authority of the nobles. Within a short time he managed to alienate much of the army by insisting on harsh disciplinary measures.

Even his most devoted supporters were shocked by his actions in regard to a policy toward the peasants and especially foreign relations. Upsetting the present peace, he joined the coalition of nations against Napoleon and then within two years he adopted an anti-British policy. As a result, by the end of 1800 Paul had so mismanaged things that he was at the same time officially at war with Napoleon, unofficially at war with England, and had broken diplomatic relations with Austria. He was also preparing to invade India.

Finally, a group of military and civil officials headed by Count Peter von Palen, the governor-general of St. Petersburg, and General Leonty Leontyevich plotted the czar's assassination. Before proceeding, they approached the czar's son and heir, Alexander, for approval to eliminate his father. Alexander gave it.

Although Paul considered himself safe inside the Mikhaylosky Palace, the plotters had no trouble penetrating the defenses by bribing the guards. Only one elderly guard remained outside the royal chambers, and he was quickly dispatched by nine conspirators, who burst in on Paul, sleeping fully dressed in uniform and boots. Paul jumped to his feet and fought desperately for his life, using a chair to ward off his sword-thrusting attackers. Finally pinned to a window, he pleaded for his life – promising to abdicate, to make them all princes and settle them with rich estates. For a moment the plotters appeared to waver, until one shouted: 'We have passed the Rubicon. If we spare his life, before the setting of tomorrow's sun we shall be his victims.'

The hapless Paul was then strangled to death. Alexander came to the throne, and none of the assassins was ever punished.

PEARLMAN, Mark David   See HAMMER, MICHAEL.

PEEL, Sir Robert   See DRUMMOND, EDWARD.

PERCEVAL, Spencer (1762–1812) Considering that he was assassinated, Spencer Perceval is a little-remembered prime minister of Great Britain. Oddly it is his assassin who is more often noted, at least in legal texts. The second son of the second earl of Egmont, Perceval entered parliament in 1796, where he enjoyed a steady rise to power through friendship with William Pitt the Younger. Through a succession of governments he served as solicitor general, attorney general and chancellor of the Exchequer. When he was appointed prime minister in 1809, Perceval became ardent in his opposition to Catholic emancipation, a singular position that marked him as among the statesmen most notorious for their extreme religious intolerance. Oddly, on all other matters Perceval was quite liberal for a Tory, refusing to prosecute the early trade unionists and supporting Wilberforce's campaign against slavery.

On May 11,1812, Prime Minister Perceval was at the House of Commons defending one of his government's positions. As he walked through the lobby of the House, an assassin stepped out from behind a pillar and shot him at point-blank range. The gunman made no effort to flee and was taken into custody. Perceval died in a matter of minutes.

The assassin was John Bellingham. Since Bellingham was an old Irish settler's name, the immediate impression was that the assassination was an Irish Catholic plot. The thought was soon dispelled. Bellingham turned out to have been a businessman who had traveled to Russia, where he ended up being imprisoned by the czarist police. He lost all his money and his business and returned home embittered by his experiences. In St. Petersburg, neither the English ambassador nor the consul general had offered him any aid. In England Bellingham sought legal redress, writing to a number of officials including the prime minister. The only response he got was that his woes in Russia had been the result of his own actions and in violation of Russian law and therefore His Majesty's Government had no cause to intervene.

Festering discontent with his situation and his inability to get help or even sympathy sent Bellingham to the House of Commons that fatal day. He stated shortly after the shooting: 'My name is Bellingham. It's a private injury. I know what I have done. It was a denial of justice on the part of the Government.'

Once it became clear that Bellingham was speaking the truth, speculation about an assassination conspiracy faded. Parliament erected a monument in Westminster Abbey for the 49-year-old Perceval, but he faded to little more than a sidebar in British history. Bellingham's name by contrast was frequently recorded in the law books. Lawyers often tried to win judgments for their clients by citing Bellingham as an example of the test of criminal insanity, that is whether the accused has sufficient capacity to distinguish good from evil when committing a crime. In Bellingham's case it was decided he did – and in record time. The assassination had taken place on May 11. Bellingham's trial ended on May 15. He was hanged on May 18.

Nevertheless Bellingham was cited often in the next three decades until one Daniel McNaughton killed Edward Drummond, the private secretary to Prime Minister Robert Peel. In this case McNaughton was acquitted of murder since it was found he was insane at the time and was incapable of distinguishing right from wrong. In a sense, John Bellingham stood as a counterpoint to what became known in British and American jurisprudence as the McNaughton Rules. (See DRUMMOND, EDWARD.)

PERTINAX, Emperor of Rome (?–193)   Publius Helvius Pertinax was the first of the rulers of Rome known as the Praetorian emperors, being raised to the throne by the Praetorians or by the legions under their command in the provinces. Many such emperors did not last long. Pertinax was a case in point.

An eminently respectable senator, Pertinax was raised to the purple on January 1, 193, hours after the assassination of the tyrant Commodus, by an ecstatic Senate. The murder of Commodus had been accomplished with the connivance of Laetus, the prefect of the Praetorian Guard, and Laetus immediately trotted forth Pertinax.

As an old soldier, Pertinax was as popular with the Praetorians as he was with the Senate. In astute moves he replenished the treasury, reduced taxes, auctioned off royal holdings of gold and silver, silks and embroideries, and beautiful slaves. 'In fact,' said the Bithynian historian of Rome, Dio Cassius, 'he did everything that a good emperor should do.' Pertinax realized that the empire was in decline, and he sought to undo as quickly as possible the misdeeds of his predecessor and to tighten the looseness that had developed. He found he also had to stiffen discipline among the Praetorians themselves.

Before Commodus was three months dead, the Praetorians mutinied, determined to rid themselves of the strict new emperor. On March 28, 193, when 300 guards broke into the palace, Pertinax fearlessly came forward to meet them. He reproached his would-be assassins, and momentarily they were shamed and immobilized. Then one of the guards charged forward and plunged his sword through the emperor. Many others followed suit and he was decapitated. The Praetorians paraded the emperor's head through the streets on a pike.

Then in one of the more bizarre incidents in Roman history, the murdering Praetorians put the imperial throne up for auction to the highest bidder. The purple would be bought by a wealthy senator, Didius Julianus, who was to succeed Pertinax for a mere 66 days, until he too was assassinated. (See DIDIUS JULIANUS, MARCUS, EMPEROR OF ROME.)

Further reading: *History of Rome*, by Dio Cassius; *History of Twenty Caesars*, by Herodian.

PETER III, Czar of Russia (1728–1762) Catherine the Great of Russia suffered the distinction of having both a husband, Peter III, and a son, Paul I, who were assassinated for reasons of state. From Catherine's view the death of her husband was far more important, since it

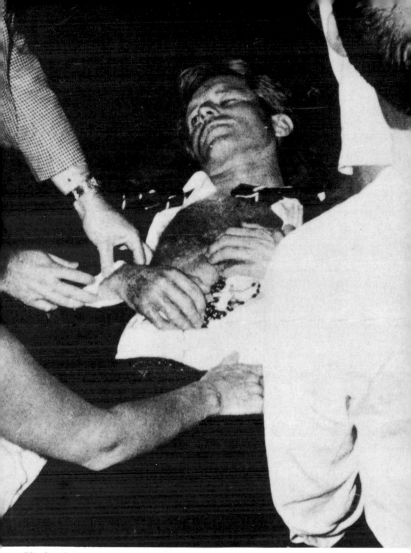

Having just scored an impressive victory in the California presidential primary, Robert Kennedy had become the clear leader for the Democratic nomination. He was struck down by a Palestinian, Sirhan Sirhan, before he left his victory headquarters.

Above: The hanging of four of the Lincoln conspirators including, at the far left, Mary Surratt whose conviction was controversial.

Left: President William McKinley was shot by anarchist Leon Czolgosz while greeting the public in a reception line. He died eight days later.

A martyr of the Mexican revolution, Francisco Madero later irritated the right and the left among the revolutionaries, as well as the U.S. government.

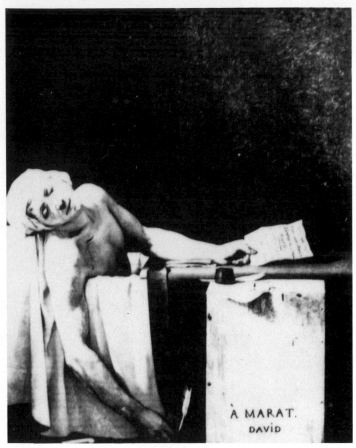

A MARAT.
DAVID

David's famed painting of Marat is an idealized treatment of a man who sat in the bath composing execution lists.

The bodies of Mussolini and his mistress, Clara Petacci, were strung up from a girder in Milan after they had been assassinated on secret orders of Italian Communist Party chief Palmiro Togliatti.

The murder of King Philip II of Macedonia was attributed variously to a disgruntled subject acting on his own and to the King's son, Alexander the Great, with his mother, Olympias.

Many bizarre tales are told of the hypnotic monk Rasputin and his influence on Russia and the imperial court. One thing was certain: his assassins had a difficult time killing him.

The treacherous assassination of rebel leader Cesar Augusto Sandino made him a martyr and gave his name to the Sandinista movement in Nicaragua.

confirmed her own role as Czarina. And indeed she ordered Peter's death.

The grandson of Peter the Great, Peter III held the Russians in contempt, a not-uncommon trait of the czars. However, Peter was so mentally enfeebled and so gallingly pro-Prussian that he managed to survive only six months on the throne.

Peter married Catherine, princess of the German principality of Anhalt-Zerbst, when he was 17. There were many who doubted if Peter ever achieved the mental age of a 17-year-old, even though he lived another 17 years. Capricious in his judgments, a drunkard and of bizarre behavior – he played constantly with toys and once had a rat executed on a specially constructed gibbet after it had gnawed on one of his favorite toys – Peter alienated his wife early in their marriage, spending much of his time with whores and mistresses. How much Catherine herself could object to this latter peccadillo is questionable considering her own legendary sexual appetite. In any event, by the time Peter acceded to the throne in late 1761, Catherine was certain that her husband planned divorce and Siberian exile for her.

Fortunately for Catherine she had room to maneuver, since her husband had within a few months of his reign managed to alienate most important blocks of Russian society. He offended the aristocracy, and even his edict relieving the gentry of compulsory state service gained him no supporters. Peter managed to alienate the Russian Orthodox Church by trying to force Lutheran religious practices on it. He made enemies of the imperial guards by making their terms of duty extremely severe and threatening to disband them. He also made peace with much-hated Prussia, withdrew from the Seven Years' War and prepared for an ill-advised conflict with Denmark, a campaign that would further German interests much more than Russian.

Exploiting this reservoir of hatred, Catherine won approval of the palace guard, the senate and the church, and with considerable aid from her lover, Grigory Grigoryevich Orlov, and his brother, Aleksey Grigoryevich Orlov, she moved quickly against her husband. Grigory arrested Peter III at his estate at Oranienbaum. Peter formally abdicated and was held in captivity in the village of Ropsha. Peter's groveling letters to Catherine were ignored, and early in July Aleksey Orlov visited Peter in his room, got him drunk and then strangled him to death.

Catherine's position as empress was now beyond dispute. In reward the brothers Orlov received huge cash endowments.

PHILIP II, King of Macedonia (382–336 B.C.) Philip II, the first successful warrior king of Macedonia and the father of the future Alexander the Great, was perhaps as great a conqueror as his son. He certainly was more tolerant of and more influenced by Greek culture.

Macedonia, a backward mountain province to the north of the great Greek city-states, was looked down upon by the Greeks. The son of a former king, Philip was seized at 15 and taken to Thebes as a hostage to guarantee the peaceful behavior of his brother, King Alexander. The young Philip was dazzled by the knowledge and culture of the Greeks and studied their literature, philosophy and military theories. In the meantime royal matters back in Macedonia were continuing in what passed for normality in that violent kingdom. Alexander was assassinated and was succeeded to the throne by Philip's elder brother Perdikkas. He too was murdered.

A struggle over the succession ensued, and the then 23-year-old Philip, having returned from Thebes, seized power with brutal efficiency and set about the task of turning Macedonia into another Greece. He converted the army into a fighting machine superior to the Thebans' and at least the equal of the Spartans'. After conquering the local hill tribes, Philip set out to take everything from the Danube to the Hellespont, including Thebes and several other cities. He left Athens untouched, wishing to make it, and especially its fleet, an important cog in a war against Persia.

One of Philip's most able generals was his son Alexander, who remained less in awe of the Greeks, despite having studied for three years under the brilliant Aristotle. It has often been observed by historians that Philip's driving ambition was to become worthy of admiration by the Greeks.

Before launching the major campaign against Persia, Philip planned to return to Aegae, Macedonia's ancient capital, for the wedding of his daughter. The capital was rife with rumors: Philip was said to be planning to take another wife and perhaps get a more 'legitimate' heir rather than Alexander. Such talk alienated his queen, Olympias, and apparently Alexander as well. While Philip did plan another of his 'political marriages,' he insisted he had no intention of jeopardizing the succession. In Aegae, he reconciled with Alexander. The question that remained was how seriously Alexander took his father's reassurances.

At the wedding of his daughter, Philip sought to show his lack of fear of his subjects by sauntering far ahead of his bodyguards. Suddenly an assassin, a young noble named Pausanias, charged forward and stabbed Philip to death. The murderer was slain before he could make a confession or reveal his motives. The official explanation was that Pausanias had a bitter grievance against the queen's uncle, Attalus, and against Philip for failing to give him justice. Nevertheless, much suspicion fell on Olympias and Alexander. Aristotle, however, disagreed with the theory, writing in his *Politics* about a monarch killed for personal and private reasons rather than for a matter of state. Acceptance of Aristotle's views must be tempered, however, by his closeness to the young Alexander.

Following the assassination of Philip II, Alexander went on to alter the map of the known world before his death at the age of 32. Rumor had it that Alexander too was murdered, but he actually died of fever. The assassination string of Macedonian kings had stopped at three in succession.

PLEHVE, Vyacheslav Konstantinovich (1846–1904)
Probably no imperial Russian statesman was more dedicated to upholding autocratic rule and suppressing liberal or revolutionary movements than Vyacheslav K. Plehve. Appointed director of the ministry of the interior police department after the assassination of Czar Alexander II in 1881, he carried out mass executions in the wake of the murder and to the public became an ogre because of his clear enthusiasm for the task.

Plehve's disrepute plunged to its lowest depths in the case of a beautiful young university student named Marie Vietrov, whose only crime was that some 'forbidden books' had been found in her room. The normal punishment was suspension from school, but instead Plehve ordered her confined in the Peter and Paul fortress. There is no stated record of what happened to Vietrov while confined over the next two months, but the standard thesis is that she was subjected to rape and torture. On February 10, 1897, the desperate prisoner soaked her mattress in paraffin, laid down on it and set it aflame. She died after two days of incalculable pain and suffering. The Vietrov family was not even informed of her death for two weeks. Revolutionary documents appeared accusing the government of torturing the girl to suicide, even though family and friends had obtained an order for her freedom, and speculating on the tortures and humiliations that had driven her to her tragic fate. In protest a huge crowd attended her funeral service, despite a warning by the police to disperse.

In spite of the scandal and many others, Plehve was promoted and by 1902 became minister of the interior. Plehve pushed a harsh Russification policy against a number of minorities, especially against the Finns and Armenians, and he fostered anti-Semitic campaigns that climaxed in a bloody pogrom in April 1903. He suppressed liberal local governments and countered labor union activities by sponsoring police-controlled unions.

Plehve's ruthlessness made him a prime target for terrorist attack, and in 1904 the Social Revolutionaries plotted his death. On July 28 Plehve was traveling to a St. Petersburg railway station when E. S. Sazonov hurled a bomb under his carriage. The explosion was so enormous that Plehve was literally atomized. Sazonov was caught and sentenced to life imprisonment. One of the leading Social Revolutionaries involved in the plot was Boris V. Savinkov, who became an important figure in the provisional government in 1917. After the Bolsheviks came to power, Savinkov fled, seeking the aid of the Allies against the new regime. He later returned to Russia and was arrested and sentenced to death in 1924. The sentence was later reduced to life imprisonment, and Savinkov died a year later in Lubyanka Prison, officially described as a suicide. (See GAPON, FATHER GEORGII.)

POMPEY THE GREAT (106–48 B.C.)   Pompey the Great carved out an illustrious military and political career in Rome but proved no match for Julius Caesar. For a time Pompey allied himself with the wealthy Crassus and Caesar, and they became the masters of Rome – an odd triumvirate, consisting of 'the egotistical general, the good-natured millionaire and the rather foppish young intellectual,' as Will Durant put it.

Pompey undoubtedly considered himself the most important of the trio. He had fought for Sulla, gaining many laurels, had claimed the major credit for the crushing of the slave revolt of Spartacus (although this was mainly done by Crassus), and had destroyed the pirates infesting the Mediterranean. In 65 B.C. he vanquished Mithridates VI of Pontus. The First Triumvirate was formed in 60 and marked the great degradation of Roman democracy.

In 54 the major tie between Pompey and Caesar was severed with the death of Pompey's wife, Julia, who was Caesar's daughter. With Crassus's death in 53 the enmity between Caesar and Pompey increased, and the latter joined forces with the Senate in opposition to the ever-growing power of Caesar.

In 49, in defiance of the Senate and Pompey, Caesar crossed the Rubicon from Gaul with his soldiers, beginning the struggle between two great men to determine who would become dictator. Pompey and his allies possessed more troops, but time after time Caesar's brilliant generalship carried the day in the civil war. The determining battle was fought at Pharsalus, on August 9, 48, with Pompey commanding 48,000 infantry and 7,000 horse, and Caesar commanding only 22,000 and 1,000, respectively. Brothers and other relatives fought on opposing sides, and Caesar bade his men spare the lives of all Romans who surrendered. He especially ordered that the young aristocrat Marcus Brutus was to be taken without injury, or to be allowed to escape if this proved impossible.

The battle was a rout, the Pompeians were overwhelmed – 15,000 were killed or wounded and 20,000 surrendered. The rest fled, including Pompey, who tore the insignia of command from his dress. He headed for Egypt by sea, hoping to join up with still potent armies of his and perhaps draw on aid from the Egyptians. At Mytilene, his wife, Cornelia, joined him, and she and the citizens urged him to remain. He refused and advised them to surrender to Caesar without fear, saying, 'Caesar is a man of great goodness and clemency.'

At Alexandria the young Ptolemy XII marched down to the sea, apparently to greet Pompey's small squadron. However, the king's counselors had determined not to risk offending the triumphant Caesar. In response to an invitation to land, Pompey entered a small boat sent to ferry him. As he prepared to step ashore, Pothinus, the eunuch vizier to the young king, gave the order for servants to stab Pompey to death. Upon Caesar's arrival, Pothinus's killers offered him his foe's severed head. Caesar turned away weeping.

Two years later Caesar himself would be assassinated as well, in a plot led by Brutus and Cassius, both of whom he had pardoned.

Further reading: *Pompey the Great*, by John D. Leach.

PONTO, Jurgen   See SCHLEYER, HANNS-MARTIN.

POPIELUSZKO, Father Jerzy (1947–1984)   While profound changes swept Eastern Europe in 1989–1990, the first fissures in the Communist bloc can be traced to Poland several years earlier and were in part the unintentional result of an assassination.

On October 29, 1984, 11 days after Polish Reverend Jerzy Popieluszko, a young activist anti-Communist clergyman, was kidnapped, his body was fished out of a reservoir. In life Father Popieluszko had been an annoyance to the Jaruzelski government, but in death he became Polish Catholics' first martyr of the postwar era.

It was an astonishing crime. Even at the height of Stalinism, the Polish secret police had not dared to kidnap and assassinate priests. Popieluszko had been one of the most ardent supporters of the then outlawed Solidarity movement. As parish priest of St. Stanislaw Kostka Church in Warsaw, Popielusko had gained considerable renown by using his pulpit to denounce the Communist rulers for their ban on trade unions and their imposition of martial law. He was abducted near the town of Torun outside Warsaw by the secret police. His recovered body showed he had been subjected to severe beatings before being killed.

The government of General Wojciech Jaruzelski moved quickly to arrest and convict the perpetrators – or at least some of them – of the brutal murder. A great deal of speculation arose that the Popieluszko assassination represented a split within the Communist Party and within the secret police, whereby the hard liners in the party were seeking to toughen the policy of the Jaruzelski leadership by causing a major fissure between church and state and by halting the rapprochement between the government and Solidarity.

Whatever the motive, the government took the surprising step of prosecuting a security police officer and three former officers for the murder. All were convicted. The three former officers, all removed from their positions shortly after the crime, were headed by Grzegorz Piotrowski, who like his two associates admitted guilt. He got 25 years' imprisonment, the second harshest penalty, after death, allowed under the law. Security men Leszek Pekala and Waldemar Chmielewski received 15 and 14 years respectively. Colonel Adam Pietruszka, the superior officer of the other defendants and the only one to deny a role in the assassination, also got 25 years. In the presiding judge's words, Pietruszka had not taken part in the kidnapping and murder per se, but his cooperation had been 'a necessary condition for the success of the whole operation.'

In passing the sentences the court lashed out at the defendants for committing their crime as the government was seeking to heal the rifts within Polish society. It said that by attacking a well-known dissident the guilty men 'could have set off a chain reaction' of unrest and confrontation.

The government prosecutor tried to place some blame for the murder on Father Popieluszko himself as well, saying he 'undertook extremist action and, like the accused, thought he was above the law.' However, this was viewed merely as a sop to Communist hardliners. The government's concessions to Solidarity continued, and Father Popieluszko's grave site became a virtual national shrine.

PRIM, Juan (1814–1870) A magnetic Spanish military and political figure, Juan Prim achieved fame by first bringing Isabella II, the Bourbon Spanish queen, to power and then a quarter of a century later dethroning her. Prim gained early military laurels in the First Carlist War (1833–39), which won the throne away from Don Carlos, Isabella's uncle. However, almost immediately Prim became opposed to the young queen's Espartero regency, and after entering the Cortes (parliament) he led a successful insurrection against Espartero. Prim became the military governor of Madrid and later of Barcelona. Later he conspired against the government of the Moderate Party's Ramón Maria Narváez.

Over the years Prim was at times under a death sentence but later won a pardon and was restored to important offices. In 1847 he was appointed governor of Puerto Rico. In 1866 he went into exile after an aborted rebellion, but two years later he returned in triumph in the 1868 revolution that toppled Isabella II. Prim emerged as the most powerful member of the new revolutionary government and had enough power to name a suitable monarch for the nation. He first backed Prussia's candidate, Prince Leopold von Hohenzollern-Sigmaringen. When Leopold stepped down, Prim pushed through the election of Amadeus of Savoy. On December 27, 1870, prior to Amadeus's arrival in Spain, Prim was shot down by a lone gunman as he was leaving the government chambers in Madrid. The assassin escaped, and Prim died three days later.

The Prim assassination undoubtedly achieved its objective of destabilizing Amadeus's reign, which lasted only two years.

PROBUS, MARCUS AURELIUS, Emperor of Rome (?–282) Of the various Roman emperors put on the throne by the legions, very few were as loyal to the Roman constitution as was Marcus Aurelius Probus. Unlike many other Praetorian emperors, Probus had taken the field as the champion of the constitution as opposed to the usurper, Emperor Florian. After Florian was murdered, the soldiers acclaimed Probus emperor.

Probus insisted on submitting his title to senatorial authority for its unfettered choice of acceptance or rejection. As emperor, Probus treated the Senate with what many historians have labeled exaggerated respect. The son of a Balkan military officer, Probus found his six-year reign continually beset by warfare with hostile tribes along the northern frontier of the empire, and he had to put down revolts in Britain, Gaul and in the East.

Probus was recognized to be as clement a statesman as he was brilliant a soldier. There was little political opposition to him. He offered a program for peace to be accomplished as the enemies of Rome were swept back. Probus forced the Germans from Gaul, drove the Vandals from Illyricum, built a wall between the Rhine and the Danube, and stopped the Persians with mere verbal warnings.

Under Probus peace broke out throughout the realm. And the emperor promised even better days. He spoke of an empire without arms and armies, without wars and with the force of law ruling everywhere.

Under this benevolent ruler, the armies took on new duties, draining marshes, clearing wastelands, planting vines for food and wine. He planned a series of other work projects and reclamations for the troops. This was new for legions used to the spoils of battle. But Probus had been placed in power by the army, and despite great support from the public, the soldiers could be a potent enemy. When a rumor, unfounded, spread that Probus planned an imminent reduction of the size of the army, the legionaires, as Durant put it, 'murdered him (282), mourned him, and built a monument to his memory.' (See FLORIAN.)

Further reading: *The Illustrated World History, Vol. II*, edited by Sir John Hammerton and Harry Elmer Barnes; *The Story of Civilization III – Caesar and Christ*, by Will Durant.

PTOLEMY XIV, King of Egypt (c.59–44 B.C.) Following the death of his older brother, Ptolemy XIII, at the conclusion of the Alexandrian War, Ptolemy XIV was elevated to corulership of Egypt together with his celebrated sister Cleopatra by the victorious Julius Caesar. After Cleopatra bore Caesar a son in 47 B.C. and accompanied Caesar to Rome the following year, Ptolemy XIV went along as well. There is little record of his activities in Rome – clearly Caesar could not leave one of Egypt's corulers behind while the other journeyed to faraway Rome – but after Caesar's assassination, Cleopatra and her brother returned to Egypt.

Unfortunately for Ptolemy XIV, Cleopatra was determined to ensure the succession of her son, Caesarion. In 44 Ptolemy XIV was assassinated, presumably on Cleopatra's orders. The queen then declared Caesarion her coruler as Ptolemy XV. After Cleopatra committed suicide following the defeat and death of Marc Antony in 30 B.C., the victorious Octavian had Ptolemy XV executed.

Q

QUINTANILLA, Roberto (1928–1971)   When on April 1, 1971, the Bolivian consul general to Hamburg was shot and killed in the Hamburg consulate by an unidentified woman, speculation centered on more than one possible motive for the crime. Quintanilla was a former chief of Bolivian police intelligence, and recent press reports had suggested that he had played a role in the suspicious 1968 heliocopter-crash death of former President Rene Barrientos, as did former President Alfredo Ovando, at the time army commander. At the time of his death, Quintanilla had officially retired from his post as consul but was remaining at his post in Germany until the arrival of his replacement, whereupon Quintanilla was expected to return to Bolivia.

The day after the Quintanilla assassination the Bolivian National Liberation Army (ELN) claimed in a communiqué that it was responsible for the deed. The ELN said it acted in vengeance for the death of guerrilla leader 'Inti' Peredo in 1969, for which it held Quintanilla responsible. However, some tended to discount the ELN claim, feeling that the rather weak revolutionary group was simply trying to capitalize on the murder to enhance its own image. The question whether Quintanilla was killed by revolutionary forces or by a conspiracy to silence him on the alleged assassination of President Barrientos remained undetermined.

R

RAMA VIII   See ANANDA MAHIDOL, KING OF SIAM

RAMUS, Petrus (1515–1572)   At the age of 21 the illustrious 16th-century French philosopher, logician and rhetorician Petrus Ramus announced his thesis at the University of Paris that 'whatever was said by Aristotle is false.' This assault on what Ramus regarded as the tyranny of Aristotelian Scholasticism was to cause ferment in the academic world and, in the view of many observers, proved to be the very death of him. Over the years Ramus's various teachings so provoked orthodox Aristotelian philosophers at the University of Paris that they successfully petitioned King Francis I in 1544 to suppress Ramus's reformed logic and forbid him to teach on the subject.

However, Ramus enjoyed the support of many academic and ecclesiastical figures, and Cardinal Charles of Lorraine succeeded in persuading King Henry II to lift the ban in 1547 – leaving Ramus 'free in both tongue and pen.' In 1551 Ramus was named regius professor of philosophy and eloquence at the College de France. Free of university control, Ramus became the most famous teacher in Paris and a foe of traditionalism. By character and personal philosophy Ramus came to sympathize with rising Protestantism, and when the Huguenots won a measure of governmental tolerance, he joined the Reformed faith in 1561. The following year some of his students tore down the religious images in the chapel of the College de Prescles. The government continued to pay Ramus his salary, but his position became more precarious, and with the outbreak of civil war in 1562 Ramus accepted a safe conduct from Catherine de' Medici and left Paris.

With the signing of peace the following year he returned, but his struggles with both ecclesiastics and academicians continued almost unabated. Twice he survived attempts on his life. When it was later ruled that only Catholics could teach at the university or College Royale, Ramus, who had fled Paris once again in 1567 and then returned, retired to private life. However, Catherine doubled his salary, and he was free to study and write.

In July 1572 Montluc, bishop of Valence, offered to take Ramus along on an embassy to Poland. The bishop appeared to foresee the Massacre of St. Bartholomew and was eager to protect the aging philosopher. Ramus declined the invitation, and one week after Montluc's departure, the bloody massacre began. Ramus was untouched during the first two days, but on the third day two men, apparently hired assassins, invaded his fifth-floor study, where they discovered the philosopher in prayer. Ramus was stabbed, shot in the head and his body heaved through the window to the street. Students or ruffians then dragged the still-living Ramus to the Seine and threw him in. Others then fished it out and hacked it to pieces.

Who ordered the assassination of Ramus? Catherine and her son Charles IX, the instigators of the great massacre, appear to have continued to favor Ramus to the very end. This leaves the ecclesiastics and the academicians as suspects. Of these there were those who openly rejoiced at Ramus's assassination. Foremost was a long-time academic foe, Jacques Charpentier, a professor of mathematics, who declared glowingly of the massacre and the murder: 'This brilliant sun, which, during the month of August, has brightened France. . . . The stuff and nonsense have disappeared with its author. All good men are full of joy.'

Durant notes: 'Two years later Charpentier himself died, some say of remorse; but perhaps this does him too much credit.'

RASPUTIN, Grigory Yefimovich (c. 1872–1916) It is probably impossible to construct a completely accurate picture of Grigory Rasputin, the Russian religious figure and courtier who rose to the status of 'czar above czars' or 'the Richelieu of Russia' before the Bolshevik Revolution. Fact and legend have become intermingled about his religious activities, his sexual exploits, his hold on the czar and the czarina, and even the details of his assassination.

Rasputin was born of peasant stock in 1872, or possibly a bit earlier in the Siberian province of Tobolsk. His real name was Novykh, but he acquired the name of Rasputin, which meant 'licentious' or 'debauched one.' As a holy man he preached salvation through repentance, and to achieve that exalted station his followers were required to practice indiscriminate sexuality so that Rasputin could 'redeem' them. Thus he offered the complete cycle of sin and redemption in one convenient package.

Rasputin was married in 1895 and had three children, but family life did not alter his religious-sexual fervor, and he absented himself from his family for long periods on pilgrimages, visiting monasteries and spreading his unusual gospel. Hordes of peasants, male and female, threw themselves at his feet, kissed his hemline and called him 'Father Grigory, our savior!' Few fathers or husbands seemed to object to Rasputin's efforts to redeem their daughters and wives since their special if earthy treatment was thought to be willed by God.

In 1904 the unwashed holy man with the hypnotic eyes, straggly hair and blackened fingernails arrived in St. Petersburg, where he met Father Feofan, inspector of the Ecclesiastical Academy, and the following year the family of Grand Duke Nikolai Nikolayevich; he also became the protege of the Grand Duchess Militsa. Not long thereafter his considerable repute as a healer led him to the imperial court, where Alexis, the young czarevitch, suffered from hemophilia. Rasputin placed his hand on the boy's forehead and prayed for him and recited endless Siberian fairy tales about humpback horses and legless riders. The boy responded, slowly, to Rasputin; his pains and swellings subsided, and his melancholy lifted. Whenever the czare-vitch's internal bleeding started again, Rasputin would be called to his bedside. Soon the grateful and superstitious empress Alexandra issued orders giving him free run of the court. Through Alexandra the slow-witted Nicholas II also came to rely on Rasputin for advice on the affairs of state.

Rasputin quickly turned his royal favor into a fulltime enterprise, opening a 'redemption center' in St. Peters-burg where he received lucrative petitions for political favors. His personal quarters were jammed with women of all classes, but he said he preferred the aristocratic ladies because 'they smelled better.' Occasionally, a woman would accuse Rasputin of rape, but the secret police ignored such claims since the czarina would brook no criticism of the savior of her son.

Most of Rasputin's intercessions in appointments con-cerned positions in the church – he provoked a scandal by forcing the appointment of an illiterate peasant friend as bishop of his native Tobolsk in Siberia – but later, when his influence extended to the political sector, he often caused chaos in the functioning of the government.

There were many attempts to assassinate Rasputin emanating from many quarters, some religious, some political-military, some from those who saw him as a threat to the monarchy. The leading priest-orator of the era, Iliodor, attacked Rasputin in a tract entitled 'The Holy Devil' and all but charged that there was a sexual relationship between the peasant monk and the czarina.

For a time Rasputin thought it wise to leave St. Petersburg. On a trip back to his home village, he was subjected to an assassination plot by a psychotic prostitute who clad herself as a pilgrim seeking alms from the monk. As Rasputin reached for some coins, she produced a 21-inch knife and stabbed him in the stomach, crying out, 'I have slain the Antichrist!' Remarkably, Rasputin did not even fall from the vicious blow, clamping his hand over the gaping wound.

The would-be assassin, Guseva, gave a series of rambling reasons for her act. She said she was seeking vengeance for the Siberian girls Rasputin had corrupted, that she wanted to restore dignity to religion, that she wanted to free the czar and czarina from his evil influence.

After an operation, Rasputin hovered between life and death for some weeks, during which time the czar was preparing for World War I. Rasputin had persuaded Nicholas to avoid getting into the Balkan war in 1912, but from his sickbed he was unable to prevent Russia's involvement in the Great War. During its first two years, after his return to the capital, he made and broke cabinet ministers at will, and those who opposed him were mired in disgrace, if not actually banished. There was considerable reason to believe that in 1915–16 Rasputin, known to be pro-German in his sympathies, was looking for a way to make peace. It was in this period that rightist elements determined to get rid of the monk. However, it is not easy to attribute their acts entirely to political motives. Clearly many felt their own position threatened by the all-powerful mystic, and probably many of them, such as the plot's leader, Prince Felix Yusupov, feared Rasputin's sin-and-redemption program might well ensnare their wives or daughters as well.

On the night of December 29–30, Yusupov, Grand Duke Dimitry Pavlovich and other nobles held a party in Rasputin's honor in the basement of the prince's castle. The conspirators baited the trap by inferring that Yusupov's wife, the beautiful princess Irene Alexandrovna, was eager to see Rasputin. Actually the princess had been sent to the Crimea.

At the party Rasputin drank glass after glass of poisoned wine and several cakes and chocolates spiked with murderous doses of potassium cyanide. The plotters watched expectantly for Rasputin to keel over dead, but he did not. Instead, Rasputin danced and sang and called on the prince to play the guitar. According to one later medical theory, Rasputin suffered alcoholic gastritis, with his stomach failing to secrete the hydrochloric acid necessary to get the cyanide compound to work.

In the meantime the only thing that seemed to show on the monk was the alcohol, and he grew ever more boisterous. Yusupov, seeing his comrades become both more impatient and disheartened, excused himself to go upstairs, allegedly to get his wife. The prince returned with a pistol and shot Rasputin. Accounts here are varied, although certainly vivid. According to some, Rasputin fell to the floor, but as the prince knelt to examine him, the mystic's eyes popped open and he seized the prince by the throat. Yusupov tore himself free and ran to the courtyard with Rasputin in pursuit on all fours. As Rasputin rose to his feet, the grand duke shot him in the chest. Another conspirator shot him in the head. Many of the officers used their sabers on Rasputin, and the prince seized an iron bar and struck the fallen victim several times with savage fury. Finally the victim lay still, although it was said one eye remained open and staring. The conspirators trussed up the body and heaved it into the Moika Canal.

Forty-eight hours later the body turned up in the ice of the Neva River. One arm had come free of the bindings, and Rasputin's lungs were filled with water. Rasputin had still been alive when dumped in the canal and had finally died by drowning.

Millions of peasants were shattered by Rasputin's murder. The Romanovs were deeply grieved, and the czarina ordered the body buried near the chapel at the imperial palace at Puskin.

It is not easy to determine what role Rasputin might have played in the revolutionary ferment of 1917 had he lived, but he did correctly prophesy 'If I die, the emperor will soon lose his crown.' As the year 1917 began, there were indications that a palace coup would be attempted to restore a measure of sanity and leadership to the state. However, a popular revolution came first.

Prince Yusupov and his wife escaped the revolution and took up residence in London, Paris and New York. The prince filed a number of lawsuits about portrayals of his role in the assassination, winning some and losing others, and in 1967 he agreed to permit a replay of the killing on television, but he died before it could be produced. Little was learned of Rasputin's family, save for his eldest daughter, Maria Grigorievna, who married a White Russian officer and fled the revolution to France. After her husband died, she became a cabaret dancer in Romania. Later she performed as an animal trainer in a circus, billed as 'the daughter of the Mad Monk.' She became an American citizen in 1945 and wrote considerably on her remembrances of imperial Russia. In 1977, the year of her death, she published *Rasputin: The Man Behind the Myth*, a curious book rather given to detailed and clinical tributes to her father's sexual prowess.

Further reading: *Nicholas and Alexandra*, by Robert K. Massie.

RATH, Ernst vom (?–1938) On November 7, 1938, a distraught 17-year-old German Jew named Herschel Grynszpan committed an assassination that was to furnish the Nazis with the ideological excuse for further persecution of the Jews in Germany and for the notorious 'Crystal Night': Grynszpan entered the German embassy in Paris, intent upon shooting the ambassador, Count Johannes von Welczeck. The youth's father had been among 10,000 Jews packed in boxcars and deported to Poland, and the younger Grynszpan decided on revenge.

He asked to see the ambassador but was rebuffed. When Ernst vom Rath, the third secretary, was sent out to see what he wanted, Grynszpan shot and fatally wounded him instead. Nazi leaders seized on the killing to launch an immediate campaign of terror. On November 9, Dr. Joseph Goebbels issued instructions that 'spontaneous demonstrations' were to be 'organized and executed' by the SS. A night of horror followed throughout Germany.

The Nazi lionizing of the slain vom Rath was steeped in irony, since he had been under surveillance by the Gestapo because of anti-Nazi beliefs and his general disapproval of anti-Semitic acts taking place in Germany.

Further reading: *The Rise and Fall of the Third Reich*, by William L. Shirer.

RATHENAU, Walther (1867–1922) In post-World War I Germany the right wing despised the illustrious statesman, social theorist, industrialist and 'Judeo-Democrat' Walther Rathenau. As the brilliant and cultured German foreign minister, Rathenau won considerable foreign accolades for his efforts to carry out at least some of the provisions of the Versailles Treaty. Rathenau was a leading industrialist and director and later president of Allgemeine Elektrizitats-Gesellschaft, a leading power company, and during the war managed the distribution of raw materials for the war effort. He was involved after the war in a number of conferences in Versailles, London and Cannes that the Right detested. The fact that he was also a Jew made him an even more attractive target for fanatic rightists seeking a way to weaken the central government and set up reactionary regimes in various parts of the country. One such center was in Bavaria, where, it was said, a plot to kill a number of moderates and liberals was concocted, among the victims Rathenau.

On January 24, 1922, Rathenau was shot down on the street as he was going to his office. Two of his killers were shot to death in a gunfight with police as they fled the country.

On May 10, 1933, four and a half months after Hitler became chancellor, there was the infamous torchlight book-burning of 20,000 volumes. Among the authors whose works were burned were Thomas and Heinrich Mann, Erich Maria Remarque, Arnold and Stefan Zweig, Albert Einstein, Jack London, Upton Sinclair, Helen Keller, Margaret Sanger, H. G. Wells, Gide, Zola, Freud, Proust, Lion Feuchtwanger, Havelock Ellis and Walther Rathenau.

REAGAN, Ronald (1911–) – Attempted Assassination John W. Hinckley was at least in part inspired to attempt to kill U.S. President Ronald Reagan after seeing a young actress with whom he was obsessed, Jodie Foster, in a film called *Taxi Driver*. In that film Robert DeNiro played an obsessed gunman who plans to assassinate a presidential candidate, a role ironically inspired by Arthur Bremer, who had attempted to kill Governor George Wallace.

A 25-year-old drifter from Evergreen, Colorado, Hinckley shot Reagan on March 30, 1981, as the president left the Washington Hilton Hotel, where he had addressed a labor audience. Hinckley was seized immediately after having fired four to six shots from a .22-caliber revolver, a weapon generally described as a Saturday Night Special. Reagan was hit by a bullet that entered under the left armpit, piercing the chest, bouncing off the seventh rib and plowing into the left lower lobe of the lung. The president froze for a moment at the door of his limousine and then was brusquely pushed inside the car by a Secret Service agent. Remarkably, the president did not realize he had been shot but thought he had simply been injured when shoved into the car. Only on the way to the hospital was it found that he had been wounded.

Wounded in the shooting as well was James S. Brady, the presidential press secretary; Timothy J. McCarthy, a Secret Service agent; and Timothy K. Delahanty, a District of Columbia police officer. All recovered, although Brady was hospitalized for months and never regained full control of his body. In ensuing years Brady and his wife would become active supporters of gun-control laws, something Reagan had long opposed and continued to do so even after the attempt on his life.

Hinckley, captured at the scene, was discovered to be the son of an oil executive. He had grown up in affluence in Dallas and moved with his family to Colorado in 1974. Off and on he attended Texas Tech University but never graduated. He made frequent trips across the country, and in 1978 he joined the National Socialist Party of America, generally referred to as the Nazi Party of America. After the attempt on Reagan's life a spokesman for the Nazis said the party had declined to renew

Hinckley's membership the next year because of his 'violent temper.'

Hinckley had apparently flown from Denver to Los Angeles and the following day, March 26, 1981, departed by Greyhound for Washington, D.C., arriving there on March 29, the day before his attack. It appeared Hinckley had a history of dogging presidents. After his arrest, it was discovered that he had been in Nashville, Tennessee, on October 9, 1980, when President Jimmy Carter was there. Hinckley was arrested at the airport after X-ray equipment revealed he had three handguns and ammunition in his hand luggage. The weapons were confiscated and Hinckley was fined $62.50. Surprisingly, federal authorities did not place Hinckley under security surveillance following this arrest. Four days after leaving Tennessee Hinckley turned up in Dallas and bought two .22-caliber handguns in a pawnshop. One of these was the weapon used in the Reagan shooting.

Investigation showed that Hinckley had been infatuated with movie star Jodie Foster, at the time a student at Yale University. He had written a number of letters to her, and investigators found an unmailed letter dated March 30, 1981, 12:45 P.M. (just one hour and 45 minutes before he shot the president) in his Washington hotel room. It read:

Dear Jodie,There is a definite possibility that I will be killed in my attempt to get Reagan. It is for this very reason that I am writing you now . . .

Hinckley went on to say that he loved her and that

although we talked on the phone a couple of times, I never had the nerve to simply approach you and introduce myself. . . . Jodie, I would abandon this idea of getting Reagan in a second if I could only win your heart and live out the rest of my life with you, whether it be in total obscurity or whatever. I will admit to you that the reason I'm going ahead with this attempt now is because I just cannot wait any longer to impress you.

I've got to do something now to make you understand in no uncertain terms that I am doing all this for your sake. By sacrificing my freedom and possibly my life, I hope to change your mind about me.

In August 1981 Hinckley was indicted for attempting to kill President Reagan. The FBI soon was satisfied that Hinckley had acted alone. The CIA director, William Casey, was not so readily convinced and launched an intensive investigation into the possibility that Russia's KGB could have been involved with Hinckley. Only the most intensive investigation by CIA experts finally convinced him otherwise.

In a verdict that shocked the country, a jury found Hinckley not guilty on grounds of insanity. He was then committed to a mental institution.

In 1987 a book by *Washington Post* reporter Bob Woodward, *Veil: The Secret Wars of the CIA 1981–1987*, caused an uproar when it disclosed that Reagan had come closer to death in Hinckley's assassination try than officially admitted and that his recovery was much more difficult. His supposedly quick, almost miraculous, recovery had been largely an act, and after the smiles and waves, he would walk 'with the hesitant steps of an old man. He was pale and disoriented.' Reagan, reported Woodward, often needed an inhalator and could concentrate for only a few minutes at a time and 'remain attentive only an hour or so a day.'

Woodward reported that the assassination attempt had made Casey especially obsessed with the president's safety and later led the CIA and the White House to overreact to unconfirmed intelligence that hit squads had been dispatched by Libyan leader Muammer al-Qaddafi to kill Reagan. Some of the hit squad stories were traced to Manucher Ghorbanifar, an arms merchant with links to Israeli and Iranian intelligence, who later played a major role in the U.S.–Iran arms sales.

In the meantime Hinckley remained in hospital confinement. In January 1987 the Secret Service revealed that over its strong objections he had been allowed to leave the hospital the previous December for a 12-hour visit with his family in a facility in Reston, Virginia. He had been escorted to the reunion by hospital personnel. The following year St. Elizabeths Hospital proposed permitting Hinckley to have a one-day, unescorted Easter visit with his family in McLean, Virginia. However, it was disclosed that Hinckley had been in correspondence with convicted murderer Theodore Bundy, at the time awaiting execution in Florida. The hospital then withdrew its request with the court.

Further reading: *American Assassins*, by James W. Clarke; *Veil: The Secret Wars of the CIA 1981–1987*, by Bob Woodward.

REMELIIK, Haruo I. (1934–1985)   The first president of the western Pacific island of Palau, Haruo I. Remeliik, elected in 1981 and reelected in 1984, was shot to death outside his home in Koror on June 30, 1985.

At first the assassination of the 51-year-old Remeliik was a mystery, although observers were aware that tensions had been growing on the island concerning the impending transition to self-government under a compact with the United States, which administered the island under a United Nations mandate.

Three weeks after the slaying a number of arrests were made, chief among these being that of Melwart Tmetuchel, the son of Roman Tmetuchel, governor of Arai state and Remeliik's chief political opponent. The younger Tmetuchel and two others, Anghenio Sabino and Leslie Tewid, were convicted of murder and were given prison terms ranging from 25 to 35 years.

REMON, Jose Antonio (1908–1955)   In a political assassination that soon developed into a genuine whodunit, President Jose Antonio Remon was machine-gunned to death while attending Franco Race Track in Panama City on the night of January 2, 1955. In an ensuing gunfight the assassin survived the Remon bodyguards' counterattack and got away, leaving in addition to the intended victim a bodyguard and a bystander dead. The following day the country remained calm, and the first vice president and foreign minister Ramon Guizado was sworn in as president.

On January 8 Professor Catalino Arrocha Gaell resigned as minister of government and justice so that the slain president's younger brother, Alejandro Remon, could be named to the office and head the hunt for the assassins. However, the Guizado government made no move to fill the post, although it did heed public opinion and bring in foreign detectives, including several from the United States.

By January 15 the case was solved. This followed the arrest two days earlier of Cadet Jose Edgardo Tejado on information received from his girlfriend. Tejado was said to have supplied the murder weapon to lawyer Ruben Miro the previous September. On the same day, the Panamanian National Assembly ousted President Guizado from office and ordered his arrest for his part in the assassination plot. The dead President's brother was given the post of minister of government and justice. Meanwhile, Miro confessed he had machine-gunned President Remon after plotting the murder with Guizado, as well as Guizado's son and Miro's business partner. Miro testified that he, his business partner and President Guizado were all deeply in debt and had decided to kill Remon to allow Guizado to run the government (and its finances) and to stall the investigation by the ministry of government and justice.

For his part in the plot ex-President Guizado was tried by the National Assembly. He was convicted of being an accomplice in the assassination, formally deprived of presidential rank and sentenced to six years and eight months in prison. He died in 1964.

RIZZIO, David (c. 1533–1566) The intrigue surrounding the murder of David Rizzio, private foreign secretary of Mary, Queen of Scots, makes it probably the most intricate and most sensational assassination in British political history.

An Italian musician, Rizzio had gained considerable influence over the young queen. On the evening of March 9, 1566, Rizzio was having dinner at the palace of Holyrood in Edinburgh with the queen, her half brother and her half sister. At the time Mary, 23 years old, was six months pregnant. If the child were born, it would crush the hopes of Henry Lord Darnley, her husband through a political marriage, to become crown matrimonial of Scotland. Together with his allies, James Douglas, the Earl of Morton, Patrick, Baron Lindsay, and William, Baron Ruthven, Darnley concocted a bizarre plot to cause his wife to miscarry by forcing her to witness the brutal murder of her favorite, Rizzio. The murder would be justified on the claim that the Italian was the queen's lover.

During the fatal dinner, six assailants, led by Morton and Lindsay, charged into the dining room and seized Rizzio, who tried desperately to clutch to the safety of Mary's skirts. They dragged him to the door and with daggers hacked him to pieces a total of 56 times. As a symbol of the attack, Darnley's own dagger was thrust and left in Rizzio's heart.

The murder may have been successful, but its motivation proved a failure. Mary was built of sterner stuff and suffered no miscarriage. With cunning the equal of her ambitious spouse, the royal mother over the next several months effected an apparent reconciliation with Darnley. On February 9 of the following year Darnley himself was strangled to death by agents of the earl of Bothwell, who was Mary's only confidant after Rizzio's murder. It was considered a certainty that Mary was aware of the plot.

Bothwell was tried but freed by a packed court. Some two months after Darnley's assassination Bothwell married Mary. The ensuing scandal forced Bothwell to flee to Denmark (where he later died insane) and Mary to abdicate. Mary went to England, where she was later imprisoned by Elizabeth and finally executed. Ironically, her only child, the real target in the Rizzio assassination, succeeded Elizabeth as James I of England.

Further reading: *Cambridge Modern History*, vol. III; *History of Scotland*, vol. II, by Andrew Lang.

ROCKWELL, George Lincoln (1918–1967) On June 27, 1967, George Lincoln Rockwell, the founder of the American Nazi Party was shot at by snipers in Arlington, Virginia, as he entered the driveway of a building. Rockwell was unhurt, and he blamed the attack on leftists. The next attempt on his life was made on August 25 as he was backing his car out of a parking space in front of a shopping center. One of two bullets fired through the windshield of the car from the roof of a laundromat hit and killed him.

Within 15 minutes of the shooting, police seized John C. Patler about three quarters of a mile from the assassination scene. Patler, a former Rockwell aide, was expelled from the party for extremism, specifically on charges that he had fomented antagonisms among party members on the basis of how fair or how dark their skin was. The 29-year-old Patler was found guilty of first-degree murder by a jury, which recommended his sentence of 20 years.

Even in death Rockwell remained a divisive figure. As a veteran, he was entitled to burial in a national cemetery (he had served as a Navy pilot in World War II and Korea but was stripped of his commission in 1960 for his Nazi activities). However, the Army blocked his burial at Culpeper National Cemetery in Virginia because American Nazi Party members refused to remove their swastikas and other Nazi insignia for the funeral, in accordance with United States army regulations. Instead, Rockwell's body was secretly cremated.

ROEHM, Ernst (1887–1934) Generally cited as the main target of Adolf Hitler's 1934 purge of his Nazi movement in 'the Night of the Long Knives,' Ernst Roehm had previously been perhaps Hitler's closest friend and ally and the only man permitted to call him 'Adolf.' Roehm was a hard-driving, ruthless Nazi, and like many of the early leaders of the movement, a homosexual. Roehm, a short, thick-necked man with a misshapen nose, part of which had been shot away in 1914, shared Hitler's hatred of democratic ideals and was perhaps as brilliant a political organizer as Hitler himself.

A professional soldier, Roehm brought into the budding Nazi movement a great number of ex-servicemen and free corps volunteers who formed the nucleus of the organization. He organized the Nazi strong-arm street fighters who grew into the SA Brownshirts. Even more important was his position in the army in Bavaria, which allowed him to give the movement considerable military protection and even at times the support of conservative and reactionary authorities. Historians agree that Hitler's campaign would never have been able to preach the overthrow of the republic without that aid, and without question he would not have been able to use intimidation and terror without the tolerance of the Bavarian government and police. About the only real difference between the two was that Roehm more than Hitler believed the real power had to come from the lower classes, and in that sense would be a more 'proletarian' party with at least as much emphasis on the 'Socialism' as upon 'National' in 'National Socialism.'

In 1931 Roehm reorganized the SA and made it a more powerful force than ever before, which angered and frightened the army officer corps. In 1933 Roehm led his SA in a revolution in Bavaria, becoming the Reich secretary of state there. He was at odds with Hitler about continuing their revolution even after Hitler became chancellor. Hitler was fearful of doing battle not only with the army but with the business interests of the nation as well. He curried their support by agreeing that the SA had to be destroyed to satisfy the army and that political elements in the Nazi movement exemplified by Gregor Strasser, the radical wing, also had to be sacrificed to placate the industrialists, whose financial support Hitler needed.

All this was accomplished during the Night of the Long Knives, June 30, 1934. Most of the killings were handled by the SS under Heinrich Himmler and special police under Hermann Goering. How many were killed was never officially determined, with estimates ranging from 401 to more than 1,000. Many Brownshirts were dragged from their beds, placed against a convenient wall and shot. Other victims were killed in their own doorways. Many, not comprehending what the purge was about, died screaming, 'Heil Hitler!'

Apparently for old times sake, Hitler ordered that Roehm be placed in a cell in Stadelheim prison in Munich with a pistol on the table. Roehm refused to use the gun, saying, 'If I am to be killed, let Adolf do it himself.' Instead, bare to the waist, Roehm stood at attention as two SS officers entered the cell and shot him at point-blank range.

Hitler used the purge night to settle some old scores, ordering the assassination of Gustav von Kahr, who had suppressed the Beer Hall Putsch in 1923, as well as many other real or perceived enemies.

In 1957 the first convictions based on the purge were obtained against Michael Lippert, who was one of the two SS men who shot Roehm, and Sepp Dietrich, who was in charge of the killings at Stadelheim prison. Dietrich had previously served 10 years of a 25-year sentence for his complicity in the massacre of captured American soldiers at Malmedy in the 1944 Battle of the Bulge. He got 18 months for the purge assassinations.

The purge accomplished everything that Hitler wanted – complete control of the Nazi movement, the support of the financial interests, and the support of and at the same time the tarring of the army for its responsibility in the barbarity of the killings. In a cunning move Hitler effectively deflected any possible criticisms within Nazi ranks that he had become a puppet of the Wehrmacht by having two army generals, Kurt von Schleicher and Kurt von

Bredow, killed during the purge. The army was helpless to protest, demonstrating quite clearly Hitler's superiority in political maneuvering and his effective use of assassination to achieve political ends. (See KAHR, GUSTAV VON; SCHLEICHER, KURT VON; STRASSER, GREGOR.)

ROMERO, Archbishop Oscar (1917–1980) In late 1979 a military junta had overthrown and exiled the president of El Salvador and seized power under Colonel Jaime Abdul Gutierrez and Adolfo Majano. By their own standards, if not those of others, the junta members regarded themselves as moderates. One who disagreed with them was the much-beloved archbishop Oscar Romero, recognized as the clergy's champion of the poor and oppressed, which encompassed the vast majority of the country's population.

The junta had promised land reform but had failed to deliver. It had also promised a return to law and order. Instead, the country was gripped by terrorism and bloodshed. Archbishop Romero continued to denounce extremists of both the Right and Left, but in El Salvador this meant primarily criticism of the former. The junta's hatred for the archbishop grew, and he and other members of his clergy received many threats, all considered to be government-inspired. In February 1980 Archbishop Romero vowed, 'I am prepared . . . to offer my blood for the redemption and resurrection of El Salvador.'

On March 24, 1980, an unknown gunman shot down the archbishop as he celebrated mass in San Salvador. There was no doubt who was behind the assassination, and antigovernment rioting and street fighting following the murder resulted in the death of at least 30 people and the wounding of some 400.

ROOSEVELT, Franklin Delano (1882–1945) – Attempted Assassination On the evening of February 15, 1933, President-elect Franklin Delano Roosevelt had come ashore in Miami, Florida from Vincent Astor's yacht after a 12-day fishing vacation. He decided to stop in a park and give a short speech. He did so by sitting on top of the right rear seat in bright light, and on concluding his 132-word address he slid down in the seat and waved to Chicago Mayor Anton J. Cermak, who was on a nearby bandstand, to join him in the car. It was then that a would-be assassin named Guiseppe Zangara stood up on a chair about 25 feet away and opened fire with a .32-caliber revolver he had purchased in a downtown Miami pawnshop for $8. Zangara got off five rapid shots, and five people were hit: three men in the head, a woman in the abdomen and Cermak by a bullet that smashed under his right armpit and entered his lung.

When he was shot, Cermak cried, 'The president, get him away!' He told Roosevelt, 'I'm glad it was me instead of you.' Roosevelt, who cradled the wounded mayor, later said, 'I held him all the way to the hospital and his pulse constantly improved. . . . I remember I said, "Tony, keep quiet – don't move – it won't hurt you if you keep quiet and remain perfectly still." '

Cermak lingered for three weeks, and from his deathbed the mayor expounded a theory, currently enjoying a new vogue, that he, not Roosevelt, was the intended victim all along. There was a seeming element of plausibility to the theory, since Cermak was feuding with the Capone gang in Chicago. According to this theory, Zangara, despite his confession to the contrary, was a hired hit man who used FDR as a cover for his successful job. Judge John H. Lyle, generally held to be the most knowledgeable non-Mafia man on Chicago crime, stated categorically that 'Zangara was a Mafia killer, sent from Sicily to do a job, and sworn to silence.' (Zangara had actually resided in the United States for a decade.)

Cermak, elected as a 'reformer' was anything but that. His war on the Capone gang was not intended to wipe out gangsterism in the Windy City but rather to replace the Capones with his own gangsters, headed by mobster Teddy Newberry. Cermak – known in political circles as Ten Percent Tony, since that figure was said to be his standard skim in kick-backs and other graft deals – went so far as to try to remove Frank Nitti, the titular successor to Capone, who was in prison. Court testimony later indicated that the mayor had dispatched some 'tough cops' to assassinate Nitti, which they attempted to do after handcuffing the unarmed gangster. Nitti was shot three times in the neck and back but made a miraculous recovery. The frightened Cermak hurriedly left Chicago for an extended Florida vacation.

The theory continues that Nitti had Newberry murdered, which was undoubtedly true, and sent a hit man – Zangara – to take care of the mayor. Since Cermak had left Chicago on December 21, 1932, and was still in Florida on February 15, 1933, the speculation by some newsmen that he never intended to return at all does have some credibility.

However, the theory of the entire Cermak assassination plot has never been proved, even though in the late 1980s some investigators who believed that John F. Kennedy was assassinated by the Mafia tried to establish a precedent by showing that the mob had also assassinated the mayor of Chicago. However, the idea that a Mafia hit man would use a handgun at 25 feet is mind-boggling to longtime Mafia watchers.

But why had Zangara missed FDR, since according to some reports, disputed by others, he was an expert shooter in the Italian army many years earlier? According to press accounts, his failure was due to the alert reaction of fearless spectators who grabbed his arm and shoved it upward as he began firing. Zangara, however, told it differently to his lawyers, saying his arm had not been seized until he fired all his shots. A police officer who helped subdue him agreed with that version of the events. Thus, it may be argued that since he hit four bystanders beside Cermak, he was not a good shot after all.

The latest to work the Zangara-Mafia lode is author David E. Scheim in his 1988 book *Contract on America*, but many found his evidence unpersuasive. In the Cermak conspiracy theory we also have our first meeting with what is to become a stock character in many assassination theories in other cases – both Kennedy murders, for example – the 'second gunman' who shoots off fatal bullets that are never recovered.

In *American Assassins*, Professor James W. Clarke turns away from the conspiracy theory and instead describes Zangara as a man whose 'emotions were severely distorted by an obsessive generalized antisocial perspective and rejection of practically everything, including his own very existence.' Zangara raved against capitalists, yet there is nothing on the record to indicate he was a socialist, communist, anarchist, or even a fascist. Despite all his ravings against 'capitalist presidents and kings,' he turned out to be a registered Republican. According to Zangara himself, he had railed against presidents since coming to America in 1923, and he claimed to have considered killing King Victor Emmanuel III before that in Italy. According to his later confession, he would have been just as likely to kill Calvin Coolidge or Herbert Hoover as Roosevelt. He happened to settle on FDR simply because he was in Miami when Roosevelt was there. 'I see Mr. Hoover first, I kill him first,' he declared at his trial. 'Make no difference, presidents just the same bunch – all same.' Zangara did not deviate from this line to the day of his execution. Of Cermak, he said, 'I wasn't shooting at him, but I'm not sorry I hit him.'

In the death chamber Zangara said: 'There is no God. It's all below . . . See, I no scared of electric chair.' Sitting down in the chair, he glared at the witnesses with contempt, saying, 'Lousy capitalists.' His last words were: 'Good-bye. *Addio* to all the world. Go ahead. Push the button.'

Further reading: *American Assassins*, by James W. Clarke; *Assassination in America*, by James McKinley; *Captive City*, by Ovid Demaris; *Contract on America*, by David E. Scheim.

ROOSEVELT, Theodore (1858–1919) – Attempted Assassination On October 14, 1912, Theodore Roosevelt, having split the Republican Party and running for president as the Progressive, or Bull Moose, candidate, emerged from a dinner at Milwaukee's Hotel Gilpatrick to head for the municipal auditorium to deliver a campaign speech. As he climbed into an open car, a roly-poly, pleasant-faced little man with receding brown hair stepped up to within six feet of the ex-president and fired a .38 Police Positive. The bullet smashed into Roosevelt's chest, and he lurched into the backseat. As the would-be assassin leveled his gun for a second shot, a Roosevelt aide, Elbert E. Martin, tackled him to the ground. Several policemen pounced on the gunman as cries of 'lynch him, kill him' rose from the crowd. Roosevelt cried out, 'Do not kill him!' And he was hauled away to the hotel kitchen to await the arrival of more police.

Roosevelt noted to one of his companions: 'He pinked me, Henry.' But he insisted to be driven to the Milwaukee Auditorium, even though on the way it was obvious the candidate was more than 'pinked.' Blood drenched his shirt and trousers and formed a puddle in his left shoe. Nevertheless, Roosevelt made his speech, announcing, 'It takes more than one bullet to kill a Bull Moose.' When some hecklers in the crowd doubted Roosevelt's claim of having been shot, he unbuttoned his vest with a flourish to expose his bloodstained shirt, scoring points as expressions of horrors swept through the audience.

Roosevelt's assailant turned out to be a 36-year-old ex-saloon owner named John Nepomuk Schrank, who it became obvious was suffering from a severe mental illness. On September 15, 1901, the day after President William McKinley died of an assassin's bullet that elevated Roosevelt to the high office, Schrank dreamed that McKinley's ghost came to him and accused Roosevelt of the murder. From that day on Schrank seethed with hatred for Roosevelt, and when Roosevelt dared to run for what Schrank regarded as a third term, his loathing reached an all-consuming level. Then one night in 1912 McKinley's ghost showed up again in Schrank's dreams and begged him: 'Let not a murderer take the presidential chair. Avenge my death.' Within a week Schrank was on the campaign trail, dogging Roosevelt around the country. He got close enough in Chicago and Chattanooga to get off a shot, but on each occasion his nerve failed him. It was different in Milwaukee.

Still, the attack failed. Doctors examining Roosevelt's chest determined that the metal glasses case and the 50-page manuscript of his speech in his jacket pocket had saved his life. However, the bullet was lodged so precariously in Roosevelt's rib cage near the heart that doctors decided it was too dangerous to try to remove it, and the ex-president carried it in his body until his death from natural causes in 1919. He frequently said he could be carrying it in his vest pocket for all the bother it gave him.

Schrank was found to be insane and was destined to remain in mental institutions in Wisconsin until his death in 1943. There was no doubt that he was psychotic; and he was labeled paranoid, although aside from the question of Theodore Roosevelt, he seemed to have a rather benign view of the world. On his way to a mental institution by train through heavy woods, Schrank was asked by his guards if he liked to hunt. 'Only Bull Moose,' he said dryly.

In one bid for more lasting fame, Schrank decreed that his pistol and the bullet that struck Roosevelt be displayed at the New York Historical Society. When informed that the bullet had to remain lodged in his victim's rib cage, Schrank was furious toward Roosevelt. 'That is my bullet,' he raged. He said he was putting it in his will that it was to go to the Historical Society.

Overall, Schrank was a model mental patient, in time dubbed 'Uncle John.' One of the few times the old fury returned was when Franklin Delano Roosevelt ran for a third term. He informed doctors that if he was turned loose, he would shoot that Roosevelt as well. Fortunately, Schrank died in 1943 before having to face an infuriating fourth term.

Further reading: *American Assassins: The Darker Side of Politics*, by James W. Clarke; *Assassination in America*, by James McKinley.

RYAN, Leo J. (1925–1978) In November 1978 U.S. Representative Leo J. Ryan, Democrat of California, went to Guyana to investigate reports that the People's Temple, a California-based religious cult led by the controversial Reverend James (Jim) Jones, was subjecting his followers to physical and psychological abuse at the cult's agrarian commune at Jonestown in that South American country. Ryan was accompanied by 17 staffers, newsmen, and relatives of Jonestown residents.

Jones, born in the Bible Belt of Indiana in 1931, gave his first fire-and-brimstone sermon to an audience of young children at the age of 12. Married in 1947, he started a mission for local Methodists in the late 1940s, aiming mainly at poor blacks. In 1954 he was ejected from the Methodist church and in 1957 set up his People's Temple in Indianapolis. Harassed by segregationists who denounced him as a 'nigger lover,' Jones moved his temple to Ukiah, California in 1965, telling his numerous followers who made the trek with him that this was one of two places in the world – that other was an area in South America – that would escape a coming nuclear holocaust. In 1970 Jones moved to San Francisco, where he could attract more followers, mostly poor blacks but also a number of whites.

With revenues pouring in, Jones opened a church in Los Angeles and flew around the country with a corps of bodyguards and devoted aides. He bought a fleet of buses for the faithful and, according to press accounts, ordered his followers to be sexually abstinent, while he himself used his congregation as a harem, fathering a number of children.

Fearful of persecution, Jones announced to his followers that they would have to move the center of their activities to Guyana, where he built Jonestown. In 1977, 1,000 members moved to the jungle retreat. A report in the *San Francisco Chronicle* the following year stated: 'The People's Temple jungle outpost in South America was portrayed yesterday as a remote realm where the Church Leader, the Rev. Jim Jones, orders public beatings, maintains a squad of fifty armed guards and has involved his 1,100 followers in a threat of mass suicide.'

Jones denied the story and through church lawyers invited Congressman Ryan, who had been demanding federal action, to visit Jonestown. When Ryan's party arrived at Jonestown on November 17, 1978, they were cordially received by Jones, who denied any abuse at the commune. He did talk about his own varied sexual activities but denied statements about sexual abstinence among his followers, pointing out that 30 children had been born since mid-1977.

However, members of the commune appeared nervous and walked away when they were approached, and the Ryan party was not permitted to roam the camp unescorted. Nevertheless, the congressman interviewed several residents and by the next day 20 had indicated a desire to leave. Jones indicated they could go, although he now appeared distraught.

As the party assembled on November 18 for the return ride to the Port Kaituma airstrip, a dispute broke out between a woman who wished to remain and her husband who wished to leave with their three children. During the controversy, a man rushed to Ryan and tried to place a knife at his throat. Ryan eluded him, and as the man was being subdued, he was wounded and his blood spurted on Ryan's shirt. Jones became more distraught by the knife incident and asked Ryan if this had altered the congressman's impression of Jonestown. Ryan said it had. In a sense the congressman was passing a death sentence on himself.

'This is terrible, this is terrible,' Jones said. It was apparently at this time, if not sooner, that Jones decided he had to take drastic action. According to a survivor of the holocaust that followed, Jones ordered Larry Layton, one of his followers, to join the defectors and to shoot the pilot of Ryan's plane while airborne so that all would die in the crash.

When the party arrived at the airstrip, there were two planes waiting and Layton boarded one, not Ryan's.

According to witnesses, Layton then began shooting before takeoff. He wounded a man and a woman before his pistol jammed, and he fled into the jungle. At the same time three men from Jonestown appeared, followed by a tractor-driven trailer. As the vehicle neared the craft, the men took guns from the trailer and commenced shooting. Ryan was hit immediately, as were NBC-TV reporter Don Harris, *San Francisco Examiner* photographer Gregory Robinson, Temple member Patricia Parks and others. Several others cowered behind the airplane's wheels or fled into the jungle. NBC cameraman Robert Brown kept filming the events until he was shot in the leg. As four Guyanese soldiers watched without taking action – they later said they were fearful of hitting innocent people if they fired – the gunmen walked over and shot point-blank into the heads of Ryan, Harris, Robinson and Brown. Then they mounted the trailer and were driven off.

When the gunmen returned to Jonestown, they informed Jones what had happened and that not all the visitors had been killed and that one of the planes had taken off. Convinced that his settlement was doomed, Jones invoked his well-rehearsed suicide plan in which all his followers were ordered to take their own lives.

Cyanide was squirted by syringes into the mouths of babies; older children lined up and accepted cups of poisoned Kool-Aid. After this, the adults drank poison. Some of the cult members tried to avoid killing themselves but were hemmed in by armed guards. Still, a few broke free and made for the jungle. After the mass suicide, Jones and his mistress, Maria Katsaris, shot themselves to death.

Guyanese troops arrived the next day and fanned out to search for survivors. Five children and about 30 adults emerged from the jungle by November 20. Among those found alive was Larry Layton.

S

SADAT, Anwar el- **(1918–1981)** While it was true that Anwar el-Sadat, the president of Egypt, had long been expecting attempts on his life, the time and place of his assassination on October 6, 1981, caught him and his security forces by surprise. Sadat, who had been president for 11 momentous years – through the Yom Kippur war of 1973 as well as the Camp David Accords, for which he and Israeli Premier Menachem Begin shared the 1978 Nobel Peace Prize – was reviewing a huge military parade in Cairo.

Security was tight, even though an assassination attempt seemed highly unlikely, with loyal troops marching by, jet fighters overhead and armed soldiers and plainclothes agents all around Sadat. There appeared to be no avenue of attack for any assassins. But they came from a direction least expected, the parade itself. A camouflaged, Russian-built army truck towing a field gun halted directly in front of the reviewing stand, and an army lieutenant and three soldiers jumped from the vehicle and ran toward the podium. The lieutenant was carrying a submachine gun, the three soldiers AK-47 assault rifles.

In those dramatic seconds there was no reaction from the VIP stand. Some on the podium were distracted by a fly-by of F-4 Phantom and Mirage trainer aircraft. President Sadat himself stood up briefly, apparently to salute the approaching soldiers. One of the soldiers threw a grenade, which exploded short of its target. A second grenade did not explode. By that time the first two attackers were at the stand and they fired their upraised automatic weapons with deadly accuracy. Eleven dignitaries, including Sadat, were either killed instantly or fatally wounded, and more than 30 others were injured. Sadat was hit four times and was flown by helicopter to a hospital for emergency surgery, but a team of 11 specialists were unable to save his life and he died some two hours later. Most of the dead were members of Sadat's party, and a prince from Oman died of his wounds.

More than 800 persons were arrested in subsequent investigations and two dozen were later indicted for murder and conspiracy. Lieutenant Khaled el Islambouly, who led the attackers, was labeled the ringleader, and he and four others were sentenced to death. Seventeen others drew prison terms ranging from five years to life at hard labor. Two defendants were acquitted.

The plotters had sought to eradicate not only Sadat but also, according to Mubarak, who succeeded Sadat, the entire political leadership of the country. The plotters intended to install a Muslim religious government, as in Iran. Mubarak accused an extremist sect, the Takfir Wal-Hajira, or Repentance of the Holy Flight, as the prime mover in the conspiracy. Unlike Iran, where a popular revolt put religious forces in power, there was no uprising in Egypt, and the assassination of Sadat produced no mass movement against secular control, perhaps another indication of the limited value of assassination in effecting major social changes unless accompanied by important complementary forces or movements.

SALAMEH, Ali Hassan (1943?–1979) Without doubt the chief assassination target for the Israelis in the 1970s was Ali Hassan Salameh, also known as Abu Hassan, a leader of the terrorist group called Black September and thought to be chief planner of the 1972 Munich Olympics massacre. Mossad, the Israeli secret intelligence service, made killing the terrorist leaders of that massacre a top priority, and in July 1973 the organization got a lead that Salameh was hiding out in the small skiing village of Lillehammer, Norway.

A special Mossad unit was sent to get him, but the

operation was botched; and the team, which included a number of amateurs, killed the wrong man, a Moroccan waiter. Further complicating matters, several of the assassins were caught, and at a sensational trial these agents revealed full details of a general revenge operation aimed at carrying out murders in Europe. The worldwide publicity had its effect, and the Lillehammer caper was said to become the last assassination to be carried out in Europe by Israeli hit teams.

Ali Hassan Salameh was not safe, however. In 1979 he was killed by a car bomb in Beirut, Lebanon. Yasser Arafat's Al Fatah blamed Israeli intelligence. No one seriously disputed the point.

Further reading: *The Mossad*, by Dennis Eisenberg, Uri Dan, and Eli Landau.

SALLUSTRO, Oberdan (1915–1971) On March 21, 1972, Oberdan Sallustro, president of Fiat of Argentina, was kidnapped by the ERP – the Ejercito Revolucionario del Pueblo, or People's Revolutionary Army of Argentina. Considered a Marxist-Leninist organization with a strong Trotskyist strain, the ERP could also be described, as Christopher Dobson and Donald Payne write in *The Terrorists*, as 'the capitalists of terror.' The organization was credited with building up a central fund estimated to be $30 million, first by robbing banks and later more lucratively by kidnapping and holding for ransom business executives under the threat of assassination.

The ERP found it easy to make a deal with Fiat for Sallustro's life. The automaker agreed to pay a $1 million ransom and reinstate 250 workers fired in an industrial dispute. However, the sticking point was the release of 50 political prisoners, on which Argentine president General Lanusse refused to yield. Three weeks later, on April 10, 1972, police and soldiers located the suburban house in Buenos Aires where Sallustro was being held. When they stormed the hideout, Sallustro was executed by his captors. Four terrorists were captured and one talked under torture, and so 26 more ERP members, more than half of them women, were brought to trial. The court upheld some of the allegations of torture and as a result the convictions were limited to 10, three persons being sentenced to life in prison and seven others receiving terms ranging from one to 12 years.

SANDINO, Cesar Augusto (1893–1934) A 1934 political assassination that was to have long-lasting repercussions in Latin America and even in the United States through the 1980s was that of rebel leader Cesar Augusto Sandino in Nicaragua. The son of a peasant, Sandino fought in the 1920s in support of Nicaraguan Vice President Juan Bautista Sacasa's claim to the presidency. Even with the intervention of U.S. Marines in 1926, Sandino did not give up the fight, although forced into the mountains from where he carried out guerrilla warfare.

The United States' new administration under Franklin D. Roosevelt decided to pull out the Marines in 1933. Meanwhile Sacasa had become president after the 1932 elections and sought peace with Sandino. Sandino demanded that he be allowed to form a semiautonomous area in his stronghold of Nueva Segovia, terms the new president was willing to accept. However, General Anastasio Somoza Garcia, commander of the Guardia Nacional, opposed the negotiations.

On February 21, 1934, following a dinner with President Sacasta, Sandino and a number of his followers were seized by Somoza's soldiers and summarily slaughtered. Shortly thereafter General Somoza seized political power himself, launching Somoza family rule that would last almost half a century. The Somozas remained dogged by the memory of Sandino, who became a martyr and a symbol of national aspirations in much of Latin America. His name was given to the Sandinistas, who finally deposed the Somozas from power in 1979. (See SOMOZA DEBAYLE, ANASTASIO.)

SCHLEICHER, Kurt von (1882–1934) The history of 'the Night of the Long Knives' is generally told in terms of the purge and assassination of the brutal leader of the Nazi SA or brownshirts, Ernst Roehm, and his followers on June 30, 1934, by order of Adolf Hitler. It can be argued that the prime victim may actually have been Gregor Strasser, and that both German business interests and the general staff of the Wehrmacht demanded the elimination of the more 'socialist' elements of the 'National Socialists' as the price of their support for Hitler. During that night of assassinations there were a number of killings the general staff had not approved of, especially those of some of their own, such as General Kurt von Schleicher.

Born in 1882, von Schleicher entered military service at the age of 18 and rose steadily in the officer corps through World War I and later in the Weimar Republic. He played a key role in the illegal free corps and the secret Black Reichswehr and was a top figure in the secret operation that established camouflaged training of German air and tank officers in the Soviet Union as well as German-controlled arms factories in that country.

Through his friendship with Oskar von Hindenburg, the son of the field marshal, with whom he served early in his military career, Schleicher gained political power as well, and he became defense minister in 1932. Late that same year, on the resignation of Franz von Papen, Schleicher became chancellor of Germany. Although a gifted manipulator and master of intrigue, Schleicher met his match in Hitler, who took over as chancellor in early 1933.

In power, Hitler continued to regard Schleicher as too gifted an opponent, and he took advantage of the Night of the Long Knives to order the assassination of the general, even though in 1934 he had no connection with either Roehm or Strasser.

On the morning of June 30, a squad of SS men in mufti came to the door of General von Schleicher's villa on the outskirts of Berlin. The general himself answered the bell, and he was shot dead on the spot. When his wife rushed to the front door, she too was murdered. Later that same evening General Kurt von Bredow, a close friend of

Schleicher, was also assassinated. According to Walter Schellenberg, the Nazi intelligence chief, Hitler had added incentives for getting rid of Schleicher 'because he knew too much of the shady financial transactions by means of which Hitler came to power.'

Journalist-historian William L. Shirer offers additional insight on the assassination of Schleicher by noting it reflected 'Hitler's contempt for the Prussian officer caste, which he held till the end of his life.' Thus, while catering to the army with his purge, Hitler callously murdered the military's own. However, the General Staff accepted the murders of von Schleicher and von Bredow 'with scarcely a murmur.' (See ROEHM, ERNST.)

Further reading: *Hitler's Secret Service*, by Walter Schellenberg; *The Rise and Fall of the Third Reich*, by William L. Shirer.

SCHLEYER, Hanns-Martin (1915–1977) On September 5, 1977, armed terrorists kidnapped West German industrialist Hanns-Martin Schleyer, killing his driver and three of his police guards in Cologne. The terrorists drove a minibus alongside two cars carrying Schleyer and his guards and opened fire with machine guns. The 62-year-old Schleyer, president of the West German Confederation of Employers' Association and president of the Federation of West German Industries, had been closely guarded since the assassination of German banker Jurgen Ponto the previously July during a kidnapping attempt. At the time Ponto's assailants had threatened further killings of members of the 'exploiting class.'

In a letter released on September 8, the terrorists threatened to execute Schleyer unless the German government of Chancellor Helmut Schmidt released 11 leftwing terrorists, including the remaining leaders of the Baader-Meinhof gang – Andreas Baader, Gundrun Ensslin and Jan-Carl Raspe. The kidnappers demanded that the prisoners each be given $43,000 and that they be provided with a plane to fly them to whatever country they wished. They also stipulated that the plane was to be accompanied by a United Nations official and the Reverend Martin Niemoller, a heroic Protestant clergyman who had been imprisoned by the Nazis.

The Schmidt government, following its pattern in dealing with terrorists, write Christopher Dobson and Ronald Payne in *The Terrorists*, 'refused to give in and played the long, hard bargaining game, demanding proof that the terrorists did indeed hold their hostage alive, while encouraging the terrorists by asking a number of Third World countries whether they would agree to the prisoners being delivered to their countries.'

The terrorists mounted a counteroffensive in the war of nerves by launching a new kidnapping in an entirely different area. Four Palestinians, two men and two women, who were members of Wadi Hadad's Popular Front for the Liberation of Palestine (PFLP)–Special Operations based in Baghdad, hijacked a Lufthansa plane bound from Majorca for Germany, loaded with German tourists and a party of six beauty queens. The kidnappers demanded the release of the same Baader-Meinhof figures the Schleyer abductors had demanded as well as two Palestinians imprisoned in Turkey. The plane was forced to fly around the Middle East, with the pilot being killed in Aden, before finally setting down in Mogadishu, Somalia.

While negotiations were going on, the West German government launched a brilliant Entebbe-style counterraid. Twenty-eight men of the GSG9, a specially trained antiterrorist force, hit the plane with cardboard-bodied grenades that stun and blind their victims for several seconds but cause no permanent damage. The grenades were developed by the British Special Air Services Regiment, and a British officer and a small contingent of British soldiers accompanied the German raiders to Mogadishu. With the terrorists temporarily blinded, the commandos were able to shoot them without harming the passengers. Three of the hijackers were killed and the fourth was seriously wounded.

In response to the Somalia raid, the Schleyer kidnappers executed the industrialist by putting three bullets in his head and slashing his throat. His abductors telephoned the French police in Mulhouse that the body could be found in the trunk of an abandoned automobile. Then, in what probably had the most devastating impact on the German government, the imprisoned Baader-Meinhof leaders, Baader, Ensslin and Raspe, managed to commit suicide in their supposedly maximum security prison at Stammheim. Their deaths were to shake the Federal Republic to its social core, and took the edge off the welcome accorded the returning GSG9 commandos. Even Chancellor Schmidt called the events at Stammheim prison 'inconceivable' and demanded an investigation of how the prisoners had managed to obtain weapons. Interior Minister Werner Maihofer (who was to resign eight months later) stated it was 'absolutely impossible' that anyone other than the prisoners were involved in their deaths, adding, 'Some people will push their treachery so far as to make their suicide look like an execution.' Schmidt noted that the terrorists 'employed the violent destruction of their own lives as a weapon' against a liberal society.

The deaths caused an upsurge of left-wing protests throughout Europe. West German property in several French and Italian cities was attacked by rioters. Office windows were shot out in Rome, Milan, Como and Turin. In Paris firebombs were thrown at West German tourist buses. Many political organizations claimed that Baader and the others had been murdered in prison, and even groups unsympathetic to the terrorists suspected that even if the authorities had not murdered the prisoners outright, they had not gone out of their way to prevent the suicides.

On September 6, 1978, the final act in the Schleyer assassination – if not in the political debate – was played out in Dusseldorf, when German police shot and killed Willy Peter Stoll, who was believed to have been the organizer of the Schleyer kidnapping.

SCHNEIDER, General Rene (1913–1970) Panic gripped

much of the right wing in Chilean politics in 1970 as it became increasingly more likely that Marxist Salvador Allende Gossens would be elected president, bringing about a triumph of the left to an extent never before witnessed in a South American country. A bastion of stability in the swirling political turmoil was the army, traditionally neutral in the nation's politics. The army's commander in chief, General Rene Schneider, was outspoken in his commitment to keep the armed forces neutral in the left–right tensions and he repeatedly pledged that he would honor the Chilean Congress's choice for president.

On October 22, 1970, Schneider was shot at least three times by an unknown assailant after three cars stopped his limousine, as he was being driven to army headquarters. Schneider's assassination was seen in the wider context of the right seeking to prevent the election of Allende by any means possible. It was a charge that would soon gain substance.

The left in Chile insisted that the general had been murdered by assailants trained by the Central Intelligence Agency in the United States. Aniceto Rodriguez, secretary-general of the Socialist Party, one of the member groups of the pro-Allende coalition, insisted, 'The CIA [is] the moral author of this crime, which is not in the Chilean character; such a crime has never been committed before in Chile.'

Within a week of the Schneider murder former General Roberto Viaux, leader of a mutiny by an army regiment in 1969, was arrested in connection with the crime. Along with Viaux at least 10 others were booked, and eventually Viaux was imprisoned and then exiled to Paraguay.

In 1975 the U.S. Senate Select Committee on Intelligence Activities issued a report stating that Schneider had died as a result of a planned coup, which U.S. officials had encouraged or were least privy to.

That same year the *New York Times* reported that the CIA had participated in two unsuccessful military plots against the Chilean government in 1970, including the

Schneider murder. The *Times* quoted U.S. government sources that the CIA had acted under orders from then President Richard Nixon to make 'a last-ditch, all-out effort' to keep Allende from gaining the presidency. Nixon reportedly gave his orders at a secret meeting on September 15, 1970, with his national security adviser Henry Kissinger, CIA director Richard Helms and Attorney General John Mitchell. Nixon was described as being 'frantic' and 'extremely anxious' about Allende's imminent legal elevation to the top office.

Nixon was said to have told Helms in 'strong language' that the CIA must 'come up with some ideas' to keep Allende from taking office, and that he authorized an initial expenditure of $10 million in the effort. After the meeting, the CIA's chief of covert operations, Thomas Karamessines, reportedly visited Chile. On his return he was said to have briefed Kissinger on a plot by General Viaux to kidnap Schneider as a prelude to a military coup. Karamessines told Kissinger the plot would most likely fail, and Kissinger recommended that the CIA try to halt the plot but 'keep the pressure up' in other ways, according to the *Times*' sources.

SCHULTZ, Dutch (1902–1935) He was one of the most powerful leaders of organized crime in America, and like many another of that ilk, he died under gangster guns himself. However, the 1935 murder of Dutch Schultz (Arthur Flegenheimer) was a pure and simple political assassination, carried out so as not to disturb the American body politic.

The underworld – more exactly, organized crime – murdered Schultz because he was planning a political assassination of his own, that of a fledgling prosecutor, Thomas E. Dewey, who would eventually use his campaign against organized crime as a stepping-stone to the governorship of New York and near election to the White House. By 1935 Dewey had succeeded in putting a number of major syndicate criminals behind bars, including the notorious Waxey Gordon, and would later get the likes of Louis Lepke, Gurrah Shapiro and, above all, Charles 'Lucky' Luciano. Before he could go after these later targets, prosecutor Dewey set his sights on Schultz, then the chief power in New York's Harlem rackets as well as many others. Schultz was also a founding member in 1931 of what came to be known as the national crime syndicate, the major decisions of which were determined by a gangster board of directors, including the Dutchman himself.

As Dewey's investigation closed in on Schultz, the gangster, known for erratic and murderous reactions, appeared before the national board with a plan to assassinate Dewey 'before he gets us all.' In 1931 the syndicate had decided on a modus operandi that forbade such killings, as stated by Lucky Luciano, that 'we wouldn't hit newspaper guys or cops or DAs. We don't want the kind of trouble everybody'd get.'

Led by the forces of Luciano and gangster Meyer Lansky, the board turned down Schultz's plan. Schultz, however, was not deterred, announcing that if the board would not agree with him, he'd carry out the killing on his own. At first, the gangsters believed Schultz was merely venting his spleen, but in October 1935 it was discovered that the mob boss was actually setting the assassination plot in motion.

Dewey's Fifth Avenue apartment was staked out by a man who posed each morning as the father of a child pedaling a velocipede, certainly a typical scene and hardly cause for any suspicion. Dewey and two bodyguards always passed them on their way to a drug store, where Dewey made his first phone call of the morning to his office from a bank of payphones. The prosecutor did not use his home telephone for fear it might be tapped.

Having learned Dewey's routine, Schultz and his men developed the rest of the plot: An assassin armed with a silencer-equipped gun would be inside the store before Dewey arrived. His bodyguards, stationed outside, would be unaware when the killer shot Dewey and then walked out past them.

Unfortunately for Schultz, he involved Albert Anastasia, a top mob killer and the 'chief executioner of Murder, Inc.' in the plot. Anastasia was virtually the only top mobster who had agreed with Schultz's motive for killing Dewey. However, Anastasia was also devoted to Luciano, to whom he revealed the extent of the developing plot. Luciano and other members of the ruling board were horrified by the plan, and an immediate death sentence was passed on the absent Schultz.

On October 23, 1935, Schultz and three of his top henchmen, Abbadabba Berman, Lulu Rosenkrantz and Abe Landau, were in a favorite hangout, the Palace Chop House and Tavern in Newark, New Jersey. Schultz went to the men's room. While he was there, two hit men charged into the Palace. One stopped at the men's room purely as a precaution and, seeing a man at a urinal, shot him to protect the killers' flank. He then charged forward, where the three Schultz aides were seated, and blazed away with two guns, killing all three. Only at that point did the gunmen discover that Schultz was not among the trio. However, when they checked the men's room, they found Schultz. The gunman who had done all the shooting lifted a considerable amount of cash from Schultz's pockets and the pair fled.

The mob leader lingered in a hospital for two days before dying. Eventually, one of the killers, Charles 'the Bug' Workman, was convicted and served 23 years in prison for the crime.

Dewey himself did not learn of the plot against him until 1940, when it was revealed to him by Murder, Inc., prosecutor Burton Turkus. Dewey listened impassively to the details, but his eyes widened perceptibly when the proud father and the tot on the velocipede were mentioned. After five years, he apparently still remembered them.

There have been those who have claimed that the real motivation for Schultz's killing had been a desire by other syndicate leaders to take over the Dutchman's racket empire. This is what in fact happened, but the overwhelming opinion among crime experts was that the principal motivation was to save Dewey's life and avoid the unwanted attention to the syndicate that the prosecutor's death would have brought.

Further reading: *The Last Testament of Lucky Luciano*, by Martin A. Gosch and Richard Hammer; *Murder, Inc.*, by Burton B. Turkus and Sid Feder. (Note: For a discussion of the validity of Luciano's *Testament* see *The Mafia Encyclopedia* by Carl Sifakis.)

SERGEI, Grand Duke (1857–1905) Of all the autocrats in the Romanov court of Nicholas II, the czar's uncle, Grand Duke Sergei, may have been the most violently reactionary. He served the czar as governor-general of Moscow, and was, writes Robert K. Massie, 'so narrow and despotic that he forbade his wife to read *Anna Karenina* for fear of arousing "unhealthy curiosity and violent emotions." '

Sergei took a certain hard-nosed joy in knowing how bitterly he was hated by the revolutionaries. On February 17, 1905, he bade goodbye to his vivacious wife, Elizabeth, the empress's sister, at their Kremlin apartment to be driven to his post. The carriage was just passing through one of the gates when a bomb exploded. Hearing the shattering blast, the grand duchess cried out, 'It's Sergei!' and rushed to him. All she found were a hundred pieces of bloody flesh, beyond all recognition. The grand duchess amazingly kept her senses and went to comfort her husband's dying coachman, easing his concerns for his master by assuring him that Sergei had survived.

The bomber was a Social Revolutionary named Kaliayev, and the courageous Elizabeth, known as Ella, even visited the assassin in prison. She offered to plead with the czar for his life if he would beg forgiveness from the czar. The revolutionary refused, declaring his death would assist in his cause, the overthrow of autocratic rule. After the assassination of her husband, Ella's character – previously she had been the gayest, most irrepressible figure at court – and life changed. She built an abbey, the

Convent of Mary and Martha, where she became abbess, discarding all worldly matters. She remained there until the revolution of 1917. Finally, as a prisoner of the triumphant Bolsheviks she was brutally murdered. (See ELIZABETH, GRAND DUCHESS.)

Further reading: *Nicholas and Alexandra*, by Robert K. Massie.

SHAKA   See CHAKA, KING OF THE ZULUS.

SHERMARKE, Abdi Rashid Ali (1919–1969)   In an assassination that 'accidentally' altered the political landscape of the country, Somalian President Abdi Rashid Ali Shermarke was murdered on October 15, 1969. After having served as the country's prime minister for five years following the establishment of the Somali Republic at the Horn of Africa, Shermarke won election as president in 1967 and won respect throughout Africa for a regime that provoked very little popular unrest. However, in 1969 Shermarke was on a visit to the city of Los Anod, north of the capital of Mogadishu, when a police officer stepped up to him and shot him to death.

The officer was 22-year-old Abulkadir Abdi Mohammed, who gave himself up. No political motive was established for the crime, but as the president and his assassin were from the same tribe, there was considerable speculation that it was the result of a tribal feud. Whatever the motive, the Somalian military took advantage of the situation and seized power, dissolving the legislature and ruling by decree. The military pledged to erase the 'inefficiency, graft and injustice of the past,' and is presumably still so occupied two decades later.

SMIT, Robert (1933–1977)   Sometime during the night of November 22/23, 1977, a killer or killers entered the Springs, South Africa, home of Robert Smit, an internationally known South African economist, and shot and stabbed Smit and his wife, Jeanne-Cora, to death. Smit, a former executive director of the International Monetary

Fund, was a candidate of the ruling National Party in the elections that were one week away and was predicted to be the nation's next finance minister.

Police said they found no indication of forced entry and no evidence for robbery as the motive, and there was growing media speculation that the murders were politically inspired. The South African government was then becoming mired in an economic scandal involving massive diversions of government funds for 'secret projects' directed by the Department of Information. The scandal ultimately led to the resignation of Prime Minister John Voster and Department of Information Minister Connie Mulder, and, despite the government's strong denial of any connection between the two matters, the Smit murder hung over the funding scandal like a question mark. However, the Smit assassination remained unsolved.

In 1990, the press speculated that the crime was committed by a police 'hit squad,' described by a defector to have operated with the approval of at least some members of the government.

SOILIH, Ali (1937–1978)   One month after the Comoros, three volcanic islands in the Mozambique Channel of the Indian Ocean, won their independence from France in 1975, leftist Ali Soilih seized power. He ousted President Ahmed Abdallah Abderemane, who fled to exile in France.

Soilih promised he would introduce socialism to the archipelago, whose main economic activity was the export of spices used for making perfumes. Most of the 300,000 islanders were Muslims, and Soilih's efforts to set up a Chinese-style revolutionary system that opposed religion angered many of them. By 1978 Soilih was being denounced as pursuing dictatorial and barbarous policies, and in early May 1978 Abdallah returned to the country. On May 13 Soilih was overthrown in a coup engineered by a mercenary Frenchman, Bob Denard. Abdallah renewed his presidency, and Soilih was placed under house arrest.

On May 29, a radio broadcast in the capital city of

Moroni announced that the 41-year-old Soilih had been fatally wounded as he tried to escape from his confinement with the aid of 'certain outside elements.'

There were accusations that Soilih had been killed by his mercenary captors. In any event, President Abdallah and Denard prospered greatly for nearly the next dozen years until President Abdallah was assassinated as well. Denard was generally accused of being the force behind that murder. (See ABDALLAH ABDEREMANE, AHMED.)

SOKOLLI, Mohammed (1505–1579) The brilliant grand vizier (chief minister) during much of the 16th-century Ottoman reigns of Sulayman the Magnificent and Selim II, Mohammed Sokolli was perhaps the real ruler of the empire from 1566 to 1574, when Selim died. He successfully martialed the forces of the Ottomans even after the naval disaster in the famed Battle of Lepanto in 1571 and indeed secured the war's chief aim, the wresting of Cyprus from the Venetians.

Had Selim II's successor, Murad III, given Sokolli continued free rein it is generally agreed the Ottomans would have continued to prosper and triumph. Instead, under Murad, Sokolli's enemies at court were able to erode the grand vizier's power. Murad, who begot 103 children from almost as many wives, allowed his favorite wife, 'Baffo,' a Venetian slave, to work her charms. Baffo charmed the sultan, took bribes to make use of her influence and interfered with matters of state. Meanwhile Sokolli had aroused the most fanatic opposition among the Turkish populace with plans to build an observatory in Stamboul. With Sokolli now in public disfavor, his foes were able to strike, and he was assassinated, almost certainly at Murad's behest, via Baffo.

SOLDEVILLA Y ROMERO (1843–1923) The Vatican's spokesman in Spain and a leading political conservative, Cardinal Soldevilla y Romero, Catholic archbishop of Saragossa, was sitting in a church car at a monastery on June 4, 1923, when he was approached by two youthful assassins who shot him to death. The assassins, two anarchists named Francisco Ascaso and Buenaventura Durruti, made good their escape. The following year the pair were unsuccessful in an assassination try against King Alfonso XIII. Although they served brief prison terms, the pair went on to commit a number of other acts of political terrorism before the outbreak of the Spanish civil war. Both died early in that conflict, Durruti rising to the command of an army column. He was shot in the back in November 1936, and it was never determined whether it was a deliberate action by his own men or just an accident.

SOMOZA DEBAYLE, Anastasio (1925–1980) For almost a half century the history of repression in Nicaragua was told through the history of the Somoza family, which dominated the country with the blessing of American political and economic interests. When a member of the dynasty did not hold the presidency, it was simply put in the hands of a front man favorable to the Somozas.

The founder of the Somoza dynasty was Anastasio Somoza Garcia, who won control of the army, the Guardia Nacional, in 1933 and a few years later ousted the elected president, Juan Bautista Sacasa. Under Somoza Garcia the country was made less dependent on banana income. The same could be said for the Somozas themselves, as over the ensuing decades the family fortunes soared as most political opponents were exiled and the family seized the ownership of land and businesses. The Somozas assumed huge interests in such areas as coffee, beer, rice, cattle and meat packing, banking, television, newspapers and hotels. They controlled all cement production, the roofing industry, the national airlines and the nation's only shipping line. Perhaps a quarter of the country's arable land belonged to the family. The Somozas were accused of unconscionably gouging the stricken populace during the Managua earthquake of 1972. With cement desperately needed for rebuilding, the Somozas price-gouged to an extent that, it was said, would have shamed America's robber barons of the 19th century.

Somoza Garcia was assassinated in 1956 by 27-year-old Rigoberto Lopez, who was in turn shot to death by Somoza's guards. As if to demonstrate the futility of assassination against the family dynasty, the presidency passed to his elder son, Luis Somoza Debayle. After a term ending in 1963, power passed for a time to Somoza puppets, who ruled until 1967, when Luis's younger brother, Anastasio, took the presidency. Although he relinquished some of the trappings of office, Anastasio Somoza remained in firm and aggressive control of the country, and his regime became a byword for repression and brutality, with graft used to hold supporters to the government in the struggle against the left-wing Sandinista rebels.

As Anastasio Somoza's power waned in the long and bloody revolution, the support of the American government also decreased, until the United States finally accused him of massive violations of human rights, including many instances of state-sponsored assassinations, such as that of newspaper editor Pedro Joaquin Chamorro, a noted opponent of the Somoza dynasty, in January 1978.

Finally, in 1979, the government crumbling, Somoza resigned and fled to Miami, taking with him a personal fortune estimated at $100 million. All Somoza gained was a few more months of life, however. Faced with recriminations and fearful of physical attack from opponents, Somoza fled Miami for the Bahamas and finally to Paraguay. Police-state protection did not suffice. On September 17, 1980, Somoza was cut down by a rain of bazooka and submachine-gun fire by an assassination squad, which made good its own escape.

The identity of the attackers was not exactly a mystery, and Paraguay broke relations with the new Sandinista government in Nicaragua. (See CHAMORRO, PEDRO JOAQUIN; SANDINO, CESAR AUGUSTO.)

SOREL, Agnes (c. 1422–1450) Agnes Sorel, the first officially recognized royal mistress in France, wielded considerable influence over King Charles VII – perhaps even as much as Joan of Arc did on that often indolent monarch. In the process Sorel made many enemies in court – including ladies whom she so greatly outshone in beauty and men opposed to many royal political decisions. Much to the irritation of female society at court, the brazen mistress introduced a new, indecorous style of 'bare to the waist' dresses at royal functions.

Charles VII showered Sorel with great wealth, castles and land and secured for her the distinctions usually reserved for queens; she was often addressed as 'Dame de Beaute,' after the estate at Beaute-sur-Marne, presented to her by the king. The resentment of those scandalized by the open recognition of a mistress grew, and intrigues were born seeking to bring down Sorel. In 1450 Sorel died, shortly after giving birth to her fourth royal child. Officially, the cause was first listed as dysentery, but it was later attributed to poison.

The administration of drugs by contending mistresses at court was a time-honored art. However, other suspects soon appeared. Enemies of the great financial ally of the king, Jacques Coeur, charged him with the poisoning of Sorel, the one offense likely to turn Charles VII against him. In 1451 Coeur was arrested, condemned for the poisoning and banished, his property confiscated for the state. Coeur fled to Rome, where he was made admiral of a papal fleet. He died fighting the Turks in 1456.

For want of another suspect, some historians laid the Sorel murder – if it really was one – to the Dauphin (later Louis XI) who, exiled from court, had launched a number of intrigues against his father. The idea of robbing him of his fabulous mistress and key adviser would seem not without a certain Machiavellian merit.

Some even saw a link between Coeur and the Dauphin, and such speculations were not quenched by Louis XI's later restoration of some of the deceased Coeur's property to his sons and his reviving of enterprises the great merchant prince had initiated.

Further reading: *Jacques Coeur*, by C. M. Chenu; *Jacques Coeur: Merchant Prince of the Middle Ages*, by

A. B. Kerr; *The Story of Civilization VI – The Reformation*, by Will Durant.

SPRETI, Count Karl von (1907–1970) On March 31, 1970, Count Karl von Spreti, the West German ambassador to Guatemala, was kidnapped from his home in Guatemala City by the FAR (Rebel Armed Forces), a left-wing terrorist group, which demanded the release of 17 political detainees for his safe return. In the 1960s the FAR had been held responsible for a number of political assassinations, including that of three U.S. officials – John Gordon Mein, the U.S. ambassador, and two American military men, Colonel John D. Webber and Lieutenant Commander Ernest A. Munro, all killed in 1968.

Despite intense pressure from the West German government to accede to the terrorists' demands, Guatemalan President Julio Cesar Mendez Montenegro refused. The kidnappers countered by upping the ante to 22 prisoners plus a cash ransom of $700,000 for von Spreti. The West German government dispatched a special envoy, William Hoppe, to handle its position, which included a secret offer to reimburse Guatemala if it would ransom the prisoners. Chancellor Willy Brandt sent a personal plea, and a delegation of foreign diplomats petitioned Foreign Minister Alberto Fuentes Mohr in an effort to save the German envoy.

Despite this, the Guatemalan president held firm, and as a result on April 4 the terrorists murdered von Spreti with a bullet to the left side of his head, leaving his corpse in a mud hut outside the capital.

The reaction by the West Germans was caustic. Chancellor Brandt publicly stated that his government had offered to pay the ransom, and he accused the Guatemalan government of the inability to protect diplomats. The Guatemalan government responded by declaring that four of the terrorists who had been subject to exchange had admitted to taking part in the murder of U.S. Ambassador Mein. Furthermore, it said, the lives of Guatemalan officials as well as the government's credibility would have been badly damaged had they acceeded to the demands.

Ironically, later that same year Guatemalan Foreign Minister Fuentes Mohr was also kidnapped by leftists. Unlike von Spreti, he was later exchanged for an imprisoned guerrilla. (See FUENTES MOHR, ALBERTO.)

STAMBOLISKI, Aleksandur (1879–1923) Before his assassination in 1923, Bulgarian Prime Minister Aleksandur Stamboliski, leader of the Agrarian Party, had a long record of opposing the monarchy. In 1908 he entered the national assembly as the head of his party and came into frequent political conflict with King Ferdinand I. He was imprisoned before Bulgaria's entry into World War I. Freed from prison in September 1918, Stamboliski led rebel forces into the capital and forced the king's abdication. Ferdinand was succeeded by his own son Boris III; Stamboliski entered the new king's cabinet and late in 1919 became prime minister. Stamboliski proved more powerful than Boris and became a virtual dictator of the nation for the next four years.

In 1923 a military coup, apparently supported by the king, ousted Stamboliski from power. He tried to flee the country, but was caught and murdered. Stamboliski's successor as party boss, Petko Petkov, was murdered in 1924, further weakening the Agrarian Party. (See BORIS III, KING OF BULGARIA.)

STELESCU, Michael (1902–1936) A longtime Romanian Fascist, Michael Stelescu was the founder and leader of the Brothers of the Cross, which merged in 1928 with another right-wing extremist group, the Legion of the Archangel Michael, to form what became known as the Iron Guard. The head of the new group was Corneliu Codreanu, the founder of Archangel Michael.

With the rise to power of Adolf Hitler, Codreanu pursued closer ties than approved of by Stelescu, who remained anti-German in deference to Romanian war memories. Stelescu was as anti-Semitic and Fascist-minded as any Iron Guardist but campaigned for a more

Romanian face on the organization.

By 1936 friction between the two Romanian leaders had become so strained that Stelescu issued dramatic predictions of an attempt on his life. He even induced the organization's newspaper to publish a list of eight men he said had been chosen by Codreanu to carry out the killing. In July 1936 Stelescu entered a hospital for an appendectomy. He was shot 38 times by the eight agents he had previously named. (See CODREANU, CORNELIU Z.)

STEUNENBERG, Frank (1861–1905) The killing of ex-Governor Frank Steunenberg of Idaho in 1905 resulted in the most important judicial confrontation between capital and labor in the United States. Had there been a conviction of radical labor leader William D. 'Big Bill' Haywood, it would have altered the history of the American labor movement. In fact, there are those laborites who insist the Steunenberg assassination was used in a cynical and naked effort to destroy the union movement with fabricated charges.

Born in Keokuk, Iowa, Steunenberg became the Democratic governor of Idaho in 1896 and was reelected in 1898. During his tenure he earned the enmity of the union movement for a number of probusiness actions, especially in the bitter labor struggle in the Coeur d'Alene mines. After retiring as governor, Steunenberg devoted his interests to the lumber company that would eventually grow into Boise Cascade.

On December 30, 1905, Steunenberg emerged from his home in Caldwell, Idaho, and as he opened the front gate, his body was shattered by a bomb.

The first man arrested in the assassination was Harry Orchard (real name Albert E. Horsley). Orchard confessed not only to the Steunenberg killing but also to a number of other murders that, if true, would have made him the greatest labor assassin in American history. The counter argument was that he cooperated in a monumental plot with the Pinkerton Detective Agency and its business-interest clients in an effort to frame America's labor leadership and save himself from execution in the process.

Orchard's story was supported by another self-confessed informer-assassin, Steve Adams. The pair linked the murder of Governor Steunenberg to Western Federation of Miners leaders Charles H. Moyers, George A. Pettibone and Haywood, the last of those also a head of the Industrial Workers of the World. All three were indicted, but before the first trial (1906–07), that of Haywood, the prosecution, headed by such legal lights as William E. Borah and James Hawley, suffered a sudden setback. Adams withdrew the confession he had made involving the trio and insisted it had been Pinkerton-inspired.

Haywood's chief defense lawyer, the legendary Clarence Darrow, in tactics still regarded as classic today, made a shambles of the prosecution's case until all that remained was Orchard's written confession, which bore a number of inked corrections, many in the hand of the noted Pinkerton operative James McParland, who 30 years earlier had played the key and controversial role in the successful prosecution of the Mollie Maguires, a secret labor society operating in the Pennsylvania coal fields.

McParland's cooperative penmanship venture with Orchard was supplemented with a conversion to religion by the self-confessed murderer. Orchard and McParland prayed together, but belief in Orchard did not dominate the jury room. From the jury's first deliberations, a majority held there could be no conviction of Haywood. His acquittal caused unbounded joy in the labor movement throughout the country.

Darrow later succeeded in gaining an acquittal of Pettibone, and Moyers was discharged. In the end the only conviction in the case was that of Harry Orchard, who was condemned to death; the sentence was later commuted to life imprisonment. Pinkerton operative McParland, until his own death in 1919, frequently appealed for a parole for Orchard, but ironically even William A. Pinkerton demurred, stating in an internal agency memo: 'I know that McParland always thought Orchard should have been released for testifying, but I still regard Orchard as a cold-blooded murderer who killed many innocent persons and who testified only to save his own skin.'

It was charged that prosecutor Hawley and Governor Gooding (who had vowed before the first trial that the accused trio 'will never leave Idaho alive') did much to make Orchard's life tolerable. Charles Steunenberg, the victim's brother, related: 'The penitentiary outfitted a room for Orchard and paid for the electricity used. Private parties gave him the money with which to buy machinery; the state permitted him to use convict labor for his own enterprise in which he manufactured shoes for prominent people in Idaho and rolled up a cash reserve of ten thousand dollars.'

In 1940, at the age of 73, Orchard was, according to Darrow biographer Irving Stone, 'still fat and sleek, oily eyed and unctuous. He told visitors to the prison chicken farm that he "just can't bring himself [sic] to kill a chicken." To anyone wanting to clear the historic record of the crime Orchard cried petulantly, "The trouble with you writers is that you never come here to write about me. You always want to use me to write about somebody else!" '

Orchard died in 1954, still in prison but perhaps the most coddled assassin in American penal history.

Further reading: *Clarence Darrow For The Defense*, by Irving Stone; *The Pinkertons: The Detective Dynasty That Made History*, by James D. Horan.

STOLYPIN, Pyotr Arkadyevich (1862–1911) Repression under the Russian czars, sparked by assassinations and terrorism against the state, achieved what can only be called monumental proportions in the 18th and 19th centuries. The army and the police were leaders in the oppression, yet even they were reputed to have been repelled by the extent of the terror sponsored by Pyotr Arkadyevich Stolypin, prime minister from 1906 to 1911.

Stolypin backed every action the police took, but he demanded much in return: mass arrests, mass deportations, mass executions. Under Stolypin a new phrase entered the language – 'the Stolypin necktie' – for the hangman's noose.

During the Stolypin era as premier and previously as minister of the interior the cycle of violence continually escalated, and while radicals and activists died in huge numbers, the same was true of the security forces. Still the prime minister pressed his campaign, insisting that the Stolypin necktie offered the ultimate solution.

Sometime around 1906 a young terrorist named Dmitri Bogroff was seized by the secret police for terrorist acts. He did not fall victim to the Stolypin necktie, instead being 'turned' by the police and going to work for them. The record here is understandably murky and has cast considerable uncertainty on the real plotters in the Stolypin assassination.

On September 14, 1911, the prime minister, along with Czar Nicholas II, was in attendance at a gala at the opera house in Kiev. The czar occupied the royal box, and Stolypin was in the front row of the stalls. Such was security at the time that tickets for the performance were not purchased at the box office, but rather at the police station. Every ticket holder had to be cleared by police investigation. Despite this, Bogroff, carried in police files as a terrorist and anarchist, easily obtained a seat in the stalls, near the prime minister. It was, to put it mildly, a breach of security by an agency not noted for a lack of jealousness.

During an intermission, Prime Minister Stolypin rose to stretch his legs. He bowed to the czar, and as he drew erect, Bogroff fired a single shot, wounding him fatally. While attendants unsuccessfully sought to save Stolypin's life, the czar hurried to the stage, where he led the audience in singing the national anthem, drawing wild applause for his bravery.

For his act Bogroff earned his Stolypin necktie, and the murdered prime minister got a lavish state funeral. However, many questions arose. Why had the assassin sought to kill the prime minister instead of the czar? Did Bogroff's police masters decide that Stolypin and his campaign of repression were simply too heavy a burden for them? There was much discontent about the Stolypin affair, and perhaps in time an exhaustive investigation might have unearthed the facts of the assassination. However, the ravages of war and revolution were to make all speculation moot.

Further reading: *The History of Assassination*, by Brian McConnell.

STRASSER, Gregor (1892–1934) Before Adolf Hitler achieved power, the number-two man in the National Socialist movement was Gregor Strasser. He was a brilliant organizer and a powerful speaker, and as William L. Shirer notes, 'With his genial Bavarian nature, he was the most popular leader in the party next to Hitler, and, unlike the Fuehrer he enjoyed the personal trust and even liking of most of his political opponents. There were a good many at the time, within and without the party, who believed that Strasser might well supplant the moody, incalculable Austrian leader.'

Not surprisingly, Hitler probably hated Strasser, but he needed him because Strasser (and his then protege Joseph Goebbels) had the ability to take the northern more radical and even 'proletarian' wing of the party with him if he left the movement. In the mid-1920s Strasser and Goebbels much more than Hitler believed in the Socialism in National Socialism. Eventually Hitler succeeded in luring the vain and admiring Goebbels to his side, but Strasser remained a thorn until the 'Night of the Long Knives' of June 30, 1934, when Hitler carried out the bloody purge of Ernst Roehm, the depraved and brutal head of the bullyboy SA Brownshirts, who he thought was plotting against him. Hitler used the purge to assassinate many other old enemies or 'traitors' as well, and under personal orders from Hermann Goering Strasser was seized at his Berlin home and murdered by the Gestapo.

Perhaps the most incisive description of the motivation behind the Strasser assassination comes from Walter Schellenberg, the Nazis's great spymaster, who states in his memoirs that while the General Staff of the Wehrmacht had pushed hard for the elimination of Roehm and the SA, they applied special pressure on Goering for 'the elimination of the more unreliable elements among the Nazis, in particular the radical wing led by Gregor Strasser, who took the socialist aspect of National Socialism too seriously.'

Strasser undoubtedly also provoked the business interests in Germany who had constantly threatened to cut off financial support for Hitler if the radicals in the party were not stopped in their campaign to nationalize industry. It was obvious that Strasser's base in the Nazi Party could not withstand the combined enmity of big business, the Wehrmacht and Hitler himself. In fact, he rather than Roehm stood out as the prime candidate for assassination in the intrigues enveloping Germany in 1934.

Further reading: *Hitler's Secret Service*, by Walter Schellenberg; *The Rise and Fall of the Third Reich*, by William L. Shire.

SUI WEN TI, Emperor of China (541–604)   Sui Wen Ti, whose contemporary name was Yang Chien, was the first emperor of China's Sui dynasty, a position he achieved following a bloody campaign of assassinations. Yang was a leading military commander for the Western Wei dynasty and had arranged for his infant daughter to be married to the crown prince. However, when the crown prince ascended to the throne in 578, friction developed between son-in-law and father-in-law. There is little doubt that Yang began actively planning to usurp power. As it happened, his son-in-law suffered a fatal stroke and was succeeded by his young son, Yang's grandson.

Yang became regent and effectively ran royal affairs, but found he had to contend with supporters of the old emperor within and without the royal family. Yang launched a carefully crafted campaign of murder, arranging the assassinations of an estimated 50 members of the royal family, including his grandson. He launched the Sui dynasty in 581 and by 589 had unified all of China under his rule, which turned out on the whole to be most progressive, setting the stage for the artistic and cultural renaissance that was to flower in the succeeding, long-lasting Tang dynasty.

Yang, or Sui Wen Ti, his posthumous title in history, died in 604, most probably an assassination victim of his son and successor, Sui Yang Ti. (See SUI YANG TI, EMPEROR OF CHINA.)

Further reading: *Companion to Chinese History*, by Hugh B. O'Neill; *The Sui Dynasty*, by Arthur F. Wright.

SUI YANG TI, Emperor of China (569–617) The second emperor of the Sui dynasty, Sui Yang Ti, was the second son of the emperor Sui Wen Ti. It is generally accepted that Yang Ti succeeded to the throne in 605 by eliminating his elder brother, the crown prince, and his father.

As emperor, Yang Ti proved to be a tyrant, and his regime was marked by rampant corruption. Under him relations with the Turks deteriorated into warfare, and in 615 the Turks dealt the Chinese a devastating defeat. Similarly, Yang Ti's forces were beaten in Vietnam, and three efforts from 612 to 614 to conquer the Korean kingdom of Koguryo and exact tribute proved unsuccessful. In 617 Yang Ti was almost captured by enemy forces, and a welter of rebellions broke out throughout the empire.

Yang Ti fled to Nanking, his queen's native city. However, intrigue now dominated the court and Yang Ti was assassinated by a member of his own entourage. His death marked the effective end of the Sui dynasty, which began with assassinations and ended in the same fashion. His weak successor, Kung Ti, reigned for a mere year, and the stage was set for the beginning of the much more illustrious Tang dynasty. (See SUI WEN TI, EMPEROR OF CHINA.)

Further reading: *Companion to Chinese History*, by

Hugh B. O'Neill; *The Sui Dynasty*, by Arthur F. Wright.

SYKES, Sir Richard (1920–1979)   On March 22, 1979, 58-year-old Sir Richard Sykes, the British ambassador to the Netherlands, was leaving his residence in The Hague when two gunmen opened fire on him and a Dutch servant, Karel Straub. Both the ambassador and Straub died of their wounds. The Provisional wing of the Irish Republican Army (Provos) took credit for the Sykes assassination, with assistance from the Dutch Red Help movement.

Sykes had been a 32-year veteran of the British foreign service, occupying a number of posts around the world. He was regarded as an expert in military, defense and security matters, and he handled the investigation in the 1976 bomb murder of Christopher Ewart-Biggs, British ambassador to Ireland. Sykes was knighted in 1977, and the same year took up his post in The Hague.

The Provos were a wing that split away from the main body of the IRA, or the 'Officials.' By the Sykes assassination as well as other killings outside Ireland, the Provos were seeking to demonstrate that Britain faced retribution anywhere in the world for its Irish policy. At the same time the Provos sought to score points against the Officials, whom they accused of having gone soft in the struggle.

SYLVESTER II, Pope   See OTTO III, HOLY ROMAN EMPEROR.

T

TALAT PASHA, Mehmed (1874–1921)   A leading member of the Ottoman government from 1913 to 1918, Mehmed Talat Pasha was a leader of the Young Turks and grand vizier in 1917–1918. The son of a minor Ottoman official, he was arrested at age 19 for subversive activities. Released from two years' imprisonment, he was active among the Young Turks and gained minor govermental posts until being dismissed for being a member of the Young Turk conspiratorial division. After the 1908 revolution he became deputy for his native Edirne in the Ottoman parliament and then moved up to minister of the interior and other posts.

Before the start of World War I, Talat leaned toward the Allied powers, but by 1914 he was swayed to the other side and agreed to enter the war on the side of Germany. As minister of the interior, Talat was required to handle the forced deportation of the Armenians from the eastern provinces. Many historians attributed to him the barbarity that brought about the deaths of some 600,000 Armenians.

In 1917 Talat became grand vizier, but shortly before the end of the war, Talat and other Ottoman governmental officials were forced to flee to Germany. Talat remained in exile in Berlin until March 15, 1921, when a 22-year-old Armenian, Saro Melikian, assassinated him, declaring he had acted to avenge the slaughter of his people. Despite his confession, a German court refused to convict him of any crime.

TARAKI, Nur Mohammad (1917–1979)   In September 1979 Nur Mohammad Taraki, president of Afghanistan, was replaced as head of state by his prime minister, Hafizullah Amin. At the time it was said that Taraki had resigned due to ill health, a line that subsequent revelations proved highly unlikely.

Taraki had come to power in 1978 with Soviet support following the bloody coup against President Daud Khan, who was murdered. Taraki's regime came under severe pressure on September 14–15, 1979, with shooting in the streets of the capital city of Kabul. On September 16 Taraki was replaced. On September 23 new President Amin insisted, despite foreign news accounts to the contrary, that Taraki had not been killed and that he was being treated for an undisclosed illness. On October 9 Kabul radio declared that Taraki had expired from 'a severe and prolonged illness.' However, independent reports from Pakistan indicated that Taraki had been shot to death on September 17, and that Amin himself had survived an ambush by pro-Taraki military men.

The Amin regime lasted only a few months. Amin proved incapable of quelling Islamic opposition to the Soviet-sponsored government, and on December 27 the Red Army rolled into Afghanistan. Amin was replaced by former Deputy Premier Babrak Karmal, who was imported from exile in Eastern Europe. It was announced that Amin had been found guilty by a revolutionary court for 'crimes against the state' and executed.

The Afghanistan invasion, finally ended in 1989, proved to be a disaster for Soviet foreign policy and came to be referred to as 'Russia's Vietnam.'

TARUC, Pedro (1907–1970) The assassination in 1970 of Pedro Taruc, the 'supremo' of the Hukbalahap guerrilla movement in the Philippines, decimated the old-guard leadership of the revolutionary group. Tarac, secretary-general of the Philippine Communist Party, had a $25,000 bounty on his head by the Marcos government. He was shot to death by two informers who had led government soldiers to his hideaway in Angeles City. Officially the government insisted Taruc was shot to death by the soldiers in a gunfight, after having been traced through intelligence work, but local citizens identified the assassins as two members of Taruc's own bodyguard who had betrayed him for the reward money.

One month earlier Taruc's top aide, Faustino del Mundo, had been captured by government forces, and with the elimination of Taruc, the old-guard faction among the Huks was all but eliminated, and control of the movement now passed to even more militant Maoist elements. Two decades later, the insurrection continued.

TELL, Wasfi (?–1971) The name of Black September – the Palestinian terrorist group – was first announced to the world in horrific fashion on November 28, 1971, with the assassination of Jordanian Prime Minister Wasfi Tell. The group took its name from September 1970, when King Hussein destroyed the Palestinian guerrilla movement in Jordan, and it was formed as the terror weapon of Yasser Arafat's Al Fatah group. At first Al Fatah denied any link with Black September solely to give Arafat deniability for terrorism, but eventually the connection became obvious and Fatah denials became little more than pro forma.

Although the first Black September acts were bombings of European commercial enterprises with Israeli connections, it was the Wasfi Tell murder that was the group's first important mission. Tell was looked upon by Palestinians as the key architect of their Jordanian debacle and therefore their chief target, aside from King Hussein himself.

Tell was on an official visit to Cairo; he was cut down in a hail of bullets on the steps of the Sheraton Hotel after he returned from a meeting of the Arab League's Joint Defense Council, which was convened, ironically, to plan joint actions against Israel. In the shooting, Jordan's foreign minister, Abdullah Saleh, was slightly wounded and an Egyptian bodyguard was more seriously injured. Four suspects were arrested, and the overall plotter was eventually identified as Fakhri-al-Umari. However, three months later the suspects were released on bail put up by the PLO after ballistics reports failed to identify the guns found on them as those that had fired the fatal bullets. After the Tell assassination Black September's terrorist raids included the Olympic massacre in Munich, the killing of diplomats in Khartoum, the hijacking of a Lufthansa jet and the letter bomb outrages against Israelis in 1972.

THATCHER, Margaret (1925–) – Attempted Assassination   In the early morning of October 12, 1984, a bomb exploded at the Grand Hotel in the southern coastal town of Brighton, England, where virtually the entire British cabinet and Conservative Party delegates were staying for their annual conference. Four persons were killed, and over 30 injured, but the principal target, Margaret Thatcher, narrowly avoided injury, having left her bathroom just before the bomb, planted five flights directly above, mangled the room.

Those killed were Sir Anthony Berry, a Conservative M.P.; Roberta Wakeman, the wife of the party's chief whip, John Wakeman, who was himself seriously injured; Jeanne Shattock, the wife of the Conservative chairman in the west of England; and Eric Taylor, a local Tory Party official.

Others managed remarkable escapes. Norman Tebbit, the trade and industry secretary, plunged two stories after floors below collapsed, and lay buried under rubble for four hours until being dug out by firefighters. Authorities said the death toll would have been much higher if more of the delegates had been in their rooms. Many were reported to have been in the hotel's bar at the time of the blast.

The attack was the most serious against the upper ranks of the British government since 1605, when Guy Fawkes and a number of English Catholics conspired to blow up Parliament and King James I.

In Dublin the Provisional Irish Republican Army claimed responsibility for the act and said the bomb had been aimed at Thatcher and her 'warmongers.' The explosion occurred just hours before the party conference was to debate Northern Ireland policy. The IRA statement declared: 'Today we were unlucky, but remember we only have to be lucky once.'

Mrs Thatcher announced one hour after the explosion that the conference would continue. Four days later Foreign Secretary Sir Geoffrey Howe denounced U.S. supporters of the Provisional IRA, saying, 'Those who provide funds to the IRA through any of their front organizations in the U.S., in the profoundly mistaken belief that they are romantic nationalists fighting in an honorable cause, should rid themselves of such delusions. Let them make no mistake – they are supporting and promoting terrorism.'

Newspapers in England also attacked the United States. The mass-circulation *Daily Mirror* charged that the United States had done little to hinder Noraid (the Irish Northern Aid Committee) and editorialized: 'The Brighton bomb may have been planted by an Irish terrorist, but the fingerprints upon it were American.'

U.S. ambassador to Britain Charles H. Price II responded that banning the work of Noraid would raise 'a constitutional question that becomes quite complicated.'

THEOCTISTUS See MICHAEL III, BYZANTINE EMPEROR.

TIBERIUS, Emperor of Rome (42 B.C.–A.D. 37) As a general before achieving the imperial purple, Tiberius had been a favorite of Emperor Augustus. Tiberius did not squander wealth and Roman blood in grand new conquests, although he was as savage in putting down provincial rebellions as any emperor before or after. He halted the drain on the imperial treasury so much that when he died he left 270 million sesterces, 20 times the sum he inherited from Augustus. Rome was also much more secure thanks to its newly strengthened navy. Tiberius also stopped the practice of providing gladiatorial games and reformed taxes, acts that were none too popular.

In time Tiberius became disgusted with life in Rome and the constant castigations heaped on him. His most trusted adviser, Sejanus, the prefect of the Praetorian Guard, convinced him to leave Rome for Capri, from where he could rule by edicts to be carried out by Sejanus. There seems little doubt that Sejanus was seeking in time to become emperor himself, with Tiberius to be assassinated when the time was ripe.

In Capri Tiberius appears to have devoted himself to sexual perversions as much as to the affairs of state, if we are to believe Suetonius and the equally venomous reports of the historian Tacitus. Some historians now regard such castigations as mere gossip but most agree that many of the charges that Tiberius threw off moral restraints are probably true.

In A.D. 23 Tiberius's son Drusus died of poisoning made to look like illness. Almost certainly the mastermind behind the assassination was the ambitious Sejanus. Sejanus's duplicity remained concealed from Tiberius for several years, but by A.D. 31 the emperor had become certain that Sejanus was plotting his overthrow and murder.

Now Tiberius's legendary cunning came into play. With the aid of Macro, Sejanus's successor as commander of the Praetorians (Sejanus had been promoted by Tiberius to co-consul of Rome), the emperor suddenly demanded that the Senate execute Sejanus. That pliant body was shocked by the sudden change in the wind, but long resentful and fearful of Sejanus – the Senate itself had erected golden statues in his honor, animals were sacrificed to him, and his birthday was celebrated as a holiday – it eagerly complied with the royal command. Under Macro's supervision the matter was handled with the utmost speed. Sejanus had awakened that morning the most powerful man in Rome and by nightfall he had been condemned, strangled and his spittle-covered corpse displayed by the Tiber for three days for the mob's abuse. Sejanus's allies were killed by the score. His three children were also executed. Since his daughter was 14 and a virgin and as such was exempt from being put to death, the executioner was obliged to rape her before killing her.

Over the final six years of his reign, Tiberius's bloodlust was unchecked. Once citizens had aroused the emperor's slightest suspicion they were tried and executed on the mildest of pretexts. Perhaps the most appalling crime of Tiberius – although it was not fully appreciated at the time – was his naming of the young Caligula as his heir. Tiberius himself realized what he was doing, however; he observed, 'I am nursing a viper in Rome's bosom.'

As the years passed, Tiberius lost the support of the few who still admired him. In A.D. 37, at the age of 78, he left Capri with plans eventually to return to Rome. Along the way he took part in a ceremonial game that required him to throw a javelin. He wrenched his shoulder badly and at Lucullus's villa in Misenum he fell into a fainting fit or coma. His physicians, whom Tiberius had barred from examining him for half a century, now viewed his emaciated body and declared he could not last another 24 hours. The courtiers immediately flocked to Caligula, paying him homage. Then suddenly Tiberius awakened, sat up and asked for food. The notables of the court were in a frenzy, and Caligula himself fled in terror. Only Macro, the Praetorian commander, remained calm. He smothered the still weakened and probably still mortally ill emperor with a pillow.

Back in Rome the populace went wild for joy at the news of the emperor's demise. 'Tiberius to the Tiber!' was the cry. It was the happiest day in the capital since Sejanus's passing. (See DRUSUS CAESAR.)

Further reading: *The Story of Civilization III – Caesar and Christ*, by Will Durant.

TISZA, Count Stephen (1861–1918) Hungarian premier in 1903–05 and 1913–17, Count Stephen Tisza was a prominent advocate of the Austro-Hungarian dualist system of government and an ardent opponent of election reform. Subject to popular approval in elections in 1905, Tisza was heavily defeated, and in 1917 he resigned when the new emperor, Charles I, decreed further suffrage reform. Tisza was popularly seen as the leading advocate of the monarchy's alliance with Germany during World War I. As such, he was popularly held to be responsible for provoking the unsuccessful war and causing the suffering inflicted on the country. Shortly before the end of the war on October 31, 1918, he was assassinated by a group of disgruntled discharged soldiers.

TOLBERT, William R., Jr. (1913–1980) On April 12, 1980, an army coup headed by Master Sergeant Samuel K. Doe overthrew what was generally regarded as the rather mild, but obviously venal government of Liberian President William R. Tolbert Jr. The country was the oldest republic in black Africa.

Tolbert was assassinated and 27 of his entourage slaughtered during the first night of the coup, as Doe led a band of rebellious troops on the palace grounds in Monrovia. Tolbert had been in Liberian politics for almost 40 years and in 1951 became vice president under President William Tubman. He succeeded to the presidency when Tubman died in July 1971. There had been growing public disenchantment with Tolbert as the country's economy declined and corruption became more prevalent.

Doe pledged to stamp out immediately all corruption and took what he considered proper steps to that end by subjecting surviving members of the coup to a quick trial before a special five-man military court. The charges were not fully spelled out, but the verdict of death was clear enough for 13 defendants, including Tolbert's brother, Frank, who was president of the nation's senate. Also condemned were Tolbert's ministers of foreign affairs, finance, justice, commerce and agriculture, as well as the speaker of the House of Representatives and the chief justice of the Liberian Supreme Court.

On April 22 the condemned men were bound to stakes along an ocean beach and executed by firing squads, whose soldiers then desecrated the bodies, reportedly to much applause and cheering by a festive crowd of citizens. On April 25, Doe having proclaimed himself president, suspended Liberia's 133-year-old constitution. (See DOE, SAMUEL KANYON.)

TOMBALBAYE, Ngarta (1918–1975) The 20th-century record for survival of the most assassination attempts perhaps belonged to Ngarta Tombalbaye, the first president of the poverty-stricken and landlocked north central African nation of Chad, which had previously been a French colony. A former schoolteacher, Tombalbaye survived eight attempts on his life in the 15 years of his despotic rule, from 1960 to 1975.

The attempts varied from the standard ones of gunfire and bombing to the 'magical' efforts of Kalthouma Guembang, the former president of the women's section of the Chadian Progressive Party, who was sentenced to seven years' imprisonment for hiring a number of wizards to pierce the eyes of a black sheep representing Tombalbaye, and then bury the animal alive.

Tombalbaye was finally killed on April 13 in the ninth assassination try against him, this by machine-gun fire and mortars aimed at his official residence by defecting army units.

Tombalbaye was replaced by a nine-man Supreme Military Council. Brigadier General Felix Malloum, who had been imprisoned by Tombalbaye in 1973 for plotting against him, was released from prison and took over as head of the council. Tombalbaye had turned extremely caustic against the military in the last few years, and for a time the revolt was ascribed to a reaction to the humiliation and ridicule heaped on the army by Tombalbaye. However, other observers detected a French hand in the assassination. The Paris newspaper *Le Monde* charged that Camille Gourvenec, the French commander of the Chadian National and Nomadic Guard and director of information services, was in a position to know of the coup plans in advance but did not warn Tombalbaye. In addition, France maintained 2,000 men in the capital city of N'Djamena, and the Chadian plotters obviously would not have dared move had they not had assurance that

France would not intervene. After the coup Gourvenec retained both his posts and was also appointed to the Military Commission, the most important body established by the new government.

Anti-French forces, such as the Chadian National Liberation Front (Frolinat) operating in the northern part of the country, were much more caustic in their charges, accusing Gourvenec of actually having directed the coup and describing him as 'the junta's mentor.'

TORRES, Juan Jose (1921–1976) On June 2, 1976, retired General Juan Jose Torres, who had been president of a leftist Bolivian government for ten months in 1970–71, was found murdered on a rural road 60 miles from Buenos Aires, Argentina, where he had been living in exile. He was blindfolded and his body was riddled with bullets. Torres had fled to Chile after his government had been toppled in a bloody right-wing military coup initiated by General Hugo Banzer Suarez, who at the time of Torres's death held the post of president himself.

Both the Argentine and Bolivian governments denounced the Torres murder, putting the blame on 'international extremists.' The Bolivian government specifically laid the crime to allies of a left-wing group that had claimed responsibility for the Paris murder the previous month of General Joaquin Zenteno Anaya, the Bolivian ambassador to France. However, there was suspicion in some quarters that the Bolivian government actually bore responsibility for both the Zenteno and the Torres killings.

Bolivian mineworkers, longtime Torres supporters, held a nationwide strike and were joined by many leftist students and workers in other cities in denouncing 'international fascists.' President Banzer at first offered Torres's widow a state funeral in Bolivia for her husband, but retracted the offer when Mrs. Torres demanded that the services be held in the headquarters of the mineworkers' union. Instead the body was flown to Mexico City for burial, and Mrs. Torres told a press conference that the

Argentine and Bolivian governments were responsible for her husband's murder. She claimed that Torres had been directly threatened by Colonel Raul Tejerina, the Bolivian military attache in Buenos Aires.

In the aftermath of the Torres assassination President Banzer offered amnesty to Bolivian political exiles who feared possible assassination abroad. Several allies of Torres and otherwise opponents of Banzer, including former cabinet ministers Jorge Gallardo, Samuel Gallardo and Ciro Humboldt, accepted the offer and returned. They were immediately arrested, and Interior Minister Juan Pereda Asbun later declared that the amnesty did not apply to persons deemed by the government to be 'extremists.' (See ZENTENO ANAYA, JOAQUIN.)

TRESCA, Carlo (1875–1943) The ability, indeed the eagerness, of the American Mafia to work with governments in assassination attempts hardly started with the infamous CIA-underworld plots to kill Fidel Castro. It goes back at least to World War II, the only difference being that the underworld cooperated with the Italian government to carry out a political murder in New York.

Technically, the murder of syndicalist editor Carlo Tresca remains a mystery. No one was convicted for the crime, although few police officials doubt the Mafia connection. This version was repeated by a number of informers and was also confirmed by Charles 'Lucky' Luciano, at the time the recognized head of Mafia activities in the United States.

Born in Pulmona, Italy to a wealthy land-owning family, Tresca gravitated to left-wing causes and in his 20s was the editor of the Socialist Party newspaper. Forced to flee the country, he emigrated to Geneva, Switzerland, where he met another young man with a reputation as a hothead, Benito Mussolini. At the time Mussolini regarded Tresca as too conservative, and Tresca regarded Mussolini as a charlatan. Tresca would later, from his exile in the United States, become an implacable foe and caustic critic of

Mussolini's Fascist regime. The record indicates that Mussolini put Tresca on a death list as early as 1931, but it would be a dozen years before the radical's murder could be carried out.

The instrument of Mussolini's revenge was Italian-American mobster Vito Genovese, who had fled a murder charge in New York in the 1930s and returned to Italy. There, laden with considerable underworld funds, Genovese curried favor with the Italian dictator by becoming a major contributor to the Fascists. Genovese further ingratiated himself to the Duce's son-in-law and Italian foreign minister, Count Galeazzo Ciano, by keeping him supplied with drugs.

When Mussolini raged about Tresca – 'Genovese's countryman' – and his New York publication *Il Martello* for constantly attacking him, Genovese saw a great opportunity to ingratiate himself even more by offering to 'take care' of Tresca. According to later police theory, Genovese, despite the war, had no difficulty passing on the orders from Rome, to his New York aides Mike Miranda and Tony Bender to have Tresca 'hit.' The actual killing was handed to a then minor Brooklyn hoodlum named Carmine Galante, who in the 1970s would rise to become boss of the Bonanno crime family.

On the evening of January 11, 1943, Tresca was shot dead in a hail of bullets while walking on Fifth Avenue near 15th Street. The gunman escaped, but Tresca's companion and other bystanders recorded the license number of the killer's automobile: 1C-9272.

Immediate newspaper speculation was that Tresca could have been assassinated by forces of either the left or the right. Eventually, though, the police traced the license number to underworld figures. They discovered that two hours before the Tresca assassination, Galante, a parolee, had made his weekly visit to his parole officer in downtown Manhattan. It was standard practice for parole officers to trail parolees out of the office in the hope of seeing them consorting with other criminal types, and Galante was followed to a car, which he entered and drove off. The parole officer recorded the license number of the car: 1C-9272.

Brought in for questioning, Galante denied getting in any car. He said he'd gone to the subway and taken a train to midtown, where he went to a Broadway movie house. The film he had allegedly been watching during the time of the Tresca killing was *Casablanca*. Galante proved singularly vague about the plot of the film. He failed even to remember the phrase 'You must remember this . . .'

Despite strong suspicions, the police were unable to develop an indictable case against Galante. In 1946 Vito Genovese was returned to the United States to face the original murder charge against him. In short order all the witnesses against him were silenced, and Genovese went free on that charge. He was grilled on the Tresca assassination but insisted he knew nothing about it. In effect he mimicked Carmine Galante's words on the case: 'Who is this guy Tresca? Never even heard of him.'

TROTSKY, Leon (1879–1940)   In 1940 Joseph Stalin, the dictator of the U.S.S.R., had one major target for assassination left – Leon Trotsky. In the preceding years Stalin had carried out a mass extermination of 'Old Bolsheviks,' whom he had regarded, whether right, left, or center, as potential rivals to his power. The Great Purge trials eliminated such revolutionary figures as Zinoviev, Kamenev, Radek, Bukharin, Piatakov and many others. Now only Stalin's archenemy Trotsky remained.

Trotsky and Lenin were the actual architects of the Russian Revolution, and Trotsky had been the organizer of the Red Army and led it to victory in the civil war against the Whites. On Lenin's death in 1924 Trotsky and Stalin, the general secretary of the Communist Party, stood as chief rivals. Stalin proved the more skillful infighter and used his control of the party apparatus to weaken Trotsky by allying himself at times with Zinoviev and Kamenev and then with Bukharin on the right. Stalin opposed Trotsky's program of world revolution in favor of the concept of 'socialism in one country,' an alternative attractive to the party bureaucrats. In 1925 Trotsky was ousted from his post of commissar of war. He was expelled from the party in 1927 and deported from the Soviet Union in 1929.

Turkey granted him asylum, and in 1933 he moved to France and then in 1935 to Norway. That country, under pressure from Russia, expelled him in 1936. Trotsky then settled in Mexico, where he faced the constant threat of assassination by Stalin's henchmen. Why did Stalin so desperately want Trotsky silenced? It went far beyond jealousy to fear. Trotsky was feverishly trying to organize a Fourth International to promote world revolution. But that was a minor threat to Stalin compared to Trotsky's most potent weapon, his pen. As George Bernard Shaw said of Trotsky, 'When he cuts off his opponent's head, he holds it up to show that there are no brains in it.'

In the last few years Trotsky had intensified his literary attacks on Stalin with such works as *Stalin's Crimes*, *The Real Situation in Russia*, and *The Stalinist School of Falsification*. Now the 60-year-old Trotsky was engaged in a full-length 'antibiography' called *Stalin*.

The Stalinist war against his tormentor was fought with weapons more lethal than the pen. In 1938 Stalin's agents murdered Trotsky's 32-year-old son Lev Sedov, either kidnapping him from a Paris hospital or first killing him in his hospital bed and then removing the corpse. Against Trotsky himself, Stalin's killers prepared a two-pronged assault. During his Stalinist phases the artist Diego Rivera would later brag that as Trotsky's original host in Mexico he had 'lured the exile to his death.'

The first attack on Trotsky came under the leadership of the famous painter and Stalinist David Alfaro Sequeiros, who led a 20-man frontal assault on Trotsky's villa on May 23, 1940. The raiders wore phony military and police uniforms and overpowered guards, threw dynamite and incendiary bombs, and blasted the Trotsky bedroom with 73 machine-gun bullets. Miraculously, neither Trotsky nor his wife was hit. With the failure of the attack, the Communists in Mexico started a drumfire of propaganda that the raid had been a fake, staged by Trotsky, but this was disproved when the body of a 23-year-old devotee of the revolutionary, wealthy American Sheldon Harte, turned up. The attackers had kidnapped Harte in the raid. Harte was traced to a house where Siqueiros and his aides had taken him, murdered him apparently in his sleep and dumped his body in a lime-filled grave. Now the Soviets heaped the blame for the raid on Mexican Communist leaders, and they in turn blamed those they had recently ousted from office. The Mexican Communists denounced Siqueiros as an uncontrollable, mad fringe element of the party. By that time Siqueiros and his accomplices had conveniently fled the country.

This left Stalin's secret police, the GPU, with their alternative plan, which had been nurtured since 1937, when the unit infiltrated an agent, Ramon Mercader, into Trotskyite circles. Using the name of Frank Jacson, he seduced Sylvia Agelof, a New York supporter of Trotsky, and in 1939 the unwitting Agelof introduced Jacson-Mercader into the Trotsky household in Mexico. Eventually, the comings and goings of Mercader exhibited little surprise from guards, even after the first murder attempt.

Mercader encouraged Trotsky's trust by attempting to write political pieces for the Trotskyite press. The old revolutionist was probably not overimpressed but did view him as an earnest follower. Meanwhile Mercader spent much time learning how to use an ice ax, while climbing high volcanoes around Mexico City.

On August 20, 1940, Trotsky was feeding his pet rabbits when Mercader approached him, clutching a raincoat. Hidden in the raincoat pocket was an ice ax. Mercader had an article, and Trotsky agreed to look at it. They went indoors to Trotsky's paper-littered study, and Trotsky sat down at a table to read the article. Mercader stationed himself to Trotsky's left, blocking him from an alarm button that would have instantly summoned some guards if pushed.

Later Mercader confessed:

> I put my raincoat on the table on purpose so that I could take out the ice axe which I had in the pocket . . . I took the *piolet* out of my raincoat, took it in my fist and, closing my eyes, I gave him a tremendous blow on the head . . . The man screamed in such a way that I will never forget as long as I live. His scream was . . . very long, infinitely long, and it still seems to me as if that scream were piercing my brains.

Mercader tried to hit Trotsky a second blow, but the old Bolsehvik grabbed his hand and arm and bit his hand to try to make him drop the weapon. Then Trotsky staggered out to the drawing room and summoned help. Guards disarmed Mercader and gave him a vicious beating. The still conscious Trotsky was asked if his assailant should be killed. Trotsky answered with difficulty: 'Impermissible to kill, he must be . . . forced . . . to . . . talk.'

Both Trotsky and his attacker were rushed to the same hospital. Trotsky died 26 hours after being attacked. Mercader recovered but did not talk. He was sentenced to 20 years' imprisonment. He was later identified as the son of a dedicated Cuban Communist woman named Caridad. The mother was waiting at a car nearby in case her son made it out of the villa. Nearby as well was Leonid Eitingon, alias General Kotov, the Kremlin agent in charge of the operation.

Someone, either Caridad or Russian agents, saw to it that money was paid to ensure Mercader relative comfort during his imprisonment. Mercader was released in 1960. He did not rejoin his mother, who was then living in Cuba. She had been to Moscow years earlier and been feted as the mother of a great Communist hero and been awarded the Order of Lenin by Stalin personally. By this time there was little pretense that Mercader had not been a Stalinist assassin. Mercader went to Communist Czechoslovakia to live. He was declared a hero of the Soviet Union before he died in Havana, Cuba on October 18, 1978.

TRUJILLO MOLINA, Rafael Leonidas (1891–1961) A few years after the assassination of the Western Hemisphere's most ruthless dictator, Rafael Trujillo, then U.S. President Lyndon Johnson was to say, 'We had been operating a damned Murder, Inc., in the Caribbean.' In the case of Trujillo, U.S. policy during the 31 years of his rule in the Dominican Republic constantly vacillated between propping him up and then seeking his downfall; in the end the United States supplied the weapons to slay him.

In early 1961 the United States was actively involved in planning the downfall of Cuba's Fidel Castro. Needing to demonstrate to other Latin countries that U.S. policy also opposed right-wing elements, it was decided to nurture a plot to remove Trujillo, a ruler who carried state terrorism to horrific depths, considered human life a cheap commodity and was compared by observers to the Roman emperor Caligula.

It was never difficult to find elements in the country eager to kill Trujillo, and the CIA and members of the U.S. diplomatic corps maintained close ties with the anti-Trujillo conspirators. The plot drew in right-wing military figures, libertarians, and, perhaps most important, members of the close-knit and affluent old Dominican family the de la Mazas. The de la Mazas were renowned for their volatile behavior and for their previous cooperative attitude toward the dictator and his enforcers, the dreaded secret police known as the SIM.

A member of the de la Mazas, a young pilot named Tavio, had assisted, wittingly or not, in the kidnapping and later assassination of the exiled Jesus de Galindez, a professor of international law at Columbia University. Tavio was involved in the 'airlift' that returned the drugged Galindez back to Trujillo. Later, to cover himself, Trujillo had Tavio conveniently 'commit suicide' while in custody during the later investigation. From that time on the de la Mazas became the most dedicated of all the anti-Trujilloists and put backbone into the others.

Somewhat less dedicated was the United States. By

early May 1961 there was less pressing need to depose Trujillo. The previous month the Bay of Pigs invasion of Cuba had ended in debacle, and if Castro and the Latin left were safe, there was less incentive for demonstrating any opposition toward the right. By this time the CIA had prepared a method to supply needed machine guns for the assassination to the conspirators. U.S. Chargé d'affaires Henry Dearborn previously reported that the dissidents were 'in no way ready to carry on any type of revolutionary activity in the foreseeable future, except the assassination of their principal enemy.'

Throughout the hectic days of May, Dearborn and the CIA pushed for the continued supply of weapons. On May 5 President John Kennedy, apprised of the plot, told a National Security Council meeting, 'The United States should not initiate the overthrow of Trujillo before knowing what kind of government would succeed him.'

On May 21 Dearborn noted in a communication to Washington that State Department officials in the Dominican Republic had been 'nurturing the effort to overthrow Trujillo and had assisted the dissidents in numerous ways, all of which were known to the Department.' Dearborn also cabled that it was 'too late to consider whether United States will initiate overthrow of Trujillo.'

The previous May 16 Dearborn had cabled a request for the release of machine guns and hand grenades already in the Dominican Republic, noting the assassination attempt was set for that evening (it was postponed to May 30) and that the machine guns might increase the chances of success beyond the estimated 80 percent. Washington's answer: 'Negative.'

Later some observers would regard the U.S. actions as intended to establish 'credible deniability.' It was clear the assassination would go forward regardless, since the dissidents had undoubtedly been schooled in the need for having contingency plans should the promised weapons be for any reason unavailable. The plot did in fact go through, even though the only U.S. weapons were two M-1 rifles previously supplied. The dissidents had managed to find enough additional firepower for their mission.

Trujillo was shot to death by automatic gunfire when his chauffeured car was ambushed outside the capital. True to his nature, Trujillo, badly wounded, insisted on his car stopping so that he could return fire rather than flee to safety. He was riddled with bullets, and later his body was taken away and dumped in Ciudad Trujillo. His chauffeur Zaszrias de la Cruz, was badly wounded but survived.

The dissidents were sure they could seize power, but delay and fear in their ranks cost valuable time. The remnants of the Trujillo family and government continued to exercise power and exacted vengeance in the ensuing months. Many of the conspirators were caught, tortured and murdered, including many members of the de la Maza family. Eventually, though, the Trujillo machine itself was finished. The argument of whether the CIA was the 'principal partner' in the tyrannicide has continued. 'Ironically,' notes journalist Bernard Diederich, 'the CIA lists the end of the Trujillo era as one of the Agency's "successes." ' (See DE GALINDEZ, JESUS.)

Further reading: *Trujillo: The Death of the Goat*, by Bernard Diederich.

TRUMAN, Harry S (1884–1972) – Attempted Assassination On November 1, 1950, while the White House was being restored and President Harry Truman was residing in Blair House across the street, Donald Birdzell, a uniformed presidential guard stationed at the bottom of the outside stairs, heard a faint metallic click. He turned his head and saw a dark-skinned man neatly dressed in a blue-green pin-striped suit, carefully pointing a German F-38 automatic pistol at him. The gun went off as Birdzell jumped toward the street – standard operating procedure to draw fire away from the house so that the president might not catch a stray bullet. The first-ever assault on a president of the United States in his Washington residence was underway.

Birdzell, ending up on the streetcar tracks on Pennsylvania Avenue, returned the gunman's fire. The attacker shot

Birdzell in the leg, dropping him to one knee. Then Birdzell took another bullet in his good leg, and he pitched forward on his face. At the same moment other guards and Secret Service agents swung into action, but their attention was drawn to a second gunman who had darted up to the lone guard in the west sentry booth, Leslie Coffelt. He opened fire on Coffelt at point-blank range. Coffelt toppled over with slugs in his chest, stomach and legs and died a short while later. Plainclothesman Joseph Downs went down next, shot in the stomach, but he survived.

Meanwhile the wounded Birdzell stretched out prone on the pavement and shot the first gunman in the chest as he frantically tried to reload. The would-be assassin went down hard, heels kicking, his hat awry. Other guards turned a raking fire on the second gunman, who lurched backward over a low boxwood hedge, dead with a bullet through his head.

The fall air fell suddenly silent. Then Secret Service agent Floyd Boring saw President Truman in his undershirt peering out the window of an upstairs room, where he had been napping. 'Get back, Mr. President!' Agent Boring yelled frantically, 'Get back!'

Truman stepped back, while additional Secret Service agents converged on the death scene. Most, however, remained alert at their posts in case of further attacks.

The wounded would-be assassin was identified as Oscar Collazo and the dead man as Griselio Torresola. In Torresola's pockets were two letters from the president of the Nationalist Party in Puerto Rico, Harvard-educated Albizu Campos.

In many respects the attempts to get to the president in his official residence was an insane idea, without doubt the hardest point of attack for an assassin. Collazo and Torresola had failed to penetrate even the outermost defenses. In a nearby office building a Secret Service man sat in a window with a clear view of the Blair House. Although armed, he had not opened fire. His job was not to protect the agents in front of the building but to bring down any attacker who made it to the door of the house.

And even had the attackers gotten past the front door, they would have faced an agent stationed just inside the entrance with a submachine gun in his lap.

There was another agent on the stairway, one in front of Truman's door, and undisclosed others in surrounding rooms. It was estimated that the assassins would have had to shoot their way past at least 20 agents before reaching the president.

Truman took the attempt on his life as having no special significance. A few hours later he presided at the unveiling of a statue before a large crowd in Arlington as though nothing untoward had occurred.

Collazo recovered from his wounds and stood trial. The Campos letters to Torresola contained some provocative thoughts of Campos but did not establish that he was involved in the assassination plot. Collazo maintained that he and Torresola had concocted the plot entirely on their own as a show of solidarity with their comrades in rebellion in Puerto Rico. His wife, Rosa, was arrested as well but later released. (In an unrelated case, several years later, she was one of 13 persons convicted of conspiracy to overthrow the government and was sentenced to six years' imprisonment.)

Collazo turned his trial into a passionate presentation of the cause for Puerto Rican freedom. He condemned what he called the economic exploitation and political manipulation of the Puerto Rican people by the United States government. 'Anything that I have done I did for the cause of the liberty of my country,' he said, 'and I still insist, even to the last, that we have the right to be free . . . I didn't come here to plead for my life. I came here to plead for the cause of the liberty of my people.'

Collazo was given the death sentence for the murder of Coffelt. As he was taken from the court his wife cried out, 'Goodbye, my dove!' Collazo rejected making any plea for clemency, but just a few days before the scheduled execution, Truman commuted his sentence to life imprisonment.

On September 10, 1979, Collazo was released from

federal prison, his sentence commuted to time served by President Jimmy Carter 'for humane reasons.' The act of clemency evoked little general objection.

TUKHACHEVSKY, Marshal Mikhail (1893–1937) Perhaps the most cunning of all assassination conspiracies carried out by the Nazi intelligence services occurred in 1937 when they succeeded in setting the stage for Joseph Stalin to execute Marshal Mikhail Tukhachevsky, a number of other generals and in fact half of the Red Army officer corps.

With considerable forged evidence, the Nazis were able to convince the always paranoid Stalin that Tukhachevsky, in league with portions of the German General Staff, was conspiring to overthrow him. This brilliant deception was masterminded by Reinhard Heydrich, Heinrich Himmler's cunning lieutenant. It can be argued otherwise; however, the most plausible thesis is that the entire affair was a Nazi fabrication. In either even, the goal was the same – to betray Tukhachevsky to Stalin to cripple the Russian officer corps for the coming war with the Soviet Union.

A great many forged documents were turned over to Stalin. According to Walter Schellenberg, the equally masterful underling to Heydrich, the letters merely fabricated portions of the evidence to make the documentary record more complete. According to Schellenberg, Heydrich was playing a double game, seeking to weaken the German General Staff as well.

The doctored evidence was turned over to Stalin's secret police, the GPU, in mid-May 1937. Tukhachevsky and his fellow-defendants were arrested on June 4, and the marshal's trial began at 10 A.M. on June 11, before a secret court composed chiefly of Soviet marshals and Red Army leaders (most of whom themselves did not survive later purges). The prosecutor was Andrei Vishinsky. The trial was over by 9 P.M. that evening. *Tass* reported that all the defendants admitted their guilt. Vishinsky's summations lasted a mere 20 minutes and concluded with a demand for the death penalty. The sentence was carried out by firing squad four hours later.

The final result of the Nazi-managed plot was the devastation of the Red Army – only two of five marshals escaped arrest, two of 15 army commanders, 28 of 58 corp commanders, 85 of 195 divisional commanders, and 195 of 406 regimental commanders. It can only be guessed how much this loss of military brainpower cost the U.S.S.R. during the early, successful onslaughts of the Wehrmacht.

Schellenberg offered in his memoirs a black-humored fillip to the affair. When Stalin was offered the bogus evidence, he inquired what price the Nazis put on it. The question caught Hitler and Heydrich unprepared, and it was hurriedly decided that to preserve appearances they should demand the payment of 3 million gold rubles. Stalin's emissary paid the money at once. Later, Schellenberg reports, he had to destroy most of the payoff money. They were in the form of high-denomination bills whose serial numbers had been recorded by the GPU, and when Nazi agents tried to spend some of the bills inside the Soviet Union, they were quickly apprehended.

Further reading: *A History of Russia*, by Nicholas V. Riasanovsky; *Hitler's Secret Service*, by Walter Schellenberg.

TYLER, Wat (?–1381) The Peasants' Revolt of 1381 was England's first great popular rebellion. It was led by Wat Tyler, an ex-soldier and, according to some, an ex-highwayman. The spiritual leader of the revolt was John Ball, the 'mad priest of Kent' who preached that 'things won't go well in England until everything is held in common, without serfs or lords.'

It was a message of resounding class conflict that earned John Ball a prison cell. However, that could not stop the peasants' uprising, and with Wat Tyler elected their captain, an army 20,000 strong set out from Kent toward London. On the way they stopped at Maidstone jail and liberated Ball, who joined the march. The rebels took Canterbury and Rochester, turning castles and manor houses to cinders on the way. They captured Savoy palace, the property of the king's uncle, John of Gaunt. The next day they were inside the walled city of London, taking London Bridge and the Tower of London.

The rebels opened the jails and set about beheading people they felt were most responsible for their plight – such as the treasurer and archbishop of Canterbury and merchant Richard Lyons, who they said had raised prices of essential goods to the point of keeping the peasants in permanent poverty.

The beleaguered king, 14-year-old Richard II, promised concessions such as the elimination of serfdom, a full pardon for those taking part in the rebellion, and the renting of land at fourpence an acre. On June 15 rebels and courtiers met in Smithfield Market, and Wat Tyler approached the king to speak.

What followed was assassination, the only argument being whether it had been premeditated. The most logical conclusion was that it had been planned, but the version offered by the courtiers was that Tyler was unduly insolent to the king. Other reports were that Tyler presented even more radical demands, including the confiscation of all church lands. According to these versions, the outraged lord mayor of London, William Walworth, struck Tyler to the ground and another of the king's men ran him through.

The chronicler Sir John Froissart cast Richard II in a heroic light, saying he then walked forward as the rebels raised their bows, telling his own men not to follow him. Then he addressed the rebels: 'Would you kill your king? I will be your leader.' The king convinced the rebels to move off to the fields of Clerkenwell. The lack of real resistance was probably due to the fact that Tyler was not dead. His followers rushed him to St. Bartholomew's Hospital. Later, however, by order of the lord mayor (who was subsequently knighted), Tyler was dragged from his hospital bed and beheaded.

The leaderless rebels – John Ball was also seized – started drifting off, some actually believing that the king had knighted Wat Tyler, in spite of the fact that his head was on display at London Bridge.

The king rescinded all the concessions he had made and troops were sent into the countryside to root out other leading rebels. There is no accurate count of the numbers killed in the bloodbath, but all estimates range upwards of 200. John Ball himself was hanged, drawn and quartered, with Richard II in attendance.

Further reading: *A Criminal History of Mankind*, by Colin Wilson; *The Great Revolt of 1381*, by Charles Oman; *The Story of Civilization VI – The Reformation*, by Will Durant.

U

UMBERTO I, King of Italy (1844–1900)   The last assassination victim of the 19th century, King Umberto I of Italy, the son of Victor Emmanuel II, had ruled since 1878 and had gained honors in the liberation movement of the 1860s. However, many observers have described his rule as tyrannical, with his treatment of individuals, associates and subjects most unsavory. Umberto filled his cabinet with military officers who swore personal allegiance to him rather than to Italy.

The king survived an assassination attempt in 1897 when a man tried to stab him in his carriage. On July 29, 1900, Umberto was distributing prizes to athletes at Monza when a man stepped up to the carriage and killed him with four revolver shots. The assassin, an avowed anarchist named Gaetano Bresci, had saved his wages as a weaver in Paterson, New Jersey to travel to Italy to commit the murder. Since Italy had no death penalty at the time, Bresci was sentenced to life in prison, where he shortly thereafter committed suicide.

The grief for the murdered monarch may be described as restrained. Even though Bresci's act was murder and the deed of an anarchist, many republicans and members of other establishment political parties clearly regarded it as a necessary and worthy sacrifice.

V

VAIDYA, General Arun (1926–1986) On August 1986, General Arun Vaidya, the retired chief of the Indian army, was shot to death in the city of Pune, an extension of the assassination violence that in 1984 cost the life of Prime Minister Indira Gandhi. The Vaidya killing was laid to Sikh extremists, as was the Gandhi assassination. No one was charged with the general's murder, however.

General Vaidya was among those who supervised the army raid on the Golden Temple in Amritsar in June 1984 that sought to crush a Sikh uprising based there. The main Sikh political demand was for an autonomous Punjab state. In the raid more than 100 troops were killed as were hundreds of militants and pilgrims inside the shrine, the main temple of the Sikh faith. Among those killed were Sant Jarnail Singh Bhindranwale, the extremist leader.

The raid prompted outrage among Sikhs across India, and Sikh cadets shot an Indian army brigadier soon after word of the attack at Amritsar was released. Some four months later Prime Minister Gandhi was also killed in revenge. General Vaidya had retired from the army in January 1986 but had remained a prime target of extremist Sikh assassins. (See GANDHI, INDIRA.)

VALENTINIAN III, Emperor of Rome (419–455) Roman Emperor Valentinian III has not been treated kindly by historians, who have viewed him as a ruler who left the running of government first to his mother, Galla Placidia, and later to the powerful patrician Flavius Aetius, the commander in chief of the army. Either of these two were far more capable than Valentinian himself, but after his mother's death and Aetius's assassination, the emperor was free to err in the first person.

The murder of Aetius essentially doomed Valentinian, yet ironically it was the emperor himself who slew the general. He was goaded to the deed by another powerful Roman, Petronius Maximus, and by the eunuch Heraclius on the grounds that Aetius was growing so powerful (which was true) and that he was seeking to dethrone Valentinian (which was most likely false). In truth the real plotter in the affair was Maximus.

After Valentinian summoned Aetius before him and personally struck him down in September 454, Maximus began planning the death of the emperor. Maximus and Heraclius then induced two bodyguards of the late Aetius, Optila and Thraustila, to avenge their master, and on March 16, 455, they murdered the emperor in the Campus Martius. Neither was punished for the assassination, as much more concern was being spent in these final, venal years of declining Rome to proclaiming a new emperor. Valentinian having no male heir, Maximus laid claim to the purple and won it through bribery, forcing the emperor's widow, Eudoxia, to marry him.

However, Maximus's reign lasted only 11 weeks. In May a Vandal fleet approached Rome, perhaps summoned by Eudoxia, and on May 31 Emperor Maximus sought to flee as the Vandals neared the gates of the city. However, he was captured in flight by enraged Romans and torn limb from limb.

The Vandals then looted the city and carried away thousands in slavery. The Vandals ruler, Gaiseric, also took Eudoxia and two of her daughters back to Africa, marrying one daughter, Eudocia, to his son. Essentially, the assassination of Valentinian III and the mob murder of Maximus marked the end of imperial Rome. Officially, the empire continued another two decades, but power thereafter, while claimed by various emperors and pretenders, actually resided in various barbarians who had enlisted as Roman soldiers.

The assassinations started in legend by Rome's cofounder Romulus, who killed his brother Remus, had finally ended with the Fall of Rome, although an accurate count of the assassinations from that time of the great and near great would represent a truly heroic task. (See AETIUS, FLAVIUS.)

VERWOERD, Hendrik Frensch (1901–1966) Hendrik Frensch Verwoerd was probably the most outspoken advocate of apartheid among the South African leadership. His racial policies provoked demonstrations by blacks and in 1960 led to the bloodbath at Sharpeville, Johannesburg, in which the police opened fire on the mob, killing more than 80 people and wounding more than 250.

Verwoerd was the son of a Dutch missionary; his family settled in South Africa when Verwoerd was three months old. A brilliant scholar, he became a professor of applied psychology at the age of 27 and later of sociology and social work. His views turned more racialist with the years, and in 1937 he became the editor of the racialist daily, the *Transvaaler*. In World War II Verwoerd, firmly committed to the view of the white peoples as the master race, supported Hitler.

Appointed a senator and later elected to the House of Assembly, he authored much of the apartheid legislation. As prime minister Verwoerd pushed apartheid to a level never achieved under the previous regimes of Malan and Strijdom. Under Verwoerd it was impossible for whites and blacks to be born of the same parent, or live, marry, work, or die as one people. Verwoerd's plan was for the eventual ejection of all blacks to so-called 'protective' states. Politically, Verwoerd also led South Africa out of the British Commonwealth.

The real criticism coming from whites and even his own right-wing extremists was the expense of Verwoerd's program; apartheid was actually a drag on a booming South African economy.

Verwoerd ignored such objections as he continued to push his social program. Ironically, it was in a sense the results of his economic policies rather than apartheid itself that led to his eventual assassination. Three weeks after the Sharpeville massacre, Verwoerd spoke at a right-wing meeting in a Johannesburg park, telling the audience, 'We shall not be killed. We shall fight for our existence.'

After he sat down, David Pratt, a local farmer, entered the speaker's stand and whispered to the prime minister, 'Dr. Verwoerd?' Verwoerd turned, and Pratt shot him twice, once in the ear and once in the cheek, before being wrestled down.

Remarkably, Verwoerd survived. Pratt later stated in court, 'I think I was shooting at the epitome of apartheid, rather than at Dr. Verwoerd.' Despite such sentiments, Pratt was declared mentally unfit and committed to a mental institution.

Within two months Verwoerd was back at his desk, undeterred by the attempt on his life and certainly unprepared to alter his polices in the slightest.

The final, and fatal, assault on Verwoerd occurred six years later, by Dimitrio Tsafendas, a parliamentary messenger of mixed racial descent. He was born in Mozambique of a mulatto woman and a Greek-Egyptian father, but had slipped through the apartheid net by convincing the authorities that he was a white European entitled to South African citizenship. It may well be that he convinced himself of the same circumstances because he constantly complained to others that the Verwoerd government was doing too much for 'coloreds' and not enough for whites. If the government restricted programs for nonwhites, he argued, it would be able to pay him more than his $140 monthly salary.

That thought festered in Tsafendas' mind until September 6, 1966. Early that afternoon he strode into the parliamentary chambers and approached Verwoerd, who assumed Tsafendas was a messenger. Tsafendas pulled out a knife and stabbed the prime minister repeatedly in the chest and neck, killing him. However, as in the case of Pratt, Tsafendas was not tried but was instead sent to a mental asylum. Some observers felt that in both instances the South African government did not want a trial because of the resulting glare of world opinion on its practice of apartheid.

VICTORIA, Queen (1819–1901) The long reign of Queen Victoria, from 1837 to 1901, was marked by the rise of industrialism at home and of imperialism abroad. By no means unrelated to those developments were more than a half-dozen attacks on the queen, some clear attempts at assassination and others acts of protest.

While some have described all the attacks as made by disturbed individuals, biographer Jasper Ridley sees them as symptoms of the social unrest during Victoria's reign, especially the early years. The tone for this was set, according to Ridley, by the callous mindset of Victoria's first prime minister, Lord Melbourne. He was 'a Whig of the old school, whose attitude to the great campaigns for the reform of the political and social systems were summed up in a phrase that he used whenever reform was suggested: "Why not leave it alone?" He showed no concern over the sufferings of the poor in the mines, factories and workhouses.'

Melbourne advised Victoria not to read Charles Dickens's *Oliver Twist*, since it dealt with paupers, criminal types and other subjects with which, he said, the queen should not be troubled.

The following are the six most serious attacks made on the queen:

June 10, 1840; Constitution Hill, Westminster. Edward Oxford, a potboy, fired two pistols at Victoria's carriage. Charged with shooting at Her Majesty, he was acquitted on grounds of insanity and confined in a mental institution.

May 30, 1842; Constitution Hill, Westminister. John Francis, a cabinetmaker, fired a pistol at the queen's carriage. He was sentenced to death for high treason, but the sentence was later reduced to transportation for life.

July 3, 1842; St. James's Park. John William Bean, 18, pointed a loaded pistol at Her Majesty's carriage. He was committed to Newgate Gaol for the assault.

May 19, 1849; Constitution Hill, Westminster. William Hamilton, an Irishman, fired a blank charge at the queen's carriage. He was sentenced to transportation for seven years.

May 27, 1850; Cambridge House, Piccadilly. Robert Pate, a former army officer, struck Victoria on the forehead with a stock. He made a defense of insanity to the charge of assaulting Her Majesty, but was convicted and sentenced to transportation for seven years.

March 2, 1882; Windsor Railway Station. Roderick McLean fired a revolver at Her Majesty's carriage. Found innocent on grounds of insanity, he was detained during Her Majesty's pleasure in a mental institution.

Further reading: *The Lives of the Kings and Queens of England*, edited by Antonia Fraser.

VICTORIA (ENA), Queen of Spain See ALFONSO XIII, KING OF SPAIN.

VIERA, Jose Rodolfo See HAMMER, MICHAEL.

VILLA, Pancho (1878–1923) One of the most sentimental and one of the most savage figures of the Mexican Revolution and civil wars of 1910–1920, Pancho Villa was a dedicated revolutionary and a brutal bandit.

Villa, born Doroteo Arango in 1878, became early in life a fugitive from the law, when, already orphaned, he killed one of the owners of an estate where he worked in revenge for the sexual assault on his sister. On the run, Villa became the head of a group of cattle thieves. But it could not be said that Villa was devoid of social consciousness, and by 1909 he was a devoted follower of the great liberal revolutionary Francisco Madero in the effort to drive from power the longtime dictator Porfirio Diaz.

By that time Villa had become a hero of the poor of northern Mexico, and he was able to furnish Madero with an entire division of trained soldiers under his personal command. After Madero succeeded in driving Diaz out of the country, Villa remained in the irregular army and was ready to do battle against insurrectionists trying to bring down Madero. In 1912 General Victoriano Huerta, a top Madero general, declared Villa a traitor and ordered his execution. However, Madero ordered a stay of execution, which arrived as Villa stood before a firing squad. It later appeared that Huerta was himself plotting against Madero and was seeking to eliminate one of the president's most loyal generals. Villa escaped prison and fled to the United States, returning after Madero was assassinated in 1913 in Huerta's coup.

He was soon at war with Huerta, seeking, along with Emiliano Zapata and the more moderate Venustiano Carranza, to restore the revolution. Villa was a terror with his foes, hanging or shooting all enemy captives. However, this was common behavior by all sides throughout Mexico's bloody decade. It was just that Villa could be more inventive in his methods. Once he permitted Rodolfo Fierro, his most ardent bloodletter, to be sole executioner of 300 prisoners, in what became known as The Carnival of the Bullets. The 300 were herded into a cattle pen in which Fierro and his orderly waited. At the far end was an adobe wall, six feet high. The prisoners were released 10 at a time and any who could reach and climb the wall could go free. Fierro fired while his orderly reloaded. 'Come on, boys,' Fierro called. 'I'm only going to shoot, and I'm a bad shot.' It was a lie. Fierro killed 299, and only one made it over the wall. The ghastly chore took two hours.

Villa himself was capable of ordering a man executed and then raping his widow. Says historian Samuel H. Mayo: 'He could be warm and friendly at one moment and ferocious the next. He could invite you to dinner and then order your execution – rescind the order and offer you coffee.'

Morally, Villa was hardly a Zapata, who can be considered the conscience and nobility of the Mexican Revolution, but Villa always chose the side of the poor Mexicans in his struggles. Unfortunately, Villa proved to be a better guerrilla fighter than a field general. After the defeat of the Huerta counterrevolution, Zapata and Villa became disenchanted with the conservatism of Carranza, who as head of the largest armies became provisional president. However, Carranza and his ally, Alvaro Obregon, after a number of battles, defeated and isolated Villa in the north and Zapata in the south. By 1916 Villa was no longer really a major player in the civil war. Yet Villa was still in the hearts of most Mexican people and was to endear himself even more in the future.

Frustrated because the United States had granted de facto recognition of the Carranza government and badly in need of supplies, Villa crossed the U.S. border to Columbus, New Mexico, and shot up the town, leaving nine civilians and eight soldiers dead. President Woodrow Wilson ordered pursuit of the guerrillas back into Mexico by Brigadier General John 'Black Jack' Pershing with 6,000 men. Villa led his pursuers on a 300-mile chase through the mountains, where he was supreme.

While Carranza may have hated Villa he could not risk the wrath of the Mexican people, and so he condemned the presence of foreign troops on Mexican soil. Finally, in February 1917 the United States ordered the frustrated Pershing home. The punitive invasion had cost $130 million, caused enormous loss of prestige and enmity from almost all Mexicans. The Villa legend grew, celebrated in the 'Ballad to Pancho Villa,' in which the Americans were derided for ending up 'with their faces full of shame.'

Throughout 1917 and 1918 Villa recouped much of his prestige and power, but it was limited to northern Mexico. He continued his guerrilla campaign against Carranza, but with Carranza's overthrow and assassination in 1920 Villa tired of warfare, and after 10 years of violence, he reached an agreement with provisional president De La Huerta that he and his men would lay down their arms. In exchange Villa's soldiers received some land and a year's pay. Villa was given a 25,000-acre rancho at Canutillo, Durango, and was allowed to maintain a 50-man body-guard from the ranks of his dorados. The Villa rancho stood as a monument to idealized reform. Villa built a hospital, chapel, school and telegraph office in the town. He was pacified, but Mexico was not.

Obregon, who had masterminded the elimination of Carranza, became the new constitutional president and established a number of reforms, perhaps not as much as Zapata (assassinated in 1919) and Villa would have wished, but certainly of considerable scope. Obregon was nevertheless threatened by several attempted coups by revolutionary generals. What if Villa would harken to their call and return to the field? The elections of 1924 would have been threatened.

There was no evidence that Villa was planning a comeback when on July 20, 1923, a group of gunmen under Mexican Congressman Jesus Salas Barrazas intercepted Villa's massive 1919 Dodge touring car (given him by the government), as it headed for town for supplies. In the Dodge were Villa and four heavily armed aides and bodyguards with two others riding on the running boards. In the deadly ambush all but one of his men were shot to pieces, the other escaping although wounded.

Barrazas was convicted for the Villa assassination and sentenced to 20 years in prison. He served only a few months and was freed by President Obregon, the grounds being that he was in mortal danger in prison. All the other participants in the raid save one died violent deaths. One in fact, was murdered in an ambush at the exact spot where Villa had been assassinated. (See also CARRANZA, VENUSTIANO; OBREGON, ALVARO; ZAPATA, EMILIANO.)

Further reading: *The Eagle and the Serpent*, by Martin Luis Guzman; *Heroic Mexico*, by William Weber Johnson; *A History of Mexico*, by Samuel H. Mayo.

VITELLIUS, Emperor of Rome (15–69) Emperor Vitellius was one of the four occupants of the Roman throne in A.D. 69. Galba, the first, was assassinated; Otho, the second, committed suicide to avoid assassination by the conquering legions of Vitellius; Vitellius, the third, did not break the cycle of violence when his end came.

Otho had come to the throne in January with the support of the Praetorians who assassinated Galba, the ruler they were sworn to protect. As Otho was given the throne by the docile and fearful Senate, the Roman legions in Germany were proclaiming Vitellius as emperor, and meanwhile the armies in Egypt were proclaiming their commander, Titus Flavius Vespasianus, as the logical successor to Galba. Germany being nearer than Egypt, Vitellius arrived first to challenge Otho, and the former's legions had no trouble defeating the northern garrisons and the Praetorians protecting Otho.

Instead of worrying about Vespasianus, Vitellius decided it was time to dine. Says Will Durant in *The Story of Civilization III – Caesar and Christ* of Vitellius: 'He was a gourmand who thought of the Principate chiefly as a feast, and made a banquet of every meal. He governed in the intervals; and as they grew shorter he left state affairs to his freedman Asiaticus, who in four months became one of the richest men in Rome.'

Even when word reached the epicurean ruler that Vespasianus's general, Antonius, had arrived in Italy to do battle, the emperor left the task of resistance to subordinates. In October Antonius won a bloody battle at Cremona and then moved slowly on Rome. Finally arriving at the capital, Antonius met stiff resistance from the remainder of Vitellius's legions, while the emperor took refuge in the palace. According to Tacitus's *Histories*, the Romans 'flocked in crowds to behold the conflict, as if a scene of carnage were no more than a public spectacle exhibited for their amusement.'

During the fighting some of the populace plundered homes and shops, and prostitutes did a land-office business. Once the tide turned decisively to Antonius, the mob joined in the bloodletting by turning on Vitellius's supporters. Antonius's men killed without quarter, except in the case of the emperor himself. He was flushed out of his hiding place and led through the streets of the city with his head in a noose. The mob was permitted to pelt him with dung and he was then tortured at his captors' leisure before being slain. The corpse was dragged through the streets on a hook and finally heaved into the Tiber.

The Senate hurriedly confirmed the new conqueror and crowned him as Vespasian. Remarkably, after the bloodletting of that year, Vespasian proved to be a most effective and popular ruler during his 10-year reign. He died in bed of natural causes, only the second of Rome's first nine emperors to do so, going back to the honored Augustus, the first of the line. (See GALBA, EMPEROR OF ROME.)

W

WALLACE, George Corley (1919–) – Attempted Assassination On the humid and warm Monday afternoon of May 15, 1972, Alabama Governor George Wallace, running for the Democratic presidential nomination, addressed an open-air rally at a shopping center in Laurel, Maryland. Wallace was very conscious of assassination attempts against him. Earlier he had been severely heckled in Wheaton, Maryland, and had later expressed concerns about his personal safety. As a precaution, Wallace generally spoke from behind a bulletproof podium and wore a bulletproof vest. Because of the weather, Wallace skipped the vest for this speech.

The address went off quite well, with a noticeable absence of heckling and the governor left the podium to move through the crowd to shake hands. A young blond crew-cut man dressed in red, white and blue combinations of shirt, tie and jacket called out several times: 'Hey, George, over here.' Wallace approached the general area of the enthusiastic young man, and as he did the youth pulled a gun and fired several shots at the candidate, hitting him four times. As Wallace's guards descended on the gunman, he emptied his weapon wounding three other persons, all of whom survived. Wallace himself remained paralyzed afterward because of a bullet that lodged near the spinal column. Not only would Wallace never walk again or control his bowels, but he would not continue in the presidential campaign, despite impressive primary wins in Michigan and Maryland (the latter coming after the shooting).

The would-be assassin was identified – how soon was to be a matter of some interest later – as Arthur Herman

Bremer, a 21-year-old youth who had worked as a janitor's assistant and a busboy in Milwaukee, Wisconsin. In November 1971 Bremer had been charged there with carrying a concealed weapon, but the offense was reduced to one of disorderly conduct and the gun was confiscated. Undeterred, Bremer went out and bought two other guns.

On March 1, 1972, Bremer started stalking the Wallace campaign trail. In a short time he ran up bills, which he paid, totaling $5,000, although his total earnings for 1971–72 amounted to only $1,611. At times he departed from the Wallace chase. On April 4 he journeyed to Canada in pursuit of Richard Nixon, then on a state visit. He stayed at the expensive Lord Elgin in Ottawa. However, Bremer was frustrated in his efforts to get near Nixon, mainly because of anti-Nixon protesters demonstrating wherever Nixon went.

Bremer went back to stalking Wallace. Where all the money came to finance his movements remained a mystery, since it was readily established that he had gotten no money from his parents.

As is frequently customary in American political assassin cases, Bremer was later reported initially to be a 'loner.' This was not accurate. He had several friends in Milwaukee, including one Dennis Cassini, a man officials never got to question. He was found dead of a heroin overdose, his body found tucked in the locked trunk of his own automobile.

Although Cassini became known to the FBI, it has been alleged that there was no indication that the agency was ever ordered to make any inquiry in the Cassini death. Other oddities in Bremer's activities surfaced. He was reported to have been seen in Ludington, Michigan in the company of a man described as having a 'New Joisey brogue.' Roger Gordon, a former member of the Secret Army Organization (SAO), a right-wing intelligence organization, said the man was Anthony Ulasewicz, a man who would later win fame as a White House operative in the Watergate scandal. Gordon later left the country.

There were reports that White House aide Charles

Colson ordered E. Howard Hunt (two more Watergate figures) to break into Bremer's apartment and plant Black Panther Party and Angela Davis literature. More explosive than that was the charge that the order was given within one hour of the attempt to kill Wallace. In later testimony before the Senate committee investigating Watergate, Hunt declared that Colson had hinted that Hunt might want to 'review the contents of Bremer's apartment.' It was reported that Colson was acting under direct orders from Nixon, but Colson denied making any such suggestion.

Commenting on these allegations, Wallace later told Barbara Walters in an interview: 'So I just wondered, if that were the case, how did anyone know where he lived within an hour after I was shot?'

Wallace's question was never answered, but of perhaps even more importance was the fact that the assassination try eliminated Wallace from the 1972 race, in which he was certain to run as a third-party candidate. A week before the election, voters were asked how they would have voted had Wallace been on the ballot. The results were Nixon 44%; McGovern 41%; Wallace 15%. Such a result, because of how the voting would most likely break down, would have very likely thrown the election into the House of Representatives, where Wallace's influence would have been very pronounced. With Wallace out of the running, virtually all his supporters went to President Nixon.

Afterwards Arthur Bremer never explained his motives in shooting Wallace. He was sentenced to 63 years, despite his legal defense that held that he was unbalanced. In prison he was described as a loner. In 1979 Warden George Collins of the Maryland State Penitentiary said, 'Bremer does not give interviews. In fact, he won't even see his mother. She came in all the way from Milwaukee at Christmas, and he talked to her for about five minutes and went on back down inside. He just doesn't want to be bothered.'

As for archsegregationist Wallace, he later won election

again as governor of Alabama. Because of his altered
political stance on race, he won the overwhelming support
of Alabama blacks, who provided him with his margin of
victory.

Further reading: *American Assassins*, by James W.
Clarke; *Assassination in America*, by James McKinley.

**WALLENSTEIN, Albrecht Eusebius Wenzel von (1583–
1634)** The greatest military figure of the Thirty Years'
War, Albrecht von Wallenstein, the owner of vast estates
in Bohemia, raised an army for Emperor Ferdinand II in
1625 and became the chief imperial general in the conflict
with Protestant forces both within and without Germany.
Wallenstein won a great number of victories for the
Catholic cause, all aimed at making Ferdinand, a Hapsburg, the most important ruler in Europe. Despite this,
Wallenstein earned the enmity of numerous Catholic
German princes who were jealous of his power and
suspicious of his ambitions and he was dismissed in 1630.
However, because of the deteriorating political and military situation Ferdinand was forced to recall him to duty
in 1632 and grant him virtually unlimited powers to
negotiate and sign treaties.

Wallenstein conducted secret peace negotiations with
Protestant leaders and even with Cardinal Richelieu, who
had brought Catholic France in on the side of the anti-
Hapsburgs. Ferdinand undoubtedly learned that Bohemian exiles were plotting to raise Wallenstein to the
Bohemian throne. By the end of 1633 Ferdinand and his
council reached a decision to remove Wallenstein permanently. Stories were spread that Wallenstein's army was
about to declare him king of Bohemia and Louis XIII
Holy Roman Emperor. On February 18 imperial orders
were issued relieving Wallenstein of command. Wallenstein fled with 1,000 of his loyal troops, realizing the stage
had been set for his assassination.

Even within his forces it was understood that his
assassin would receive limitless beneficence from the
emperor. On February 25 a handful of Wallenstein's

soldiers burst into his quarters, and, finding him unarmed and without guards, they ran him through with their swords. 'Presently,' a contemporary account reads, 'they drew him out by the heels, his head knocking on every stair.' The murderers hurried to Vienna, where a grateful emperor, 'having spent days and nights in fear and prayer, thanked God for His cooperation.' The assassins received promotions, lands and money.

Some authorities say that had not Ferdinand mistrusted his most successful general, he might well have won the war. As it was, the conflict limped on another 14 indecisive if bloody years until the Peace of Westphalia, leaving the Holy Roman Empire and Hapsburg power in a state of permanent decline.

Further reading: *The Story of Civilization VII – The Age of Reason Begins*, by Will and Ariel Durant.

WEBBER, John D. See MEIN, JOHN GORDON.

WELCH, Richard S. (1929–1975) The 1975 assassination of Richard S. Welch, the chief of the American CIA station in Greece, made him the 32nd CIA officer known to have died in the line of duty since 1947. What made the 46-year-old Welch's murder a cause celebre was the way his identity was alleged to have been revealed to his assassins, who were never caught.

Tweedy, erudite and witty, Welch had risen high in the CIA hierarchy and was considered to be destined to reach one of the agency's top posts. 'In fact,' *Newsweek* reported, 'Welch had risen to an executive level at which – by the unwritten rules of the intelligence game – he should have been safe from the assassins who killed him. . . .'

What may be regarded as the official CIA version of the assassination was offered by Dr. Ray S. Cline, former deputy director of the CIA, in a 1981 book, *The CIA Under Reagan, Bush & Casey*:

Philip Agee, a CIA employee who resigned and then went to Cuba, instigated some of the most devastating assaults. He allegedly experienced a political conversion to Communism, definitely worked closely with Soviet and Cuban intelligence agents, and, in 1974, published a hostile book, *Inside the Company: CIA Diary*, about covert political operations in Latin America. He helped to organize *Counterspy* and *Covert Action Information Bulletin*, two publications dedicated to exposing the names and addresses of CIA undercover officers stationed abroad. Two days before Christmas in 1975, Welch was killed on his own doorstep after being identified by *Counterspy* and later by a local Athenian newspaper.

It should be noted, however, that CIA activities in Greece were hardly as secret as they might have been. Welch had been laboring in Athens under what the media referred to as 'light cover.' The residence of the CIA station chief was well known in the Greek capital, and bus tours even pointed it out. Under those circumstances the Welch murder to some observers bore a certain flavor of negligence.

Yet it may be said that, as *Washington Post* reporter Bob Woodward put it, 'Welch, dead, rendered a final service to his CIA,' because the killing produced a surge of public sympathy and support for the agency in the United States and Welch became a martyr. His body was returned to the United States with live television coverage, and he was given a funeral with full military honors, his caisson the same one that had borne the body of assassinated President John F. Kennedy.

In 1977, much to the distress and anger of old CIA hands, the U.S. Justice Department informed Agee, who had been expelled from Great Britain for endangering national security and public order and then barred from residence in the Netherlands and France, that he was not involved in any crime for which he could be prosecuted in the United States.

WILLIAM RUFUS, King of England (c. 1056–1100) The

second and favorite son of William the Conquerer, William Rufus was hardly held in such high esteem by others in his realm. Many Norman barons wanted both England and Normandy to remain under one ruler. William the Conquerer had left Normandy to his eldest son, the incompetent Robert Curthose, and these barons conspired to back him in a revolt. William Rufus triumphed in the ensuing conflict, mainly by gaining the support of the native English by promising to cut taxes and institute a fairer regime. Typically, the victorious Rufus did not keep that pledge.

In 1095 the Norman barons staged a second revolt. Once more Rufus triumphed, and he punished the ringleaders with such brutality that all further resistance to his reign ended. By 1096 William Rufus had extended his control in Normandy, reducing his brother to a subordinate role. Rufus also solidified his hold on Scotland and over the English church by driving out Anselm, the archbishop of Canterbury.

On August 2, 1100, William Rufus was eliminated by an arrow in the back. The act was carried out by a knight, Walter Tirel, while the tyrant king was hunting in the New Forest in Hampshire. Tirel insisted it had been an accident, and no one, highborn or peasant, seemed to belabor Tirel for his poor marksmanship or to be eager to label the act for what it most likely was, an assassination. It is now considered likely that Tirel was acting under the orders of the king's younger brother, Henry, who promptly seized the throne as Henry I.

WILLIAM THE SILENT (1533–1584) Perhaps no man so exemplified the Protestant cause – especially in the view of the Catholic leaders of church and state – than William the Silent of the Netherlands, who as William of Orange opposed the oppressive outside rule of Spain's Philip II in the latter 16th century. As the prince of the Netherlands, he was accused of heresy by the Spanish Inquisition, and his assassination was long plotted by Philip and his representatives in the Netherlands, first the duke of Alva and then the duke of Parma.

Assassination attempts abounded, especially after William announced the Act of Abjuration, which renounced any allegiance to the king of Spain. In the landmark document, the Dutch under William declared that a ruler who destroys the liberty of his subjects and treats them as slaves was not legitimate and could lawfully be deposed.

A price of 25,000 crowns was offered for anyone who assassinated William, and in March 1582 one Jean Jaureguy armed himself with a pistol, prayed for God's assistance (in exchange for a portion of the reward), made his way to Antwerp and shot William in the head. William's aides killed the assassin, and William hovered near death for weeks. Under the care of his devoted wife, Charlotte, who herself would die of exhaustion and fever during the ordeal, William slowly recovered.

In July of the same year, two conspirators worked out a plot to poison both Orange and his ally the duke of Anjou. The plot was uncovered in time and the pair arrested. One killed himself in his cell, while the other was convicted and drawn and quartered.

In March 1583 an ambush attempt on William's life failed, and, feeling unsafe in Antwerp, he shifted his headquarters to Delft. Assassins followed. In April 1584 one Hans Hanszoom of Flushing tried to kill Orange with explosives, but failed and was executed. Then a 20-year-old religious zealot, Balthasar Gerard of Burgundy, appeared before Parma and offered to kill William, asking for a small sum on account. Palma doubted the youth's capability and declined the advance, but he did promise Gerard the full reward if he succeeded. Gerard went to William's court in Delft in the guise of an impoverished Calvinist. William gave him alms of 12 crowns, and Gerard then hid in a room instead of leaving. When William entered that chamber, Gerard shot him three times. William cried, 'My God, have pity on my soul . . . Have pity on this poor people.' He died in a matter of minutes.

The Protestants of the nation were stunned. Gerard, expressing great joy at his deed, was put to death with the extreme torture reserved for regicides. A grateful Parma saw to it that the full reward was paid to the assassin's parents, and Dutch Catholics rejoiced in what they described as God's vengeance for the deaths of priests and the desecration of churches.

They secured the executed man's head and shipped it off to Cologne as a precious relic. For 50 years, even after Claudio Aquaviva, the general of the Society of Jesus, in 1610 condemned the teachings of the Jesuit scholar Juan de Mariana on tyrannicide, the Dutch Catholics sought to have Gerard declared a saint. (See HENRY IV [HENRY OF NAVARRE], KING OF FRANCE.)

WILSON, Sir Henry (1854–1922) Few Englishmen achieved the level of hatred from the Irish Republican Army as much as Field Marshal Sir Henry Wilson, former chief of the Imperial General Staff. To IRA activists such as Michael Collins, Wilson epitomized their charges of cruelty and racism by the English against Irish Catholics battling for their freedom. After retiring from the army in February 1922, Wilson stood for the House of Commons from Ulster and was elected in a tide of Protestant votes. He also visited Belfast as an adviser to the Northern Ireland government on methods of suppressing bombings and other acts of terrorists.

On June 22, 1922, Wilson, wearing uniform and sword, unveiled a memorial honoring railway workers killed during World War I. He returned to his home at 36 Eaton Place about 2:30 P.M. and was about to unlock his front door when a revolver shot fired at short range crashed into the paneled door. A second shot struck Wilson as he tried to draw his sword. At least six more shots were fired, several hitting Wilson, who collapsed on his doorstep. Lady Wilson rushed to the door and aided her husband inside, where he died minutes later.

Meanwhile the two assassins, 25-year-old Reginald Dunn and fellow Irishman 24-year-old Joseph O'Sullivan, fled down Eaton Place, firing their revolvers and downing two police officers and a civilian chasing them. The pair were finally captured and only spirited defense by police prevented their being lynched by a hostile mob.

As a mark of respect for Sir Henry, the House of Commons adjourned upon hearing of the murder. In the political aftermath, Lloyd George's government came under strong criticism for a recent decision to withdraw police protection from virtually all persons involved in the 'Irish troubles.'

Dunn and O'Sullivan were brought to trial less than a month after the assassination. Although neither implicated the IRA in their murder plot, they were linked by authorities to Michael Collins. Dunn was denied the opportunity to make a statement to the jury since the court held it was merely a 'political manifesto' offering a 'justification of the right to kill.' After a guilty verdict, Dunn was cut off once more when he tried to make a speech. However, the defendant did get in the last word when the judge pronounced the customary 'And may the Lord have mercy on your soul.' Dunn cried out, 'He will, my Lord.'

Dunn and O'Sullivan were hanged on August 10, 1922.

Y

YANG CHIEN See SUI WEN TI, EMPEROR OF CHINA.

Z

ZAHRA, Colonel Ali Kannas   See HAMIDI, IBRAHIM AL-.

ZAPATA, Emiliano (1879–1919)   A Mexican revolutionary of Native American birth, Emiliano Zapata is considered by many as the noblest hero of the country's revolutionary and civil wars that raged from 1910 to 1920. As a youth, his radical spirit was molded by comparing the dirt-floor hovel in which he lived while working as a stable hand on a large hacienda to the clean, tiled stables provided for the horses in his charge.

In 1897 he became a leader in a peasants' protest against the hacienda that had appropriated their land. Arrested and then released, Zapata continued his activities and was finally drafted into the army. That tour of duty did not cool his revolutionary ardor, and by 1909 he was president of the board of defense for his village and soon led peasants on campaigns that seized hacienda lands and restored them to the people.

Meanwhile Francisco Madero had launched a revolution against the reactionary national government of Porfirio Diaz, and Zapata eagerly joined that campaign, not, however, abandoning his own rebellion. He soon came to regard Madero's reform programs as far too moderate. Still, Zapata played a key role in defeating the counterrevolution under General Victoriano Huerta. His forces, known as the Liberation Army, numbered 25,000, and after Huerta's flight, Zapata notified the more moderate revolutionaries under Venustiano Carranza and Alvaro Obregon that he would continue his own revolutionary struggle. In that he was supported by another revolutionary, the often savage Pancho Villa. Zapata's forces were responsible for a number of brutal excesses, but these often paled compared to those of almost all other armies on both sides. When in 1914 the Zapatistas occupied Mexico City, his men did not commit the bloody actions that had turned the populace against all the other forces of the period. Historian Ronald Atkin described their behavior: 'But the Army of the South made no attempt to loot stores or homes, even though their meager rations were soon exhausted. Instead they knocked on doors, asking humbly for a little food, or approached a passerby to beg a peso.'

Efforts by the Carranza forces to buy off Zapata proved without avail, and Zapata was destined to die poor. However, in the ensuing struggles, Carranza and the independent Obregon forces gained the military advantage, weakening Villa especially. Zapata also was weakened but still remained master of his own territory. Finally, Carranza became constitutional president in 1917 and determined to wipe out all the rebels. He sent General Gonzalez to Morelos to destroy Zapata. Zapata met the challenge on the battlefield, and as government troops burned villages and crops and hanged peasants, Zapata warred on the haciendas, putting great numbers to the torch. The result was a genuine Mexican standoff, Gonzalez controlling the cities but Zapata the king of the hills.

Finding himself unable to overcome Zapata's masterful guerrilla tactics, Gonzalez turned to duplicity and sent Colonel Jesus Guajardo to feign interest in joining Zapata. Zapata could not help but be interested since it would mean the addition of 800 soldiers and much-needed munitions. Guajardo demonstrated his sincerity to Zapata by actually seizing a town occupied by government troops and killing many of them in a fake mutiny. Among the federals Guajardo captured were 50 former Zapatistas who had previously gone over to the government and provided much assistance against Zapata. In a further demonstration of his good faith, Guajardo had these expendable 50 executed on the spot.

That evening Zapata, with a heavy guard, met Guajardo for the first time. Guajardo presented Zapata with a handsome sorrel stallion, and Zapata agreed that they would meet the following day at the Chinameca hacienda to plan their joint actions. On April 10, 1919, Zapata arrived with 150 men, but entered the hacienda with only 10 of them. The rest remained outside to guard the hacienda, since it was believed federal forces might be in the area.

Inside the hacienda Guajardo's men assembled in 'present arms' formation to honor Zapata. The bugle sounded three times, at the end of which the massive formation turned their guns on Zapata, who fell from the sorrel riddled with bullets. His 10 companions were all killed or wounded, and his soldiers outside had no choice but to flee.

General Gonzalez, who had masterminded the ambush, notified President Carranza of its success the same day. The president replied: 'I received with satisfaction your report telling of the death of Emiliano Zapata as a result of the plan executed so well by Colonel Jesus M. Guajardo. . . . Because of Colonel Guajardo's conduct I have dictated . . . a promotion in grade for Colonel Guajardo and his officers.'

While it can be said that the movement for immediate land reform died with Zapata, his death gave birth to a legend and slogan that has long survived him – *Tierra y libertad*, or 'Land and Liberty.' Zapata's name is now inscribed in gold in the Mexican Chamber of Deputies.

The killings did not stop with Zapata. In May 1920 Carranza was assassinated by followers of Obregon, who then came to power. Caught in the changing tides of power, General Gonzalez was imprisoned and Colonel Guajardo went before a firing squad, not for the assassination of Zapata but allegedly for seeking to free Gonzalez. (See also CARRANZA, VENUSTIANO; OBREGON, ALVARO; VILLA, PANCHO.)

Further reading: *Zapata*, by Roger Parkinson; *Zapata and the Mexican Revolution*, by John Womack; *Heroic*

Mexico, by William Weber Johnson.

ZENTENO ANAYA, Joaquin (1923–1976) General Joaquin Zenteno Anaya, the Bolivian ambassador to France, was gunned down by terrorists on a Paris street on May 11, 1976. Following the assassination, a group identifying itself as the International 'Che' Guevara Brigade issued a telephone communique to Agence France-Presse, the French news service, declaring the murder was in retaliation for the 1967 slaying of Ernesto 'Che' Guevara. Zenteno had commanded the controversial expedition that killed the Latin American revolutionary in Bolivia.

The story made a neat little package, but other possible motives for the Zenteno killing came to the surface. Zenteno was alleged to have been deeply involved in attempts to prevent the French government from seeking the extradition from Bolivia of German war criminal Klaus Barbie.

In Buenos Aires six days after the killing, General Luis Reque Teran, who had commanded the army division that tracked down Guevara's guerrilla band, charged that the killing of Zenteno had been ordered by rightist Bolivian President Hugo Banzer Suarez. General Reque had previously charged that the Guevara execution had actually been ordered by General Alfredo Ovando Candia, who later became president of Bolivia.

Bolivia's current army commander, General Raul Alvarez, denounced Reque for revealing 'military secrets,' and stated that he would be dismissed from the army for treason and that his revelations had led to Zenteno's assassination – a peculiar statement since Zenteno's position had been well publicized at the time of Guevara's slaying.

Reque countered that in addition to the Zenteno murder, Banzer and Alvarez were guilty of 'genocide' in the slaying of hundreds of political prisoners and Bolivian peasants.

President Banzer warned the Bolivian press that he would impose sanctions on the media after they published accounts of the charges made by Reque. On May 22 radio stations and newspapers went on strike across the country in protest to Banzer's threat, which he then withdrew.

Who had really ordered Ambassador Zenteno's assassination was left unclear. (See TORRES, JUAN JOSE.)

ZIAUR RAHMAN, General (1936–1981) General Ziaur Rahman, who became president of Bangladesh after the assassination of the country's first chief executive, Sheik Mujibur Rahman, in 1975, was himself assassinated on May 30, 1981. President Ziaur, two aides, and six bodyguards were all slain after they had gone to sleep in a guest house in Chittagong. The assassination represented an unsuccessful coup attempt led by Major General Manzur Ahmed, whose power base was in the city of Chittagong.

Hours after the assassination Manzur went on radio to announce the firing of the army chief of staff and eight other generals. However, much of the army remained loyal to Ziaur's memory as well as to 75-year-old Vice President Abdus Sattar in the capital city of Dacca. When after two days of bloody fighting – 50 police officers in Chittagong alone were killed – it became apparent the rebels were not gaining strength, General Manzur and some of his supporters fled the city. On June 1 Manzur and two other high-ranking generals were captured by government soldiers, and it was announced the following day that after their arrests the trio had been killed by enraged guards.

Ziaur was buried on a plot before the parliament building in Dacca. Although he ran a stern, even brutal regime, Ziaur was credited with giving poverty-stricken Bangladesh some elements of stability. By the late 1980s most Bangladeshis were giving the late president positive ratings. However, his widow, Khaleda, who took over the reins of her husband's political organization, had not been able to build a strong government. The same could be said of Sheik Hasina Wazed – the daughter of Bangladesh's first leader, Mujibur – who assumed leadership of her father's Awami League. Always in the background in

Bangladesh was the threat of yet another military coup, since in the first 19 years of Bangladesh's history no constitutional head of government had been able to complete a presidential term. (See MUJIBUR RAHMAN, SHEIK.)

APPENDIX

The following index of assassinations and attempted assassinations by country contains a number of duplications since it reflects both the nationality of the victim and the place of assassination. For instance, Elizabeth, Empress of Austria, is listed of course under Austria but also under Switzerland, where she was fatally attacked.

Michael III, Byzantine
  Emperor
Nicephorus II Phocas,
  Byzantine Emperor
Theoctistus (see MICHAEL III,
  BYZANTINE EMPEROR)

CANADA
Cross, James R. (see
  LAPORTE, PIERRE)
Laporte, Pierre

CEYLON
Bandaranaike, Solomon West
  Ridgway Dias

CHAD
Tombalbaye, Ngarta

CHILE
Allende Gossens, Salvador
Letelier, Orlando
Schneider, General Rene

CHINA
Lin Piao
Sui Wen Ti, Emperor of
  China
Sui Yank Ti, Emperor of
  China
Yang Chien (see SUI WEN TI,
  EMPEROR OF CHINA)

COMORO ISLANDS
Abdallah Abderemane,
  Ahmed
Soilih, Ali

CONGO (Zaire)
Biayenda, Emile Cardinal
  (see NGOUABI, MARIEN)
Lumumba, Patrice
Ngouabi, Marien

CUBA
Castro, Fidel
Guevara, Ernesto 'Che'

DOMINICAN REPUBLIC
Caceres, Ramon (see
  HEUREAUX, ULISES)
De Galindez, Jesus
Heureaux, Ulises
Trujillo Molina, Rafael
  Leonidas

ECUADOR
Garcia Moreno, Gabriel

EGYPT
Atrakchi, Albert
Arsinoe III, Queen of Egypt
Maher Pasha, Ahmed
Nokrashy Pasha, Mahmoud
  Fahmy
Pompey the Great
Ptolemy XIV, King of Egypt
Sadat, Anwar el-Tell, Wasfi

EL SALVADOR
Aguirre Salinas, Osmin
Hammer, Michael
Pearlman, Mark David (see
  HAMMER, MICHAEL)
Romero, Archbishop Oscar
Viera, Jose Rodolfo

FRANCE
Alexander I, King of
  Yugoslavia
Ben Barka, Mehdi
Carnot, Sadi
Coligny, Admiral Gaspard de
Darlan, Jean
De Gaulle, Charles
Guise, Henry, Duke of
  Henry III, King of France

GREECE
Alcibiades
Ephialtes
George I, King of Greece
Lambrakis, Gregory
Welch, Richard S.

GUATEMALA
Castillo Armas, Carlos
Fuentes Mohr, Alberto
Mein, John Gordon
Munro, Ernest A. (see MEIN, JOHN GORDON)
Spreti, Count Karl von
Webber, John D. (see MEIN, JOHN GORDON)

HUNGARIA
Tisza, Count Stephen

INDIA
Dass, Arjun
Gandhi, Indira
Gandhi, Mohandas Karamchand (Mahatma)
Kumar, Major General B. N.
Longowal, Harchand Singh
Maken, Lalit (see DASS, ARJUN)
Vaidya, General Arun

IRAQ
Faisal II, King of Iraq

IRELAND
Barnhill, John
Cavendish, Lord Frederick Charles
Collins, Michael
Costello, Seamus
Doyle, William
Ewart-Biggs, Christopher
Fox, William

Mountbatten, Louis, Earl of Burma
O'Higgins, Kevin

ITALY
Alfonso of Aragon
Borgia, Juan
Dalla Chiesa, General Alberto (see LA TORRE, PIO)
Gregory V, Pope (see OTTO III, HOLY ROMAN EMPEROR)
Humbert I, King (see UMBERTO I, KING OF ITALY)
John Paul I, Pope
John Paul II, Pope
La Torre, Pio
Leo X, Pope
Matteotti, Giacomo
Medici, Alessandro de'
Medici, Ippolito de' (see MEDICI, ALESSANDRO DE')
Medici, Lorenzino de' (see MEDICI, ALESSANDRO DE')
Medici, Lorenzo de'
Moro, Aldo
Mussolini, Benito
Otto III, Holy Roman Emperor
Sylvester II, Pope (see OTTO III, HOLY ROMAN EMPEROR)
Tresca, Carlo
Umberto I, King of Italy

JAPAN
Inukai Tsuyoshi
Ito Hirobumi, Prince of Japan
Okubo Toshimichi

JORDAN
Adbdullah Ibn Hussein

TUNISIA
Hached, Farhat

TURKESTAN
Alp Arslan, Seljuq Sultan of Persia
Bahram VI Chubin, King of Persia

TURKEY
Abdul-Aziz, Ottoman Sultan
Hussein Avni Pasha (see ABDUL-AZIZ, OTTOMAN SULTAN; MIDHAT PASA)
Midhat Pasa
Sokolli, Mohammed
Talat Pasha, Mehmed

UGANDA
Luwum, Janani

UNITED STATES
Buckley, William
Canby, Brigadier General Edward R. S.
Cermak, Anton J. (see ROOSEVELT, FRANKLIN DELANO)
De Galindez, Jesus
Dewey, Thomas E. (see SCHULTZ, DUTCH)
Dubs, Adolph
Evers, Medgar W.
Ford, Gerald
Frick, Henry Clay
Garfield, James A.
Gaynor, William Jay
Goebel, William
Haig, General Alexander
Hammer, Michael
Jackson, Andrew
James, Jesse
Kennedy, Caroline (see FRASER, HUGH)
Kennedy, John F.
Kennedy, Robert F.
King Martin Luther, Jr.
Letelier, Orlando
Lincoln, Abraham
Long, Huey
McKinley, William
Malcolm X
Mein, John Gordon
Milk, Harvey
Mitrione, Daniel A.
Moore, George C.
Moscone, George (see MILK, HARVEY)
Munro, Ernest A. (see MEIN, JOHN GORDON)
Nixon, Richard M.
Noel, Cleo A., Jr.
Pearlman, Mark David (see HAMMER, MICHAEL)
Reagan, Ronald
Rockwell, George Lincoln
Roosevelt, Franklin Delano
Roosevelt, Theodore
Ryan, Leo J.
Schultz, Dutch
Steunenberg, Frank
Tresca, Carlo
Truman, Harry S
Wallace, George Corley
Webber, John D. (see MEIN, JOHN GORDON)
Welch, Richard S.

VENEZUELA
Betancourt, Romulo

VIETNAM
Diem, Ngo Dinh (see NGO DINH DIEM)
Ngo Dinh Diem

A SELECTED BIBLIOGRAPHY

The following bibliography represents works that were most helpful for this compilation and that provided comprehensive coverage of several assassinations. In addition, the sources of limited information and quotations are mentioned in the main text. Of course innumerable news sources — newspaper and periodicals — and standard reference works were relied upon heavily. Among these are the *Encyclopaedia Britannica*, the *Encyclopedia Americana, Facts On File News Digest*, the *New York Times*, the *Washington Post, Time, Newsweek* and *Current History*.

Ault, Warren O. *Europe in Modern Times*. Boston: D.C. Heath, 1946.

Belin, David W. *Final Disclosure*. New York: Charles Scribner's Sons, 1988.

Blakey, G. Robert, and Billings, Richard N. *The Plot to Kill the President*. New York: Times Books, 1981.

Bowder, Diana, ed. *Who Was Who in the Roman World*. New York: Washington Square Press, 1984.

Carey, Jane Perry Clark, and Carey, Andrew Galbraith. *The Web of Modern Greek Politics*. New York: Columbia University Press, 1968.

Cambridge Ancient History, The. 3rd ed. Cambridge, England: Cambridge University Press, 1970.

Cambridge Medieval History, The. Cambridge, England: Cambridge University Press, 1936.

Cambridge Modern History, The New. Cambridge, England: Cambridge University Press, 1957.

Clarke, James W. *American Assassins: The Darker Side of Politics*. Princeton, N.J.: Princeton University Press, 1982.

Cline, Dr. Ray S. *The CIA Under Reagan, Bush & Casey*. Washington, D.C.: Acropolis Books, 1981.

Cohen, Mickey, with Nugent, John Peer. *Mickey Cohen, In My*

Own Words. Englewood Cliffs, N.J.: Prentice-Hall, 1975.

Conquest, Robert. *Stalin and the Kirov Murder*. New York: Oxford University Press, 1989.

Davis, John H. *Mafia Kingfish. Carlos Marcello and the Assassination of John F. Kennedy*. New York: McGraw Hill, 1989.

Demaris, Ovid. *Captive City: Chicago in Chains*. New York: Lyle Stuart, 1969.

——. *The Last Mafioso: 'Jimmy the Weasel' Fratianno*. New York: Times Books, 1981.

Diederich, Bernard. *Trujillo: The Death of the Goat*. Boston: Little, Brown, 1978.

Dio Cassius. *History of Rome*. Cambridge, Mass.: Harvard University Press, 1961.

Dobson, Christopher, and Payne, Ronald. *Counterattack*. New York: Facts On File, 1982.

——. *The Terrorists*. New York: Facts On File, 1980.

Durant, Will (and Durant, Ariel, vols. VII–X). *The Story of Civilization* (10 volumes). New York: Simon and Schuster:

I.	*Our Oriental Heritage*, 1935.
II.	*The Life of Greece*, 1939.
III.	*Caesar and Christ*, 1944.
IV.	*The Age of Faith*, 1950.
V.	*The Renaissance*, 1953.
VI.	*The Reformation*, 1957.
VII.	*The Age of Reason Begins*, 1961.
VIII.	*The Age of Louis XIV*, 1963.
IX.	*The Age of Voltaire*, 1965.
X.	*Rousseau and Revolution*, 1967.

Ergang, Robert. *Europe Since Waterloo*. 3rd ed. Boston: Heath, 1967.

Ford, Franklin L. *Political Murder: From Tyrannicide to Terrorism*. Cambridge, Mass.: Harvard University Press, 1985.

Fraser, Antonia, ed. *The Lives of the Kings & Queens of England*. New York: Knopf, 1975.

Gibbon, Edward. *The Decline and Fall of the Roman Empire*. New York: Penguin, 1977.

Goldman, Emma. *Living My Life*. New York: New American Library, 1977.

Gutteridge, William, ed. *Contemporary Terrorism*. New York: Facts On File, 1986.

Hammerton, Sir John, and Barnes, Dr. Harry Elmer, eds. *The Illustrated World History*. New York, 1940.

Hibbert, Christopher. *The House of Medici: Its Rise & Fall*. New York: Morrow, 1975.

Horan, James D., and Sann, Paul. *Pictorial History of the Wild West*. New York: Crown, 1954.

Huie, William Bradford. *He Slew the Dreamer*. New York: Delacorte Press, 1970.

Kee, Robert. *The Green Flag*. New York: Delacorte Press, 1972.

Jenkins, Romilly. *Byzantium: The Imperial Centuries A.D. 610–1071*. New York: Random House, 1966.

Johnson, William Weber. *Heroic Mexico*. Garden City, N.Y.: Doubleday, 1968.

Lankenvich, George J., and Furer, Howard B. *A Brief History of New York City*. Port Washington, N.Y.: Associated Faculty Press, 1984.

Lentz III, Harris M. *Assassinations and Executions: An Encyclopedia of Political Violence 1865–1986*. Jefferson, N.C.: McFarland, 1988.

Lesberg, Sandy. *Assassination in Our Time*. London: Preebles Press International, 1976.

Liston, Robert A. *Terrorism*. Nashville: Thomas Nelson, 1977.

McKinley, James. *Assassination in America*. New York: Harper & Row, 1977.

McMillan, George. *The Making of an Assassin*. Boston: Little, Brown, 1976.

Machiavelli, Niccolo. *The Prince*. New York: New American Library, 1952.

Mallet, Michael. *The Borgias*. New York: Barnes & Noble, 1969.

Massie, Robert K. *Nicholas and Alexandra*. New York: Atheneum, 1967.

Mayo, Samuel H. *A History of Mexico*. Englewood Cliffs, N.J.: Prentice-Hall, 1978.

Melanson, Philip H. *The Murkin Conspiracy*. New York: Praeger, 1989.

Murray, Jane. *The Kings & Queens of England*. New York: Scribner's, 1974.

O'Neill, Hugh B. *Companion to Chinese History*. New York: Facts On File, 1987.

Petherick, Maurice. *Restoration Rogues*. London: Hollis & Carter, 1951.

Plutarch's Lives. New York: Dutton, 1957.

Riasanovsky, Nicholas V. *A History of Russia*. New York: Oxford University Press, 1984.

Scheim, David E. *Contract on America*. New York: Shapolsky, 1988.

Schellenberg, Walter. *Hitler's Secret Service*. New York: Jove/ HBJ, 1977.

Schevill, Ferdinand. *A History of Europe from the Reformation to the Present Day*. New York: Harcourt, Brace, 1947.

Shirer, William L. *The Rise and Fall of the Third Reich*. New York: Simon and Schuster, 1960.

Sifakis, Carl. *The Mafia Encyclopedia*. New York: Facts On File, 1987.

Sykes, Sir Percy. *History of Persia*. London: Macmillan, 1930.

Toland, John. *The Last 100 Days*. New York: Random House, 1966.

Tuchman, Barbara W. *The Guns of August*. New York: Macmillan, 1962.

——. *The March of Folly*. New York: Knopf, 1984.

Tucker, H. H., ed. *Combating the Terrorists*. New York: Facts On File, 1988.

Ulam, Adam B. *The Bolsheviks*. New York: Collier Books, 1976.

Wilson, Colin. *A Criminal History of Mankind*. New York: G. P. Putnam's, 1984.

Wilson, Colin, and Seaman, Donald. *Encyclopedia of Modern Murder 1962–1982*. London: Arthur Barker, 1983.

Woodward, Bob. *Veil: The Secret Wars of the CIA 1981–1987*. New York: Pocket Books, 1987.

Young, George F. *The Medici*. New York: Modern Library, 1930.

INDEX

Note: Page numbers in *italics indicate the main entry* of that individual. When a page number appears more than once under a listing, it indicates that the subject appears in different entries on the same page.

I

J